Partakers
of
the Divine Nature

Partakers of the Divine Nature

The History and Development of Deification in the Christian Traditions

Edited by

Michael J. Christensen and Jeffery A. Wittung

Paperback edition published in 2008 by Baker Academic
a division of Baker Publishing Group
P.O. Box 6287, Grand Rapids, MI 49516-6287
www.bakeracademic.com

Hardcover edition published in 2007 in Cranbury, New Jersey, by Associated University Presses

Printed in the United States of America

Library of Congress Cataloging-in-Publication Data
Partakers of the divine nature : the history and development of deification in the Christian traditions / edited by Michael J. Christensen and Jeffery A. Wittung. — Paperback ed.
p. cm.
Proceedings of a conference held May 21-22, 2004 at Drew University.
Originally published: Madison : Fairleigh Dickinson University Press, c2007.
Includes bibliographical references and index.
ISBN 978-0-8010-3440-4 (pbk.)
1. Deification (Christianity)—History of doctrines—Congresses. I. Christensen, Michael J. II. Wittung, Jeffery A.
BT767.8.P38 2008
234—dc22 2007047669

Contents

Acknowledgments

THE EDITORS AND CONTRIBUTORS WISH TO ACKNOWLEDGE AND THANK the following publishers for granting permissions to quote from the following sources:

Excerpts from *Union with Christ: The New Finnish Interpretation of Luther,* edited by Carl E. Braaten and Robert W. Jenson, Copyright 1998, reprinted by permission of William B. Eerdmans Publishing Co., Grand Rapids, MI.

Excerpts from *Old Possum's Book of Practical Cats,* copyright 1939 by T. S. Eliot and renewed by Esme Valerie Eliot, reprinted by permission of Harcourt, Inc.

Excerpts from Plato's *Theaetetus and Sophist* are reprinted by permission of the publishers and the Trustees of the Loeb Classical Library from *Plato: Vol. VIII,* LCL 123, translated by H. N. Fowler, Cambridge, MA: Harvard University Press, Copyright 1921 by the president and Fellows of Harvard College. The Loeb Classical Library [R] is a registered trademark of the President and Fellows of Harvard College.

Excerpts from Plutarch's *Themistocles and Camillus, Aristides and Cato Major, Cimon and Lucullus* are reprinted by permission of the publishers and the Trustees of the Loeb Classical Library from *Plutarch: Vol. II,* LCL 47, translated by B. Perrin, Cambridge, MA: Harvard University Press, Copyright 1914 by the president and Fellows of Harvard College. The Loeb Classical Library [R] is a registered trademark of the President and Fellows of Harvard College.

Excerpts from Plutarch's *De sera 550DE* is reprinted by permission of the publishers and the Trustees of the Loeb Classical Library from *Plutarch: Vol. VIII,* LCL 405, translated by Philip H. DeLacy and Benedict Einarson, Cambridge, MA: Harvard University Press, Copyright 1959 by the president and Fellows of Harvard College. The Loeb Classical Library® is a registered trademark of the President and Fellows of Harvard College.

Excerpts from *St. Ephrem the Syrian: Hymns on Paradise* translated by S. P. Brock, Copyright 1990 pp. 49, 60–61, 73, 78, 80, 81, 134–35, 111–12;

and *The Mystical Theology of the Eastern Church* by Vladimir Lossky, Copyright 1998, pp. 50, 67, 69–70, 73–74, 77–78, 88–89, 94–96, 117, 158, 238, used by permission of St. Vladimir's Seminary Press, 575 Scarsdale Road, Crestwood, N.Y., 1-800-204-2665, www.svspress.com.

Excerpts from *Spirit in the World* by Karl Rahner, translated by W. V. Dych, English translation copyright 1968 by Herder and Herder, used by permission of the publisher, The Continuum International Publishing Group.

Excerpts from *Foundations of Christian Faith* by Karl Rahner, translated by W. V. Dych, Copyright 1978, used by permission of the publisher, Seabury Press, NY.

Excerpts from *St. Ephrem the Syrian, Selected Prose Works: Commentary on Genesis, Commentary on Exodus, Homily on Our Lord, Letter to Publius,* FC 91, edited by K. E. McVey and translated by E. G. Mathews, Jr. and J. P. Amar, Copyright 1994, used with permission: The Catholic University of America Press, Washington, DC.

Excerpts from *St. Cyril of Alexandria: The Christological Controversy: Its History, Theology, and Texts,* translated by John A. McGuckin, Copyright 1994, used with permission of the publisher, Brill Academic Publishers, Leiden.

New Revised Standard Version Bible quotations, Copyright 1989 by the Division of Christian Education of the National Council of the Churches of Christ in the U.S.A., used by permission.

Excerpts from *Sergius Bulgakov: Apoctastasis and Transfiguration,* edited by Boris Jakim, Copyright 1995, used by permission of The Variable Press, New Haven, IL.

The editors would also like to express their appreciation to the following persons for their invaluable assistance in the careful preparation and production of this volume: Dean James Pain, Rev. Joel Elowsky, Vladimir Kharlamov, Warren "Cal" Robertson, and Boris Jakim at Drew University; and to Harry Keyishian, Julien Yoseloff, Christine Retz, and Cathy Slovensky, the directors and editors at Fairleigh Dickinson University Press and Associated University Presses.

Preface

THE IDEA FOR THIS PUBLISHED WORK HAD ITS GENESIS WITH TWO GRADUATE students at Drew University who had done research and writing on patristic notions of *theosis.* Recognizing the growing academic interest in the subject, Vladimir Kharlamov and Jeffery Wittung of the Caspersen School of Graduate Studies at Drew University proposed the idea of holding a colloquium for and by students of Drew on the topic of *theosis*/deification. As the plans for the colloquium developed, however, interest began to arise beyond the walls of Drew. In light of this surprising development, James Pain, dean of the Caspersen School, Dr. Thomas Oden, head of the Ancient Christian Commentary on Scripture project, and Dr. Michael Christensen, director of the Doctor of Ministry Program at Drew, agreed to fund and cosponsor an academic conference that would explore the history and development of the concept within the broadly Christian traditions. Paper proposals were received from scholars on four continents, and over one hundred scholars and interested clergy and laypersons attended the "Partakers of the Divine Nature" conference held at Drew University on May 21–22, 2004.

Out of the conference proceedings, a publishable manuscript was organized and edited. The essays included in this volume were selected from an internationally open process of proposal by committee, vetting, academic presentation to peers, and evaluation of thematic suitability for publication by the editors and a faculty committee from Drew University. None of the essays in their present form have been previously published. Thus, the volume in part and as a whole represents a new and significant contribution to scholarly discourse in the field of historical and philosophical theology.

The contributors to this volume find the idea and history of *theosis* to be a compelling vision of human wholeness and spiritual transformation, worthy of serious study and relevant for our contemporary culture. Further, the editors find the idea and history of *theosis* not merely an academic or scholastic enterprise, but an experiential possibility that includes every seeker of salvation. *Partaking of the Divine Nature,* first conceived and experienced by ancient philosophers, Christian saints, and mystical theologians, has functional value if not ontological reality for humanity today in illuminating our intellectual path and transforming our spiritual lives. In this spirit we delight in offering this unique volume and labor of love to a larger readership.

Michael J. Christensen
Feast of Pentecost, 2006

Introduction

Michael J. Christensen
and
Jeffery A. Wittung

EASTERN ORTHODOX SPIRITUALITY HAS BECOME INCREASINGLY POPULAR in academic and lay circles, as has the ancient Christian idea of becoming "partakers of the divine nature" (2 Pt 1:4) and of "becoming god" (Athanasius).[1] Western Protestant and Roman Catholic theologians are now in dialogue with Eastern Orthodox theologians on the subject of *theosis.*[2] Popular and academic interest in this compelling vision of human potential for transformation and spiritual perfectibility is evidenced by increasing numbers of contemporary books, journal articles, academic conferences, and edited volumes on the topic. At the same time, the idea of deification has been tarnished in the West by much of the "New Age" movement, so that many have forgotten or simply do not know the importance and history of *theosis* in Christian tradition. It is to the renewed interest in a neglected doctrine that the present volume is directed, with the hope that it will serve as a worthy partner in both scholarly conversations and lay explorations.

The topic of deification in the past was largely confined to patristic studies and discussions within Eastern Christianity. Recent publications have focused on particular traditions and contexts of the topic.[3] There has been no full study of *theosis* across cultures and historical periods within the Christian traditions until now. This multiauthored volume achieves what no one writer probably could have achieved alone: it treats the various visions of deification (from its early Greek origins to modern constructions), related theological conceptions of "participation in the divine nature" (transfiguration, sanctification, perfection, glorification, sophianization), and multiple trajectories of their development (East and West) in the rich history of ideas.

Included in this volume are critical essays by leading scholars on the concept of deification in the New Testament; its place in the ancient Greek, Syriac, and Copto-Arabic Christian traditions; and its development in patristic, Orthodox, Roman Catholic, and a variety of Protestant traditions. Attention is given to the development of the theme of *theosis* over a span of more than a millennium and a half in the works of such prominent theologians as Athanasius, Ephrem the Syrian, Basil the Great, Gregory of Nyssa, Gregory of Nazianzus, Maximus the Confessor, Gregory Palamas, St. Anselm, Martin Luther, John Calvin, John Wesley, Sergius Bulgakov, and Karl Rahner. The result, the editors believe, is an important and distinctive contribution to the scholarly literature on the subject, as well as a useful text for general courses in historical theology.

Volume co-editor Michael Christensen sets the stage for the essays that follow by locating the idea of deification in its functional context as a bold and viable doctrine of salvation. By organizing this complex concept under three simple categories—the *promise, process,* and *problem* of *theosis*—the topic is introduced and explored in a contemporary biblical and theological context for both Eastern and Western traditions.

Andrew Louth investigates the place of *theosis* in the tradition of the East, presenting it in relation to the other elements that comprise the mosaic of this tradition's theology, and identifying three ways this doctrine functions within the overall Orthodox experience: (1) as a complement to the doctrine of the Incarnation in the economy and plan of God; (2) as a way to stress the real change involved in the transformation of the human nature; and (3) as a witness to the grounding of theology in the transforming encounter with God. Louth demonstrates that the doctrine of deification has "structural" significance in Orthodox theology and goes on to argue that it determines the shape of that theology.

John Lenz provides a careful, foundational study of deification in classical Greece. Recognizing that deification is a neglected but essential theme in Greek philosophy, and arguing that Plato makes the participation of human beings in the divine nature open to all through contemplation and the development of one's soul, Lenz identifies philosophical antecedents of *theosis* in Greek and classical literature by presenting two major themes: (1) the union of reason and spirituality in Greek thought; and (2) the continuity of Greek philosophy, particularly Plato, and Christian thought.

In the context of scriptural exegesis and reasoning, Stephen Finlan explores the possibility of *theosis* in the Epistles of Paul in the New Testament. He examines Paul's idea of a "spiritual" and "glorified" body, and argues that what Paul is attempting to do is to delineate differing levels of substance and kinds of life force, and thus differing levels and kinds of bodies. In the "Christification" process of being conformed and transformed by the renewing of one's "mind," the believer receives the promised spiritual body, produced first as a *cruciform* and then as an *anastiform* body.

James Starr offers an exegesis of 2 Peter 1:4 within its contemporary context to determine whether it teaches *theosis* or *apotheosis* (i.e., a migration from humanity to divinity). Starr argues that the phrase "partakers of the divine nature" stands for a "constellation of ideas" suggesting participation in specific divine attributes that are only received through knowledge of

Christ and thus cannot be achieved by human effort alone. He concludes that 2 Peter 1:4 neither relapses into Hellenistic dualism nor teaches *apotheosis,* and provides a nonontological understanding of deification.

Through a close reading of the Cappadocians, J. A. McGuckin argues that Gregory of Nazianzus and Gregory of Nyssa, whose thought came to dominate Byzantine theology, critically appropriated Origen's mystical vision of the soul's journey to union with God. McGuckin shows how, while retaining this vision, both thinkers attempted to clarify the language of *theosis* in order to more clearly demonstrate the critical difference between Christian deification theory and Platonic assimilation language.

Vladimir Kharlamov, one of the instigators of the Drew conference on *theosis,* examines the use of the concept of *theosis* in fourth-century Greek patristic theology, using Athanasius and Gregory of Nazianzus as case studies. He argues that the language of deification was treated more as a rhetorical tool applied to various aspects of Christian spirituality and less as an independent theological topic for discussion. The resulting lack of coherent systematic theological treatment led to *theosis* assuming a variety of modes, often within the same writer, without proper supporting explication.

Elena Vishnevskaya explicates the vision and reality of deification as *perichoresis*—an "interpenetrating" dynamic embrace of divinity and humanity in the mystical theology of Maximus the Confessor. The *perichoretic* hypostatic union as evidenced in the person of the Logos serves as a prototype, Vishnevskaya argues, for the *perichoresis* of God and the believer. This deific union appears in Maximus as "an organic relation of human freedom and divine grace" that coinheres in a dynamic embrace between divine and human.

Thomas Buchan explores *theosis* in the thought of Ephrem the Syrian by focusing on his use of the biblical image of paradise and the Garden of God as the landscape for understanding the meaning of deification. For Ephrem, paradise was a place originally intended to facilitate human union with the divine and whose cosmic geography assumed the shape of a mountain, the ascent of which brought one increasingly closer to God. While paradise was lost in the Fall, the way has been reopened by Christ; so too, the possibility of *theosis.*

Stephen Davis offers a Eucharistic reading of John 3 in the Copto-Arabic tradition and considers the relationship of Coptic Christology to human participation in divinity. While not *explicitly* addressing the concept of *theosis* in the Gospel of John, the essay transports the reader into an underrepresented area of Christian literature on the nature of Christ and its implications for deification.

Nathan Kerr examines Anselm's *Proslogion* as a theological bridge between Eastern and Western Christianity. For Anslem, deification is an essential constituent of the doctrine of God, which of necessity must involve a doctrine of creaturely deification. *Theoria,* or contemplation, of God can only come about through participation in that which is contemplated, so that creaturely participation in the divine nature, or deification, lies at the very heart of theology.

In the Finnish school of Luther studies within the Reformed tradition, Jonathan Linman explores Martin Luther's vision of *theosis* as believers becoming "little Christs" for the world. He posits a Lutheran understanding of *theosis* that is rooted in the doctrine of justification by faith, whereby justification is removed from forensic preoccupations and becomes the means of enacting *theosis* while faith functions as the source of this union. The sacraments, which play a crucial role in the creation and nurture of faith, remain central in the dynamic process of *theosis.*

J. Todd Billings suggests, in his contribution, that *theosis* indeed is present in the thought of John Calvin. Arguing that Byzantine theology cannot be made the only lens through which deification is understood, Billings focuses specifically on the language of "participation" in the *Institutes* and affirms a particular "type" of *theosis* in Calvin that is consistent with the rest of his theological system and distinct from the notions of *theosis* in late Byzantine theology.

Michael Christensen's essay on John Wesley's doctrine of entire sanctification and Christian perfection, explores this doctrine's similarity to (and perhaps, continuity with) older ideas of deification in selected patristic writers of the East. If Wesleyan perfection as "faith filled with the energy of love" functions in the same way as Clement's and Origin's vision of spiritual "union" between God and humanity, then the similarity of ideas implies the same means—deifying faith, perfecting love and sanctifying grace—toward the goal of "entire sanctification" and "full salvation," as both John and Charles Wesley understood their Eastern sources to have taught and practiced.

Theosis in the history of ideas would not be complete without modern theological reflections. Jeffrey Finch explores the neo-Palamite tradition of divinizing grace and its effects on the continued division between Eastern and Western Christianity. He attempts to show that the neo-Palamite distinction between divine energies and essence, and its critique of Western theology, is grounded in a false alternative; and that Eastern and Western conceptions of deification are complementary.

Boris Jakim, a translator into English of several Russian religious philosophers, captures the spirit of *theosis* in Russian thought by focusing on its formulation in the works of Sergius Bulgakov. Bulgakov's doctrine of deification, in continuity with Solovyov's vision of Divine-humanity, is explored from the viewpoint of sophiology and the divinizing process of sophianization.

Francis Caponi turns to an exploration of deification as it is formulated in the Roman Catholic tradition through the scholastic lens of Karl Rahner. With a detailed examination of the thought of this twentieth-century German

Jesuit, who has been extremely influential in the Roman Church over the last fifty years, Caponi concludes that a symbol of *theopoiesis* lies at the very core of Rahner's theology, acting as the center of gravity around which the rest of the elements of his theology orbit.

Gösta Hallonsten concludes the volume with a critique of recent *theosis* research in the West. By focusing on the more recent scholarly work of Tuomo Mannermaa and A. N. Williams, he argues for a distinction to be made between the theme and a doctrine of *theosis,* and calls for an appropriate scholarly differentiation between the two as well as a careful use of terms.

Volume co-editor Jeffery Wittung, instigator and co-coordinator of the acacdemic conference on *theosis* at Drew University, contributes an extensive bibliography of works on *theosis* for further study.

Read individually, each chapter provides intellectual, social, cultural, and theological insights and resources for understanding the idea and development of deification in particular historical and contemporary settings. Taken together, the various essays serve as a matrix of meaning for both scholarly conversation and lay exploration.

Notes

1. *On the Incarnation* 54: "God became man so that man might become God."

2. *Theosis*/deification is the preferred theological term for what the New Testament describes as "becoming partakers of the divine nature" (2 Pt 1:4) and Eastern Orthodox theologians refer to as "becoming god." There are other related terms used in scholarly discourse to point to this ancient vision, including: transfiguration, perfection, sanctification, glorification, Christification, sophianization, ingoding, and Divine-humanity. In this volume, contributors use the terms *theosis* and deification interchangeably, even as they nuance related terms and concepts.

3. Recent academic publications on the topic of *theosis* include: Jules Gross, *The Divinization of the Christian according to the Greek Fathers* (1938; translated and published in English by A&C Press, 2002); Norman Russell, *The Doctrine of Deification in the Greek Patristic Tradition* (Oxford University Press, 2005); Stephen Finlan and Vladimir Kharlamov, eds., *Theosis: Deification in Christian Theology* (Wipf and Stock, 2006); see also "Resources on *Theosis*" in the present volume. Recent conferences on *theosis* include: "Consultation on Orthodox and Wesleyan Spirituality" at Saint Vladimir's Orthodox Theological Seminary (1999), sections at the American Academy of Religion (2001), and "Partakers of the Divine Nature" at Drew University (2004).

Abbreviations

AB	The Anchor Bible Commentary Series. Garden City, NY: Doubleday, 1964–.
ANF	Ante-Nicene Fathers. 10 vols. Edited by A. Roberts and J. Donaldson. Buffalo, NY: Christian Literature, 1885–96. Reprint, Grand Rapids, MI: Eerdmans, 1951–56; Reprint, Peabody, MA: Hendrickson, 1994.
CC	John Calvin. *Commentaries.* Edited by David Torrance and Thomas Torrance. Edinburgh: Oliver and Boyd, 1959.
CCL	Corpus Christianorum. Series Latina. Turnhout, Belgium: Brepols, 1953–.
CCSG	Corpus Christianorum. Series Graeca. Brepols: Leuven University Press, 1977–.
CS	Cistercian Studies Series. Kalamazoo, MI: Cistercian Publications, 1973–.
CSCO	Corpus Scriptorum Christianorum Orientalium. Louvain, Belgium, 1903–.
CTS	John Calvin. *Commentaries.* Calvin Translation Society. Edited by John King et al. Grand Rapids, MI: Baker, reprinted 1981.
CWS	The Classics of Western Spirituality Series. Mahwah, NJ: Paulist Press.
FC	Fathers of the Church: A New Translation. Washington, DC: Catholic University of America Press, 1947–.
ICC	International Critical Commentary
JSNT	*Journal for the Study of the New Testament*
JSNT Sup	*Journal for the Study of the New Testament,* Supplement Series
JSOT Sup	*Journal for the Study of the Old Testament,* Supplement Series
JTS	*Journal of Theological Studies*
LCL	Loeb Classical Library. Cambridge, MA: Harvard University Press; London: Heinemann, 1912–.
LXX	Septuagint
MC	*Maximus the Confessor.* Edited by Andrew Louth. New York: Routledge, 1996.
m. Yoma	The Mishnah tractate *Yoma*

NPNF — A Select Library of the Nicene and Post-Nicene Fathers of the Christian Church. 2 series (14 vols. each). Edited by P. Schaff et al. Buffalo, NY: Christian Literature, 1887–94; Reprint, Grand Rapids, MI: Eerdmans, 1952–56; Reprint, Peabody, MA: Hendrickson, 1994.

OS — John Calvin. *Joannis Calvini Opera Selecta.* Edited by Peter Barth and Wilhelm Niesel. Munich: Chr. Kaiser, 1926.

PG — Patrologia Graeca. 166 vols. Edited by J.-P. Migne. Paris: Migne, 1857–86.

PPS — *St. Maximus the Confessor: On the Cosmic Mystery of Jesus Christ.* Translated by Paul Blowers and Robert Louis Wilken. Popular Patristic Series. Crestwood, NY: St. Vladimir's Seminary Press, 2003.

SC — Sources Chrétiennes. Edited by H. de Lubac, J. Daniélou et al. Paris: Editions du Cerf, 1941–.

SW — *Maximus the Confessor: Selected Writings.* Translated by George Berthold, CWS. Mahwah, NJ: Paulist Press, 1985.

TDNT — *Theological Dictionary of the New Testament.* 10 vols. Edited by Gerhard Kittel. Grand Rapids, MI: Wm. B. Eerdmans, 1964–76.

W — Martin Luther. *Werke.* Weimar: Hermann Boehlaus Nachfolger, 1893–.

See individual essays for additional primary source abbreviations used.

Partakers
of
the Divine Nature

I
The Context of *Theosis* in Christianity

The Problem, Promise, and Process of *Theosis*

Michael J. Christensen

> *When a sunbeam falls on a transparent substance, the substance itself becomes brilliant, and radiates light from itself. So too Spirit-bearing souls, illumined by Him, finally become spiritual themselves, and their grace is sent forth to others. From this comes knowledge of the future, understanding of mysteries, apprehension of hidden things, distribution of wonderful gifts, heavenly citizenship, a place in the choir of angels, endless joy in the presence of God, becoming like God, and, the highest of all desires,* ***becoming God.***
>
> St. Basil the Great of Caesarea, 330–79

A HUMAN BEING BECOMING DIVINE IS AN ENGAGING, INSPIRING, AND POWERful religious idea. But what exactly is meant by *becoming god* (*theosis*)? What is the origin of the term and the development of the concept in the intellectual history of ideas? What are the original visions behind and subsequent interpretations of the *promise* in 2 Peter 1:4 of becoming a "partaker of the divine nature"? What did Irenaeus of Lyon mean when he said: "God the Logos became what we are, in order that we may become what he himself is," and Athanasius mean when he declared that "God became Man so that Man could become God"?[1] What is the *process* of human deification in the soteriology of Basil the Great as quoted above? And what are the contemporary philosophical and theological *problems,* if any, with human beings becoming divine? These are among the many questions raised and issues surveyed in this general, introductory chapter. These questions and issues will be sharpened, contextualized, and addressed in the essays that follow by specialists as they explore, document, and explicate the nature and development of *theosis*/deification as a vision and doctrine within the various Christian traditions.

What Does It Mean to Become God?

To simplify and provide an overview of the subject, I have summarized some of the issues under three headings: (1) the promise; (2) the process; and (3) the problem of *theosis* as they relate to what the author of 2 Peter 1:4 meant by the phrase "becoming partakers of the divine nature."

The Promise of Theosis

Is there a divine *promise* of human deification implicit in the teachings of the Scriptures? If we associate the idea of deification with divine intention, as many patristic theologians do, the promise of *theosis* may be found in several scriptural passages, including: Gen 1:26–27; Gen 3:5; Ps 82:6; Jn 10:34–35; Mt 5:48; 2 Cor 3:18; 2 Pt 1:4; and 1 Jn 3:1–2.

According to Jaroslav Pelikan, the promise of salvation has been understood as *theosis* on the basis of two principal passages of the Bible: the declaration of Psalm 82:6, "I say, 'You are gods,'" which Jesus quoted in John 10:34–35; and the "exceedingly great promise" in 2 Peter 1:4 that believers would become "partakers of the divine nature and thus escape the corruption of the world and its passions."[2] The first of these promises, writes Pelikan, "meant that righteous men and angels would become divine, the second that 'being united with Christ' was the means of deification. For similarity to Christ was a deifying force, making men divine. Greek paganism had already known that one should rise from the active life to the contemplative, but Greek Christianity discovered that there was a third step beyond both of these, when one was taken up and was made divine."[3]

In the Genesis story of creation, according to Gregory of Nyssa, humanity first is created in the image and likeness of God, neither male nor female. Sexual differentiation emerges from the archetype, creating a dual nature: "God made them male and female." Our likeness to God was lost in the differentiation, but is restored in Christ, in whom "there is neither male nor female."[4] Origen argues similarly: "man received the honor of God's image in his first creation, whereas the perfection of God's likeness was reserved for him at the consummation."[5] Irenaeus considered that, although it was created in a state of innocence and did not know good and evil, infant humanity had the natural capacity to grow into full maturity in God.[6] "Ye shall be like God,"[7] though spoken from the mouth of the serpent, was indeed the promise of God, but it was to be actualized through obedience, not disobedience. The serpent, in appealing to Adam and Eve's pride, offered a shortcut, a premature and forbidden means to the end God had promised. Thus pride is the originating sin, according to Augustine,[8] thwarting (or perhaps only delaying) the promise made to Adam and Eve to grow up into their full humanity.

In Psalm 82, the Lord God is envisioned presiding over the great assembly of gathered gods and mortals. What God says to mortal humanity is meant to shock: "I declare, 'Ye are gods; you are all sons of the Most High'" (Ps 82:6). In its scriptural context, it is a call to humanity, created in the image and likeness of God, to act in justice as God would act: "to defend the cause of the weak and needy, and deliver them from the hand of the wicked." When Jesus cites this verse in the Gospel of John, he is responding to criticisms that "he, being a man, made himself to be God" (10:34). Jesus turns the accusation around and repeats the declaration of the psalmist: "I say, 'Ye are gods.'" Similarly, in the Gospel of Matthew (Mt 5:48), Jesus tells his disciples: "Be ye perfect as your Father in heaven is perfect." Perfection and deification in patristic soteriology are often seen as closely related if not synonymous terms, though individual writers vary on how they understand deification, and careful, nuanced use of the terms and symbols of *theosis* is important.[9]

Second Peter 1:4 is sometimes interpreted to reveal the promise of *theosis:* God's divine power has been given to us in Christ in order for us to live a godly life. In receiving God's "exceeding great and precious promises," we become "partakers of the divine nature" and thus escape the corruption that is in the world.[10] What God is in nature, it is commonly argued and debated in the Eastern Orthodox tradition, humanity can become by *participation,* first in image and then in likeness, following the prototype of Christ, "the first born of a large family" (Rom 8:29). The writer of 1 John states: "Now we are the children of God, and it does not yet appear what we shall be. But we know that when he appears, we shall be like him, for we shall see him as he is" (1 Jn 3:2). When this occurs, Paul adds, "we all, with unveiled faces, beholding the glory of the Lord, will be changed into his likeness, from glory to glory" (2 Cor 3:18). These and other texts, according to proponents of the doctrine, point to the divine promise of *theosis* as the fullness of salvation.[11]

The Process of Theosis

Plato had identified the highest aim of humanity as *eudaimonia* (to be blessed with a good internal divinity) and defined deification as "likeness to God so far as possible."[12] "How far is possible" continued to be debated by proponents of the doctrine in the Neoplatonic Christian tradition for centuries.

Clement of Alexandria (150–215) understood deification as "assimilation to God as far as possible" in the progressive order of salvation. The process is identified as a prolepsis in the Christian initiation rite: "Being baptized, we are illuminated; illuminated, we become sons; being made sons, we are made perfect; being made perfect, we are made immortal. 'I,' says He, 'have said that ye are gods, and all sons of the Highest.'"[13]

For Origen (145–254), human deification is possible because of God's prior humanization in Christ. In the descent of divinity, a spiritual merging occurred—"human and divine began to be woven together, so that by prolonged fellowship with divinity, human nature might become divine."[18] His vision of *theosis* is one of education of souls, transformation of nature, and unification with God. Progressively, the soul is perfected in time until all is reconciled, and time is no more. Then "God is all in all."[15]

Humanity partakes of divinity in stages of ascent—purified in wisdom, perfected in love, glorified in spirit. The image is one of flight: Souls take wings and "return like an eagle to the house of their master." The journey to paradise is through the "flaming sword" of the cherubim that guards the gate to the tree of life (Gen 3:21).[16]

Ephrem, the fourth-century Syrian poet (306–73) whose poems are preserved as Armenian hymns, weaves the images of deification together in memorable hymns of ascent. As in the story of the Rich Man and Lazarus, a great "chasm" divides humanity from divinity. However, there is a celestial ladder of descent and ascent to reunite what has been severed and restore humanity to paradise. God comes down so that humanity may be drawn up to God. Or, God, like a mother bird, teaches her young to fly:

> A bird grows up in three stages,
> From womb to egg,
> Then to the nest where it sings;
> And once it is fully grown it flies in the air,
> Opening its wings in the symbol of the Cross.[17]

Similarly, the human soul grows in stages into divinity: from physical birth to spiritual birth (baptism), from mother's milk to the meat of the Gospel, by learning to "sing" (praise) and feed on divinity (Eucharist), the purified soul soars and returns in flight to God in the form of the Cross. Other images of deification in Ephrem include: seeing with the "luminous eye," blessing the One that has "polished our mirror," drinking the "medicine of life," "putting on the garments of light," wearing the "robe of glory," and passing through the "flaming sword" of the Cherub guarding the gates to the "Tree of Paradise."

Gregory of Nazianzus (328–90), in his contemplation of the Trinity, compares the process of deification to the polishing of a mirror. The *imago Dei* within humanity may become so clear and polished that it perfectly reflects its divine source of Light. The divine magnificence that can be contemplated, Vladimir Lossky interprets Gregory to mean, "is only a little ray of that great light." No one sees God in his essence or nature, rather, "we will discover God when the godlike image, our spirit, is elevated to its Archetype and joined to that with which it is familiar, when we know even as we are known."[19]

According to Gregory of Nyssa (335–99), there are no limits to the degree of perfection, knowledge of God, or Godlikeness that can be progressively achieved. Grace restores the *image* and appropriates the *likeness* of God "as far as possible" in this life and in the next, as St. Paul suggests in 2 Corinthians 3:18. Deification, for Gregory, quoting Paul, is a life of gradual transformation and perfection, "from glory to glory" without limitation. Our heart's desire to see God constantly expands as we progress toward the Good. "This truly is the vision of God: never to be satisfied in the desire to see him. . . . Thus, no limit would interrupt growth in the ascent to God."[20]

Cyril of Alexandria (370–444) spoke of deification as the supreme goal of created beings. By progressive participation and interpenetration, God and humanity are unified. Cyril employs the image of "melted wax" and "iron in the fire" in speaking about *theosis:* "Just as if someone were to entwine two pieces of wax together and melt them with a fire, so that both are made one, so too through participation in the Body of Christ and in His Precious Blood, He is united in us and we too in Him."[21] To be deified is to be "penetrated by divinity." Just as the "red-hot iron in the fire is penetrated by the heat of the fire—allowing the beauty of the inexpressible nature of the Trinity to shine in us," we are deified by the Holy Spirit who conforms us into the perfect image of the Father.[22]

In the sixth century, Maximus the Confessor (580–662) also understood the process of *theosis* as *perichoresis*—an "interpenetration" of God and humanity. First, a spiritual relationship of *communion* in Christ is established; then progressively, a mystical state of *union* is achieved, which in the end tends to blur, but not collapse, the essential distinction between Creator and creation. Thus, while remaining entirely human in nature, we become entirely divine by grace, progressively in this life and fully in the life to come.[23]

Theosis in the Russian mystical tradition goes beyond union language to the notion of a new creation of Divine-humanity. As Boris Jakim explains, "The Divine-humanity is a particular form of the Divinity's consciousness of itself through humanity; the Divine-humanity likewise is a particular form of humanity's consciousness of itself through the Divinity. It is the fusion of the Creator and creation, a fusion that is simultaneously the *kenosis* of the Divinity and the *theosis* of the humanity, and that concludes with the perfect glorification of the God-Man."[24]

Likeness to God as far as possible, climbing the ladder of divine accent, crossing the chasm that divides, learning to fly, putting on the robe, interweaving threads of God and humanity, interpenetration, the wax of humanity and divinity melting together, the polished human mirror reflecting its divine source, the red-hot iron receiving heat from the divine fire, fusion into a new Divine-humanity—these are the common images and symbols of deification in the Eastern and Western mystical traditions.[25] Although the process of *theosis* in the order of salvation, the stages of divine ascent, and the extent of the transformation are articulated and nuanced differently in the various Christian traditions, what has been commonly agreed upon is that human beings are creatures called, in some way, to become god.

The Problem of Theosis

In the Orthodox Study Bible, on a page between 1 and 2 Peter entitled "Deification," are these words of theological qualification:

> *What deification is not:* When the Church calls us to pursue godliness, to be more like God, this does not mean that human beings then become divine. We do not become like God in His nature. That would not only be heresy, it would be impossible. For we are human, always have been human, and always will be human. We cannot take on the nature of God.[26]

What is the *problem* with *theosis* that requires such a cautionary commentary? There are, of course, psychological, philosophical, and theological problems with and objections to "creatures becoming gods" or humans becoming divine in nature.

Modern psychology, for example, has moved beyond the ancient study of the psyche (or essential soul), with its capacity to transcend human nature, to the psychoanalysis of the relational or constructed self in the process of becoming an integrated whole. Depth psychologists, like Carl Jung, come closer to the ancient vision of the self and its capacity for transcendence and transformation. However, human *individuation* (to use Jung's term) applied to spiritual deification may be too bold and optimistic a vision of human wholeness and perfectibility for most depth psychologists.[27]

Philosophically, the problem of *theosis* is the classical problem of the One and the many. How can the phenomenon of multiplicity be reconciled with the vision of a foundational reality of unity at the summit of being? In post-structuralism, there can be no essential self or foundational reality, either as unity or plurality. While in Greek philosophy contemplation of the Beautiful and the Good was a deifying activity, in modern philosophy rational inquiry and reflection have replaced perfection as the highest order.

Theologically, human deification understood ontologically is objectionable in most Western Christian traditions. How could a human being become divine without negating the essential divine-human distinction in classical theological reasoning? Progressively perfected human beings may assume some qualities, attributes, or "energies" of divinity (namely holiness, love, and wisdom), but never become divine in substance or essence, according to Palamite reasoning.[28] One may become perfected in a spirit of love but not in body or nature; one will remain always creature in relation to Creator. Thus, whatever Athanasius meant when he declared that "God became Man so that Man could become God," he could not have meant it ontologically, given systematic theology's required distinctions between Creator and creation, Divinity and humanity, and the limits of sanctification and perfection in this life. As Orthodox bishop Kallistos Ware writes, "In the Age to come,

God is 'all in all' but Peter is Peter and Paul is Paul." Each retains his or her own nature and personal identity. Yet all are filled with God's spirit and perfected as creature.[29]

Finally, those who object to the ancient understanding of *theosis* on "enlightened" theological grounds sometimes try to dilute or domesticate it, or modernize it by finding a more reasonable substitute or dynamic theological equivalent to the term (e.g., Christian perfection, entire sanctification, imputed and imparted righteousness, glorification, Christification, spiritual individuation).[30] Some contemporary translators solve the problem of *theosis* by simply omitting the term from their modern translations and editions, or objecting to passages about *theosis* in the ancient texts.[31] Other scholars seek to explain the patristic concepts of deification in their historical settings. Still others attempt to reconstruct the ancient vision in a new context in continuity with its original meaning.

In this volume, the promise, process, and problem of *theosis* are explored in both their historical and contemporary contexts within the various Christian traditions under the general topic of becoming "partakers of the divine nature." The need for more precise usage of the terms, symbols, and concepts related to deification in contemporary theology is highlighted in this academic study. The functional nature and rhetorical applications of *theosis* language in the various Christian traditions are emphasized as a significant and enduring contribution to a centuries-long conversation on what it means to *become god.*

Notes

Quote in the epilogue is from *On the Spirit* 9.23; emphasis mine. Cf. NPNF 2 8:15–16. A version of this essay appeared in the *Journal of Christian Education and Information Technology* 8 (Oct. 30, 2005): 15–30.

1. These bold and memorable words, which first appear in Christian theology in the writing of Ireneaus (*Against Heresies* 5, pref.; ANF 1:526), are rephrased and repeated by Athanasius in *Incarnation of the Word* 54, in NPNF 2 4:65.

2. "I have said, 'Ye are gods; and all of you are children of the most High.'"; Jesus answered them, "Is it not written in your law, I said, Ye are gods?" (Jn 10:34).

3. Jaroslav Pelikan, *The Spirit of Eastern Christendom (600–1700),* The Christian Tradition, vol. 2 (Chicago: University of Chicago Press, 1974), 10.

4. Gregory of Nyssa, *On the Making of Man* 16; NPNF 2 5:405.

5. Origen, *On First Principles* 3.6.1; see also *Origen: On First Principles,* trans. G. W. Butterworth (Gloucester, MA: Peter Smith, 1973), 244.

6. Ireneaus, *Against Heresies* 4.38.1–3; see also ANF 1:521–22.

7. "and you will be like God (or the gods), knowing good and evil" (Gen 3:5).

8. "Pride is the beginning of all sin." Sir 10:15, quoted by Augustine in *On Nature and Grace* 29.33. FC 86:46.

9. See Vladimir Kharlamov on the diversity of understandings of *theosis* in rhetorical application of Greek patristic theology in this volume; see Gösta Hallonsten on the need for clarification of terms in this volume.

10. See James Starr for an exegesis of 2 Pt 1:4 in this volume.

11. See Vladimir Lossky, *The Vision of God,* trans. Asheleigh Moorhouse (Crestwood, NY: St. Vladimir's Seminary Press, 1983).

12. *Theaetetus* 176b. See *The Collected Dialogues of Plato,* ed. Edith Hamilton and Huntington Cairns (New York: Pantheon Books, 1961), 881.

13. Clement, *Christ the Educator* 1.6. ANF 2:215. Cf. FC 23:26: "and becoming perfect, we are made divine."

14. Origin, *Against Celsus* 3.28. See ANF 4:475.

15. Origen, *An Exhortation to Martyrdom* 15. *Origen: An Exhortation to Martyrdom, Prayer and Selected Works,* trans. Rowan Greer, CWS (Mahwah, NJ: Paulist Press, 1979), 52.

16. Ibid. 36. CWS 67.

17. *Hymns on Faith* 18.2. Sebastian Brock, *The Luminous Eye: The Spiritual World Vision of Saint Ephrem the Syrian,* rev. ed., CS 124 (Kalamazoo: Cistercian Publications, 1992), 79.

18. Ibid.

19. Lossky, *Vision of God,* 81.

20. Gregory of Nyssa, *The Life of Moses* 2.239. *Gregroy of Nyssa: The Life of Moses,* trans. Abraham Malherbe and Everett Ferguson, CWS (Mahwah, NJ: Paulist Press, 1978), 116–17. John McGuckin argues that Gregory of Nyssa and Gregory of Nazianzus appropriated Origin's vision of *theosis* as union with the Divine, but distinguished Christian deification from Platonic participation and assimilation to the Divine. See John McGuckin in this volume.

21. See *Commentary on the Gospel according to St. John,* vol. 2, Library of the Fathers 48 (London: Walter Smith, 1885), 370–71.

22. See Lossky, *Vision of God,* 98.

23. See Lossky, *Vision of God,* 134. For a nuanced understanding of divinization as *perichoresis* in Maximus the Confessor, see Elena Vishnevskaya, later in this volume.

24. See Boris Jakim on Sergius Bulgakov and Vladimir Solovyov's vision of Divine-humanity in chapter 16 of this volume.

25. Lossky summarizes the way of union in the process of attaining deification as a synergistic cooperation of divinity and humanity, through the action of the Holy Spirit, in three stages: *penitence, purification,* and *perfection.* The first stage involves conversion of the will; the second, liberation from the passions; and the third, "acquisition of that perfect love which is the fullness of grace." However, the "deification . . . of the creature will be realized in its fullness only in the age to come." *The Mystical Theology of the Eastern Church,* 204, 196.

26. The Orthodox Study Bible (Nashville, TN: Thomas Nelson Publishers, 1993), 561.

27. Carl Jung may be among the notable exceptions in modern psychology in his work on the archetypes in the human psyche, particularly the archetype of the Self. "In the world of Christian ideas," Jung writes, "Christ undoubtedly represents the self. As the apotheosis (elevation to divine status) of individuality, the self has the attributes of uniqueness and of occurring once only in time." As an archetypal symbol, "it is a God-image and therefore universal and eternal." "The Self," in *Aion,* par. 116. Jung also cites the patristic vision of "apokatatasis" as the "restoration of an original condition" and the "completion of all things," saying: "This is in exact agreement with the empirical findings of psychology, that there is an ever-present archetype of wholeness which may easily disappear from the purview of consciousness or may never be perceived at all until a consciousness illuminated by conversion recognizes it in the figure of Christ." As a result of this "anamnesis" the original state of oneness with the God-image is restored. It brings about integration, a bridging of the split in the personality . . . (and) an all embracing totality." *Aion* V, in *The Collected Works of Jung* (Princeton, NJ: Princeton University Press, 1970), par. 73–74.

28. See Jeffrey Finch on neo-Palamism later in this volume.

29. *The Orthodox Way* (Crestwood, NY: St. Vladimir's Seminary Press, 1986), 168.

30. Wesleyan reconstructions, for example, are comfortable substituting the term sanctification for *theosis.* See my essay in this volume on John Wesley.

31. For example, Martin Werner views deification as part of the Hellenization of Christian belief. *The Formation of Christian Dogma* (New York: Harper, 1957), 168. According to Ben Drewery, the concept of deification in the fathers, from Clement through Gregory Palamas, presents "an inherent dilemma that defies resolution." "Deification," in *Christian Spirituality: Essays in Honour of Gordon Rupp,* ed. Peter Books 33–62 (London: SCM Press, 1975), 57. The idea of deification sounds blasphemous or too pretentious to some and totally absurd and non-Christian to others. See Francis J. Hall, *The Incarnation* (New York: Longmans, Green and Company, 1915), 192; Donald E. Gowan, *When Man Becomes God: Humanism and Hubris in the Old Testament* (Pittsburgh: Pickwick Press, 1975), 1. I am indebted to Vladimir Kharlamov for pointing these objections out to me.

The Place of *Theosis* in Orthodox Theology

Andrew Louth

It is often claimed that the doctrine of θέωσις, or deification, is distinctive to Greek Patristic or to Orthodox theology; and that claim is made both negatively and positively. Negatively it has often been claimed that deification stands in the sharpest possible contrast to the biblical doctrine of justification and represents most clearly the way in which Greek and Orthodox theology has strayed from authentic Christianity. Positively the claim is often made by Orthodox theologians that deification is distinctive to Orthodox theology, and by other Christians, Protestant and Catholic, that it is in the doctrine of θέωσις that Western Christians will find what they are most in need of from the Orthodox tradition. It was in these terms that Professor Cunliffe-Jones, many years ago, commended "the Christian humanism of the conception of *theosis*—the transformation and re-creation of mankind by the power of God";[1] it is doubtless something of the same hope that has lain behind the publication of the present volume.

This perception of the centrality of deification for Orthodox theology is borne out by the fact that three important studies on this subject have recently been published. The first, Emil Bartos's *Deification in Eastern Orthodox Theology,*[2] focuses on the work of the Romanian priest, Fr. Dumitru Stăniloae—a figure often considered to be the greatest Orthodox theologian of the last century. The second book is Bishop Joachim Giosanu's *La Déification de l'homme d'après la pensée du Père Dumitru Stăniloaë.*[3] The third is Dr. Norman Russell's major study of deification, which I have read more than once on its journey toward the published text.[4] I could not express my thoughts on the subject of *theosis* without drawing deeply on what I have learned from that reading. Instead of building on this illuminating and thorough analysis of the history of the doctrine of deification in the Greek Fathers, I will content myself to look at the *place* of deification in Orthodox theology.

It has often struck me that in theology—as in other subjects—analysis of concepts can seem to miss the point in a tantalizing way. One breaks the concept down into its constituent parts and analyzes each of these parts—historically and conceptually—and then puts it all back together again, but still one seems to have missed the significance that it holds for those who value it. This is notably true in the literature on deification of Ben Drewery's elegant and concise paper on deification, contributed to the Festschrift for Gordon Rupp.[5] The concept of deification is analyzed in a way that displays Drewery's excellent grasp of the meaning given to this term in various Greek theologians; his criticism is sharp and clearly put. But what is interesting about his presentation is that when he comes to express his own perception of the truth with which deification is meant to be bound up, he does not himself attempt to present an alternative concept—his understanding of justification, for instance, a doctrine I don't think he mentions—rather he quotes from hymns, especially those of Charles Wesley, that characterize his own Methodist tradition. Deification is a concept that he can analyze and for which he does not much care; what matters to him is the doctrine of scriptural holiness, not analyzed as a concept, but expressed in the devotional verse of hymns. The Methodist Drewery grasps very well the *place* of the doctrine of scriptural holiness, the Methodist doctrine that others have argued displays many points of convergence with the doctrine of deification, but has no feel at all for the place of the doctrine of deification, which appears to him a concept of dubious lineage and dangerous connotations. What I want to do in this essay is to say something about the *place* of deification in Orthodox theology.

What I mean by "place" is the way the doctrine functions in the whole Orthodox experience, including the pattern of theology. In studying the history of Christian theology, we have often paid too little attention to what I would call the pattern of theology: the mosaic, as it were, that emerges when the various doctrines of the faith are fitted together. We tend to take for granted the pattern of theology that we are familiar with from our own Christian experience, or from what we have picked up in our reading and thinking, and impose that pattern on whatever it is we are studying. If the pattern does not fit, we complain that there seems to be an inadequate grasp of whatever is involved in that lack of fit. It takes a lot of humility and patience to revise our framework, and try and work out what framework was assumed, or adopted, by whomever it is or whatever tradition it is that we are trying to understand. This is, I think, particularly true of attempts on the part of non-Orthodox to understand the doctrine of deification.

For whatever reasons, the doctrine of deification ceased to have a central role in Western theology from about the twelfth century, though it had a continuing place among the mystics, with all the marginalization, and suspicion, and also allure, that such relegation entailed.[6] It is no longer part of the pattern of either contemporary Catholic or Protestant theology; Western attempts to understand it have consequently assimilated it to an alien framework, and not surprisingly, it fits very awkwardly. How does it fit into the pattern of theology found in the Greek Fathers and in modern Orthodox theology? (I am not confusing these, as if they were the same, but I do think that in this case the answers are much the same, which is not surprising, given the importance to modern Orthodox theology of the vision of the Greek Fathers.)

Incarnation: The Cosmic Dimension of *Theosis*

I want to proceed by suggesting various ways in which deification finds a significant place in Orthodox theology, in relation to other doctrines, and indeed—perhaps more important—in relation to Orthodox experience as a whole. Let me start by looking at the most famous patristic assertion of the doctrine of deification, St. Athanasius's words toward the end of *De Incarnatione:* "He [the Word of God] became human that we might become God; and he revealed himself through a body that we might receive an idea of the invisible Father; and he endured insults from humans that we might inherit incorruption."[7] Here, the doctrine of deification is presented as a counterpart of the doctrine of the Incarnation. It might, however, be better to speak of the *event* of deification and the *event* of the Incarnation, for Athanasius is talking about something that happened; he is talking about the engagement between God and humankind in the Incarnation, and its consequences. Deification expresses the full extent of the consequences of the Incarnation; as in the Incarnation God the Word shared with us in what it is to be human, so in deification we shall come to share in what it is to be God—as St. Irenaeus put it, "in his immense love he became what we are, that he might make us what he is."[8] He shared our life, to the point of death, that we might be redeemed from death and come to share the divine life. This notion of an exchange, of what the Latin Fathers called *admirabile commercium* (wonderful exchange), is the place where deification fits; it is not so much a doctrine to be analyzed, as a way of capturing the nature and extent of our response to the Incarnation. The rest of the sentence quoted draws out something of the nature of the exchange: the Word becoming visible through a body, so that we might find access to the invisible Godhead; the Word in the body submitting to insult and outrage that we might attain a state beyond all that outrage and insult entail, the state he calls incorruption, ἀφθαρσία. We shall explore a little later on more of what this entails.

Deification, then, has to do with human destiny, a destiny that finds its fulfillment in a face-to-face encounter with God, an encounter in which God takes the initiative by meeting us in the Incarnation, where we behold "the glory as of the Only-Begotten from the Father" (Jn 1:14), "the glory of God in the face of Jesus Christ" (2 Cor 4:6). It is important for a full grasp of what this means to realize that deification is not to be equated with redemption. Christ certainly came to save us, and in our response to his saving action and word we are redeemed; but deification belongs to a broader conception of the divine οἰκονομία: deification is the fulfillment of creation, not just the rectification of the Fall. One way of putting this is to think in terms of an arch stretching from creation to deification, representing what is and remains God's intention: the creation of the cosmos that, through humankind, is destined to share in the divine life, to be deified. Progress along this arch has been frustrated by humankind, in Adam, failing to work with God's purposes, leading to the Fall, which needs to be put right by redemption. There is, then, what one might think of as a lesser arch, leading from Fall to redemption, the purpose of which is to restore the function of the greater arch, from creation to deification. The loss of the notion of deification leads to lack of awareness of the greater arch from creation to deification, and thereby to concentration on the lower arch, from Fall to redemption; it is, I think, not unfair to suggest that such a concentration on the lesser arch at the expense of the greater arch has been characteristic of much Western theology. The consequences are evident: a loss of the sense of the cosmic dimension of theology, a tendency to see the created order as little more than a background for the great drama of redemption, with the result that the Incarnation is seen simply as a means of redemption, the putting right of the Fall of Adam: *O certe necessarium Adae peccatum, quod Christi morte deletum est! O felix culpa, quae talem ac tantum meruit habere Redemptorem!*—as the *Praeconium Pascale* has it: "O certainly necessary sin of Adam, which Christ has destroyed by death! O happy fault, which deserved to have such and so great a Redeemer!"[9]

Orthodox theology has never lost sight of the greater arch, leading from creation to deification. One can see this in the theology of Fr. Sergius Bulgakov, whose patristic learning is often—unjustly, I think—impuned. In the first volume of the last, great trilogy, *The Divine Wisdom and the Divine Humanity,* he has this to say about deification in the context of the Incarnation:

> God wants to communicate to the world his divine life and himself to "dwell" in the world, to become human, in order to make of human kind a god, too. That transcends the limits of human imagination and daring, it is the mystery of the love of God "hidden from the beginning in God" (Eph 3:9), unknown to the angels themselves (Eph 3:10; 1 Pt 1:12; 1 Tim 3:16). The love of God knows no limits and cannot reach its furthest limit in the fullness of the divine abnegation for the sake of the world: the Incarnation. And if the very nature of the world, raised from non-being to its created state, does not appear here as an obstacle, its *fallen* state is not one either. God comes even to a fallen world; the love of God is not repelled by the powerlessness of the creature, nor by his fallen image, nor even by the sin of the world: the Lamb of God, who voluntarily bears the sins of the world, is manifest in him. In this way, God gives all for the divinization of the world and its salvation, and nothing remains that he has not given. Such is the love of God, such is Love.
>
> Such it is in the interior life of the Trinity, in the reciprocal surrender of the three hypostases, and such it is in the relation of God to the world. If it is *in such*

> *a way* that we are to understand the Incarnation—and Christ himself teaches us to understand it *in such a way* (Jn 3:16)—there is no longer any room to ask if the Incarnation would have taken place apart from the Fall. The greater contains the lesser, the conclusion presupposes the antecedent, and the concrete includes the general. The love of God for *fallen* humankind, which finds it in no way repugnant to take the failed nature of Adam, already contains the love of stainless humankind.
>
> And that is expressed in the wisdom of the brief words of the Nicene Creed: "for our sake and for our salvation." This *and,* in all the diversity and all the generality of its meaning, contains the theology of the Incarnation. In particular, this *and* can be taken in the sense of identification (as *that is to say*). So it is understood by those who consider that *salvation* is the reason for the Incarnation; in fact, concretely, that is indeed what it signifies for fallen humanity. But this *and* can equally be understood in a distinctive sense (that is to say "and in particular," or similar expressions), separating the general from the particular, in other words without limiting the power of the Incarnation nor exhausting it solely in redemption. *The Word became flesh:* one must understand this in all the plenitude of its meaning, from the theological point of view and the cosmic, the anthropological, the Christological and the soteriological. The last, the most concrete, includes and does not exclude the other meanings; so, too, the theology of the Incarnation cannot be limited to the bounds of soteriology; that would be, moreover, impossible, as the history of dogma bears witness. . . .
>
> The Incarnation is the interior basis of creation, its *final cause.* God did not create the world to hold it at a distance from him, at that insurmountable metaphysical distance that separates the Creator from the creation, but in order to surmount that distance and unite himself completely with the world; not only from the outside, as Creator, nor even as providence, but from within: "the Word became flesh." That is why the Incarnation is already predetermined in human kind.[10]

The doctrine of deification preserves this sense that God created the world to unite it to himself; it preserves the sense that the purpose of creation is to achieve union with God. Humankind, fashioned in his image to be a microcosm and bond of the cosmos, was to have a key role in that process of deification; in the Incarnation, the Word comes to humankind as a human being to take on this role himself, to fulfill the human purpose for the cosmos—something on which St. Maximus the Confessor meditated in the forty-first of his *Ambigua,* or "Difficulties."

Deification is a way of expressing a sense of the "plan—οἰκονομία—of the mystery hidden for ages in God who created all things" (Eph 3:9), a plan that is not exhausted in redemption made necessary by the Fall of humankind; it is a way of summing up the purpose of creation. Consciousness of the arch that stretches from creation to deification is essential to preserving a sense of the cosmic dimension of the divine economy. Another way of "placing" the doctrine of deification emerges if we consider more deeply the quotation from St. Athanasius already cited. Deification is presented as the effect of the Incarnation, the result of human response to the Word's becoming flesh. What is envisaged is a transformation, a transfiguration, of human beings. Those are big words, but what is certainly meant is a real *change*: a change that is the result of coming to share in the life of God. This change involves a kind of reconstitution of our humanity, a reshaping, a straightening out of all the distortions and corruptions that we have brought upon our humanity by misusing—abusing—our human capacities, and by living out our lives in accordance with values and principles that fall a long way short of the values and principles inherent in creation as God intended it. This reconstitution of human nature is something impossible without the grace of God, without everything implied in God the Word's living out what it is to be human, and thereby on the one hand showing us what it is to be truly human, and on the other experiencing and overcoming the accumulated power of evil that has manifested itself in human nature and human affairs—ultimately experiencing and overcoming the power of death itself. This reconstitution of our human nature is therefore something beyond our human powers—no self-help will be anywhere near adequate—but on the other hand it is something that involves the most profound commitment of our human powers; it is not a change in which we will be passively put right—some sort of moral and spiritual surgery—it is a change that requires our utmost cooperation, that calls for truly ascetic struggle. No theology can call itself Orthodox in the true sense that does not embrace such an ascetic commitment.

It is for this reason that the most important work for Orthodox theology published in modern times is not any of the so-called "Symbolical Books," which defined the Orthodox faith in relation to Catholicism and Protestantism in the seventeenth and eighteenth centuries, nor even any of the works of the Russian émigré theologians of the last century—great though many of these are—but a compilation of ascetic texts made by St. Makarios of Corinth and St. Nicodimos of the Holy Mountain, called the *Philokalia,* published in 1782. One could indeed argue that everything that is most vital about modern Orthodoxy can be traced back to that work, such is its towering importance.[11] The title page of the *Philokalia* reads: "Anthology [*Philokalia*] of the holy ascetics [or: watchful ones], gathered from our holy and god-bearing Fathers, in which, through ethical philosophy in accordance with practice and contemplation, the intellect is purified, illumined and perfected . . ." The purpose of the book, then, is the purification, illumination, and perfection of the intellect—a process that will render it capable of pure prayer, that is, authentic communication with God, in which the intellect or the heart, the spiritual principle of the human person, attains its ultimate goal. This process is not possible apart from the body, nor indeed without attention to communion with others made possible through the body; the purpose of asceticism is to restore the original faculties of created reality, which involves individual effort, but which cannot be achieved on one's own, nor indeed apart from the whole of God's creation in which the human is to play a key role.

It is to one of the works contained in the *Philokalia* that I want to turn to develop a little the ascetic implications of St. Athanasius's fundamental assertion that the Word "became human that we might become God." It is one of the shorter works in the collection, St. Maximus the Confessor's treatise, *On the Lord's Prayer.* As Fr. Gabriel Bunge observes, in his wonderful book on prayer in the patristic tradition recently translated into English, it is striking that the Lord left us, not a creed, but a prayer: it is in and through a prayer that the most fundamental summary of our beliefs are contained.[12] It is this insight that St. Maximus develops in his short treatise. Of the Lord's Prayer, he remarks:

> For hidden within a limited compass this prayer contains the whole purpose and aim of which we have just spoken; or, rather, it openly proclaims this purpose and aim to those whose intellects are strong enough to perceive them. The prayer includes petitions for everything that the divine Logos effected through his self-emptying in the Incarnation, and it teaches us to strive for those blessings of which the true provider is God the Father alone through the natural mediation of the Son in the Holy Spirit.[13]

He goes on to say a little later that our response to the Incarnation, through which we receive deification, imitates the action of the Word in the Incarnation—our deification mirrors his Incarnation, the principle St. Athanasius enunciated—and, in particular, our response involves a κένωσις, a self-emptying, that mirrors the κένωσις through which the Word of God assumed humanity:

> The Logos bestows adoption on us when He grants us that birth which, transcending nature, comes by grace from above through the Spirit. The guarding and preservation of this with God depends on the resolve of those thus born: on their sincere acceptance of the grace bestowed on them and, through the practice of the commandments, on their cultivation of the beauty given to them by grace. Moreover, by emptying themselves of the passions they lay hold of the divine to the same degree as that to which, deliberately emptying Himself of His own sublime glory, the Logos of God truly became man.[14]

Our κένωσις is a self-emptying of the passions, passions that St. Maximus defines as "impulses of the soul contrary to nature."[15] Emptied of such passions, the soul is restored to its natural state—the Logos, Maximus says, "restores human nature to itself"[16]—so that, to quote from a little later on in the treatise, "our whole intellect be directed towards God, tensed by our incensive power as if by some nerve, and fired with longing by our desire at its most ardent."[17] In this restored state, the beauty of the soul, lent it by grace, is revealed. But this self-emptying of the passions, of all distortions and corruptions that lay waste our nature, cannot take place without serious ascetic struggle, because it involves a real change in our nature: a change that restores it to its truly natural state.

Here is perhaps a good place to clear up a misconception about deification, namely, that it involves the transformation of our human nature into something other than human, some kind of *apotheosis* that removes our humanity: to quote some frequently quoted words, "If the aim of the Christian is to cease to be 'human, all too human,' it would be a natural corollary in Christology to regard the humanity of our Lord as a problem rather than a datum."[18] For the Orthodox tradition, and for St. Maximus in particular, nothing could be further from the truth: the aim of the Christian is to become once again truly human, to become the human partners of God as we were originally created, and as human partners to share in the divine life. It may well be that Nietzsche's "menschliches, allzumenschliches" ("human, all too human") is hardly a good way of summing up what this entails, but that is perhaps not surprising; better, perhaps, is the remark of Bulgakov's: "God comes in the cool of the day to talk with man, as with a friend, and that 'conversation' was no *donum superadditum* [gift provided in addition] in relation to his incorrupt nature, but, on the contrary, that conversation was something quite normal."[19] That is, part of what it is to be human is to speak with God as "with a friend" and all that such intimacy with God entails: which is what deification means. Deification, then, is not a transcending of what it means to be human, but the fulfillment of what it is to be human. Although we need to realize how far we are from that fulfilment, that realization is greatly impeded by the conviction that to be human is to be fallen and frail ("all too human"). As Nikolai Berdyaev remarked, "There can be no question of the work of a great artist being poor, low and insignificant simply because it is created. But the Creator of the world is the greatest of artists, and there is no reason why it should be denied that He can create something divine and lofty."[20] Deification reveals the divine and lofty purpose for which humankind was created. This is the first way in which I would suggest we should think of the *place* of deification in the Orthodox understanding of things.

Transformation: The Human Dimension of *Theosis*

The second way in which I suggest we can see the doctrine of deification "placed" in Orthodox theology lays stress on the real change involved in the transfiguration of human nature that deification entails, a change only possible through the transfiguring power of God combined with a genuine and costly commitment to ascetic struggle on our part. Orthodox theology wants to speak of this change in terms of ontology, not because this change involves a conversion into something other than human, but rather because the change involved is fundamental, radical, a rebuilding of what it is to be human from the roots up. It is not a matter of some superficial change in patterns of behavior—though it involves a radical change in our way of life—still less is it a matter of our simply being regarded in a different light by God, as justification by faith alone is sometimes taken to imply. Rather, it is something fundamental, and ontological language is often used to express this. This change restores human nature to its true purpose, to be companions of God, through Christ in the Holy Spirit, and to be partakers of the divine life and the divine nature. Human beings are to speak with God as "with a friend," as Bulgakov put it in the passage just quoted. In the Old Testament, Moses is spoken of as enjoying such a relationship with God: as we read in Exodus, "Thus the Lord used to speak with Moses face to face, as a man speaks to his friend" (Ex 33:11). It is for this reason that Moses came to be, for many of the fathers, the archetype for the human encounter with God. "Face-to-face": in these terms the fulfillment of our relationship with God is represented. "Now we see through a glass darkly; but then face to face: now I know in part; but then I shall know even as I am known" (1 Cor 13:12). The Transfiguration of the Lord, at which significantly Moses was present, is the great Gospel account in which the chosen disciples come face-to-face with Jesus as God. In the fourth Gospel, in which, as has often been remarked, the event of the Transfiguration does not occur because the reality of the Transfiguration is always present, Jesus calls his disciples friends (Jn 15:15).

What is meant by this face-to-face vision of God? First of all, it must mean that God has a face: the face revealed in the Transfiguration, the face of which the Apostle Paul speaks when he talks of God "who has shone in our hearts to give the light of the knowledge of the glory of God in the face of Jesus Christ" (2 Cor 4:6). Second, our final encounter with God is an encounter, an engagement, with an Other; it is not to be dissolved in the Ultimate. But that encounter is on our part also a transfiguration: "when he appears we shall be like him, for we shall see him as he is" (1 Jn 3:2)—a transfiguration in which we shall become "like him."

It is striking that it is in conjunction with a reference to the Transfiguration that the Apostle Peter speaks of our becoming "partakers of the divine nature." What does this mean? What kind of transfiguration—transformation—is envisaged? When we speak of becoming partakers of the divine nature, or of becoming God, we are speaking of what we know not, something beyond any human conception. As the Prophet Isaiah professed, "Truly, thou art a God who hidest thyself" (Is 45:15), and, as Dionysius the Areopagite reminds us, as revealed in Jesus Christ, "he is hidden after his manifestation or, to speak more divinely, even in his manifestation. For even this mystery of Jesus is hidden, and what it is in itself can be expressed by no word or concept, and what can be spoken remains ineffable and what can be understood remains unknown."[21] What it is to be divine is beyond our comprehension, and indeed is revealed as precisely beyond our comprehension: deification is not becoming something we know and understand (as seems to be suggested by those who are sure that becoming divine means to cease to be human), it is to enter into a mystery, beyond anything we can understand. This is often called an apophatic approach, attitude, or way of union.

Apophatic Theology: The Divine-Human Union

There are, it seems to me, two sides—at least—to what is meant by such prizing of the apophatic. One on side, to quote the great living Greek philosopher, Christos Yannaras,

> The apophatic attitude leads Christian theology to use the language of poetry and images for the interpretation of dogmas much more than the language of conventional logic and schematic concepts. The conventional logic of everyday understanding can very easily give man a false sense of a sure knowledge which, being won by the intellect, is already exhausted by it, completely possessed by it. While poetry, with the symbolisms and images which it uses, always exhibits a sense from within the words and beyond the words, a concept which corresponds more to common experiences of life and less to cerebral conceptions.[22]

Historically, this perception has been most evident in Orthodoxy in the symbolism that has come to surround the celebration of the Divine Liturgy, and in the wealth of liturgical poetry that characterizes Orthodox worship. The mystery of God is not something explored by the "flight of the alone to the Alone," but rather something celebrated in the hymns and ritual actions of the Christian community, as no one has seen more clearly than Dionysius the Areopagite. The beauty of the soul that Maximus sees created by our ascetic struggle is a response to the beauty of God, manifest in creation and celebrated in the liturgy, a beauty that calls us back to God (here the Greek has a convenient play of words between κάλλος, beauty, and καλεῖν, to call). That is one side of the apophatic approach we need to grasp if we are to construe deification properly.

The other side is the rejection itself of the ultimacy of our concepts, the entry into darkness and unknowing, evoked by Dionysius the Areopagite in his brief and pregnant treatise, *Mystical Theology.*

> Trinity, beyond being, beyond godhead, beyond goodness! Guardian of the divine wisdom of Christians! Lead us up beyond unknowing and light, up to the highest peak of the hidden oracles, where the mysteries of theology lie simple, absolute and unchangeable in the dazzling darkness of hidden silence. In the deepest darkness

> they pour overwhelming light on what transcends manifestation, and in what is wholly beyond touch and sight they fill to overflowing our sightless minds with splendors beyond all beauty.[23]

Dionysius goes on to compare those who pursue this path to sculptors, who bring beauty out of stone by cutting away: "like those who make a natural statue by removing every hindrance that gets in the way of the pure vision of the hidden object, and simply by cutting away from itself make manifest the concealed beauty."[24] It is a familiar image, going back through Gregory of Nyssa to Plotinus,[25] and that lineage is important, for Dionysius's allusion to it makes clear that this process of cutting away is not simply a matter of refining, and ultimately rejecting, concepts, but a matter of cutting away and refining oneself, or as Gregory himself expresses it, submitting oneself to Christ himself who cuts away whatever it is in us that hides the true image of God in which we were created. That Dionysius has in mind a process by which we are transformed, rather than simply some sort of dialectic process, becomes clear in the next chapter of the *Mystical Theology,* where he asserts that

> the more we look upwards, the more our words are confined to the simple vision of the intelligible; so that now as we plunge into that darkness that is beyond intellect, we shall find ourselves not simply running short of words but actually speechless and unknowing . . . ascending from below to what is transcendent, the more it climbs, the more language falters, and passing beyond any ascent it will be wholly speechless and wholly united to the One who is ineffable.[26]

What is the nature of this being reduced to silence as we find ourselves closer and closer—ultimately united with—the One who is beyond any human conception? It is certainly the failure of language expressive of awe before the divine: the same awe that can find expression in a babbling overflow of symbols and similes. But it is not the divine over against us, it is the divine with which we are being united, the divine grace that penetrates within, cutting away all that is opposed to it, and revealing within the divine image in which we have been created in all its glory and beauty. This sense of the apophatic attitude as not constituting some limitation to our knowledge, but rather as disclosing the transforming encounter with God himself, is perhaps best expressed in some words of Vladimir Lossky, in the concluding chapter of his *Mystical Theology of the Eastern Church:*

> We have had again and again, in the course of our study of the mystical theology of the Eastern Church, to refer to the apophatic attitude which is characteristic of its religious thought. As we have seen, the negations which draw attention to the divine incomprehensibility are not prohibitions upon knowledge: apophaticism, so far from being a limitation, enables us to transcend all concepts, every sphere

> of philosophical speculation. It is a tendency towards an ever-greater plenitude, in which knowledge is transformed into ignorance, the theology of concepts into contemplation, dogmas into experience of ineffable mysteries. It is, moreover, an existential theology involving man's entire being, which sets him upon the way of union, which obliges him to be changed, to transform his nature that he may attain to the true *gnosis* which is contemplation of the Holy Trinity. Now, this "change of heart," this μετανοια, means repentance. The apophatic way of Eastern theology is the repentance of the human person before the face of the living God. It is the constant transformation of the creature tending towards its completeness: towards that union with God which is brought about through divine grace and human freedom.[27]

This then, I would suggest, is a further way in which deification may be "placed" in Orthodox theology: deification witnesses to the rooting of theology in the transforming encounter with God, now known most fully in the Incarnation, and approached through the "gates of repentance."

Conclusion

What I have attempted to demonstrate in this essay is that the doctrine of deification in Orthodox theology is not some isolated *theologoumenon,* but has what one might call structural significance. In various ways, I have suggested that deification, by the place it occupies in Orthodox theology, determines the shape of that theology: first, it is a counterpart to the doctrine of the Incarnation, and also anchors the greater arch of the divine economy, which reaches from creation to deification, thereby securing the cosmic dimension of theology; second, it witnesses to the human side of *theosis* in the transformation involved in responding to the encounter with God offered in Christ through the Holy Spirit—a real change that requires a serious ascetic commitment on our part; and finally, deification witnesses to the deeper meaning of the apophatic way found in Orthodox theology, a meaning rooted in the "repentance of the human person before the face of the living God."

Notes

1. H. Cunliffe-Jones, *Christian Theology since 1600* (Duckworth, 1970), 124.
2. Emil Bartos, *Deification in Eastern Orthodox Theology: An Evaluation and Critique of the Theology of Dumitru Stăniloaë* (Carlisle, Cumbria: Paternoster Press, 1999).
3. Évêque Joachim Giosanu, *La Déification de l'homme d'après la pensée du Père Stăniloaë* (Iassy: Trinitas, 2003).
4. Norman Russell, *The Doctrine of Deification in Greek Patristic Theology,* Oxford Early Christian Studies (Oxford: Oxford University Press, 2004).

5. Ben Drewery, "Deification," in *Christian Spirituality: Essays in Honour of Gordon Rupp,* ed. Peter Brooks, 33–62 (London: SCM Press, 1975).

6. While it is still important in the mystic Bernard of Clairvaux, it is absent from Peter Lombard, and Aquinas only uses the language of *deificatio* of Christ's human nature, not of human beings.

7. Athanasius, *De Incarnatione* 54.

8. Irenaeus, *Adversus Haereses* 5. *praef.*

9. The *Praeconium Paschale* is part of the Easter Vigil in the Western Church; see *Missale Romanum* (Ratisbon: F. Pustet, 1963), 227–28; translation is mine.

10. S. Boulgakoff, *Du Verbe incarné* (Paris: Aubier, 1943), 97–98; translation is mine. The echoes of Barth's doctrine of the covenant as the inner ground of creation are pre-echoes; Bulgakov's work was first published in 1933, when only the first volume of Barth's *Kirchliche Dogmatik* had been published.

11. See my contribution to the Festschrift for Bishop Kallistos of Diokleia: "The Theology of the *Philokalia,*" in *Abba: The Tradition of Orthodoxy in the West,* ed. John Behr, Andrew Louth, and Dimitri Conomos, 351–61 (Crestwood, NY: St. Vladimir's Seminary Press, 2003).

12. Gabriel Bunge OSB, *Earthen Vessels: The Practice of Personal Prayer according to the Patristic Tradition* (San Francisco: Ignatius Press, 2002), 11.

13. Maximus the Confessor, *On the Lord's Prayer,* ed. P. Van Deun, CCSG 23, lines 62–69 (Turnhout: Brepols/Leuven: University Press, 1991); translation in *The Philokalia: The Complete Text,* ed. and trans. G. E. H. Palmer, Philip Sherrard, and Kallistos Ware, vol. 2 (London: Faber and Faber, 1981), 286.

14. Ibid., lines 97–106; translation modified in *Philokalia,* 287.

15. Maximus, *Centuries on Love* 1.35.

16. Maximus, *On the Lord's Prayer,* line 135; *Philokalia,* 288.

17. Ibid., lines 542–45; *Philokalia,* 298.

18. Quoted from Drewery, "Deification," 61, where he is quoting from H. E. W. Turner, *The Patristic Doctrine of Redemption* (London: Mowbray, 1952), 82–83, who is himself quoting J. L. Haire, "On Behalf of Chalcedon," in *Essays in Christology for Karl Barth,* ed. T. H. L. Parker, 104–5 (London: Lutterworth Press, 1956).

19. S. Bulgakov, *Kupina Neopalimaya* (Paris: YMCA Press, 1927), 25.

20. N. Berdyaev, *The Destiny of Man* (London: Geoffrey Bles, 1937), 27.

21. Dionysius the Areopagite, *Ep.* 3. Translations from Dionysius the Areopagite are my own, sometimes based on the Luibheid-Rorem translation in *Pseudo-Dionysios: The Complete Works,* CWS (Mahwah, NJ: Paulist Press, 1987).

22. C. Yannaras, *The Elements of Faith* (Edinburgh: T. & T. Clark, 1991), 17.

23. Dionysius the Areopagite, *Mystical Theology* 1.

24. Ibid. 2.

25. Cf. Gregory of Nyssa, *Life of Moses* 2.313, *Inscriptions of the Psalms* 2.11, *Homilies on the Song of Songs* 14; and Plotinus, *Enneads* 1.6.9.

26. Dionysius, *Mystical Theology* 3.

27. V. Lossky, *The Mystical Theology of the Eastern Church* (London: James Clarke, 1957), 238.

II

Theosis in Classical and Late Antiquity

Deification of the Philosopher in Classical Greece

John R. Lenz

Greek philosophy, specifically Plato, has a central place in religious history in general and the Neoplatonic Christian tradition in particular. Plato, in the context of early Greek religion and contemplative spirituality, makes the idea of deification—or the participation of human beings in the divine nature—open to all through personal contemplation and the development of the soul. Deification is a neglected but essential theme in Greek philosoply. If we look only to Neoplatonic Hellenistic philosophy for antecedents of Christian thought and of *theosis* in particular, and not to the earlier period of classical Greek religion and philosophy, we will miss the origins of *theosis*. This paper presents two major themes: (1) the union of reason and spirituality in early Greek thought as evidenced by the Platonic vision of *theosis*; and (2) the continuity of Greek philosophy and Christian thought.

(1) Classical Greek thought displays a union of mysticism and rationality, and also of knowledge and praxis. The human capacity for reason provides the basis and potential for divinity in human beings. *Nous* (mind, reason) is the highest and most godlike part of us, according to Plato, Aristotle, the Epicureans and the Stoics. Since all human beings share a capacity for reason, and participate in divine reason through contemplation, deification is possible for all people, though only achieved by true philosophers like Socrates.

The theme of the deification of the sage or philosopher in ancient Greece has received little attention in Western scholarship; typically it is relegated to dark corners where Orphic cults and mystery religions lurk. Thus marginalized, or disparaged (falsely) as non-Hellenic, deification has come to be regarded as mere metaphor (the common way, for example, of accommodating Socrates' *daimonion*) or otherwise domesticated.[1] To the contrary, Peter Kingsley has explored and articulated the mystical foundations of Western thought, which has a positive place for *theosis*.[2] Pierre Hadot, more generally, has reminded that Greek philosophy is less about propositions than about a way of life.[3] What kind? A *spiritual* way of life: a pursuit of the best, most perfect life, comparable to that of the gods.

(2) The continuity of Greek philosophy, particularly Plato, and Christianity is well established. Christianity arose in the Greek world and its texts were

written in Greek. The Eastern church fathers made much use of Plato,[4] and Neoplatonism is found in early Western Christian thought, particulary in the Hellenistic period (323–30 BC). However, scholars should examine deification more carefully not only in its Hellenistic context, but also in earlier Hellenic thought (c. 550–323 BC).

Classical thought and religion are distinct from the Neoplatonic Christian tradition. In the study of the background of Christianity, the Hellenistic era has received attention for its blending of East and West. The union of Greek and Near Eastern cultures at the time is a problem that admits various solutions, depending on one's view of the early church. I wish to avoid a common view that a divine revelation was at some time infused with Greek "reason" or "rhetoric," as if Greek culture only provided Christianity with outward, stylistic embellishments. The continuities are deeper. Greek thought is richly spiritual from the Presocratics (sixth century BC) on; it does not just appear in the Hellenistic age. Typically, Greek spiritual interests of the Hellenistic age (such as mystery religions and soteriological beliefs) are regarded as new, exotic, quasi-Eastern innovations. This marginalizes them with respect to the Greek tradition itself.[5] The Hellenistic period is a barrier erected between classical Greek and Christian thought. A broader perspective views classical Greek philosophy as providing an important background for the historical study of Christianity.

Reason and spirituality are united in early Greek thought, and Hellenistic Greek philosophy is in continuity with Christian thought. After providing some initial background, I will present these two themes through a brief survey of the thought of leading Greek philosophers.

Background

Classical Greek thought typically stresses the existential boundary between mortals and immortals. Homer portrays the "mortal hero" (the Mesopotamian *Epic of Gilgamesh* had set the tone) together with the bleak picture of miserable shades in the underworld in book 11 of the *Odyssey.* In the *Iliad,* for example, a demigod such as Achilles is inescapably mortal, despite being the son of a goddess. And even Zeus is told he cannot overrule fate and raise his son Sarpedon from death. Naturally, given this basic binary opposition between humans and gods, which is defined by the irrevocable boundary line of death (i.e., fate), deification involves the making immortal of a mortal. We find this notion of deification in ancient Greek thought perhaps more than is commonly assumed. The topic of deification naturally overlaps with questions of immortalization or attainment of a blessed afterlife.

In Greek religion, a hero (*hērōs*) was a mortal who became a minor deity after death, was worshipped and could exert power in the world (bearing comparison with a Christian saint). Herakles achieved an *apotheosis* to Mount Olympus, as did Oedipus in Sophocles.[6] An *apotheosis* (elevation to divine status) was an exceptional grant by a god to a favored individual. Some of the heroes of Hesiod's fourth generation of mankind, the one preceding the contemporary age, passed to the Islands of the Blessed. More ambiguously, Homeric kings are sometimes likened to gods (among several genuine echoes of divine kingship in the epics). In addition, many myths tell of heroes transformed into stars or constellations, which are eternal: for example, the hope Ovid expresses for the emperor Augustus at the conclusion of his *Metamorphoses.* The latter is a more spiritual view since such an individual does not live on bodily.

However, in early Greek literature and myth/religion, the hope of achieving a life of the gods after death was something a few heroes of early times might once have attained by a special dispensation from gods, but it was thought to be no longer generally accessible to mortals. Hence the bleak view of Homer mentioned above, of Hesiod, and of the Mesopotamian *Gilgamesh.* Mortals live in the real world after the decline and fall from the golden age and the age of heroes. The structural similarity with the biblical pattern of the Fall of mankind is not coincidental, nor is a comparison of the Greek *hērōs* to the Hebrew Nephilim, or giants (Gen 6:4). And the biblical Fall consists above all of a fall into mortality (Gen 3). Greek literature, like Judeo-Christian literature, teaches how to be mortal in a fallen state.

Yet a desire for immortality, or a return to the golden age before the Fall, is surely rooted biologically and psychologically in human nature, that is, in instinctual desire and the will to live forever. If so, this would be a feature of that soul called the *thumos,* the so-called life-soul, bodily life force, or "mortal soul."[7] (In Homer, the psyche does not play a role in a living person, but appears only at death; this is the so-called "death-soul.")[8] The Roman poet and Epicurean philosopher Lucretius wrote that religion is based on human emotions, particularly the fear of death.[9]

Given that we have such desires, a problem with nature is that whatever is born eventually dies. This is the primary sense of the Greek word "nature" (*phusis* and the verb *phuein*), which refers to the natural process of birth, nurture, growth, and decay: physical, bodily, mortal processes. In Greek mythology, even the gods are born. Both in Greek and in Mesopotamian myth, the gods are neither creators of the universe nor the first things created. Although they possess an indefinite life span, they can sometimes die by experiencing a type of death or disabling.[10]

Over time, the Greek gods began to change due to the criticisms of philosophical thought. Beginning in the sixth century BC, in the archaic period, from the first Presocratics on, Greek thinkers began to criticize the traditional and civic religion in favor of a more spiritual "road" or "path" (a Pythagorean cult term) accessible to the mind and worthy of moral, intelligent beings.

We might call them "not religious, but spiritual." Yet the historical magnitude of this theme is not fully appreciated,[11] partly because it falls astride the academic boundaries of philosophy, classics, and religion.

In time the gods became less physical, less anthropomorphic, and less sharing in human passions that were thought to be unworthy of divinity. Xenophanes expressed this radical shift in the sixth century BC: "One god, greatest among gods and men, in no way similar to mortals either in body or in thought."[12] Xenophanes even *increases* the unbridgeable gap between gods and mortals: for if (as this implies) the gods have no desires, what good are ours in trying to reach them?

Precisely here, a new possibility of deification opens up. Humans might achieve, not the *life* of the gods rooted in nature (*phusis*) and potential death, but the unchanging essence of divinity. When speaking of "divine nature," this second meaning of "nature" comes into play: the meaning of "essence," the fixed nature or being of a thing, its "nature" in an abstract or logical sense. Although sometimes criticized as a scholastic notion that fixes fluxing reality in an overly logical scheme, this seems to be equally an original and inherent meaning of the word *phusis.*[13] Indeed the Presocratics were interested in both senses of nature: flux and underlying reality (or cause). The latter sense dominates in Plato's overriding concern with the real as that which abides and endures as opposed to what suffers change and decay. The natural world of birth and death became something temporal to overcome. Reason, *logos,* could provide access to another realm of eternal essence.

As a consequence of increasingly spiritual views of deities, and of human beings, the philosophers we will consider here exhibit two trends in Greek thought. Empedocles and Plato see the sage as a deity, a *daimon* or like a *daimon,* a transcendent being who lives on after death. Following them, Aristotle, the Epicureans, and the Stoics stress living a life of godlike qualities in this life rather than necessarily a life after death, about which they have varying and sometimes ambiguous views, due no doubt to the strong tradition of nature-philosophy of the first type mentioned. Given this background discussion, we will illustrate various philosophers' views of human and divine natures and how to cross the great divide (*apotheosis* or *theosis*) or to realize in this life one's essential divine nature. These philosophers span the archaic, classical, and Hellenistic periods of ancient Greece.

Deification in Greek Philosophers

Empedocles: The Philosopher as Daimon

The fifth-century-BC Presocratic philosopher, Empedocles, refers to himself as having become "an undying god, mortal no more."[14] Such talk is not simply a poetic or rhetorical device. Peter Kingsley has been one of the few scholars taking seriously Empedocles' claim of divinity. His work serves the purpose of seriously restoring mysticism and magic to Greek, and the roots of Western, thought. He writes, "Empedocles presents himself quite openly as a *daimon,* as someone who knows he is divine."[15] A *daimon* is a deity (or divinity); in this case, a spirit who has fallen, incarnated, and seeks to escape the physical world altogether and return to its original abode with the gods. Empedocles wrote of "purifications" that might enable a sage to achieve this.

Shortly before Empedocles, Parmenides was perhaps the first to draw attention to a world of eternity as a religious or spiritual goal for humans. His poem relates a revelation he received from a goddess after he had been conveyed by divine escorts to a divine, perhaps celestial, realm beyond the border of fate, that is of death.[16] Pythagoras, too, is relevant here, in his teaching that the soul (psyche) is immortal. Perhaps more prevalent in this period than we commonly credit to a "pagan" age were spiritual beliefs of the type represented by the still problematic Orphic and Dionysiac mysteries. That such ideas were current in classical Greece is shown also by the fifth-century poet Pindar: "we do have some likeness to immortals in mighty mind or nature." And Euripides (reputedly a friend of Socrates) says: "The mind (*nous*) belonging to us is in each person a god."[17] These crucially important figures illustrate major influences on Plato and through him on early Christianity.

Plato and Socrates: The Philosopher Cultivates the Immortal Soul

Plato, of course, holds a prominent place in the history of religious thought. He presents the first lengthy argument for the immortality of the soul, a system of rewards and punishments after death, divinity as ultimate goodness, intimations of monotheism, and the first use of the word "theology."[18] Plato develops two important themes related to deification of human beings. The highest and most godlike part of our soul is our mind or reason (*nous*), which is immortal. All human beings can seek immortality through the cultivation of the highest part of their soul, reason, in the pursuit of wisdom and knowledge of the Good.

Plato's Socrates holds that the job of philosophy is to care for the soul "for all time."[19] Its only hope of achieving the "best and highest good" of "becoming as good and wise as it possibly can," is through "education and training" for the benefit of its "journey to the other world."[20] Indeed, we could argue that this gives us the ideal of liberal arts education, of developing the inner person as both a secular and an idealistic pursuit. Strictly speaking, the mind is not developed but present innately and drawn out over time, since the soul must have preexisted the body. The belief that the soul lives on after death requires that it be eternal and preexistent.

Plato's position should be called *theosis* and not *apotheosis*. The previous Greek notion of an *apotheosis* entailed the promotion of a mortal being to divine status through a special and rare heroic dispensation. For Plato, all human beings possess an innate divinity which we should seek to free from the body by our own efforts. Normally, the soul is tainted by contact with the body, expressed by the slogan *soma sema,* "the body (is) a tomb (of the soul)." Being immortal, it enters into successive incarnations. Only the philosopher, the perfect sage, will achieve the ultimate escape from the cycle of the soul's continual rebirth and reincarnation. Three successive lives of purity are required to achieve this.[21] In Plato's *Republic* Socrates says, "the argument concerns no ordinary topic, but the way we ought to live."[22] That is, to live with the ultimate end (telos) in view, of becoming godlike, entails caring for the soul above all.[23] An ascetic ethics is tied to a religious metaphysics.

The philosopher aspires to ultimate wisdom (*sophia*), which only the gods possess.[24] For Plato's Socrates, the philosopher is not yet a perfect sage (*sophos*) but rather a *lover* of wisdom (*philosophos*). Only the gods have wisdom; humans have love, desire, and *eros.* (The role of these bodily passions contributes to Plato's enduring fascination, considering that the goal is disembodied reason.) As Socrates says, "Skill in this area is what makes a person spiritual."[25] Any other skill is merely technical.

Indeed, the *religious* pursuit of wisdom is what most separated Socrates from other sophists. Plato describes the philosopher as a being mediating between gods and men, comparable to a *daimon.*[26] Socrates even has his own personal deity, his *daimonion.* Uncomfortable with this notion, many scholars domesticate it by calling it Socrates' personified conscience or higher reason. It is much more than that if taken seriously as spiritual rather than secular ethics.

Historically, conscience itself is often regarded as spiritual. This is a recurring theme in religion and what is called mysticism. One may trace it in the history of the word *synteresis,* which means conscience, divine spark, or reason.[27] Conscience, so conceived as in touch with a higher power, is regarded as knowledge of good and evil. The notion of knowledge appears in the etymology of the Latin word *con-scientia.* Similarly, we can understand why the God of the Hebrew Bible, Yahweh, says that a special knowledge is what makes human beings godlike (if not yet, in this case, immortal): "See, the man has become like one of us, knowing good and evil" (Gen 3:22, NRSV). Plato's Socrates holds a similar view. Socrates is a moral teacher above all, stressing true knowledge of the good; he argues that virtue is knowledge. His *daimonion* provides access to divinity, to a divine, more than human reason.

Plato grounds the immortality of the soul in an elaborate tripartite psychology: mind, bodily spirit, bodily appetites.[28] The soul of a living being may be said to be one's inner life: from top to bottom, head, breast, and belly. The highest part of the soul is mind or reason (*nous, to logistikon*). It should rule the other two parts, *thumos* or "spirit" (such as courage), and the lower bodily desires or appetites (*epithumia*).[29]

Reason, the most godlike and ruling part of our souls, is akin to the gods.[30] This is the soul that can be ultimately disembodied through purification by means of education and philosophy (seeking wisdom) and proper living. Knowledge and praxis are joined. One must both be morally good, just, and pure (i.e., pursuing a certain spiritual way of life), and pursue pure knowledge. With the mind we grasp divinity in the form of eternal, changeless objects of true knowledge, as opposed to perception and opinion that characterize the ephemeral world of nature.[31] This privileging of reason as the most spiritual part of us characterizes the major trends of Greek thought discussed in this paper as essential background for Christian thought. Christianity is a very rational religion in this sense.

Reason does not mean merely technical or ratiocinative calculation. For Plato reason is partly intellectual and partly something higher. Plato does speak of the mind using reasoned arguments (*logos, logistikos*); we exercise our souls with dialectic, learning, and true wisdom.[32] However, the ultimate reward for disembodied reason is noetic *vision.* Contemplation (*theoria*) of regions above the heavens, the so-called *noētos topos,* or place accessible to the intellect, can occur for blessed souls just as it does for the gods.[33] The souls of the good follow the path of the gods, whom they are most like.[34] Thus, the reward of *logos* (reason) is not logic but vision, an intelligible awareness of true knowledge, goodness, and being.[35] This is the realm of Platonic "forms" or "ideas." Perhaps we should translate the famous Platonic forms as "visions."

Patristic Reflection on Platonic Thought

Greek patristic theology stresses the fact that Plato's soul is akin to the divine by nature, whereas in Western Christianity immortality is conferred as a gift from God.[36] In fact, one can draw Plato closer to Christianity on this point in two particular ways. First, the idea of a special gift makes *theosis* more like *apotheosis* (discussed briefly above) rather than being a contrast to it, as the patristic apologetic line holds. The difference, besides obvious doctrinal ones of who gives the gift and how it is earned, is that mythical *apotheosis* was rarer and not open to any and all. But in Plato, all people have access to it through their souls. Thus, divinization open to all is an important similarity between Christianity and Plato. Second, Plato does have the creator-god, his Demiurge, put an intelligent soul in the world, and (ultimately) in human beings, out of his perfect goodness, because "he desired that all things should come as near as possible to being like himself."[37] The human soul comes from heaven; true, this is a matter of the physics of the universe, but nevertheless still a gift of divine favor.[38] The gods favor "anyone . . . who makes himself as much like a god as a human can."[39]

Humans then "rival the gods."[40] Which gods? Not the creator. However much people share in, or the soul is akin to, the divine nature, they do not partake of an essential feature of God as creator and governor of the universe.[41] This is true of Christianity as well. (Perhaps partly for this reason Mormons, who have countless deifications amounting to polytheism, do not make their God the creator.)[42] Plato's creator-god, the Demiurge, creates the traditional anthropomorphic gods, who like humans are born (as in myth), have bodies, and share in *phusis* as "nature" in the nonlogical sense (i.e., subject to becoming, sharing in bodily passions, birth and death).[43] However, besides these crude, anthropomorphic deities, the heavenly bodies such as the planets and stars are often seen as deities, and therefore serve to provide a more spiritual model for disembodied souls. The Demiurge created human souls from the same ingredients as the world soul, although he used less pure leftovers.[44] To that extent human souls are of "second and third grades of purity" just as there are grades of deities.[45] The blessed immortal souls of human beings who have lived a good life, having become freed from the body after death, may ultimately reach the gods in heaven and travel "upon the back of the world" to visions of *hyperouranion* (beyond the heavens) reality;[46] that is, to the sources of creation.

Cultivating reason, true knowledge and goodness as much as possible (granted our less-than-perfect purity) by having a philosophical soul (mind), is "the extent that human nature can partake of immortality."[47] "That is why a man should make all haste to escape from earth to heaven; and escape means becoming as like God as possible; and a man becomes like God when he becomes just and pure, with understanding."[48] One may dwell with the gods in bliss: "This soul brings calm to the sea of desires by following Reason . . . and by contemplating the true and divine . . . and drawing inspiration from it; because such a soul believes that this is the right way to live . . . and that after death it reaches a place which is similar and kindred to its own nature, and there is rid for ever of human ills."[49]

Theoretically (indeed), all human beings have access to the immortal soul planted in them at birth. All can achieve it through virtue or human excellence (*aretē*). But to be sure, the road is difficult for most. Although often criticized as a hierarchical and rather elitist model of ascent to ultimate fixed values, this view paradoxically democratizes the notion of divinity in human beings. Politically, it is a democratic elitism. This is another major move in the history of religion. Both human beings and the traditional Olympian deities become more spiritual through philosophy.

Aristotle: An Afterlife of Platonic Idealism

Aristotle was largely an empiricist in physics, but not when it came to metaphysics of the higher heavenly bodies. There he incorporates some features of Platonic idealism. Even in his secular discussion of practical virtues, he speaks of godlike sages.

Aristotle's *Nicomachean Ethics* concerns virtue, human excellence, and the good life, culminating in a discussion of happiness.[50] The Greek word for "happiness," *eudaimonia,* means literally, "having, or favored by, a good *daimon.*" Happiness is an activity, but activity of the best or ruling part of us, the mind (*nous*), and therefore contemplative (*theōrētikē*) activity.[51] "The activity of intellect, which is contemplative," in his words, possesses the following divine attributes: it aims at no end (*telos*) beyond itself, it has its proper pleasure, it has self-sufficiency and leisure, is unwearied, and has all the other attributes of the "blessed" (*makarios*) man.[52] These are the qualities both of a god, and of a man who has attained a godlike life; above all, the activity of god is contemplation.[53] Contemplation is the human activity "most akin" to divine.[54]

"Complete happiness"—or "perfect (*teleia*) happiness"[55]—of human life consists in attaining something divine:

> he [the man who has attained the above] will live so [i.e., in the way just described] . . . in so far as something divine is present in him . . . If intellect is divine, then, in comparison with man, the life according to it is divine in comparison with human life. But we must not follow those who advise us, being men, to think of human things, and, being mortal, of mortal things, but must, so far as we can, make ourselves immortal, and strain every nerve to live in accordance with the best thing in us . . .[56]

Thus we would live happily, having "some likeness" of "the blessed life" of the gods.[57]

Such a view, an obvious legacy of Plato, sprinkled throughout other writings of Aristotle,[58] complicates understanding both of him as an empiricist, and of Greek "humanism" in general. Now, Aristotle is talking about human life—not life after death or a disembodied soul. But he makes clear that mind (or reason) enters the body from outside, is divine, and has no connection with bodily activity.[59] It might outlive the body,[60] presumably (and necessarily) because it preexisted. However, whether this entails *individual, personal* immortality became a thorny point of contention in the twelfth century AD, when Aristotelian learning encountered Christian orthodoxy in the West and ultimately became assimilated with it through the efforts of Aquinas.[61]

Again, note the theme that our mind, our reason, is the highest and most godlike part of us. Reason is also the most spiritual and celestial, the least bodily part of our souls. In contrast with Plato who stresses the lover (*philo-*) of wisdom, for Aristotle the gods favor the reasonable man.[62] The intellectual, the wise man (*sophos*), is the one who cultivates reason and is possessed by the gods. Aristotle's happiest man is the one who strives after wisdom and eventually attains godlike wisdom (*sophia*) in his life.

The Hellenistic Period between Classical and Christian

If we wish to argue for a continuous tradition of thought from classical Greek, through Hellenistic, to important features in Christianity, this requires addressing the problem of what kind of break or new beginning "Hellenistic" represents. The Hellenistic period (323–30 BC) is the age when Greek rule and culture (Hellenism) spread throughout the Near East in the wake of the conquests of Alexander the Great. We often artificially erect historical periods as barriers, and this is a big one that deserves to be reconsidered. Even within classics, Hellenistic thought is poorly explained as a product of new political conditions (basically, that Hellenistic kingdoms caused escapist or individual philosophies). Rather, as Long shows, both Epicureans and Stoics (and Cynics, with whom some New Testament scholars have compared Jesus) regarded Socrates as a master and exemplar of the philosophical life.[63] That is, trends in thought continue from the previous period.

The Hellenistic period was for a long time neglected due to a privileging of the classical era. It was commonly said that Classical Greek culture ended with the deaths of Alexander and Aristotle in 323 and 322 BC, respectively. In fact, it may be that this ridiculous old bugbear was designed precisely to avoid the embarrassment of drawing Greek pagan thought too close to Christianity. The Hellenistic period provided a convenient insulating barrier. It was seen as a time when new "Oriental" or "mystery religions" developed from some meeting of East and West. Thus, the Hellenistic period is routinely studied as "background" to Christianity, but classical Greek philosophy is not.

In fact, the term "Hellenistic" was coined by Droysen originally for religious motives. The field is vexed by ideological debates of what is Oriental or Hellenic, relevant for the nature of the early church. In the metaphoric formulation of Droysen, the Christian church resulted from a merger of a holy spirit with a Greek body; Harnack, the historian of "dogma," reverses the image, with the Greek spirit (of philosophy) infusing the church (i.e., the body).[64] Either way, this is Platonic language of incarnated spirit; the dichotomies of body and spirit, or matter and form, correspond to secular and eternal. In such images, one of the two elements is usually downgraded. These metaphors all represent rather awkward attempts to credit the role of history and the Greek tradition in the formulation of Christianity. Rather, this essay wishes to point out a substantive continuity of thought, offering many comparisons of similarities as well as differences to be sure, from Greek philosophy to Christian thought. We should not divide classical from Christian content. Seen the other way around, we might not have classics without this religious legacy.

The two main schools of Hellenistic thought to be considered here are the Epicureans and the Stoics: the very ones with which Paul disputed in Athens (Acts 17:18). Each presents a complete worldview comparable to those of religious traditions. These schools exerted powerful forces for centuries, even into modern times. Stoicism in particular bears some comparison with Christianity.

Epicureans

Epicureanism and Stoicism, established respectively by Epicurus and Zeno in Athens shortly before 300 BC, both follow the legacy of Socrates (as noted above). Although they were rivals, and had different notions of the universe and gods, they developed generally similar views of the perfect sage being like a god. Although their conceptions of the gods differ, we can see common tendencies and a shared tradition.

Following a trend begun by some Presocratics, and seen in Plato and Aristotle, gods are more spiritual, nonworking, perfect beings. Gods have wisdom and human beings do not. Hence being a philosopher meant aspiring to live and think like a god. That was the legacy of Socrates. Epicureans and Stoics both aspired to achieve a wisdom and rational calm characteristic of gods. Epicureans aspired to the divine state of perfect peace of mind (Greek *ataraxia,* literally "freedom from disturbance"; Latin *tranquillitas*).

Epicureans held a radically materialist position according to which everything was composed of atoms. Typically for ancient Greek philosophical thought, ethics relied on proper understanding of physics and the universe. Understanding nature would give us peace of mind and freedom from false fears and superstitions. Yet, although they were as secular as can be, they still spoke of godlike sages.

Epicurus writes that if you practice his teachings by day and night (even in your dreams), "you shall live as [*or* like] a god among men. For quite unlike a mortal animal is a man who lives among immortal gods."[65] This is more than mere metaphor. It is more than high-minded ethical talk about how to live practically in the secular world. It implies a philosophical-religious view of the world that we must take seriously.[66] Like all the views considered here, it attempts to explain the values of the mind in a material world. Mind, as noted above, generally suggests both intellect (understanding) and conscience (the moral knowledge of good and evil).

By all indications the Epicureans took this seriously. Epicurus's followers worshipped him as a god. Lucretius, in the first century BC, wrote (in the longest surviving Epicurean text), "he was a god, a god."[67] What made him divine were his reason (*ratio*), "divine mind" (*divina mens*), and words "ever most worthy of life eternal."[68] The Epicurean sage possesses "lofty sanctuaries (*templa*) serene, well fortified by the teachings of the wise, whence you may look down upon others," while "the mind, kept away from care and fear, enjoy(s) a feeling of delight."[69] That is the life of the gods and the aim of philosophy. Further, although this is attained with difficulty as a result of a study, of therapy, of ethical praxis, we all have the capacity in us, because all human beings have a share of reason.

Of course, one becomes the Epicurean idea of god, just as earlier one became an Aristotelian god. But perfection still means, in this tradition, the ultimate of reason and virtue. Epicurus "purged" or "purified" the gods, and himself, of base passions (cares, lust, greed, etc.), of all but reason and wisdom.[70] The Epicurean gods improve on the silly anthropomorphic gods of myth, and we are told that Epicurus himself has done greater good than those old gods supposedly did even if stories of them are true![71]

The path to this life lies in proper understanding. Again, reason is universal: in nature and in us. Proper understanding of the laws of nature brings peace of mind. Lucretius adds that for those who heed the teachings, "nothing hinders our living a life worthy of gods."[72] We are exalted "to heaven."[73] We will not live on after death—naturally for Epicureans who are thoroughgoing materialists—but we will pass our lives in a godlike state.

In the second century AD, the Epicurean Diogenes of Oenoanda (in Lycia) wrote a letter to reassure his mother who was afraid due to visions she was having of him. He later inscribed his teachings on a large public monument in his hometown for the benefit of others: "Therefore, mother, take heart. . . . Rather consider that I am daily acquiring useful help towards advancing further towards happiness. Not slight or of no avail are the advantages that accrue to me, such that they make my condition equal to the divine and show that not even mortality can make me inferior to the indestructible and blessed nature. For as long as I live I rejoice even as do the gods."[74] Even Epicurus died, but his discoveries live on in the form of words that aspire to immortality—sacred words to heal all souls, a spiritual therapy of philosophy.[75]

Stoics

The Stoics follow, in a different way, the path blazed by earlier philosophers, especially Plato's Socrates. They carried this tradition into the Roman Empire and further in time. A useful surviving author is Epictetus (ca. AD 50–130).

Like Plato, Aristotle, and their opponents the Epicureans, the Stoics were concerned with the ruling part (*hēgemonikon*) of our soul. Here alone, in our judgment or faculty of choice, are we free and autonomous. Socrates, writes Epictetus, "became fully perfect (*apetelesthē*) . . . by not paying attention to anything but his reason. . . . You . . . ought to live as someone wanting to be Socrates."[76] Socrates was *the* sage, the most godlike human who had lived, that is. If you hold fast to philosophy, you will be, like Socrates, "as someone assigned by god to this place."[77]

Epictetus talks of the "kinship (*sungeneia*) of god and men."[78] Aristotle had used the same language of kinship, following Plato.[79] "Epictetus believed that our reasoning powers and moral sense are an 'offshoot' of [God,] the world's divine governor.":

> And if our minds [or souls, *psychai*] are so connected and attached to God, as parts and offshoots of his being, does he not perceive their every movement as something belonging to him and sharing in his nature (*sumphuēs*)? . . . you are an offshoot of God; you have within you a part of him. Why, then, are you ignorant of your own kinship? . . . You are carrying God around. . . . You are carrying him around inside yourself.[80]

Reason is "the internal divinity."[81] Oddly, the Stoics considered the emotions as outside of us, because they are part of the body (and a feature of what would be Plato's lower soul) and outside the mind or soul, which they considered to be our true selves.[82] The spiritual soul, a permanent nature, must be disembodied, because matter is subject to the physical process of nature that brings decay and death. This is consistent with what we have seen in Plato, but it goes further: the soul is mind only.

God directs the *logos,* "the universal reason."[83] God is essentially the soul of the world. The Stoics equated spirit (*pneuma*), reason (*logos*), and God.[84] Rather typical of this whole ancient tradition, each individual is like a microcosm; one must understand the world to know oneself; humanities (ethics) depends on science (physics and metaphysics).

Stoics believed in divine providence. Slightly paradoxically, we must rule ourselves to achieve freedom and autonomy. Controlling our piece of the world-reason empowers the individual: "the Stoic sage is the *only* king."[85] The Stoic sage is the equal of Zeus in virtue.[86] To be sure, this is an austere goal; Epictetus even advises, "Avoid banquets given by those outside philosophy."[87]

Cicero (106–43 BC), it may be noted, picked up the Platonic and Stoic notion of humans and gods being akin by virtue of their participation in reason.[88] Classicists often take the texts discussed here as metaphoric, as poetic, or as reflective of social and political interests. The reductionist dismissive method typically used in the study of ancient Greek religion today reduces it to society and politics. However, we must regard it as religious thought of great significance and influence, as constitutive of a tradition far beyond the uses it has served as supposed stylistic, cultural, or rhetorical embellishment. Such visions move people. Writes Kingsley, "This tradition is an endless source of surprises."[89]

Christians and Neoplatonists

The tradition sketched here exerted great influence. With embarrassing exaggeration the classicist Barry Powell writes, "Much of what we think of as Christianity is Platonic philosophy, some of it Orphic in origin."[90] Whatever truth this expresses is better appreciated in the Eastern than in the Western church. At the least, we should take classical content and subject matter seriously in a broad view of the continuities in the history of thought and of religion, and not only focus on contrasts. We must study the great importance and influence of Greek philosophy as in part constitutive of a tradition and not mere rhetorical decoration or shape.[91] Christianity is in crucial ways a highly philosophical religion, and it was written first in ancient Greek.

Second Peter 1:4 is a foundational passage used for the notion of *theosis* in this volume and the conference upon which it is based. The passage echoes Platonic language. In advocating becoming "partakers of the divine nature" (*theias koinōnoi phuseōs*), it talks about fleeing destruction (*phthora*) present in the world in "lust" (*epithumiai*). "Nature" is used in the sense of an unchanging essence. The language echoes that of Greek philosophy. The sentiment parallels Plato's concern with what abides and endures as opposed to what suffers change and decay. Destruction and "lust" characterize the physical world of things that experience birth, decay and death. *Epithumia* is a word for the third or lowest part of Plato's tripartite soul, the seat of bodily appetites (residing, say, in the belly and groins). We are urged to overcome *phusis* as natural process (of birth, growth, and death) through a move to "nature" as abstract, unchanging essence. However, a major difference is that reason does not play an explicit role here. Reason developed this line of thought (in general), but now it is a matter of faith.

These truths are said to be in the heart rather than as, previously, known to the mind. Paul in Galatians 4:3–6 says that "we were enslaved to the elements (*stoicheia*) of the world" before God sent the spirit (*pneuma*) of his son into our hearts, so that we are now heirs of God. This parallels the formative Socratic move from physics ("elements" is a term from nature-philosophy) to metaphysics linked with ethics and concern for the soul. Metaphysics, the spirit, is placed in the "heart." Although thoroughly familiar and commonplace, this nevertheless suggests a remarkable image. "Heart," it is true, means "seat of life," and perhaps (for the sake of comparison) recalls Plato's use of desire and the spirit (his *thumos*) as ancillary to reason (which is absent here). The image invokes love of god, a notion found in their own ways in both Plato and Aristotle. But the heart, after all, is an organ of flesh, the seat of those very passions we need to overcome. For the Greeks, words, thoughts, and *pneuma* (a key Stoic term) belonged to the mind, the highest, disembodied soul. Here, the notion of spirit is *naturalized.* Today, "reason" is suspect. It is cold and limiting compared to truths in the heart or breast or (colloquially) "gut"—paradoxically, in the body. This move in imagery, quite brilliantly, proved to be more acceptable and more democratic: one need not learn to be a sage in the former way.

If we recall the opening verses of the Gospel of John, we are reminded that many of the central concepts in the Christian tradition have deep roots in Greek thought: "In the beginning was the *logos, and the logos was with god and the logos* was god" (Jn 1:1). *Logos* refers to reason, mind; it is a Stoic term for "spirit" or the ruling world-soul. Further, *sophia* is a philosophical ideal that is holy in Christianity. Both concepts are central to the theme of immortality or deification, which humans who share in *logos* or *sophia* may attain.

Philosophical paganism and Christianity often meet metaphysically. Recent work in the topic of so-called "pagan monotheism" draws attention to their "organic unity" in late antiquity.[92] The word *theosis* crosses boundaries as well. Said to be a coinage of church fathers designed to avoid the pagan connotations of the Greek word *apotheosis,* meaning mythical "deification," the word *theosis* apparently occurs only once in "pagan" Greek, in the Neoplatonist Damascius.[93] Damascius was the last head of the Academy founded by Plato in fourth-century BC Athens at the time Justinian closed it in AD 529.[94] Damascius therefore appears to be adopting a Christian term. He also, interestingly, makes use of the same threefold hierarchy of *logos, thumos,* and *epithumia* found in Plato and suggested in 2 Peter.

Conclusions

The broad tradition of belief in deification stemming from archaic and classical Greek philosophy continues into early Christianity and points us back above all to Plato. By studying the full tradition we see similarities of intellectual content and core ideas, and not only the differences of emphases among sects.[95] Greek philosophy, that is, *classical* Greek rationalism, provides deep roots of spiritual thought. Therefore, we should not look only to the Hellenistic period for "antecedents" to Christianity.

Classical Greek philosophy (for better or worse) privileged reason, both as a method and as a goal. Through philosophy, both divine nature and human nature became more spiritual in each other's images. In the psychology of Plato, glimpsed in his Presocratic predecessors and rightly attributable to Socrates, we find the view that all human beings "partake of the divine nature," that all may in fact become divinities through the development of the highest part of their souls. Reason (*logos*) itself is spiritual. It includes goodness, because the mind knows the good (the idea of the conscience, comparable to the biblical "knowing of good and evil") and properly controls baser (more bodily, secular) passions. The philosopher, of whom Socrates is the prototype, provides a model and a guide for how to live here and now in order to become, ultimately, for the truly wise (*sophos*), like a god in another realm after death. With changes in various schools and systems of belief, this tradition exerted tremendous influence throughout the ancient world, a period we still regard as providing formative ethical and religious teachings for the present day. Thus, Classical Greek thought provides deep roots, essential and inescapable, for the Christian tradition.

Notes

1. E.g., A. A. Long, "The Concept of Daimon and the Soul's Divinity" (unpublished lecture, Princeton University, Princeton, NJ, March, 2002), 26–27, on the Stoic idea "that our reasoning powers and moral sense are an 'offshoot' of the world's divine governor." D. N. Sedley ("The Ideal of Godlikeness," in *Plato 2: Ethics, Politics, Religion, and the Soul,* ed. Gail Fine, 309–28 [Oxford: Oxford University Press, 1999]), by contrast, does take seriously the notion of godlikeness in Plato (and provides a few other references at 309n1). He shows that the ancients regarded this as Plato's central teaching of the *telos* (fulfillment) of a human life. Sedley himself writes from the perspective of analytical philosophy, which tends to do only partial justice to Plato by making the ideas more secular. This, in a different way, is a broad trend in twentieth-century Continental antimetaphysical readings of Plato as well. Thus, godlikeness, which Sedley regards as an ethical notion of how to live one's life, is treated in a fine way as epistemology, physics, and ethics of the incarnate (only) soul, but not as ontology, metaphysics, eschatology, and religion (e.g., the disembodied soul in Plato). Other scholars talking about the theme of the soul's divinity in Greek philosophy have been Long, "Concept of Daimon," and Elizabeth F. Cooke, "The Moral and Intellectual Development of the Philosopher in Plato's *Republic,*" *Ancient Philosophy* 19 (1999): 37–44, who shows that the philosopher aims to become godlike.

2. Peter Kingsley, *Ancient Philosophy, Mystery, and Magic: Empedocles and Pythagorean Tradition* (Oxford: Oxford University Press, 1995); Kingsley, *In the Dark Places of Wisdom* (Inverness, CA: Golden Sufi Center, 1999); and Kingsley, *Reality* (Inverness, CA: Golden Sufi Center, 2003).

3. Pierre Hadot, *What Is Ancient Philosophy?* trans. M. Chase (Cambridge, MA: Harvard University Press, 2002; originally published 1995). Also of interest are John Cottingham, *Philosophy and the Good Life: Reason and the Passions in Greek, Cartesian and Psychoanalytic Ethics* (Cambridge, MA: Cambridge University Press, 1998); William V. Harris, *Restraining Rage: The Ideology of Anger Control in Classical Antiquity* (Cambridge: Harvard University Press, 2001).

4. See the essay by J. A. McGuckin, "The Strategic Adaptation of Deification in the Cappadocians," in this volume. A book on the use of Plato by the Cappadocian fathers is forthcoming.

5. Similarly, John Scheid has recently written that elements that are often called "new" or "foreign," such as mystery cults, should be seen as more integral and, shall we say, routine

parts of ancient classical religious culture. Scheid, *An Introduction to Roman Religion,* trans. J. Lloyd (Bloomington, IN: Indiana University Press, 2003), 8, 14.

6. *Oedipus at Colonus.*

7. The latter is the term of J. Lenz and V. Adluri, used in Adluri, "Mortal Knowledge in Parmenides and Plato: A Study in *Phusis,* Journey, *Thumos* and *Eros*" (PhD diss., New School University, 2002). *Thumos* is usually translated "spirit," and later becomes demoted as second to mind in Plato's tripartite soul.

8. Jan N. Bremmer, *The Early Greek Concept of the Soul* (Princeton, NJ: Princeton University Press, 1983).

9. *De Rerum Natura* 3.37ff.

10. Diana Burton, "The Death of Gods in Greek Succession Myths," in *Homer, Tragedy and Beyond: Essays in Honour of P. E. Easterling,* ed. Felix Budelmann and Pantelis Michelakis, 43–55 (London: Society for the Promotion of Hellenic Studies, 2001).

11. But see Werner Jaeger, *The Theology of the Early Greek Philosophers* (Oxford: Clarendon Press, 1947).

12. Xenophanes, *Fr.* 23, trans. Kirk and Raven in G. S. Kirk, J. E. Raven, and Malcolm Schofield, *The Presocratic Philosophers: A Critical History with a Selection of Texts,* 2nd ed. (New York: Cambridge University Press, 1983), 169.

13. At least, it is hard to see one meaning ("essence") evolving in archaic Greek times from another supposedly earlier one ("natural growth, "life cycle"), because both senses are present in the Indo-European root "*bheud-.*" Calvert Watkins, *The American Heritage Dictionary of Indo-European Roots,* 2nd ed. (Boston: Houghton Mifflin, 2000), s.v., 11–12. Some try to argue along the former line (Adluri, "Mortal Knowledge," interestingly contrasts *physis* with *logos*). For sophisticated criticisms of "nature denatured" in Western thought, see Reiner Schürmann, *Broken Hegemonies,* trans. R. Lilly (Bloomington, IN: Indiana University Press, 2003; originally published in 1996).

14. *Fr.* 112.

15. Kingsley, *Reality,* 58; see also Kingsley, *Ancient Philosophy.*

16. Kingsley, *Places of Wisdom;* Kinglsey, *Reality;* Adluri, "Mortal Knowledge." Adluri shows that in line 1 of frag. 1, Parmenides' *thumos* (mortal soul) prompted him to seek transcendence.

17. Pindar, *Nemean* 6.4–5; Euripides, *Fr.* 1007 as reported by Cicero, *Tusculanae disputationes* 1.65. I owe these references and translations to Long, "Concept of Daimon." Some classical scholars hold that *nous* does not mean "mind" here, relating it to a line of Heraclitus (*ēthos*) rather than to Plato (as I do).

18. In the *Euthyphro* Plato's Socrates virtually presents an argument for monotheism. Scholars fail in interpretation when they treat the frequent uses of "the god" (*ho theos*) in the singular in Plato, Plato's Socrates, and Aristotle, as a grammatical oddity, an unexplained coincidence, or a matter of scholarly *aporia.* On Plato's use of the word "theology," see *Rep.* 379a; see also below on the Demiurge. Plato's works I have deliberately treated without getting into questions of supposed inconsistencies or genetic links between various works; that becomes unduly convoluted.

19. *Phaed.* 107c; 95c.

20. Ibid. 97d; 107d.

21. *Phaedr.* 249a. This takes 3,000 years total, since a soul spends 1,000 years between lives in an early version of heaven and hell. For normal souls, it takes ten lives or 10,000 years (*Phaedr.* 248e). Language of "purifications" points to the Pythagoreans, the mysterious Orphics, and Empedocles.

22. *Rep.* 352d. Plato, *Republic,* trans. C. D. C. Reeve (Indianapolis: Hackett, 2004).

23. Plato, *Apol.* 30a-b.

24. Ibid. 20d, 23a.

25. *Symp.* 203a.

26. Ibid. 202e–203a, trans. Robin Waterfield, *Plato: Republic,* Oxford World's Classics Series (Oxford: Oxford University Press, 1998); general discussion in Hadot, *Ancient Philosophy,* chap. 4.

27. *The Oxford English Dictionary,* s.v. "synteresis" and "synderesis," attests these meanings; (e.g.): conscience in the sense of a guide of conduct; the spark of knowledge, of good and evil, natural in mankind (1594); the purer part of the soul, the will to good (1637); "The divine nucleus, the point of contact between man's life and the divine life. . . ." (1911). The variant spelling "synderesis" means (e.g.) "the higher part of reason" (1426), moving to good not evil (1531), and the like. In the Greek etymology, by the way, "*-tērēsis*" means "keep guard, watch"; that is precisely the role Socrates assigns to his *daimonion.*

28. *Rep.* 435ff. Aspects of Plato's psychology remain controversial; see W. K. C. Guthrie, "Plato's Views on the Nature of the Soul," in *Plato: A Collection of Critical Essays II,* ed. G. Vlastos (Garden City, NY: Doubleday, 1971), 230–43, and T. M. Robinson, *Plato's Psychology,* 2nd ed. (Toronto: University of Toronto Press, 1995).

29. The term *thumos* has an interesting history. In Homer and early Greek literature, it is *the* general term for the life-soul. Plato makes it subordinate to the mind, in furtherance of his generally spiritual and idealistic interests.

30. *Rep.* 611e, for example.

31. *Tim.* 28a, for example.

32. Indeed Plato is responsible for the crucial shift in the meaning of *logos* from "speech" to "logical reasoning." Kingsley, *Reality,* 129, 566; on exercising our soul, see *Tim.* 90b.

33. *Phaedr.* 247c; *Rep.* 508c.

34. Ibid. 250b–c and 248a.

35. Kingsley, *Reality,* 20. I suggest "vision" as a translation of the Platonic form or idea (the Greek word *idea*—the basis of Platonic "idealism"—is etymologically related to "vision" and "wise").

36. Henry A. Wolfson, "Immortality and Resurrection in the Philosophy of the Church Fathers," *Harvard Divinity School Bulletin* (1956–57): 7–40; J. A. McGuckin in the present volume. On *Timaeus* generally, see also Riemer Roukema, *Gnosis and Faith in Early Christianity,* trans. J. Bowden (Harrisburg, PA: Trinity Press International, 1999), 76–81.

37. With the Demiurge, writes F. M. Cornford, "Plato is introducing into philosophy for the first time the image of a creator god." *Plato's Cosmology: The Timaeus of Plato Translated with a Running Commentary* (London: Routledge & Kegan Paul, 1937), 34. Cornford, however, regards it as a mythical, poetic figure, typically of scholars uneasy with seeing Plato as crucial for religious history; *Tim.* 29e–30b, with 41c–d.

38. Ibid., 90a; as Sedley calls it in "Ideal of Godlikeness," 326–27.

39. *Rep.* 613a, trans. Reeve.

40. *Tim.* 41c.

41. Other passages, among many, in which Plato speaks of the soul being "akin" to the divine include *Laws* 892a, 896a, 957a; *Meno* 81c; *Phaed.* 79b-c, 86a; *Pol.* 309c; cf. *Prot.* 337c: like is akin to like by nature; Sedley, "Ideal of Godlikeness," 323–27: the world-soul governs both being and becoming, sameness and difference, in the world, unlike the human soul, which partakes only of the eternal, pure intellect (when disembodied, that is). However, there is more to this since in the human body, the rational part (incarnate) does rule the "lower" parts of the soul for Plato.

42. Harold Bloom, *The American Religion: The Emergence of the Post-Christian Nation* (New York: Simon & Schuster, 1992), chaps. 4–6; on *theosis,* see Jordan Vajda, *"Partakers of the Divine Nature": A Comparative Analysis of Patristic and Mormon Doctrines of Divinization* (Provo, UT: Foundation for Ancient Research and Mormon Studies, 2002).

43. *Tim.* 40c; Nalin Ranasinghe wonders how these beliefs relate to the traditional Olympian deities, along rather different lines, in the last paragraph of *The Soul of Socrates* (Ithaca, NY: Cornell University Press, 2000), 178.

44. *Tim.* 41d.

45. Ibid.

46. *Phaedr.* 247b.

47. *Tim.* 90c.

48. *Theaet.* 176a–b, trans. M. J. Levett and M. Burnyeat, in *Plato: Complete Works,* ed. John M. Cooper (Indianapolis: Hackett, 1997); [sic]; note the capitalization of "God." "Heaven" (*ouranos*) means "sky."

49. *Phaed.* 84a–b.

50. *Eth. nic.* 10.6–9.

51. Ibid. 10.7.1177a12ff.

52. Ibid. 10.7.1177b19–23.

53. Ibid. 10.7.1178b21–23.

54. Ibid. 10.7.1178b23.

55. Ibid. 10.7.1177b24.

56. Ibid. 10.7.1177b26–34.

57. Ibid. 10.7.1178b26–27. Aristotle's highest god, the prime mover, moves the universe in an unusual way: "it produces motion by being loved, and it [thus] moves the other moving things." *Metaph.* 1072b3–4, trans. W. D. Ross, in *The Complete Works of Aristotle: The Revised Oxford Translation,* ed. Jonathan Barnes, vol. 2 (Princeton, NJ: Princeton University Press, 1984). Heavenly bodies seek to imitate its perfection. David Lindberg, *The Beginnings of Western Science* (Chicago: University of Chicago Press, 1992), 62; Sedley, "Ideal of Godlikeness," 325.

58. For parallels, see e.g., Guthrie, "Plato's Views," 243. For Aristotle and Plato, see Sedley, "Ideal of Godlikeness," 324–28.

59. *Gen. an.* 736b27–29.

60. *Metaph.* 1070a25–26.

61. See Lindberg, *Western Science,* chap. 10, and Richard A. Rubinstein, *Aristotle's Children* (New York: Harcourt, 2003).

62. *Eth. nic.* 1179a24–32.

63. A. A. Long, "Socrates in Hellenistic Philosophy," in *Stoic Studies* (Berkeley: University of California Press, 1996), 1–34; and Long, "Hellenistic Ethics and Philosophical Power," in *Hellenistic History and Culture,* ed. Peter Green, 138–56 (Berkeley: University of California Press, 1993). W. V. Harris, *Restraining Rage,* 362–63, rightly shows the inadequacies and the prejudices in the commonplace political explanation for a supposed rise in individualism.

64. Werner Jaeger, *Early Christianity and Greek Paideia* (Cambridge, MA: Belknap Press, 1961), 5; A. D. Momigliano, "J. D. Droysen between Greeks and Jews," in *Studies on Modern Scholarship,* ed. G. W. Bowersock and T. J. Cornell, 147–61 (Berkeley: University of California Press, 1994); William V. Rowe, "Adolf von Harnack and the Concept of Hellenization," in *Hellenization Revisited: Shaping a Christian Response within the Greco-Roman World,* ed. W. E. Helleman, 69–98 (Lanham, MD: University Press of America, 1994). E.g., Droysen wrote in 1843: "history has . . . created the body for the Holy Spirit" (quoted in Momigliano, "J. D. Droysen," 152). Momigliano criticizes Droysen for ignoring the Jewishness of Christianity. Harnack reversed the metaphor, calling the Christian church "a work of the Greek spirit on the soil of the Gospel." Rowe, "Adolf von Harnack," 79. Jaeger, a rare classicist with patristic interests, uses similar metaphors of form and matter (which are Platonic and Aristotelian), although these vary, e.g., writing that Greek culture (*paideia*) provided the "form" to Christian doctrines (Jaeger, *Early Greek Philosophers,* 4, 20–21, and 81–85 on Basil). Generally he argues that Hellenism provides only intellectual and literary culture,

shape, not substance. Specific issues of the formation of Christian "dogma" are not our concern here.

65. Epicurus, *Letter to Menoeceus* 135, text 23J in A. A. Long and D. N. Sedley, eds., *The Hellenistic Philosophers* (Cambridge, MA: Cambridge University Press, 1987).

66. Cicero criticized it in *Tusc.* 1.21.48; M. F. Smith, ed., *Lucretius: De Rerum Natura,* LCL 181, rev. 2nd ed. (Cambridge MA: Harvard University Press, 1992), 378n.

67. *De Rerum Natura* 5.8; also 19.

68. Ibid. 3.12–15.

69. Ibid. 3.7–9, 18–19.

70. Ibid. 5.18, 43ff; 5.10.

71. Ibid. 5.13ff.; cf. Epicurus, *Letter to Menoeceus,* 123–24, text 23B in Long and Sedley, *Hellenistic Philosophers.* On the status of Epicurus, see Bernard Frischer, *The Sculpted Word: Epicureanism and Philosophical Recruitment in Ancient Greece* (Berkeley: University of California Press, 1982).

72. Ibid. 3.321.

73. Ibid. 1.79.

74. *Fr.* 52. C. W. Chilton, *Diogenes of Oenoanda, the Fragments* (Oxford: Oxford University Press for the University of Hull, 1971).

75. Lucretius, *De Rerum Natura* 3.1042; 6.7.

76. *Ench.* 51.

77. *Ench.* 22. The language echoes Plato's *Apology of Socrates* 30a, e.

78. *Diatr.* 1.9.1.

79. Above, *Eth. nic.* 10.7.1178b23.

80. Long, "Concept of Daimon," 26, words introducing the quotations; Epictetus, *Discourses* 1.14.6, trans. Long, "Concept of Daimon," 25; and *Discourses* 2.8.11–13.

81. Long, "Concept of Daimon," chap. 6.5.

82. The wording of this sentence makes use of Nicholas P. White, *Handbook of Epictetus* (Indianapolis: Hackett, 1983), 25n23.

83. Cleanthes, *Hymn to Zeus* 2, found as text 54I in Long and Sedley, *The Hellenistic Philosophers.*

84. See Lindberg, *Western Science,* 81–82.

85. Long, "Hellenistic Ethics," 146. A theme that could be traced beyond the present paper is the prevalence of the imagery of cosmic and divine "kingship" and "majesty."

86. Chrysippus at text 61J in Long and Sedley, *Hellenistic Philosophers*; Long, "Hellenistic Ethics," 151.

87. *Ench.* 33, trans. White, *Handbook of Epictetus.*

88. A. Ben Mansour, "Aspects de la religion de Cicéron," *Bulletin de l'Association Guillaume Budé* (1970): 359–73, explains (insufficiently, but typically) Cicero's thought as social and political ideology. Cicero, note, also presents sympathetic arguments (in dialogues) for the immortality of the soul (*De Amicitia* 13–14, citing Pythagorean precedent, and the influential ending of *De Republica* 6, known from Macrobius in the fifth century AD, known as *Somnium Scipionis,* "Dream of Scipio," which begins by recalling Plato's myth of Er's vision of the afterlife).

89. Kingsley, *Reality,* 474.

90. Barry B. Powell, *Classical Myth,* 4th ed. (Upper Saddle River, NJ: Prentice-Hall, 2004), 306.

91. In the words of a fifth-century AD character in a recent novel who represents the last pagan aristocracy in Rome, "such mysteries as the Incarnation, the Trinity, the Holy Spirit were given shape in our minds through the teachings of the Academies." Iain Pears, *The Dream of Scipio* (New York: Riverhead Books, 2002), 8.

92. Polymnia Athanassiadi, "Persecution and Response in Late Paganism: The Evidence

of Damascius," *Journal of Hellenic Studies* 113 (1993): 3; and P. Athanassiadi and M. Frede, ed., *Pagan Monotheism in Late Antiquity* (Oxford: Oxford University Press, 1999).

93. See J. A. McGuckin in the present volume. *Apotheosis* and its comparison with *theosis* are discussed above.

94. Damascius, *de Principiis* 100 (used in the plural).

95. The philosopher Gadamer writes of "a shared, continuous tradition" to which Plato and Aristotle belong, "a continuous line of thought" (in the words of his translator) or a "unitary effect." Hans-Georg Gadamer, *The Idea of the Good in Platonic-Aristotelian Philosophy,* trans. P. Christopher Smith (New Haven: Yale University Press, 1986), viin2, 1n1, and 1. We may extend this from Plato to the Eastern church fathers.

Can We Speak of *Theosis* in Paul?

Stephen Finlan

THE QUESTION OF WHETHER OR NOT PAUL TAUGHT A DOCTRINE OF *THEOSIS* is entirely dependent upon what one means by the term. There certainly are some meanings of the term *theosis* that do fit what Paul taught, so we need to clarify his teaching in relation to deification.

Paul has a number of passages that speak of believers reflecting God's glory. They either "behold" or they "reflect" God's glory; they "have the mind of Christ"; they are shaped "to the image of God's Son"; they were even "prepared beforehand for glory" (2 Cor 3:18; 1 Cor 2:16; Rom 8:29, 9:23).[1] In 1 Corinthians 15, believers will receive "spiritual," "imperishable" bodies (1 Cor 15:42–44). In Philippians 3:21, the Lord Jesus Christ will transform our humble bodies "into conformity with the body of His glory" (NASB). What, then, is this spiritual and glorious body?

There may be a certain resistance to the central point of this chapter because of the difficulty of imagining a *spiritual body.* British New Testament scholar N. T. Wright exemplifies this resistance, so I will focus on an inadequacy in his interpretation. I will then present more positively Paul's articulation of a spiritual and glorious body, which theologically constitutes divinization.

THE SPIRITUAL BODY: 1 CORINTHIANS 15

But someone will ask, 'How are the dead raised? With what kind of body do they come?' Fool! What you sow does not come to life unless it dies. And as for what you sow, you do not sow the body that is to be, but a bare seed, perhaps of wheat or of some other grain. But God gives it a body as he has chosen, and to each kind of seed its own body. Not all flesh is alike. . . . What is sown is perishable, what is raised is imperishable. It is sown in dishonor, it is raised in glory. It is sown in weakness, it is raised in power. It is sown a physical body, it is raised a spiritual body. If there is a physical body, there is also a spiritual body. . . . What I am saying, brothers and sisters, is this: flesh and blood cannot inherit the kingdom of God, nor does the perishable inherit the imperishable. Listen, I will tell you a mystery! We will not all die, but we will all be changed. . . . For this perish-

> *able body must put on imperishablility, and this mortal body must put on immortality.* (1 Cor 15:35–39a, 42b–44, 50–51, 53)

Apologies may be in order to Wright for seeming to dwell on his work, but he is, in fact, representative of many scholars who have difficulty with the idea of a spiritual body.

Wright not only resists but vehemently rejects the possibility that Paul's contrast between *psychic* body and *pneumatic* body could possibly indicate a contrast between physical and nonphysical. Of course, "psychic" does not mean physical, it means, literally, "soulish,"[2] but one should not overlook the equation of psychic with physical in vv. 40, 48, 50, and 53, nor fail to pick up on the implications of Paul's intensely dualistic presentation. However, in the twenty verses of 1 Corinthians 15:35–54, I count twenty contrasts made about bodies, eighteen of which are dualistic contrasts:

- A present-future contrast is made in v. 37;
- A terrestrial-celestial or earthly-heavenly contrast occurs in vv. 40, 47, 48, 49;
- A perishable-imperishable or mortal-immortal contrast is found in vv. 42, 50, 53 (twice), 54 (twice);
- A body for dishonor is contrasted with one for glory in v. 43, a weak one with a powerful one, in the same verse;
- A living being is contrasted with a life-giving spirit in v. 45;
- Finally, a psychic body (σῶμα ψυχικόν) and a pneumatic body (σῶμα πνευματικόν) are contrasted twice in v. 44 and once in v. 46.

In addition to these 18 dualistic contrasts, vv. 39 and 41 emphasize the point that "not all flesh is alike" and not all kinds of glory are alike, giving four examples of different kinds of flesh or glory. The opening question for all this (v. 35), was: "ποίῳ δὲ σώματι ἔρχονται—with what kind of body do they come?" What *kind* of body is clearly under question, but Wright says this refers to "the animating principle" of the body,[3] a body animated by spirit as opposed to one animated by soul. Certainly this is implied, but "what *kind* of body" is asking about more than motivation. Paul repeatedly returns to different kinds of bodies, places of origin, and levels of mortality. Why spend time forming twenty contrasts to make a point that he elsewhere can make in a short sentence (Rom 8:6, e.g.)? Paul is not just spelling out different animating principles, but entirely different *levels and kinds of life force, nativity,* and *substance:*

life force: one is subject to corruption and death, the other is not;
nativity: one earthly or from earth, the other is heavenly or from heaven;
substance: one is *psychic,* the other is *pneumatic* and possesses characteristics that are not like those of any bodies *we* know.

Wright does acknowledge that "Paul's main purpose here is to establish that there are different kinds of physicality," but he then underplays this, emphasizing the body's "animating principle."[4] But Paul is answering a question specifically about the bodies of the resurrected, not about motivation, which would be a question for *this* life. He begins by telling the foolish reader that what he sows does not come to life unless it dies, and that what he sows is *not* "the body that is to be (τὸ σῶμα τὸ γενησόμενον)," but is a "bare seed (γυμνὸν κόκκον)" (vv. 36–37).

Paul could hardly make it any clearer that he is talking about two different bodies. Still, he goes on to say that "not all flesh is alike"; that there are heavenly bodies and earthly bodies; that they have a different "glory" (vv. 39–41); the *psychic* body is perishable, weak, and "of dust," while the *pneumatic* body is imperishable, powerful, and "of heaven (ἐπουράνιοι)" (vv. 42–44, 48).

While *psychic* is not a synonym of "physical," it is associated with the "first man," the "man of dust" (vv. 45–49). The dusty (χοϊκός) man is a clear reference to Genesis 2:7, where the cognate noun, χοῦς, is used in the LXX. In this verse it is said that God made man a "living being (ψυχὴν ζῶσαν)," which Paul quotes in v. 45, contrasting this with the "last Adam," who is a "life-giving spirit." Of the psychic body, he says "flesh and blood cannot inherit the kingdom of God" (v. 50); *sarx* by itself can indicate motivation, but flesh *and* blood emphasizes mortality or physicality.[5] The verses that follow seem to imply transformation of the existing temporal body into a new body that can no longer perish: "we will be changed. For this perishable body must put on imperishability" (vv. 52–53). This is an ontological change, from dust to something else, something "of heaven" (v. 48).

Second Corinthians 5 describes the same events but with a mixed metaphor of dwelling and enclothing: "the earthly tent" will be destroyed, and we will receive a new "house (οἰκία)" (v. 1) or "be clothed with our heavenly dwelling (τὸ οἰκητήριον . . . τὸ ἐξ οὐρανοῦ)" (v. 2). Again, in vv. 3–4, he speaks of "taking off" one body and being "clothed" with another.

Wright's principle of being animated by spirit is as true of the earthly life as it is of the afterlife. To say "the *psychikos/pneumatikos* contrast" simply indicates "'ordinary human life' contrasted with 'a life indwelt by the Spirit of God,'" is to dodge the afterlife question.[6] But we must let Paul be eschatological. Not everything is reducible to *this*-worldly realities.

The problem with Wright's analysis is that he allows only two conceptions: either a physical body on the one hand, or a "ghost" or disembodied spirit on the other.[7] In fact there are other possibilities. He accuses scholars of agreeing "to drive a steamroller through what Paul actually says . . . to make room for a different worldview in which the aim of Christian faith is 'to go to heaven when you die.'"[8] I think, in fact, Wright drives a steamroller over the possibility of a new and bold idea being expressed by Paul: namely, that the "spiritual body" is neither physical body nor a disembodied spirit; it involves neither Pharisaic resuscitation nor Platonic immortality. God is doing a "new thing" in the new creation of a spiritual body.

Paul, for all his rhetorical dualities, is trying to express something that has never been expressed before, and that does not fit into prior dualities (an *embodied* form that is not *physical*), while Wright, for all his learnedness and insight, is trying to force simplistic and dualistic choices upon the interpreter (either physicality or ghostliness). Wright forces Paul and Jesus into the narrow category of what he calls the Second Temple Jewish hope, where all spiritual values, all hope, all salvation images must fit the paradigm of Sin-Exile-Return, where Jewish hope is entirely a subcategory of nationalist ideology and where there is no hint of Hellenism. Anyone who does not put Jesus and Paul into this ideology must join the ranks of marginal scholars who engage in "an unwarranted platonizing of Christian hope."[9] But Christian "platonizing" has always been a *Christian* project, from the earliest days of Greek-speaking Christianity.[10] The whole biblical message cannot be tucked into the bed of Sin-Exile-Return, with no loose edges and no trace of platonizing.

Wright's image of Platonism is shallow; it is simply a foil for his Sin-Exile-Return ideology. When Wright speaks of the "heavenly life chang[ing] the present earthly reality," he specifically distinguishes this from "all kinds of Platonism ancient and modern. The point is not to escape from earth."[11] Yet this in no way appears to be the same Plato who explicitly writes that "the best minds," after they "ascend to a vision of the Good," must not be allowed to "remain in the upper world," but must return and share their rewards with society, for the good "of the whole community."[12]

Christification Process

The scholar whom Wright uses as support for his "animating" position is less rigid than Wright on the question of an ontological difference between bodies. Murray Harris at one point concedes that the resurrection body "will be neither fleshly nor fleshy."[13] One of those adjectives must concern the question of substance. Harris allows on the next page that Paul felt pressure from "the objections constantly leveled by cultured Greeks against the idea of a physical resurrection."[14] However, he sees Paul retaining not just embodiment, but "corporeality,"[15] and so does not allow Paul to envision a different *kind* of embodiment. This is a tricky subject, of course, not least because Paul seems to be saying one thing (new body) in 1 Corinthians 15, and another thing (*changed* body) in Philippians 3. In either case, though, Paul is not talking about resuscitated corpses, but resurrected persons. Harris writes that 1 Corinthians 15:44 "justifies only the concept of 'the resurrection of the (spiritual) body'!"[16] He intriguingly describes this as "an acceleration of the process of christification," and says the "inward person" is "the embryo of his spiritual body."[17]

So What Is the Body Like?

It is necessary to acknowledge that the resurrection body has some continuity, as well as some discontinuity, with the earthly body.[18] It grows out of the latter as a plant grows out of a seed, but it belongs somewhere else (heaven, not earth), it is linked with a different model (Christ, not Adam). The discontinuity is perhaps most clearly indicated in dualities such as that in 1 Corinthians 15:49: "Just as we have borne the image of the man of dust, we will also bear the image of the man of heaven."

This transformation into "the image of his Son" (Rom 8:29) in the afterlife could be called *theosis*. But the process of transformation, at least in terms of character, loyalty, and spiritual fruits, is initiated during this lifetime. Paul's message is primarily one of transformation and its associated process, *con*formation.

Conformation and Transformation

*Trans*forming is not identical with *con*forming, a term Paul uses in Romans and Philippians in reference to radical spiritual change.[19] In Romans 8:29 Paul uses the adjective σύμμορφος to speak of believers being "conformed to the image of his Son." Numerous statements in Romans 8 show that this involves a moral and spiritual reshaping, a strengthening of character (mind is set on the Spirit in 8:5; body given new life in 8:11; Spirit helps us in our weakness in 8:26; believers are glorified in 8:30), and a change of status before the Lord ("no condemnation" in 8:1 and 33; "children of God" in 8:14). All this change in status and character is accomplished by the Spirit, who is mentioned twenty-one times in this chapter. There is a resulting severance from the life of the flesh, from the "dead body" of v. 10 and the death-oriented mind of v. 6. The reception of new life requires concrete ascetic practice to "put to death the deeds of the body" in v. 13. Thus, *conformation* has to do with reorientation from fleshly living to spiritual living.

In Philippians

In Philippians 3:10, the participle συμμορφιζόμενος describes the believer being "conformed to his death" (KJV). There is an unmistakable linkage between Christ's death to sin and the believer's death to sinful sensuality; the believer gets his righteousness by faith; it is a "from-God-righteousness, upon faith," to translate literally Philippians 3:9b: τὴν ἐκ θεοῦ δικαιοσύνην ἐπὶ τῇ πίστει. These two *con-forming* passages then, both tie in to the Christ pattern of dying and rising. For believers, this means a necessary renunciation of fleshly living, and its replacement by Spirit living.

Finally, in Philippians 3:21 we find that the Savior Jesus Christ will "transform (μετασχηματίσει) the body of our humble state into conformity (σύμμορφον) with the body of His glory" (NASB).[20] The transformation of the physical body makes the human body conform to Christ's body. Thus, first there is an earthly conformation to the Christlike pattern of dying to sin; then there is reception of godly righteousness and light; and finally there is physical death and resurrection, which entails receiving a transformed body modeled on Christ's body. This is no mere metaphor, but a straightforward attempt to describe the resurrected body the believer will receive. One reason for Paul's confidence on this point is, presumably, his experience of having seen the Savior in this resurrected form on the Damascus road. Forever after he retained the idea of the resurrection body as glorious; neither an ordinary earthly body, nor a disembodied spirit.

We must not neglect the middle stage in this metamorphosis, where one reflects God's glory while still in the flesh. Transformation refers to a fundamental change in one's nature. In Romans 12, believers are told to offer themselves up wholly to God in order to "be transformed (μεταμορφοῦσθε) by the renewing (ἀνακαίνωσις)[21] of your minds, so that you may discern what is the will of God—what is good and acceptable and perfect." Loyalty leads to transformation, which leads to discernment. It is more than just training the mind to think spiritually; it means an ability to actually discern the *qualities of God* and choose them, similar to the process described in 2 Corinthians 3:18: *beholding* the glory and being transformed into its image; here discernment precedes transformation.

In Philippians 1:9–10, Paul prays that "your love may overflow more and more with knowledge and full insight (περισσεύῃ ἐν ἐπιγνώσει καὶ πάσῃ αἰσθήσει) to help you to determine what is best, so that in the day of Christ you may be pure (εἰλικρινεῖς) and blameless." Here insight leads to discernment, which leads to transformation. The Greek here and in the Septuagint is rich with meaning. Ἐπίγνωσις is the essential knowledge of God in Hosea 4:1, 4:6, 6:6, and Proverbs 2:5, while αἴσθησις is used in Proverbs 1:7 to speak of piety being "the beginning of discernment." The only LXX occurrence of εἰλικρινής is where Wisdom is described as "a pure emanation of the glory of the Almighty" (Wis 7:25).

Paul describes a "moral change in the believer."[22] This blamelessness is clearly the product of Christ-faith, as the next verse of Philippians makes clear: "the harvest of righteousness . . . comes through Jesus Christ." This hardly contradicts the statement in Philippians 3:9 that the believer receives righteousness from *God*; every gift from Christ *is* a gift from God.

What must be noticed in Philippians is that the believer receives an ability to discern what is good, what is righteous, and what is conducive of love; and with this ability, the believer is able to stand pure and blameless "in the day of Christ" (1:10). It is not that the believer will be *declared* blameless on that day; the believer already *is* blameless, already *is* righteous, already *is* possessed of ἐπίγνωσις to discern what is best, because of the re-formation wrought upon the believer in this lifetime, and because of the righteousness received from God in this lifetime. Such a change is truly a re-*formation* of the person. The insight of 1:9 and the faith-receptivity of 1:11 and 3:9 lead to the power of discernment and the blamelessness of 1:10, and to conformation to the Savior's resurrection body in 3:21. But, of course, all this is a "from-God-righteousness" (3:9). In what may be Paul's final letter, then, he makes clear that transformation takes place both in this life and in the next. But he had already said in Romans that believers can discern the will of God, can test or examine or interpret or discover—for these are all acceptable translations of δοκιμάζω—what is good and acceptable and perfect (12:2). Each one, he says in the next verse, has received a "measure of faith" (μέτρον πίστεως) from God.

This is part of what Paul means by saying that believers have the "mind of Christ" (1 Cor 2:16). Having the "mind of Christ," which also appears in Philippians 2:5, is used by Paul to make two different points. In 1 Corinthians, the remark occurs as a contradiction of the stock rhetorical question, "who can know the Lord's mind?"—giving the surprising answer, "we can." In Philippians the phrase refers to self-giving service to others. "Having the mind of Christ," then, can refer either to an ability to discern God's will or a willingness to manifest God's love. This echoes the affective and cognitive capabilities—love and knowledge—given in Philippians 1:9–10.

Anastiform Transformation

To summarize the sequence of events as given in Philippians: in chapter 1, love and knowledge lead to correct discernment and blameless character; and in chapter 2, "having the mind of Christ" refers to having the unselfish character of Christ. In chapter 3, the believer's re-formation or conformation begins with sharing in Christ's sufferings and death, and *then* with participation in resurrection. Conformity with Christ, then, is first "cruciform," and then "anastiform," to coin a term derived from ἀνάστασις, resurrection. *Theosis* has to do with "anastiform" experience, both in this life and the next. If we want to call Paul's gospel "cruciform," as Michael

Gorman does, we must also call it "anastiform," or we leave out half his message.[23]

A Glorious Transformation

Eschatological hope informs every step in Paul's soterio-logic. Even "the creation itself will be set free from its bondage to decay" (Rom 8:21), a hope that recalls the cosmic restoration in Isaiah 65:17–25 and in some apocalyptic literature.

One cannot help noticing Paul's repeated reference to receiving, beholding, and reflecting God's glory or light or righteousness. In 2 Corinthians 4:6, God "has shone (ἔλαμψεν) in our hearts to give the light of the knowledge of the glory of God in the face of Jesus Christ." Here, Christ *transmits* God's light to believers, who shine with Christ's glory. Of course, this raises the question of just what this light is, whether Paul has a "materialistic notion of God's glory," as Koenig thinks,[24] or whether this light consists of spiritual knowledge and character, as many think, or whether Paul sees it as *both* an inward quality and an outward radiance, as I think. The experience of being conformed to the image of the Son in Romans 8:29 seems to be equivalent to being justified and glorified in Christ, which appear in the next verse. In this eschatological passage, conformation, heavenly acquittal, and glorification seem to be simultaneous.

This process, however, occurs in this lifetime. Brief but stunning indicators of believers being made Christlike in this life are described in most of the letters of Paul. In 2 Corinthians 3:18 believers are "transformed . . . from one degree of glory to another." In Philippians 1:6–7, "the one who began a good work in you will bring it to completion," for believers are "partakers of grace" (RSV). The "new Adam" referred to in Romans 5:17–19 means a new humanity, "a new creation" in which believers "become the righteousness of God" (2 Cor 5:17, 21). Describing Paul's soteriology as "justification," therefore, is inadequate; mere acquittal would not empower people to *become the righteousness of God.* Believers see God's glory, they experience the mind of Christ, they even take on the character of God. Can we not speak of *theosis* in Paul?

Divinization in 2 Corinthians 3:18

The most frankly theotic passage in Paul is 2 Corinthians 3:18: "all of us, with unveiled faces, seeing the glory of the Lord as though reflected in a mirror, are being transformed into the same image from one degree of glory to another; for this comes from the Lord, the Spirit." There has been a prolonged scholarly debate about whether the verb κατοπτρίζομαι refers to "seeing" or "reflecting." Of course, either *seeing* God's radiance or *reflecting* it has staggering implications.

Gordon Fee argues that κατοπτρίζομαι "ordinarily has to do with 'looking into' a mirror, not with the mirror's reflecting an image."[25] Lambrecht says "the idea of mirror-image is present" in the verb but agrees that believers "behold" more than "reflect" his glory.[26] The reason believers behold "as in a mirror" is that it is impossible to see God directly; he is highlighting the fact that humans can only see God by "indirect vision."[27] Corinth was famous for its highly reflective bronze mirrors, in which images could be seen clearly.[28] So the significance of the mirror analogy is not *distorted* viewing, but *indirect* viewing. Humans *can* see an *image* of God, namely Christ; and this is not a *muddled* transmission, but a *stepped* transmission. Moses also had reflected God's glory, but Christians can do it with confidence and boldness (παρρησία). The Christ believer can fearlessly approach that which frightened Aaron and the Israelites. Moreover, believers go on to embody and to reflect the glory that they have beheld. God works within them and metamorphosizes them. While beholding Christ, believers are transformed into that same image. Μεταμορφόομαι in 2 Corinthians 3:18 and Romans 12:2 really does mean "change of form," or "transform."[29] "If anyone is in Christ there is a new creation!"—or new *creature*—as Paul shouts in 2 Corinthians 5:17.[30]

This gives rise to the question as to whether this transformation is progressive or immediate. Scharlemann claims that "from glory to glory . . . does not suggest constant progress," but only "indicates sequence: the glory moves from the Lord to us," similar to the expression "from generation to generation."[31] Yet this explanation seems muddled. The sequence from generation to generation is between comparable realities—humans—while Paul's sequence is between entirely different levels of reality—God and humans. Both take time, but we can only expect that the adequate human reflection of divine glory will take more time than the human reflection of parental teaching. It must therefore involve a *progressive* reflection of new glory. The phrase "from glory to glory" highlights the "ever-increasing dimension of the glory," according to Fee; denotes "progression," according to Wong; signifies "the continuous operation" of the Spirit, according to Stegmann.[32]

"The same image" (τὴν αὐτὴν εἰκόνα) of 2 Corinthians 3:18, into which we are being transformed, seems to be Christ, who, in v. 14, takes away the veil for readers of the Old Covenant and who, a few verses later in 4:4, is called the image of God (ὅς ἐστιν εἰκὼν τοῦ θεοῦ).[33] The transformation described here is "going on in the present."[34] Even now, believers have confidence, competence, life, boldness, and freedom (2 Cor 3:4–6, 12, 17); they are renewed every day (4:16).[35] Such renewal, with the ability to read the

Bible unveiled, and with capacity to reflect the character of God, is truly *anastiform*: living as though already in the kingdom of God and receiving eternal light and truth.

Formation and Freedom in Galatians

The transformation passages in the Corinthian, Philippian, and Roman correspondence describe in more detail what is probably intended in Galatians 4:19 where Paul calls for Christ to be *formed* within Christians, using the passive of the verb μορφόω. If Christ had been formed in the Galatians, they would not have considered putting themselves in subjection to the law. Failure to be transformed led to bad choice. Paul goes on to allegorize (*his* word, in 4:24), saying that real transformation makes one into a child of the free woman and a citizen of the Jerusalem above, rather than a child of the enslaved and a citizen of the earthly realm. This identification with a heavenly Jerusalem is reframed in other letters: the believer's true loyalty or citizenship (πολίτευμα) is in heaven in Philippians 3:20, and the resurrected believers "bear the image of the man of heaven" in 1 Corinthians 15:49.

In Galatians, though, the stress is on liberation from the law. "For freedom Christ has set us free," he says (Gal 5:1). That, too, is a transformation, a new *condition,* not just a new status; an ability to resist the "yoke of slavery," not just a *legal* re-inscription. The believer is changed inwardly and outwardly, but not because of outward action taken upon the body. "Neither circumcision nor uncircumcision is anything; but a new creation (καινὴ κτίσις) is everything" (Gal 6:15).

An essential, even a structural, part of transformation, for Paul, is the believer's consent: "you are all children of God through faith" (Gal 3:26). Believers must do certain things; they must present their members "as instruments of righteousness"; they are to set their minds on the Spirit, and "put to death the deeds of the body" (Rom 6:13; 8:6, 13). Recognition of what Christ has done, then, leads believers to be grateful and loyal, and to no longer live for themselves (2 Cor 5:15).

The Atoning Action

The real saving work was done for humanity by Christ while they were helplessly lost in sin. In Romans 3:25, Christ was put forward as the ἱλαστήριον, the new place of atonement, by means of his blood. This passage is full of the imagery of Yom Kippur. The ἱλαστήριον, in the innermost sanctuary, is the lid of the ark of the covenant, and is the place where the blood of the purification sacrifice was sprinkled on Yom Kippur (Lev 16:14). If Christ is the new ἱλαστήριον, then, by implication, his death was a kind of sacrifice, perhaps purifying the community, perhaps providing recompense for sin. Both cleansing of impurity and making a payment for sin are themes in Levitical sacrifice and should not be treated as antithetical interpretations, since the main cause of impurity was sin and the word used for cleansing the sanctuary, *kipper* כִּפֶּר, is cognate with the word for payment, *kopher* כֹּפֶר, sometimes designating a cultic gift and sometimes a noncultic payment.[36]

A different metaphor, but with the same end result, occurs in the crucial chapter, 2 Corinthians 5. Speaking of God's action, Paul says, "For our sake he made him to be sin who knew no sin, so that in him we might become the righteousness of God" (2 Cor 5:21). The sinless Christ takes on sin so that sinful believers might take on God's righteousness. This interchange is at the heart of Paul's soteriology.[37] It is fundamentally a scapegoat metaphor, where there is an exchange of conditions; the sinless Christ takes on the sin of the community, and the community takes on the sinless righteousness of Christ.

Paul mixes his metaphors: Christ is a new sacrifice of purification; and he is a new scapegoat who carries away sin. Paul also uses metaphors of redemption and martyrdom to describe this death as a saving event that brings about an interchange of conditions. One could say that Christ is temporarily de-divinized so that believers might be permanently divinized. Similarly, he rescued others from a curse by *becoming* temporarily a curse (Gal 3:13), another scapegoat image.[38]

Theosis comes at the end of this sacrificial process. The culmination is proclaimed in 2 Corinthians 5:21, "so that in him we might become the righteousness of God"—one of the most striking transformative statements of Paul! One can dismiss it as hyperbole, or downplay it, but the transformation of the believer is a central Pauline teaching.[39] It is, however, logically secondary to the soteriological transaction that took place at the cross, which accomplished both substitution and interchange. This action is fundamentally a cultic transaction, like the purification sacrifice or like the scapegoat, a sin-expulsion ritual. Transformation becomes possible *after* this transaction.

It proves to be impossible, therefore, to discuss *theosis* in Paul without considering, however briefly, the sacrificial interchange accomplished by the death of Christ, and without spelling out the believer's necessary participation in the Savior's cruciform life so that one may also share in his *anastiform* living. Since the *anastiform* benefits begin already in this lifetime, an exclusive focus on sin and deliverance would suppress a crucial aspect of Paul's teaching: gaining an ability to discern the will of God, and being transformed into Christlikeness, which can truly be called *theosis*. Thus, *theosis* in Paul always involves both cruciform and *anastiform* living, but points to a thoroughly *anastiform* destiny, when the believer will "be with Christ" (Phil 1:23).

Note, however, that the believer does not *become* Christ. This is where Paul's viewpoint is to be distinguished from a Gnostic one such as that in *Corpus Hermeticum,* where the mystic blends identities with a god.[40] Becoming Christified does not mean becoming Christ, but rather Christlike in substance and character.

Notes

1. NRSV is my default translation.
2. Correctly, N. T. Wright, *The Resurrection of the Son of God,* Christian Origins and the Question of God, vol. 3 (Minneapolis: Fortress Press, 2003), 351.
3. Ibid., 346, probably relying on Murray J. Harris, *Raised Immortal: Resurrection and Immortality in the New Testament* (Grand Rapids: W. B. Eerdmans, 1983), 120.
4. Ibid., 344, 346.
5. Archibald Robertson and Alfred Plummer, *A Critical and Exegetical Commentary on the First Epistle of St. Paul to the Corinthians,* ICC, 2nd ed. (Edinburgh: T & T Clark, 1914), 375–76.
6. Wright, *Resurrection,* 350.
7. Ibid., 355n130.
8. Ibid., 367–68.
9. Ibid., 367.
10. The most obvious Platonism is in Hebrews where the earthly temple is "a sketch and shadow of the heavenly one," "a mere copy" (8:5; 9:23, 24; 10:1; cf. Plato's visible things as mere "passing shadows" of unseen realities. *Rep* 7.515C), but Paul's dualities can also look Platonic, or at least Hellenistic. Paul's contrasting of inner/outer, visible/invisible, mortal/immortal, decaying/renewing, can be called Hellenistic, or even "'Platonic' antithesis." David E. Aune, "Anthropological Duality in the Eschatology of 2 Cor 4:16–5:10," in *Paul Beyond the Judaism/Hellenism Divide,* ed. Troels Engberg-Pedersen (Louisville: Westminster, 2001), 216–17, 221. The inner/outer contrast is made in a well known passage of Plato's (*Rep.* 9.588; Aune, "Duality," 220–21). Of course, "Hellenism and early Judaism are hardly mutually exclusive contexts," and observation of Hellenisms does not mean that Jewish features are "subordinated" (Aune, "Duality," 216, 238).
11. Wright, *Resurrection,* 355.
12. *Republic* 519E; *The Republic,* trans. H. D. P. Lee (Baltimore: Penguin Books, 1955), 284–85.
13. Murray J. Harris, *Raised Immortal: Resurrection and Immortality in the New Testament* (Grand Rapids, MI: Eerdmans, 1983), 124.
14. Ibid., 125.
15. Ibid., 142.
16. Ibid., 133.
17. Ibid., 130
18. Cf. good discussion in Harris, *Raised,* 125–31.
19. J. Lambrecht, "Transformation in 2 Cor 3:18," *Biblica* 64 (1983): 251.
20. Occurring in the intensely martyrological passage 4 Macc 9:22, where the first brother is "transformed by fire into immortality." This document, however, may be more recent than Paul's writings. The NRSV's "body of our humiliation" gives a negative connotation to humility, in contrast to its positive connotation in Phil 2:3, 8. Peter Doble, "'Vile Bodies' or Transformed Persons? Philippians 3.21 in Context," *JSNT* 86 (2002): 3–27.
21. Used for renewal and restoration in Ps 103:5, 104:30; Lam 5:21.

22. James M. Starr, *Sharers in Divine Nature: 2 Peter 1:4 in Its Helenistic Context.* Coniectanea Biblical Series 33 (Stockholm: Almqvist & Wiksell International, 2003), 175; the openings of 1 Corinthians, Colossians, Philemon, and 1 Thessalonians also reflect this moral change (ibid).

23. Michael J. Gorman, *Cruciformity: Paul's Narrative Spirituality of the Cross* (Grand Rapids, MI: Eerdmans, 2001).

24. John Koenig, "The Knowing of Glory and Its Consequences (2 Corinthians 3–5)," in *The Conversation Continues: Studies in Paul and John in Honor of J. Louis Martyn,* ed. Robert T. Fortna and Beverly R. Gaventa (Nashville, TN: Abingdon, 1990), 161.

25. Gordon D. Fee, *God's Empowering Presence: The Holy Spirit in the Letters of Paul* (Peabody, MA: Hendrickson, 1994), 316.

26. Lambrecht, "Transformation," 245, 247–48.

27. Ibid., 249. He also "introduces the mirror motif" in his Moses reference in 1 Cor 13:12a. Ibid., 250.

28. Fee, *God's Empowering,* 316.

29. It is also the word for Jesus's Transfiguring in Mark 9:2 and Matt 17:2.

30. "Creatures" is more appropriate contextually, since he is talking about believer transformation.

31. Martin H. Scharlemann, "'Of Surpassing Splendor': An Exegetical Study of 2 Corinthians 3:4–18," *Concordia Journal* 4 (1978): 114.

32. Fee, *God's Empowering,* 318; E. Wong, "The Lord Is the Spirit (2 Cor 3:17a)," *Ephemerides Theologiae Lovanienses* 61 (1985): 67–68; he cites, in support, Plummer, Bultmann, Hermann, Feuillet, Lambrecht, and others; Basil Augustine Stegmann, *Christ, the "Man from Heaven": A Study of 1 Cor. 15, 45–47 in the Light of the Anthropology of Philo Judaeus* (Washington, DC: Catholic University of America, 1927), 74.

33. Wong, "Lord is the Spirit," 67; Lambrecht, "Transformation," 245–46.

34. Victor Paul Furnish, *II Corinthians,* AB 32A (Garden City, NY: Doubleday, 1984), 239.

35. Koenig, "Knowing of Glory," 166.

36. Jacob Milgrom, *Leviticus 1–16,* AB 3 (Garden City, NY: Doubleday, 1991), 1079–84. The Hebrew and the Greek are discussed together by Stanislas Lyonnet, "The Terminology of Redemption," in *Sin, Redemption and Sacrifice: A Biblical and Patristic Study,* ed. Stanislas Lyonnet and Leopold Sabourin, 123–46. Analecta Biblica 48 (Rome: Biblical Institute, 1970); Frank H. Gorman Jr., *The Ideology of Ritual: Space, Time and Status in the Priestly Theology,* JSOT Sup 91 (Sheffield: Sheffield Academic, 1990), 184; Herbert Chanan Brichto, "On Slaughter and Sacrifice, Blood and Atonement," *Hebrew Union College Annual* 47 (1976): 28, 34. Even כֹּפֶר can sometimes indicate a ransom payment (Ex 30:16; Num 31:50) or aversion of God's wrath (Num 1:53; 8:19). Milgrom, *Leviticus 1–16,* 1082–83; cf. 441.

37. Utilizing the term effectively used by M. D. Hooker in "Interchange in Christ," *JTS* 22 (1971): 352, 355. Hooker, however, never mentions that this interchange of conditions is derived from cultic concepts.

38. B. Hudson McLean, *The Cursed Christ: Mediterranean Expulsion Rituals and Pauline Soteriology,* JSNT Sup 126 (Sheffield: Sheffield Academic, 1996), 113–31. The scapegoat is specifically said to be *cursed* in *Epistle of Barnabas* 7:7, 9; *m. Yoma* 6:4.

39. As N. T. Wright says that it simply refers to an ambassador embodying the person who sent him. "On Becoming the Righteousness of God: 2 Corinthians 5:21," in *Pauline Theology,* vol. 2, *1 & 2 Corinthians,* ed. David M. Hay (Minneapolis: Fortress, 1993), 206. But this verse is not focused on apostleship but on salvation (Christ dying "for *all,*" as in v. 14). Starr shares my view (*Sharers,* 170).

40. The mystic says to Hermes, "You are I, and I am you" (*Corpus Hermeticum* 8.49–50); Alfred Wikenhauser, *Pauline Mysticism: Christ in the Mystical Teaching of St. Paul* (Edinburgh: Nelson, 1960), 188.

Does 2 Peter 1:4 Speak of Deification?

James Starr

THE SECOND EPISTLE OF PETER, ASIDE FROM ONE BRIEF BUT BOLD THEOlogical comment, might be thought a theologically *unassuming* letter. Early in the letter the author states that his readers may become "sharers in divine nature" (γένησθε θείας κοινωνοὶ φύσεως), and with that remark he seemingly took a step that no other writer of the New Testament dared take. Uniquely, 2 Peter alone speaks of "divine nature," which in its Hellenistic context appears to mean an impersonal, objectifiable essence of God. And 2 Peter alone appears to suggest that we can and should escape the material world and our mortal humanity, and take on nothing less than divinity.

Ernst Käsemann's famous response was that if 2 Peter 1:4 actually means this, then it provides a clear example of Hellenistic, non-Christian thought insidiously working its way into the New Testament. Käsemann writes, "It would be hard to find in the whole New Testament a sentence which . . . more clearly marks the relapse of Christianity into Hellenistic dualism."[1] For Käsemann, this theological slip on the part of 2 Peter was simply another indication of the author's "early Catholicism" and an explanation for why 2 Peter's standing in the New Testament canon is dubious, and deservedly so in Käsemann's estimation.[2]

Is this an accurate reflection of 2 Peter's thought? In what follows I wish to examine whether Käsemann was right. Does 2 Peter 1:4 teach deification, or *apotheosis* in the sense of a migration from humanity to divinity, as Käsemann suggests? And is this a relapse into Hellenistic dualism? In the rest of his letter 2 Peter neither repeats the phrase nor refers again to it, at least not explicitly, so in what follows we will have to proceed inductively.[3]

THE DIVINE NATURE

We begin by considering what 2 Peter means by "divine nature" (θεία φύσις). What does it look like? The immediate context mentions at least five different qualities that are attributed to or associated with God or the divine, all of which are mentioned in the letter's introduction:

- 1:1 God and Christ's *righteousness* or *justice* (δικαιοσύνη)
- 1:3 "His" divine *power* (δύναμις)[4]
- 1:3b Divine *glory* (δόξα)
- 1:3b Divine *excellence* or *virtue* (ἀρετή)
- 1:4 Divine nature is contrasted with its opposite: this world's corruption. Here lies the author's emphasis: divine nature is that which is *incorruptible* or *eternal.*

These five attributes are thus explicitly linked with divinity, and by association, with divine nature: incorruptibility, power, glory, excellence or virtue, and righteousness or justice, which in the context has moral connotations.[5] In what follows we shall examine several of these characteristics more closely.

Another way to open up 2 Peter's thought behind the phrase "sharers in divine nature" is to see how he describes the person who has become or will become a partaker of divine nature. What does sharing in divine nature *do* for a person? The central statement we have already observed: it means to escape the corruption that is in the world because of passion, or desire (ἐπιθυμία). Accordingly, the sharer of divine nature (1) is *not governed by passion* and (2) will enjoy *incorruptibility.* The letter's introduction ends with the reader's ultimate hope of entry into Christ's eternal kingdom, which repeats the understanding that sharing in divine nature means incorruptibility.

Further, 2 Peter writes that his readers have received a number of things from God or Christ, that is, the one who has divine power (1:3). They have received divine promises (that is, an indication of God's intention to provide a way for those whom he calls [1:3] to share divine nature), promises that the readers believe (1:1). More importantly, for our purposes, God is said to have given them "all things that pertain to life and godliness/piety." This is possibly a hendiadys—a "godly life" or "pious life"—which some have argued. That is possible, but I suspect that the better reading is "life and piety." The reason for this is the content of 1:4: the gift of "things that pertain to life" corresponds to the freedom from corruptibility and death, and the gift of "things that pertain to piety" (εὐσέβεια), or right, reverential thinking, stands in contrast to passion and corrupt desires.

Finally, 2 Peter's words in 1:4 about sharing in divine nature are immediately followed in 1:5–7 by an exhortation to embrace a number of virtues, with love being named last, not because love is the last virtue to be embraced, but for emphasis: love is the crown of the virtuous life. It is plain from 2 Peter's perspective that a life of virtue and love is eminently suitable to the one who shares in divine nature; such a life is attendant upon a life of faith.

Alternate descriptions of the hope of sharing in divine nature thus include (1) escaping from corruption and death, (2) escaping from passionate desire, and (3) having piety and life eternally. Our brief survey of the attributes of divinity and the new or promised attributes of 2 Peter's readers overlap in two major areas. One is the enjoyment of eternity, a life that is not subject to physical decay and death. The other is its moral forerunner: a complete distancing of oneself from the sphere of passion and the rooting of oneself in the sphere of piety or righteousness or virtue.[6] A major focus of his letter is to enjoin the readers to "make every effort" to let their knowledge of Christ bear fruit through a clearer alignment with the good.

Participation in Divine Nature

How can this participation in divine nature be attained? The catalyst is, in 2 Peter's words, "the knowledge of our Lord and Savior Jesus Christ." This is a favorite refrain in the letter, being repeated with variations five times (1:2, 3, 8; 2:20; 3:18). It refers not to knowledge in the sense of "acknowledgment shown to a benefactor" (so Jerome H. Neyrey and Frederick W. Danker, but there is scant evidence for this in the text),[7] but to the knowledge of Christ in his capacities as Savior and Lord. This knowledge is gained through acquaintance with Christ by faith (1:1) and trusts the promises of Christ's return and of a provision for an entry into the eternal kingdom (1:11) "where righteousness dwells" (3:13). The traditional reading is correct, that ἐπίγνωσις (particular knowledge) in 2 Peter signifies a knowledge that is of another order than the knowledge of γνῶσις. It is an *effective* knowing of Christ, received at conversion,[8] that leads ultimately to eternal life. There are at least three signs of its presence in the readers' lives: they remember their forgiveness of sins (1:9, presumably a reference to their conversion); the power of sinful desire is broken for them (1:3–4; 2:19–20); and they make every effort to add virtue and so forth to their faith (1:8). The ἐπίγνωσις of Christ as Lord and Savior effects a process of moral change that culminates in incorruptibility and eternal life.

The participles in 1:4 do not of themselves indicate whether the participation in divine nature is past, present, or future,[9] but the consensus view that 2 Peter writes solely of the future, of an eschatological entry into a state of divine incorruption, fails to take seriously the juxtaposition of the divine attribute of virtue mentioned in 1:3 and the exhortation for the readers to enter into virtue *now* (1:5–7). The readers have already now been given everything that is necessary for piety and therefore are no longer subject to the tyranny of passionate desire. The interpretation that 2 Peter envisions sharing in divine nature as something belonging solely to the future cannot be supported from the immediate context and suggests mistakenly that a departure from the physical world is requisite for participation in divine nature. This is clearly not 2 Peter's intention, as can be seen from subsequent comments in the letter.

For example, 2 Peter argues that its author is an eyewitness of Christ's majesty at the transfiguration (1:16), a moment when the glory of God's Son was visible in the present material world. This would presumably not have been possible if divinity could not associate with matter. A few lines later 2 Peter speaks of men being moved by the Holy Spirit (1:21), a tantalizing comment about the inspiration of Scripture that sadly does not divulge *how* the human speakers were moved by the Spirit, but shows importantly that mortals were favored to be the heralds of divine revelation. The rehearsal in chapter 2 of God's various judgments throughout history point consistently to the fact that God's judgment of the world is related not to the world's material nature but to the problem of unrighteousness and rebellion (2:2–10, and note the vice catalog in 2:12–19). In fact, judgment has already fallen in the spiritual world (2:4), so the problem of corrupting passion is not limited to physical beings. Further, 2 Peter confirms that God created the material world (3:5), that the reason for its impending judgment is humanity's ungodliness (3:7), and that although this material world will pass away, it will be replaced with a new creation, "a new earth in which righteousness dwells" (3:13). Consequently, there is no reason to conclude that 2 Peter envisions divine nature as being in opposition to physical nature. He may even have intentionally tried to guard himself from that misunderstanding when he wrote in 1:4 that what we escape is "the corruption that is in the world *because of passion.*" The issue is not for the readers to escape from the physical world but to escape from passion and the corruption and judgment that inevitably follow.

Building our case solely from 2 Peter's own statements, we find that participation in divine nature follows from knowing Christ as salvific sovereign, that participation has a *present* component in the readers' progressive assimilation to Christ's virtue or moral excellence or righteousness. And participation has a *future* component in the readers' entry into the incorruption of Christ's eternity.

I propose that "sharers in divine nature" should be read as theological shorthand for a constellation of ideas: knowledge of Christ producing escape *from* passion and decay *to* divine moral excellence and divine immortality, both of which are in the process of being realized already now. Helpfully, 2 Peter repeats the constellation of ideas at the midpoint of the letter, though without the shorthand formulation from 1:4. Second Peter writes about the threat to the church caused by false teachers who confuse and entice those who—because of their knowledge of Christ as Lord and Savior—are presently escaping (ἀποφυγόντες, 2:20; cf. 1:4) the world's corruption. These opponents entice the Christians with antinomian freedom so that they are *again* entangled in passion and corruption. Second Peter warns them not to be like those who have known the way of righteousness and then turn their backs on that knowledge (2:20–21). The escape from the slavery of desire is envisaged as a *present* reality, and the readers are already now on the way of righteousness, which involves a moral transformation.

Again, knowledge of the divine (i.e., of Christ) enables an escape in the present from desires of the flesh (2:18) and effects the acquisition of divine righteousness and divine incorruption. The theological shorthand in 1:4, though not repeated verbatim, is fleshed out enough both here and in the course of the letter to show that 2 Peter is not speaking in 1:4 of *apotheosis* in the sense of becoming a part of God's essence or ceasing to be human, but of the partaking in specific divine attributes, seen perfectly in Christ. The participation in divine righteousness begins now in the progressive moral transformation experienced by the one who knows Christ (note the injunction to "*grow* in Christ's grace" in 3:18), but perfect righteousness will only be enjoyed in the new creation ("where righteousness dwells," 3:13). The concern of the present life is to see the knowledge of Christ bear fruit in one's moral dealings (1:8).

Hellenistic Dualism or Apostolic Kerygma?

Is this a sub-Christian thought, a relapse from the apostolic kerygma to Hellenistic dualism? Most modern scholars look to Hellenistic Judaism as the supposed filter through which pagan thought came in contact with the early church, particularly the Old Testament Apocrypha; Jewish thought is formulated, not without undergoing certain inevitable changes, in terms of Greek philosophy.

One text frequently referred to in the literature as being comparable to 2 Peter 1:4 is 4 Maccabees 18:3: "Therefore, those who gave over their bodies in suffering for the sake of piety (διὰ τὴν εὐσέβειαν) were deemed worthy to share in a divine inheritance (θείας μερίδος κατηξιώθησαν)." The text in 4 Maccabees indeed has the same nexus of ideas as 2 Peter, but they are arranged somewhat differently. The "divine inheritance" is specified as "endless life" (17:11–12; cf. 18:23 looking forward to the martyrs' reward of "pure immortal souls"). The end of the process is largely the same, though 4 Maccabees shows no notion of a resurrection, only of a continued life of the soul.[10]

What is markedly unlike 2 Peter is the outset of the process. If the notion in 2 Peter were parallel to 4 Maccabees, we would expect to find the Jewish author stating that the knowledge of God is the catalyst for participation in God, just as the knowledge of Christ is for 2 Peter. Instead, we find that 4 Maccabees makes no mention here of the knowledge of God, but that "devout reason" (ὁ εὐσεβὴς λογισμός) stands at the outset (18:2), and the faithful person holds fast to devout reason. For the author of 4 Maccabees, reason shows its power in conquering passion (1:14), and since reason is an *innate* human capacity, all that is needed is for reason to be educated and trained (1:15–17). Knowledge of God is bypassed. Reason's proper exercise leads one to piety; it quells passion and results in virtue, the reward of which is immortality.

For 4 Maccabees, the initial "knowledge" that can set in motion the process toward gaining a divine inheritance is simply human reason, educated and rightly directed, which leads to piety and virtue, and which is rewarded with the immortality of the soul. This is comparable to the thought of 2 Peter, and 4 Maccabees uses some of the same language, but the possibility of sharing divine nature depends in 2 Peter exclusively on a *new* knowledge entering from the outside. The encounter with Christ in his capacities as Lord and Savior leads to certain gifts (piety and life), which propel the believer into virtue and love and finally usher him into eternal life. But 2 Peter lacks any confidence in human reason per se, and nowhere does he envision immortality as a *reward* for virtue; the gift of life is given at the time one comes to the knowledge of Christ (1:3).

Similar comments could be made about Wisdom 2:23, where the goal of human life is incorruption, to be an image (εἰκών) of God's eternity. But, again, the path begins from human reason, leading to piety and holiness of life, which is ultimately rewarded by God with incorruption (2:21–23). Philo of Alexandria follows a comparable line of thought, but with the important distinction that reason itself is divine, God's Logos. By embracing divine reason, God's people can leave behind this profane world and envision God through the mind (νοῦς), which is true κοινονία with God and "the cause of a life of immortality."[11] Philo explains that we have an innate kinship with God because of our common possession of reason, and as we follow it to immortality, passion is brought under control and one's character is marked by virtue.[12] The new feature in Philo is that human reason is aligned with divine reason, which explains why it is to be trusted and followed.

Since 2 Peter 1:4 shows essential differences from contemporary Hellenistic Judaism, it is worth looking at the inspiration behind these Jewish texts. All of these examples from Hellenistic Judaism build on understandings of God and the human person found in Greek philosophical thought—the earliest and clearest example of which is found in Plato's *Theaetetus*.[13] Here we find, if not 2 Peter's exact expression, the same constellation of ideas: the desire to escape from this corrupt world to God's world, which is a future hope, where the present is characterized by progressively conforming oneself to God's perfect righteousness (δικαιότατος)—a moral assimilation that is the means to the assimilation to incorruptibility.

This standard motif in Plato, of assimilation to God's goodness (now) and eternity (potentially), informs much of what first-century Hellenistic philosophers, such as Plutarch, were writing about at the end of the first century. In his biography of Aristides, Plutarch pauses to consider peoples' feelings toward divinity, and compares the ways people endeavor to become godlike to the only way people actually can become like God. The passage is worth quoting at length:

> [D]ivinity, to which such men are eager to adapt and conform themselves, is believed to have three elements of superiority—incorruption, power, and virtue; and the most reverend, the divinest of these, is virtue. . . . [3] Therefore, considering the three feelings which are generally entertained towards divinity—envy, fear, and honorable regard—men seem to envy and felicitate the deities for their *incorruption and perpetuity*; to dread and fear them for their *sovereignty and power*; but to love and honor and revere them for their *justice.* [4] And yet, although men are thus disposed, it is immortality, of which our nature is not capable, and power, the chief disposal of which is in the hands of fortune, that they eagerly desire; while as for *virtue, the only divine excellence within our reach,* they put it at the bottom of the list, unwisely too, since a life passed in power and great fortune and authority needs justice to make it divine; by injustice it is made bestial.[14]

According to Plutarch, the aim of life, as for Plato, is assimilation to God by bringing the contours of one's life into line with the contours of God's character. Divine nature has many attributes—eternity, incorruptibility, power, reason, virtue, justice, righteousness. Reason is the part of divinity that we have by nature, and in its perfection it is moral excellence, or virtue. Moreover, this is the only divine attribute within our reach, and since virtue is the greatest of all God's attributes, it should above all be a person's first aim to attain it, if a person aspires to become like God.

There is a great optimism in Plutarch about the possibility of becoming "settled in virtue" because of his Platonic conviction, shared by the Stoics, that the human soul has a portion of divine reason, and that human reason by nature has an inclination toward virtue. More than what is meant today by the concepts of "reason" and "mind," here humanity's rational faculty is a divine spark that gives us an innate kinship to divinity, and when it is listened to and followed it leads us into virtue. There is a faint hope in Plutarch of ultimately attaining to God's eternity, but aside from a few exceptional figures, like Socrates, the normal person can expect a series of reincarnations to allow him time to progress in virtue by becoming increasingly rational (and increasingly in control of passion).[15]

Two significant differences from 2 Peter should be noted. First, 2 Peter lacks any indication that human beings by nature have a kinship to God due to their rational faculty, as if the mind is naturally inclined toward the good. Rather, the cornerstone of 2 Peter's message is that the knowledge of Christ (as divine), which is received from the apostolic and prophetic word, works out a transformation in believers by giving them "all things necessary for piety and life." Thus, unlike Hellenistic philosophy, "participating in the divine nature" is the result of knowing Christ, not an innate quality of human nature. Second, while a person aspires in both 2 Peter and in the Hellenistic Stoics and Middle Platonists to assimilate the same divine attributes—virtue and incorruptibility—these attributes function differently. For Plutarch and philosophers like him, virtue is the *means* to achieving incorruption/immortality, and exercising the reason develops virtue. This means that any moral imperfection blocks further participation in divine nature.

Second Peter, by contrast, expects that the knowledge of Christ—if embraced and cherished—will prove "fruitful" and "effective" in the expression of love and faith and virtue. The emphasis is on holding fast and enduring so that the knower of Christ does not relapse into forgetfulness and error (1:9–10; 3:11–12, 14, 17). The expectation is not moral perfection but steady growth (3:18) in the knowledge of Christ (with the moral fruit that knowledge bears). In fact, 2 Peter tends to minimize the moral side of sharing in divine nature to such an extent that it has not generally been observed in the twentieth century (though nineteenth-century and earlier theologians were readily aware of it).[16] Second Peter's confident hope of entering Christ's kingdom is strong evidence that he does not view the attainment of eternity to be contingent on a prior moral perfection.

Second Peter is thus not simply restating Platonic thought or Stoicism. There are major shifts in 2 Peter's epistemology, in his eschatology, and in his ethics. It is not that he is using Hellenistic language and filling them with Christian content, as if that could ever be a recipe for successful communication. Rather, 2 Peter is changing the way some of the philosophical pieces fit together, which gives the whole matter a new frame of reference, namely, the knowledge of Christ rather than innate divine reason. Sharing in divine nature is not something 2 Peter's readers achieve but something they receive as a result of their knowledge of Christ.

Contrasting 2 Peter and Paul

How are we to understand 2 Peter's thought here? Before we conclude that he is creating something entirely new, there is another first-century voice worth considering, one that wrote on the same constellation of ideas, and that is the apostle Paul.[17] We do not have space here to develop a detailed contrast, but will briefly note the following:

- While Paul doesn't use the phrase "partakers of divine nature" (nor does any other writer in antiquity), Paul does write repeatedly that the aim of the Christian life is transformation into the image of God's Son, with the privilege of sharing some of his attributes.[18]

- Paul bolsters his congregations' hopes of sharing Christ's eternal life, which he generally depicts in terms of a bodily resurrection, but which he also speaks of in terms of "incorruptibility."[19]
- Paul assumes that the starting point for this transformation is the position of being "in Christ," or "faith in Christ," which he on occasion describes in noetic terms as "knowing God" or Christ.[20]
- This knowledge of Christ involves liberation from the power of sinful desire, the flesh, and the putting on of the love of Christ.[21]
- While this moral assimilation to Christ's character is a natural consequence of being "in Christ," Paul never suggests that moral perfection is prerequisite to incorruptibility or joining Christ's resurrection.

As is well known, however, there are significant differences between Paul and 2 Peter. With regard to sharing in divine nature, we may note that 2 Peter lacks two of Paul's typical ways of speaking of the Christian's participation in Christ: the hope of sharing Christ's glory and the possession of the Holy Spirit.[22] Although 2 Peter notes that glory is an attribute of both Christ and God (1:3–4, 16–17), and that prophecy in Scripture is inspired by the Holy Spirit (1:21), 2 Peter never suggests that the readers enjoy *doxa* or God's Spirit directly. A possible explanation for this is that 2 Peter wished to present Paul's teaching (see below) in terms that carried weight with his readers (that is, in popular philosophical jargon). But he did so in a way that would not allow them to confuse Christian participation in divine nature with Stoic or Middle Platonic notions either of matter's unimportance or of the person's assimilation into divine reason.

Second Peter and Paul work with the same constellation of ideas, and here we find that the components fit together in the same way, although 2 Peter highlights connections with Hellenistic philosophy by using some of their vocabulary, but not *all* of it—he significantly omits talk of reason and spirit in connection with the Christian hope.

What is 2 Peter's relationship to Paul? In 2 Peter 3:15–16 he concludes the letter by noting that Paul has written the same message, but that unstable and ignorant people distort Paul's words, to their own destruction. There has been a deliberate misinterpretation and misapplication of Paul's teachings, and 2 Peter is writing to correct these problems. How did they misinterpret Paul? Second Peter warns the readers against libertarians who entice young Christians with promises of freedom from moral expectations, but that this freedom is in fact a new slavery to desire and lust (in all its manifestations, described in 2 Pt 2). This is an error that surfaced in Paul's own congregations: Romans 3:8 "Why not say—as we are being slanderously reported as saying—'Let us do evil that good may result'?" Romans 6:1 "Shall we go on sinning so that grace may abound? By no means!" and 1 Corinthians 6:12 "'Everything is permissible for me'—but not everything is beneficial. 'Everything is permissible for me'—but I will not be mastered by anything."[23]

We have ample evidence that Paul's gospel of grace could be understood as license to follow one's passions, and 2 Peter warns repeatedly of the dangers of licentiousness. It cannot of course be proven, but it is historically plausible that 2 Peter formulated his theology in the way that he did because his congregation was in a social context where a rearticulation of Paul's teaching about the Christian hope, with an implicit appeal to Hellenistic wisdom through the use of some Hellenistic philosophical terms, made the strongest argument rhetorically. What can be stated with more confidence, though, is that the line of 2 Peter's thought follows the line of Paul's thought far more closely than any other ancient writer on sharing in divine nature.

Conclusion

What, then, are the answers to our questions? Does 2 Peter relapse into Hellenistic dualism? No. The author follows a Pauline and early Christian view of the world. Corruption is a consequence of sin, not something inherent to matter per se. A new earth (γῆν καινὴν) is coming (3:13), and creation will be renewed. Second Peter is not simply repeating first-century Hellenistic philosophy. Käsemann did not read 2 Peter 1:4 closely enough in its own literary context.

Does 2 Peter mean deification? The answer to that question is that it depends on what is meant by deification. If the term means equality with God or elevation to divine status or absorption into God's essence, the answer is no. If it means the participation in and enjoyment of specific divine attributes and qualities, in part now and fully at Christ's return, then the answer is—most certainly—yes.

Notes

1. Ernst Käsemann, "An Apologia for Primitive Christian Eschatology," in *Essays on New Testament Themes* (London: SCM, 1964), 179–80, originally published in *Zeitschrift für Theologie und Kirche* 49 (1952): 272–96. This viewpoint has at times been advanced by other scholars; see Hubert Merki, *Homoiōsis Theōi: Von der Platonischen Angleichung an Gott zur Gottähnlichkeit bei Gregor von Nyssa* (Freiburg, CH: Paulus, 1952), 112n2; Pier Cesare Bori, *Koinōnia: L'idea della communione nell'ecclesiologia recente e nel Nuovo Testamento* (Brescia: Paideaia, 1972), 87–88.

2. Käsemann, "An Apologia," 169, 195. Cf. his "The New Testament Canon and the Unity of the Church," in *Essays on New Testament Themes,* 95–107.

3. This essay sketches, with several additions, certain conclusions of my previous *Sharers in Divine Nature: 2 Peter 1:4 in Its Hellenistic Context* (Stockholm: Almqvist & Wiksell, 2000).

4. The pronoun "his" refers to "Jesus our Lord," in 1:2, but 2 Peter is notoriously unconcerned with distinguishing between Christ and God. Christ is called God in 1:1, and "Lord"

refers first to Christ (1:8, 11, 14, 16), then to the God of the Old Testament (2:9, 11), and then to Christ again (2:20; 3:2, 8, 9, 10, 15, 18).

5. I will speak of divine "attributes" or "characteristics" for inherent qualities possessed by God or Christ, although divine "energies" is a valid alternate term supported by a long tradition in Orthodox theology. The disadvantage of the term "energy" from an exegetical standpoint is that it echoes the Pauline term ἐνέργεια, which refers to God's salvific power at work in the Christian (Eph 1:19, 3:7, 4:16; Phil 3:21; Col 1:29, 2:12) and never describes God *a se.* In either case the choice of terminology is heuristic, since 2 Peter does not speak objectively about God or Christ.

6. Note that virtue (αρετή) is used to describe both the divine (1:3) and 2 Peter's readers (1:5).

7. Jerome H. Neyrey, *2 Peter, Jude* (New York: Doubleday, 1993), 150–62, following the cue of Frederick W. Danker, "2 Peter 1: A Solemn Decree," *Catholic Biblical Quarterly* 40 (1978): 453–67. For a critique of this reading, see Starr, *Sharers in Divine Nature,* 37–38.

8. See Richard J. Bauckham, *Jude, 2 Peter* (Waco: Word, 1983), 169–70, building on the discussion of Rudolf Bultmann, "γινώσκω κτλ.," *TDNT* 1:707.

9. Γένησθε is a subjunctive aorist participle, and ἀποφυγόντες is an inductive aorist participle.

10. Second Peter is silent on whether incorruption is limited to the soul or includes the body, although the idiom in 1:14, "putting off of my tent (σκήνωμα)," may be interpreted as reflecting the Maccabean view. The hope of a recreated material world in 3:13, however, suggests that the metaphor in 1:14 should not be read woodenly.

11. *Quaestiones in Exodum* 2.39 on Ex 24:11b.

12. *De specialibus legibus* 4:14; *De virtute* 9.

13. The relevant passage is this: [176A] "Socrates: But it is impossible that evils should be done away with, Theodorus, for there must always be something opposed to the good; and they cannot have their place among the gods, but must inevitably hover about mortal nature and this earth. Therefore we ought to try to escape from earth to the dwelling of the gods as quickly as we can; [176B] and *to escape is to become like God,* so far as this is possible, and *to become like God is to become righteous and holy and wise. . . .* [176C] Let us give the true reason. God is in no wise and in no manner unrighteous, but utterly and perfectly righteous, and *there is nothing so like him as that one of us who in turn becomes most nearly perfect in righteousness.* It is herein that the true cleverness of a man is found and also his worthlessness and cowardice; for the knowledge of this is wisdom or true virtue" (emphases mine). *Theaetetus; Sophist,* trans. Harold N. Fowler, *Plato in Twelve Volumes,* vol. 7, LCL 123 (Cambridge, MA: Harvard University Press; London: Heinemann, 1921).

14. *Aristides* 6.2–4 (emphases mine), *Themistocles and Camillus, Aristides and Cato Major, Cimon and Lucullus,* trans. Bernadotte Perrin, *Plutarch's Lives in Eleven Volumes,* vol. 2, LCL 47 (Cambridge, MA: Harvard University Press; London: Heinemann, 1914). A passage from Plutarch's *De sera numinis vindicta* argues for the same viewpoint, here making explicit Plutarch's debt to Plato: "Consider first that god, as Plato says [*Theaetetus* 176], offers himself to all as a pattern of every excellence, thus rendering human virtue, which is in some sort *an assimilation to himself,* accessible to all who can 'follow God.' Indeed this was the origin of the change whereby universal nature, disordered before, became a 'cosmos': it came to resemble after a fashion and *participate in the form and excellence of God.* The same philosopher says further that nature kindled vision in us so that the soul, beholding the heavenly motions and wondering at the sight, should grow to accept and cherish all that moves in stateliness and order, and thus come to hate discordant and errant passions and to shun the aimless and haphazard as source of all vice and jarring error; for man is fitted to derive from God no greater blessing than to become *settled in virtue through copying and aspiring to the beauty and goodness that are his.*" *De sera* 550DE (emphases mine), trans. Phillip H. De Lacy and

Benedict Einarson, *Plutarch's Moralia in Sixteen Volumes,* vol. 7, *523c-612b,* LCL 405 (Cambridge, MA: Harvard University Press; London: Heinemann, 1959). For further discussion of these passages and Plutarch's thought in relation to 2 Peter, see Starr, *Sharers in Divine Nature,* 119–43.

15. Similar comments could be made of Stoicism, with examples from Epictetus (see *Dissertationes* 1.9; 2), Musonius Rufus (see Fragments 3, 16, 17, 18), Cicero (see the Dream of Scipio in *De Republica* 6; *De finibus* 3.75; *Nature of the Gods* 2), and Seneca (see *Epistulae Morales* 73 and 76). See the discussion in Starr, *Sharers in Divine Nature,* 144–66.

16. See, for example, Hugo Grotius, *Annotationes in Novum Testamentum* (Groningen, 1830), 8:115.

17. The following is a summary statement of my findings in *Sharers in Divine Nature,* 167–216.

18. Rom 8:29–30; Phil 3:20–21; 1 Thess 2:12.

19. See 1 Cor 15 and Rom 8.

20. For example, Rom 1:19–28; 1 Cor 13:12–13; 2 Cor 1:13–14, 13:5; Phil 1:9.

21. See Rom 8:5–10, 12:2; 2 Cor 3:18, 4:6; Phil 1:9–10, 2:5, 3:10, 4:7; Phlm 6.

22. Rom 3:23, 8:29–30, 9:23–24; 1 Thess 2:12; 2 Thess 2:14 (so also Eph 1:18) speak of the Christ-believers share in Christ's resurrected, eternal life. Cf. Heinrich Schlier, "Doxa bei Paulus als heilsgeschichtlicher Begriff," *Studiorum Paulinorum Congressus Internationalis Catholicus 1961* (Rome: Pontifical Biblical Institute, 1963), 1:50–55.

23. For a survey of other views of how the false teachers in 2 Peter misinterpreted Paul, see Bauckham, *Jude, 2 Peter,* 332.

III
Theosis in Patristic Thought

The Strategic Adaptation of Deification in the Cappadocians

J. A. McGuckin

IN THE GREEK CHRISTIAN UNDERSTANDING, THE CONCEPT OF DEIFICATION is the process of the sanctification of Christians whereby they become progressively conformed to God; a conformation that is ultimately demonstrated in the glorious transfiguration of the "just" in the heavenly kingdom, when immortality and a more perfect vision (and knowledge and experience) of God are clearly manifested in the glorification (δόξα) of the faithful.[1] This should serve as a working definition and as a brief initial introduction to a notion that moves with a tensile dynamic from the moral domain into the anthropological in a profoundly suggestive way that closely relates it to the parallel Christian notion of transfiguration (*metamorphosis*).[2] In the hands of several of the later Greek theologians the two ideas are explicitly related. In the work of Origen and the Cappadocians, especially Gregory of Nyssa, we see the insightful reminder that to differentiate the moral from the anthropological is a mistake; or to put it in other words, to imagine that the life of virtue is something other than our graced existential energy, is an "unredeemed" notion unfitting for a Christian.

Deification (Greek: *theosis, theopoiesis*) was a bold use of language, deliberately evocative of the pagan acclamations of *apotheosis* (humans, especially heroes, great sages, and latterly emperors, being advanced to the rank of deity) although that precise term was always strictly avoided by Christian writers because of its fundamentally pagan conceptions of creatures transgressing on divine prerogative: a blasphemous notion that several of the ancient Hellenes themselves, not least Arrian, found worthy of denunciation. Deification in classical Greek Christian thought is always careful to speak of the ascent of the creature to communion with the divine by virtue of the prior divine election and divine summoning of the creature for fullness of life. In other words, in all Christian conceptions of the notion, the divine initiation and priority is always at the basis of the creaturely ascent (at once both a moral and ontological ascent) and that progress is part and parcel of the very understanding of what salvation is. Deification theory is, therefore, a basic element of Greek patristic theology's articulation of the process of salvific revelation: put more simply, how the epiphany of a gracious

God is experienced within the world (more precisely within the church) as a call to more abundantly energized life. It is in this juxtaposition of the ideas of life and revelation (the revelation of life that is) that Christian deification theory assumes its true grandeur, for it breaks down, at least in the best of Greek patristic thought, the limiting "differentiation" between soteriology and creation theology. In speaking of fullness of communion as the "true life" of the creature, deification language shows that the restoration of communion (salvation as redemption) is at root one and the same movement and motive of the God who seeks to disburse the gift of the fullness of life to his rational creatures: the gift of life and the experience of divine communion being synonyms for the enlightened saint who finally sees the purposes of creation (and the motives of redemption) as they really are.

A Brief Prehistory

Let me sketch, with very broad strokes, the prehistory of this key term as it came into the purview of the Cappadocians.[3] We could, of course, trace the origins of the concept of *theosis* to the New Testament itself, as it reflects on the Psalms and on other biblical passages (particularly texts such as Jn 10:34–36). Often commentators have singled out the passage in 2 Peter 1:4 which speaks of believers becoming "participants in the divine nature," and one might particularly note the rootedness of the idea in the Johannine notions of the *anabasis* and *katabasis* of the revelatory Word. But that is not our charge here,[4] and it remains evident enough that the term *theosis* itself is not explicitly advanced by scriptural authority—something that makes Gregory Nazianzen apologize for his "boldness" in using it to sum up the message and meaning of the Scriptures.

Irenaeus was the theologian who developed the notion imaginatively, and with freshness of insight, from the scriptural bases. In a few places, but with resonant language, Irenaeus sketched out many of the chief lineaments that would comprise the nexus of *theosis* theory: its dynamic as a soteriological term, its rootedness in the concept of creation's purposes, its close relation to the ideas of corruption and immortality; its essential closeness to the concept of transactive substitution in the doctrine of the Incarnation of the Logos. All these primary elements are already noticeably assembled in Irenaeus, but in lapidary phrases that will require centuries of exegesis. No prizes for knowing the following: "God made himself man, that man might become God."[5] But other *sententiae* might not be so well known: "When a man sees God," Irenaeus says, "the vision confers incorruptibility, because it glorifies the creature with the divine glory."[6] And again: "The Word of God was made man and he who was Son of God was made Son of Man united to the Word of God, in order that man should receive adoption and thereby become the Son of God. How else could we have received incorruption?"[7]

It was, nevertheless, the Alexandrian theologians, Clement,[8] Origen,[9] and Athanasius,[10] who really elevated the soteriological theory of *theosis* to new heights, each of them nailing it within the doctrine of the Incarnation of the Divine Word, wherein the eternal Logos assumed flesh so that all humankind could be lifted up into the mystery of his personal divinity.[11] The heavy Christological accent to this schema ensured that deification would be commonly understood, after the mid-fourth century, as predominantly a "hypostatic" term of reference: to do with communion of hypostases, and the results of such. In relation to Christ that means how the presence of the divine hypostasis in the flesh deified the very body of the Lord so that it became, in Cyril's powerful language, "Life-Giving flesh."[12] In the case of the church it means how the communion of created and uncreated hypostases in the new life of the transcendent kingdom refashioned the very boundaries of creaturely existences by extending their capacities beyond earlier limitations. Salvation, therefore, was more than the forgiveness of sins, rather a profound reworking and *anakephalaiosis* of the terms of ordinary humanity, into a divinely graced life-form that would experience an ascentive metamorphosis. It is not surprising that many commentators from the mid-twentieth century onward have been enthralled by this scheme of *theosis* as a key to the so-called "mystical theology" of the Eastern Church. Even so, it is wise to remember that such a categorization of "mystical" is an odd one, and in describing it instead as the heart of Greek Christian salvation and creation theology, we are surely closer to the syntax of the fathers themselves.

I will return shortly to the contribution of the Cappadocians, so will pass over them here. Suffice it to say that they are probably best understood as the theologians who successfully transformed this largely Alexandrian theologoumenon into a universalized tradition of the church. In spite of the fact that the Syrians at large sternly refused to employ the notion (preferring instead terms of adoptive sonship),[13] the Cappadocians were collectively taken by the idea; led there in no small part by Gregory of Nazianzus's enthusiastic reading of Origen, and his equal determination to take Athanasian theology as a standard on which to build the neo-Nicene settlement in the late fourth century.

By the time of Dionysius the Areopagite in the early sixth century, deification was a relatively frequent soteriological term.[14] No longer was it felt necessary to apologize for the surprise effect of the words, an attitude that we still find in Gregory of Nazianzus. After Dionysius the idea became almost a commonplace in most Eastern writers, used to connote the transformative effects of salvation. Maximus the Confessor brought the concept of *theosis* to a peak of development in the early seventh century.[15] He had learned much from the Christological controversies of his own day, and in reference to *theosis* theory, he employed the language of *hypostasis,* as it had been immensely refined in the post-Chalcedonian debates. This he did in order to clarify what he saw to be the essential points of the earlier debates on deification; first, that the term described the spiritual nature of the redeemed creature who, by a mysterious process of the communication of the divine life is called back to the original destiny of creation; second, that this is a beneficent and totally free gift on the part of God; and third, that the gift proceeds from God alone who commands, initiates, and determines this wondrously generous economy.[16] Last, but not least, this powerful theologian amplified the ascetical context of the doctrine (something that became constitutive of it from his time onward), by noting that the exercise of love on earth allows the eschatological mystery of divinization to shine out even in the present moment.[17] Maximus was able to make this lasting synthesis from his close reading of Gregory of Nazianzus, whose works he annotated in his *Ambigua.*

To end the series, as it were, we should mention John of Damascus, who once more consolidated the theory of deification by expounding it in his summative systematics, underlining the achievements of Maximus, but particularly reading them once again through the resolving lens of the theology of Gregory of Nazianzus, whom the Damascene, at those instances in his *De Fide Orthodoxa* where he expounds the idea,[18] has clearly studied and has himself annotated closely. Gregory's *Oration* 11.11–13 is John's primary authority, and his way even into an understanding of Maximus's synthesis. This fertile theme, therefore, beginning with Irenaeus, loops its way forward rather than being linearly or progressively developed. Where in that overarching scheme should we locate the Cappadocian contribution exactly? It will be my thesis that it belongs precisely to an explicit rereading of Origen. Designed as a learned commentary on Plato, it was partly meant to show to learned Christians a refined synopsis of their faith; and partly meant to offer learned Hellenists, of that class of wealthy rhetoricians to which the Cappadocians themselves belonged, that in the newly ascendant church of the fourth century, they could find a worthy home for the deepest religious aspirations they had nurtured through the late Platonic tradition. In the aftermath of the recent collapse of Julian's revolt against the ascendancy of Christianity, that outreach to the rhetoricians was a strategic choice, a deliberate missionary strategy on the part of two theologians, the older mentor Gregory the Theologian and his rhetorical disciple the younger Gregory, who were themselves much involved in the anti-Julian intellectual propaganda. The project of rhetorics as missionary strategy is also the reason why it is the two Gregories who sustain that dialogue, more so than Basil, whose horizons are more set within the Christian camp itself, and who does not have much to offer on the explicit theme of *theosis,* though what he does say is most memorable, as we shall see.[19]

To elucidate the meaning of the two friends we ought to understand their common enthusiasms and avowed agendas: that both wished to re-present Plato as a "door into Christianity,"[20] through the medium of the genius of Origen. Not only did Plato have to be nuanced, however, but by the late fourth century so did Origen, whose very name caused a frisson in a church much traumatized by the Arian crisis. The Cappadocians were not willing to let his insights be lost, however, and if the *Philokalia Origenis* can rightly be seen as Gregory Nazianzen's joint project with Basil to rehabilitate the great Alexandrian (though it was really Gregory foisting the idea of such a book on Basil), then the respective doctrines of the two on *theosis* ought perhaps to be seen as another common effort to work again over the same ground. The two have not often been placed together, side by side, in respect of this teaching, but there are grounds to do so. We should not forget how Gregory of Nazianzus was an important mentor for Basil's younger brother, nor how the two of them claimed responsibility for mentoring Evagrius, who also is joined in with this same work though he takes it across more dramatic tangents. It is clear when we put the two Gregories in tandem how much more insistent is Gregory of Nazianzus on the bold language of deification, while Gregory of Nyssa is more intent on the wider implications of assimilation theory. Both, however, emerge in their respective teachings as entirely absorbed by the same overall task: the rereading of Origen on how to Christianize Plato, as part and parcel of the evangelization of the educated classes of their day.

New School Platonism

Let us begin, then, by considering Plato's views, which are the raw material of the Greek theologians, and which continued well into the late fourth century to be the common reading of Christian and Hellenist religious theorists. Plato's description in the *Phaedrus* of the initiate's ascent to Beauty was much admired in the period. One of the most notable rewritings of it was the rhapsodic "Ode on the Ascent to Beauty" that features in Plotinus's Sixth Tractate of the First Ennead.[21] The academician himself describes the ascent of the pure mind to a transcendent condition of communion with ideal Beauty, saying:

> How resplendent was Beauty to behold in such a time as some have had that beatific vision, when united to the choir of the blessed . . . when they were initiated in that initiation in which one can rightly say that one attains the supreme beatitude; the mystery that we celebrate in the integrity of our true nature, and exempt from all those limitations which attend on us in the later extension of time, in integrity, simplicity, immobility, and in that happiness deriving from the perception of those

> apparitions which the initiation has at last unveiled to us in the form of a pure and radiant light.[22]

Here the phrase "integrity of the true nature" signifies for Plato the ideal condition of preexistent noetic being. The theme of initiation signifies also that the philosopher has the opportunity to return, by spiritual ascent, to the clarity and radiance of the authentic state of being, which was the *stasis,* the foundational condition, of the transcendent mind, and to this extent the real and godlike nature of noetic being. This episode becomes a core passage that Gregory of Nazianzus directly alludes to and, in a sense, gives a commentary on when speaking about his own doctrine of *theosis.* For Plato the Soul was given the condition of immortality in its origin when it was able to contemplate the ideal forms. That idea ran on influentially into Origen, who continues to see *theosis* in the manner of the Soul's return to its unfallen condition. Gregory Nazianzen is determined to adapt this, changing the emphasis to a return to the transcendent condition when God purifies the soul of the believer, so that it can attain a more clarified insight into divine beauty. This is the initiation of the Christian philosopher,[23] the ascetic life (not monastic exactly but certainly including the circle of refined intellects Gregory knew would recognize his quoted sources) that Gregory is inviting his readership to belong to: to make a step toward the church, as it were. But he will also teach that there is another purification awaiting the faithful soul,[24] to give it a more capacious insight than is possible in the time of its enfleshment. Throughout his work Gregory implies that the postdeath transfiguration of the human soul will involve, for the best and greatest of the initiates, a transfiguration of ontological order, moving up and out of humanity as such, into a *stasis* more directly comparable to angelic being. The third creation (humans) is in some cases, he will argue, admitted to become the first creation (angelicals) who more surely contemplate the mysteries of God. The path to such transcendence is begun on earth by the philosophical life. The outlines of that theory, based upon the Platonic principle that "only like can know like" are set out in clear form in Gregory's first two *Theological Orations.*[25]

Basil equally stressed that idea of "like assimilated to like" in his famous account of the soul's deification by the grace of the Holy Spirit as being comparable to an eye flooded with radiant light.[26] That passage in Basil, culminating as it does with the claim that even beyond "resemblance to God" lies the "supremely desired goal of becoming god," owes much to the *Timaeus* and the *Theatetus,* with many passing allusions to Plotinus.[27] But this remarkable passage is really the most overt use he will make of the term *theosis* itself. The two Gregories are much freer than him in that regard.

Plato reprised his idea of the purified ascent of the soul in his *Timaeus,* which again was closely studied by the two Gregories, and formed a common text for their wider circle, both in and outside the church. He describes it in these terms:

> When a man has cultivated in himself the love of knowledge and true thinking; when with all his faculties he has exercised principally the capacity to think on things immortal and divine, then such a man, if he comes to touch upon the truth, will find it absolutely necessary to enjoy that truth entirely, at least in so far as human nature is capable of participating in immortality. For incessantly he shall give worship to the divinity in so far as he constantly engages with the god who is within him . . . whosoever contemplates, renders himself like the object which he contemplates, in conformity with its original nature; and being thus rendered similar to it such a man attains, both for present and future, the perfect fulfillment of life which the gods have proposed to humans.[28]

Contemplation (θεωρία) is the engine that drives the process of *theosis*. Origen is clearly at one with him in this when he says in his turn: "The nous which is purified is lifted above all material realities so as to have a clear Vision of God, and it is deified by its vision (ἐν οἷς θεωρεῖ θεοποιεῖται)."[29] Origen feels it is necessary to say that even the Logos is deified by his incessant contemplation of the Father's divinity,[30] and it was sentiments like that which required the two Gregories to rehabilitate the very idea of "degrees of participation" for a later Christian generation that was deeply scarred by the Arian crisis. Gregory of Nyssa, in particular, will take the concept of contemplative penetration into the deifying mystery of the Godhead to new depths in his remarkable notion of *epektasis*. Let us consider the two Gregories, briefly, in turn.

Gregory of Nazianzus

In a poem entitled *De Incarnatione,* Gregory is not averse to repeating Athanasius's maxim that "God became man so that man might become god,"[31] but he cannot resist cleaning up the syntax and meter, just as he cannot resist pointing out how Athanasius *ought* to have solved the problem of the attributed soul of Christ, but did not. In the end, and typically so, Gregory makes an even better syllogism by classicizing it:

> Ἐπεὶ γὰρ οὖν ἐγίγνετ' ἄνθρωπος Θεὸς,
> Θεὸς τελεῖτ' ἄνθρωπος εἰς τιμὴν ἐμήν.[32]
>
> [And since, then, God is made man,
> so man is perfected as God, and that is my glory.]

Throughout his *Orations* and poetry Gregory is very enthusiastic about the language describing the soul's "kinship" or "affinity" with the divine nature.

He regularly describes the soul as a "breath of God"[32] or a "spirit emanating from the invisible deity," or an "offshoot of the divine."[33] Adam was deified, he says, by his inborn propensity toward God and it is that natural kinship that is at the root of our return to God and the deified life;[34] but understood as a gift of God the creator, not the reassertion of any divine element innate within creaturely nature. To live the life of the true philosopher is, par excellence, the life lived in God. Already on this earth it is a deification, but for Gregory this transformation begun is only a harbinger of a greater glory to come when we are transfigured after this life.[35]

Sometimes he apologizes for the language,[36] knowing that it is pressing the envelope, but clearly delights in doing so. This is no careless theologian who blurs the distinction between creature and the Uncreated. His *Five Theological Orations* are masterpieces in drawing those distinctions, but it is with a poet's eye for paradoxical expression of mysteries that his poetry seeks to match the rapture of Plato's own poetic conception of the initiate's communion with the Godhead, and thus Gregory powerfully presses home on the implications of the Holy Spirit's deifying work in the soul.[37] This theme he learned from Athanasius but took to its logical end in his clarified doctrine of the *homoousion* of the Spirit and the coequal divine Trinity, itself the archetype of all transcendence of duality and matter, which is the goal of the enlightened and restored *nous.*

It is in *Oration* 21, however, that Gregory gives his most dramatic account of *theosis.*[38] Here he speaks of the possible ascent of a soul to God, even in the present life, which can be taken as a type of the soul's ascent to deification. Referring to Plato he designates this process as "assimilation to the divine." The idea, nakedly expressed in that way, was perhaps troubling to Gregory of Nyssa, who probably heard this oration read out in the great Symposium the Nazianzen arranged for his friends who attended the Council of Constantinople in 381, on which occasion Gregory of Nyssa himself read selections from his *Contra Eunomium.* In a telling phrase in his *Catechetical Oration* Gregory of Nyssa alludes to the concept of assimilation with a note to the effect that when humans attain to immortality they do not find that which Socrates spoke of in Plato's *Phaedrus,* rather that which God has given them as a gratuitous gift, which was far above the limits of material natures.[39] Gregory Nazianzen's reference to deification in this passage also troubled Maximus the Confessor in the seventh century, so much so that he devoted one of the longest sections of his *Ambigua* to explicating what he thought Gregory "must" have meant.[40]

Gregory's *Oration* begins with a loud and deliberate reference to Plato's *Republic:* "God," he says, "is to intelligible things what the sun is to sensory things. The one lightens the visible, the other the invisible, world."[41] Through the philosopher, Gregory sets the terms of reference of what he means by divine assimilation—*theosis.* In his preface to the *Oration* he elevates Athanasius as a prime example of illuminated saint, and singles out, from all the graces that form a plethora of blessings in this world, "the highest and kindliest of all blessings, which is our inclination and relationship to God." "Enlightenment," Gregory says, "is akin to God himself, who gives virtue to humans and thereby exalts them to himself."[42]

The noetic power of the human soul is compared by Gregory to a light that is ascentive and naturally restless in its quest for the God it relentlessly desires, because its desire can have no limit. It is thus a form of authentic experience of the illimitable by the limited creature, and a participation in God's infinity.[43] Gregory's *Oration* continues as follows:

> Just as the sun (which bestows on things which see and are seen, the very power of seeing and being seen), is itself the most beautiful of all visible things: just so is God (who creates for those who think and are thought of, the very power of thinking and being thought about) himself the highest of all objects of thought, in whom every desire finds its limit, beyond which it cannot pass. For not even the most philosophical, the most acute, and curious intellect has, or ever can have, a more exalted object, since God is the apex of all that can be desired, and those who arrive here find total rest from theoria.[44]

This "rest" (ἀνάπαυσις) is that beatific cessation of the eighth age, which on numerous occasions elsewhere he compares to the soul's advent to the true temple of God; an entering of the heavenly sanctuary where finally one can see, with unveiled eyes, the holy of holies where God dwells. Such an image, clothed in Gregory's habitual liturgical idioms, is meant to imply his overarching (yet here lightly handled) supposition that the posthumous condition of the ascended *nous* is not simply the same ontological *stasis* of personhood in a disembodied state, but rather that the saint in the next age undergoes a transfiguration into angelical form, entrance into a new ontological *stasis* that permits a greater capacity for spiritual vision, and a priestly access to the inner sanctum of the divine that is not possible to earthbound intellects.

Again using deliberate text-markers from Plato's *Timaeus, Phaedrus,* and *Symposium,*[45] in the second paragraph of the same twenty-first *Oration,* Gregory sets out his concept of the noetic ascent that deifies, saying:

> Whoever has been permitted to escape from matter, and from the fleshly cloud (or should we call it a veil?) by means of reason and contemplation, so as to hold communion with God, and be associated with the purest light (in so far as human nature can attain to it): such a man is truly blessed: both in terms of his ascent from here, and in terms of his deification there, a deification which is conferred by true philosophy, and by virtue of his rising above all the duality of matter through that unity which is perceived in the Trinity.[46]

No one reading this can fail to be impressed by the fine synthesis it makes between the Platonic themes of ascent, communion, and contemplation, on the one hand, and on the other the biblical paradigms of the generous love of the Trinity, and the access of the divine presence through the image of liturgical service in the transcendent holy of holies. The concept of the deified person being the "priest" of the cosmos is a theme that Gregory of Nyssa will further develop, and it is to his work that we now finally turn.[47]

Gregory of Nyssa

The idea of deification is as much in the fabric of Gregory Nyssen's thought as it was in the teaching of his older mentor, Gregory of Nazianzus. Although his employment of the actual word *theosis* is very limited, a praxis in which he imitates his brother Basil, this shows that he feels more constrained than the "boldness" of the Nazianzen. In the theology of Gregory of Nyssa, there is more of an explicit concern to mark the great difference and distance (διάστημα) between the creature and the divine archetype,[48] and in this he is more faithful to Origen than Gregory of Nazianzus sometimes "appeared" to be. That vast difference between the two,[49] and the dynamic spiritual energies that connect them, is a keynote of his thought and this is probably why Gregory Nyssen uses the exact term "deification" only once, and in his *Catechetical Oration,* to suggest it is an image with which we can begin but not end. Once more in this insight he is being very faithful to Origen's teachings on the multitude of levels comprising the soul's entrance into the fathomless abyss of God. When he does use the word *theosis,* it is simply to reiterate the basic teaching we find in Athanasius's *De Incarnatione* 54, that the Incarnation of the Logos is the deification of the human race.[50] Elsewhere he replaces *theosis* with the concept of μετουσία θεοῦ—participation in God.

Yet even if it was intended as an introductory primer, the text in the *Catechetical Oration* where he introduces this idea is one of remarkable profundity.[51] It was clearly a book being offered to Christian initiates who were not of the common order. Borrowing the image of the radiant eye from his brother Basil, and also from Plato's *Timaeus,*[52] which he thereby signals to his attentive readers as a significant parallel, he describes how humanity was created to find communion with God:

> Since he was created to take part (μέτοχος) in divine blessings, man must have a natural affinity (κατασκευάζεται) with that object in which he has participation (μετουσία). It is just like an eye which, thanks to the luminous rays which nature provides it, is enabled to have communion (κοινωνία) in the light. . . . It is just so with man, who since he was created to enjoy the divine blessings must have some affinity with that in which he has been called to participate. And so he has been endowed with life, reason, wisdom, and all those truly divine advantages so that each one of them should cause that innate desire of his to be demonstrated within him. Since immortality is one of those benefits that are appropriate to deity,

> it follows that our nature cannot be deprived even of this in its constitution, but must possess within itself the disposition to immortality in order that (thanks to this innate capacity) it might be able to recognise that which is transcendent far beyond it (ὑπερκείμενον) and might thus experience the desire for divine eternity.[53]

The doctrine of spiritual kinship (συγγένεια) is once again taken far beyond Plato's idea of ontological assonance by the telling context of the divine invitation and the creator's grace that supplies the means to the creature to rise up to its challenging vocation to transcendent life.

In a parallel passage in the *Discourse on Children* Gregory returns to the concept of affinity at the heart of participation, and to Platonic *Mimesis* doctrine, but he welds them both to the biblical doctrine of the Image—a consummately clever way of retaining Platonic resonances while simultaneously transcending them. This he has learned from Origen: "'To allow participation in God,' he says, 'there must, of necessity, be something in the nature of the participant which is akin to that in which it participates. This is why Scripture says that man was born in the image of God. It was surely that he could see as like does to like. For the vision of God is unquestionably the life of the soul.'"[54] But the largest departure of the two Gregories from Origen is that they both reject the presupposition that sin happened before embodiment, and thus that the fall of the body to mortality is a punishment of guilt. Both Gregories understand the constitution of the human condition (what the Nazianzen calls the peculiar μίχις of the "Third Order") as a creation of grace.[55] It is Gregory Nyssen's guiding light to insist that it is within this grace of the fundament of humanity's being, not despite it, or outside it, or after its annihilation, that the divine gift of communion takes place. This is not to say, of course, that Gregory imagines our true nature is exactly that which we now represent within the cosmos. This is why resurrection plays so central a role in his thought about the restoration of the human race to its original design. He understands humanity's reconstitution and renewal (ἀνακεφαλαίωσις) as a gift of the resurrection of Christ, beginning in a person's moral life, and consummated in our bodily resurrection from the dead, but also having much deeper implications as a symbol of the wholesale return of the alienated created order to unity with God. This radical consummation of the kingdom is referred to by Gregory, using many of the ideas of Origen, as "the reconstitution" (ἀποκατάστασις).

Gregory's notion of *apokatastasis* is evidently related in fundamental ways to the generic idea of deification. He is so concerned that the growing Christian reaction against the Origenian ideas of *apokatastasis* (which were deeply rooted in ideas of precosmic fall) might threaten the continuance of this whole scheme of cosmic soteriology, that he takes decisive action to distance himself from Origen at this point. It is the only instance where Gregory explicitly attacks his great Alexandrian mentor by name.[56] He still keeps the word *apokatastasis,* of course, thus signifying to all and sundry that he is a believer in Origen's great scheme even while he makes the necessary corrections to the master.[57]

While Origen taught that the physical body and the spiritual body of the just saints after death were two different *somata,* Gregory insisted that they were two different states of the same body.[58] And yet, in the *apokatastasis,* or total restoration of all the creation, Gregory, like Origen before him, envisages the whole assembly of the saints restored to full and total communion with each other and with the divinity through endless contemplation of the blessed and absolute glory of God. His self-distancing from Origen was not so radical as some would have liked, of course, and in the *De Anima* he taught that even the wicked would be restored to the choir of saints in the end, so that God's glory will be entirely triumphant in fulfilling the purposes of creation.[59]

Another of Gregory of Nyssa's quiet, though extensive, corrections of Origenian ideas is his replacement of the latter's concept of perfection as a conditional *stasis* with his own dynamic notion of perfection as an endless progress (προκόπη) into the divine life.[60] This theology of the endless progress of a limited creature into the boundless infinity of God, and the resultant dynamic tension of the creaturely "stretching out" (ἐπέκτασις) in the authentic but paradoxical experience of the limited directly knowing the illimitable, is something that has been extensively studied in recent decades and has accounted for a large revival in the popularity of Gregory.[61] The key notion here is the thoroughgoing replacement of the Platonic term of assimilation, by Gregory's Christianized keyword "participation" (μετουσία θεοῦ).[62]

The Life of Moses is, in fact, an extended revision of Origen's ideas on this theme, and can be considered as a major source for Gregory's doctrine of deification couched in other terms. Here he describes the dynamic of participation in God:

> The prime and chief good whose nature is goodness itself, is God himself. And whatever one may think about the deity, nevertheless it both exists and can be named. Since, therefore, no limit (ὅρος) of virtue can ever be demonstrated, except evil (though the divine is, of course, unreceptive of its opposite), just so the divine nature must be understood to be limitless (ἀορίστης) and boundless (ἀπεράτωτος). Even so, the man who pursues true virtue participates in nothing other than God, because God is perfect virtue. That which is good by nature is altogether desirable to those who recognise it and want to participate in it, and since it has no set limit, then the desire of the one participating, as it stretches out alongside the limitless, finds that it too has no necessary stopping point (στάσις).[63]

While many of the earlier Greek Fathers had spoken of participating in God himself through the grace of the Divine Spirit, and though Gregory of Nazianzus had set this on a new foundation by his insistence on the *homoou-*

sion of the Divine Spirit,[64] it was Gregory of Nyssa who developed this insight more speculatively by identifying goodness as one of the essential perfections of God. It followed then, that participation in sanctity was, in fact, participation in true being. At a stroke, the distinction between morality and ontology in the case of a divinely graced creature became a false one. It was an illumined insight the Christian ascetic tradition did not fail to take to heart, as well as one that modern theology is in great need of rediscovering.

The concept of participation is also elaborated in the *Treatise on the Making of Man.* Gregory designed this work to complete Basil's *Hexaemeron* after the sudden death of his brother. It thus takes its whole impetus from the words of Genesis 2: "Let us make man in our own image and likeness." Here Gregory's chief argument is one that simplifies Origen's two-fold doctrine of the εἰκὼν θεοῦ,[65] arguing instead that the divine image in humanity means essentially that human beings possess within themselves all the divine perfections as part of that constitutive nature that God appointed for the race. But whereas these perfections are found in God ontologically, or essentially (ὄντως), and as something that is proper to him (ἴδιον), humans possess the same things, or at least their copies (as types from the archetype), as a gift by participation.[66] Gregory pushes the ontological implications of this endowed charism, nonetheless, by insisting that it would not be proper to say that God "gave" such gifts to humankind but rather that he imparted them (μετέδοκε) to his own Image, saying that: "He added to the image the proper ornament of his very own nature."[67] For Gregory the participation of humanity in the being of God is nothing short of the entire purpose and point of the creation of mankind,[68] and thus the whole purpose of our individual ontology. In fulfilling that destiny of μετουσία θεοῦ, humanity in general and individual persons are called to become priests of the cosmos, rendering by their dynamic engagement with the world's order, a degree of divine life, a sacred blessing as it were, to all the fabric of God's created existence.

For Gregory, this dynamism of the μετουσία θεοῦ changes a person progressively even in this lifetime, but especially so in the life of the kingdom. In this life, the μετουσία progressively increases the capacity of humans for the infinite, thereby deepening their desire for it:

> It was for this reason that rational nature was brought into existence, namely that the riches of the divine benefits should not lie by idly. The all-creating Wisdom fashioned souls as vessels, so to say, endowed with freedom, for this purpose alone that there should be some receptacle for the reception of those benefits, a vessel which always becomes larger according to the increase of what is poured into it. For such is the *metousia* of the divine, that God makes the person who shares in it ever larger and more capable of receiving.[69]

Is Gregory's doctrine of μετουσία the same as the concept of deification, under a more moral and philosophic term of reference? I believe it is. In the

Contra Eunomium, which he brought out after Basil's death to defend his honor posthumously from continuing attacks by the neo-Arians, Gregory returns to defend the concept of deification as an important anti-Arian argument when set within the context of the Christological controversy. Here he combines the ideas of *metousia* and *theosis,* showing their essential synonymity by saying that, while deity does not participate in anything as of itself, since it transcends all other realities, nevertheless in Christ the humanity was indeed "brought to participate in the very deity itself" (εἰς τὴν τῆς θεότητος μετουσίαν); and in his treatise *De Perfectione Hominis,* he goes further and explicitly says that Christ did not merely unite his own nature to Godhead but through the dynamic of the Incarnation will also admit human beings to participation in deity (πρὸς μετουσίαν τῆς θεότητος), at least if we are purified of sin.[70]

Conclusion

The two Gregories are clearly enthusiastic disciples of Origen's great and mystical vision of the cosmic mystery, which is the soul's long journey to union with God. But they are not uncritical disciples. Both of them, in different ways, in relation to the tradition of deification theory which was already established before them, show themselves to be simultaneously respectful of the tradition, yet willing to advance it in new directions and for new ends.

Gregory of Nazianzus more enthusiastically endorses *theosis* language. In his *Orations* and his poetic corpus he clearly addressed himself more directly to a circle of readership he knew to be steeped in Platonic literature and its concomitant religious philosophy, and (I suggest) was deliberately appealing to that circle of initiates to make the step forward to accepting Christianity as a suitably serious vehicle for articulating religious philosophy in the new world of the Christian imperium.

Gregory of Nyssa was less of a theologian *in camera* than his older tutor and friend from Nazianzus. His teachings are modeled more from the sterner stuff of his other tutors, Macrina and Basil, who had both tried (in vain) to curb his love of philosophical speculation. The lessons seem to have been learned nonetheless, for Gregory's doctrine of μετουσία θεοῦ is clearly the Origenian doctrine of *theosis* but now with a new language code, designed to clear up once and for all the critical differences between Christian deification theory and Platonic assimilation language. It was something Gregory felt that Origen had not been able to do because he had not distanced himself sufficiently from the myth of the fall of preexistent souls into the material cosmos.

Gregory of Nyssa's audience comprised many of the same readers that were to be found in the frequent Symposia, which the Nazianzen arranged in Cappadocia and Constantinople, but it also spilled out further afield because of the extensive episcopal duties he undertook in his maturity, which involved many travels and much pastorally sensitive "brokering" in the years after the Council of Constantinople, when he was appointed by Theodosius to be one of the imperial arbiters of Orthodox theology in the East.

The juxtaposition of the thought of these two very "close" theologians shows essential similarities of approach, but also a clear line of differentiation. Gregory of Nazianzus regularly presumes that the postdeath transfiguration of the deified saint-philosopher-ascete will be comparable to a "promotion" to the much higher priestly capacity of the angelic order, which is able to see God's life-giving vision with greater acuity than the flesh-bound *nous* finds possible. He imagines the heavenly metamorphosis as an eventual "clarification" of the peculiar problem of human nature in the earthbound condition, that it is *nous* "mixed with" clay. In the day of deified glory all will be light. The spiritual body will not be one of clay (as Paul also taught in 1 Corinthians) but will have the same harmony and focus as the First Creation—the angelicals. His stress, in the doctrine of deification, therefore, is to use the strong idioms of a poet to emphasize the metamorphosis involved in glorification. On the part of Gregory of Nyssa, however, we see a concern to temper the language to clarify an aspect of the authentic Christian tradition of deification, which will remain an important element of the doctrine for all time to come. The deification, he suggests, is not a posthumous transcending of human nature, but a passing beyond the limits of human nature, in that glorified nature. The restricting limitations that were once imposed on human nature by long ages of its common experience as a "nature that was separated from God" will be lifted, in Gregory Nyssen's understanding, by the admission of the creature into the radiant fullness of the very purpose of creaturely human being, which is intimate communion with the endless mystery of the Life-Giving Presence.

It was to be Gregory Nazianzen's destiny to become the standard theological authority for the Byzantine world, and an undoubted overshadowing of Gregory of Nyssa's work came about after his death. It was ironical in many respects that the younger theologian who felt he ought to tone down Nazianzen's enthusiastic Greek on the subject of *theosis,* was himself to be put in the shade because of his retention of the Origenian belief in universal restoration.[71] The situation has today rather been reversed. A long overshadowing of interest in Gregory of Nazianzus has been a mark of Western scholarship in the twentieth century, which has also witnessed a revival of attention to Gregory of Nyssa among scholars of great acumen. Can an intelligent consideration of all the Greek Fathers, in an age when we finally possess the textual resources to call for this, bring us at last to a point when we can truly appreciate the "symphonicity" of the two Gregories and their common agenda? Because of their work, Christian theorists of the later

Byzantine age were able to see the potentiality of the rich language of *theosis,* apply the best of the heritage of Platonism to the illumination of the faith, and still have the answers to all those who, perhaps from a narrower basis of Christian culture, wanted to know how this dynamic approach of Greek patristics was to be differentiated from the old paganisms of *apotheosis* rituals. They also needed some reassurance before they could be led out into a cosmically enlarged perception that the exegesis of a biblical faith need not be fundamentalistic in order to be true.

Notes

1. The language of deification was never quite as dominant in the West, where it did not carry the main burden of redemption theory as it did with the Greek Fathers, but it is a notion certainly found in parts of Augustine (*Sermon* 192; *Exposition of Ps 49; Exposition of Ps 146*) who uses it to denote the transformative effects of grace. See J. A. McGuckin, "Deification," in *The Oxford Companion to Christian Thought,* ed. A. Hastings (Oxford: Oxford University Press, 2000).

2. Gregory of Nyssa applies that richly evocative word *epektasis* to this end: the stretching out of the blessed soul alongside the endlessly fathomless being of God, in whose participation it finds itself rendered, though creaturely, in a truly authentic "illimitability."

3. I. H. Dalmais gives a good discussion of many of the chief texts of the Greek patristic tradition relating to the concept of *theosis,* in his article "Divinisation," in *Dictionnaire de Spiritualité,* vol. 3 (Paris, 1957), cols. 1376–89.

4. A good biblical survey is given in J. Gross, *The Divinization of the Christian according to the Greek Fathers,* trans. P. Onica (Anahiem, CA: A&C Press, 2002), 61–92. Originally published as *La divinisation du chrétien d'après les Pères grecs: Contribution historique à la doctrine de la grace* (Paris: J. Gabalda, 1938).

5. Irenaeus, *Adversus Haereses* 5 (praef.). The idea and phrase were reprised and thereby made even more famous in Athanasius's *De Incarnatione* 54.

6. Irenaeus, *Adversus Haereses* 4.38.3–4; 5.8.1.

7. Ibid. 3.19.1.

8. Clement's theological aphorisms are as lapidary as those of Irenaeus in this regard. "The Word of God became man," he says, "So that you should learn from a man, how it is that man can become a god (ἄνθρωπος γίνεται θεοῦ)" (*Protreptikos* 1.8). Clement says that God divinizes (θεοποιει) man by means of his heavenly teaching, given as a beneficent and free gift out of his paternal love for his creatures (*Protreptikos* 11.14; see also *Pedagogus* 1.6.26; and *Stromata* 7.10.57). Clement, much more so than Irenaeus, is playing with the philosophical implications of the doctrine of "deification," which he knows to have a loud resonance in contemporary Middle Platonism (Numenius and Posidonius expressly). But his play is in a very identifiable Christian modality. Not only does he root the concept in the theology of the Incarnation of Logos, but he makes a profoundly biblical stress on the gracious priority of God's fatherly love. Human deification for Clement and his school does not grow out of any ontological capacity of the soul's primal nature, but from the gift of salvation. It is this constant emphasis on the divine priority that will identify all later Christians on the theme, and always radically distinguish Christian deification theory from the many varieties of paganism. Further on this, see G. W. Butterworth, "The Deification of Man in Clement of Alexandria," *JTS* 17 (1916): 157–69; see also Gross, *Divinization,* 131–41.

9. Origen's *Commentary on John* is the main book where he expands on this theme (based on Jn 10:34), but it is one that permeates much of his writing (cf. *Homily on Exodus* 6.5; *De Principiis* praef. 3; 1.3.4; 1.3.8; 1.7.5; 2.3.1–2; 2.10.1–3; 2.6.6; 4.4.4; 4.4.9; *Commentary on John* 1.288; 2.219; 32.338; *Contra Celsum* 6.13; 7.44). Cf. P. Martens, "Divinization," in *The Westminster Handbook to Origen,* ed. J. A. McGuckin, 91–93 (Louisville, KY: Westminster John Knox Press, 2004). See also J. Gross, *Divinization,* 142–49.

10. Athanasius signals his reading of Irenaeus most dramatically when he more or less repeats his aphorism: "The Word became man that man might become god." *De Incarnatione* 54. The notion of *theosis* appears throughout his writings in a consistent and clearly enunciated form (*De Incarnatione* 54; *De Decretis* 14; *Contra Arianos* 1.39; 2.70; 3.19; 3.33; 3.53; *Ep. Ad Serapionem* 1.24; *De Synodis* 51; *Ep. Ad Adelphium* 4). Athanasius's contribution is to emphasize the elements he chiefly found in Irenaeus, namely that the vision of God immortalizes mankind, and to combine them with the gloriously "cosmic" incarnational soteriology of Origen, whom he knows well but seeks to simplify and "bring back home." For Athanasius there tends to be a binary emphasis in all his passages on the theme: something that becomes definitive for most patristic commentators after him. The first of these emphases is Pedagogic (the Word becomes man to show once more the lost Image of the Father); and the second has often been called "Physical," that is, the Word enters into our humanity in order to restore the lost gift of immortality to the race, in the deepest levels of its being. Athanasius brings a simpler clarity to the underlying thesis that the vision of God is indeed immortalizing and life-giving, and that this is a noetic process that is worked out in and through the enfleshment of the Logos. Further on this, see Gross, *Divinization,* 163–75.

11. Origen, despite a common misbelief that he underestimates the economy in the flesh, is very determined to note how the Incarnation of the Logos is the root of the hopes for the *theosis* of the human race. In discussing the body of Christ he says, "The divine nature and the human nature became very closely bonded together (συνυφαίνεσθαι) in order that, by its communion with that which was more divine, human nature itself might become divine; and this not only in the case of Jesus, but also in the case of all those who in faith have embraced the life which Jesus taught, that life which leads to friendship and community with God." *Contra Celsum* 3.38. Cyril of Alexandria would be the heir to this language and would reexpress the implications of deification theory most strongly in his robust defense of Alexandrian thought, in the Christological domain, at the Council of Ephesus. See J. A. McGuckin, *St. Cyril of Alexandria and the Christological Controversy* (Leiden: E. J. Brill, 1994; repr., Crestwood, NY: St. Vladimir's Seminary Press, 2004).

12. The sacramental implications of this are not lost on the patristic theologians, especially John Chrysostom (who in his eucharistic doctrine most nearly approximates to the concept of *theosis* he otherwise avoids). Gregory of Nyssa regards the sacramental "seals" of baptism and Eucharist as absolutely essential for growth in the divine life (cf. *Catechetical Oration* c. 37). Cyril of Alexandria sees the Eucharist as the preeminent paradigm of deification as well as its primary energy when transmitted to the church. See *Homily on the Gospel of Luke 142,* trans. R. Payne-Smith, in *A Commentary upon the Gospel according to Luke by St. Cyril of Alexandria,* 664–69 (Oxford, 1859); text revised in D. J. Sheerin, ed., *The Eucharist,* vol. 7, Message of the Fathers of the Church (Wilmington, DE: M. Glazier 1986), 229–35. See also E. Gebremedhin, *Life-Giving Blessing: An Enquiry into the Eucharistic Doctrine of S. Cyril of Alexandria* (Uppsala: Almqvist & Wiksell International, 1977).

13. See Gross, *Divinization,* 200–214.

14. Dionysius Areopagita, *Ecclesiastical Hierarchy* 1.3.

15. Maximus gives a classical exposition of the doctrine of *theosis* in his *Questions to Thalassius* 59, PG 90:608d–9b; see also *Ambigua,* PG 91:1237b–c; and *Questions to Thalassius* 22, PG 90:321a. I. H. Dalmais offers a useful overview of his doctrine in *Dictionnaire de Spiritualité,* col. 1387.

16. Maximus, *Ambigua,* PG 91:1237bc; *Questions to Thalassius* 22, PG 90:321a; ibid. 60, PG 90:620.

17. Maximus, *Ambigua,* PG 91:1113bc; ibid. 1385bc.

18. John Damascene, *De Fide Orthodoxa* 2.11–12, PG 94:909–29; ibid. 3.1, PG 94:981–84; ibid. 4.13, PG 94:1136–53.

19. See n. 25.

20. I think this missionary motive is the correct perspective—the concept of "Christianizing Plato" is not born out by the evidence of how both theologians treat the philosopher (eclectically and incidentally in the main), nor is it seen in Origen's approach either. These learned Christians use Platonic resonances, certainly, but only as these are directed and shaped by their Christian agendas. Plato becomes, as it were, the rhetorical hook to catch new fish. The strategy was described by Amphilokius of Iconium, Gregory Nazianzen's cousin, as "Stripping the roses of Hellenism of all their thorns." The recent study of M. J. Edwards, *Origen against Plato* (Aldershot, Hants, England: Ashgate, 2002), sustains that argument with abundant evidence sufficient (one hopes) to overturn decades of scholarly misreadings of the agenda.

21. English translation in S. McKenna, *Plotinus: The Enneads* (New York: Pantheon Books, 1969), 56–64.

22. *Phaedrus* 250bc.

23. Gregory regularly describes Christianity as "philosophia nostra."

24. Just as the purification of fire will await the unfaithful soul.

25. *Orations* 26–27. I have commented on them in J. A. McGuckin, *St. Gregory of Nazianzus: An Intellectual Biography* (Crestwood, NY: St. Vladimir's Seminary Press, 2003); and also covered related aspects of this idea of transfigured initiation in "The Vision of God in St. Gregory Nazianzen," *Studia Patristica* 32, ed. E. A. Livingstone, 145–52 (Leuven: Peeters, 1996).

26. "The Paraclete takes possession of a pure eye, as the sun does, and will show you in Himself, the Image of the Invisible One. In blessed contemplation of the Image, you will see the ineffable beauty of the Archetype. It is He who shines in those that are cleansed of every impurity to make them spiritual through communion with Him. Just as bright and transparent bodies themselves become scintillating when light falls upon them, and reflect another brightness from themselves, just so Spirit-bearing souls, illuminated by the Spirit, become spiritual themselves, and send forth grace to others. . . . That form is the source of all that flows therefrom: the foreseeing of the future, the understanding of mysteries, the understanding of things that are hidden, the distribution of charisms, the participation in heavenly life, the chanting in the choir of angels, endless joy, the permanent indwelling within God, resemblance to God, and finally that supremely desired goal—to become god." St. Basil of Caesarea, *On the Holy Spirit* 9.23.

27. *Theatetus* 176; *Enneads* 6.9.9.

28. *Timaeus* 90 bd.

29. *Commentary on John* 32.27.

30. "The Word himself would not have remained divine if he had not persisted in his uninterrupted contemplation of the abyss of the Father." *Commentary on John* 2.2.

31. Athanasius, *De Incarnatione* 54; cf. Gregory, *Oration* 29.19: "I may become god in so far as he became man."

32. Gregory, *Carmina Dogmatica* 10.5–9. *De Incarnatione,* PG 37:465.

33. *Carmina Dogmatica* 8.1–3, PG 37:446; *Carmina Moralia* 1.156, PG 37:534; *Carmina Dogmatica* 8.70–77, PG 37:452; *Carmina Moralia* 10.135, PG 37:690; *Oratio de Amore Pauperum* 24.7, PG 35:865c.

34. τῇ πρὸς θεὸν νεύσει θεούμενον. *Orat.* 38.11, 13, PG 36:324; cf. parallels in *Orat.* 45.7, PG 36:632b.

35. *Carmina Dogmatica* 10.140–43, PG 37:690.

36. Cf. *Orat.* 11.5, PG 35:837c; *Orat.* 14.23, PG 35:888a.
37. *Orations* 27–31; Cf. *Orat.* 31.4.
38. This oration is also a Panegyric for Athanasius.
40. *Catechetical Oration* 5.4.
45. Maximus, *Ambigua* 10; It is not our primary concern here, but we can note that Maximus is most concerned not to read this as a motion to divine assimilation that dispenses with asceticism and moral effort, a path that he thought the Origenists of the generations after Gregory had more or less taken. It is clear, nonetheless, that Gregory's overt use of Plato disturbed Maximus at this juncture, and the later Origenists appealed to Gregory for support in their Platonic-Origenian reading of the idea of noetic assimilation.
41. Gregory Nazianzen, *Orat.* 21.1; *Republic,* bk. 6, trans. B. Jowett, *The Works of Plato.* vol. 2 (Oxford, 1875; repr., New York: Tudor Publications, 1937), 261.
42. Cf. 1 Jn 1:5.
43. The idea will be reprised and developed to great effect in Gregory of Nyssa's doctrine of *Epektasis,* which we shall come to momentarily.
44. *Orat.* 21.1.
45. *Timaeus* 90; *Phaedrus* 250 bc; The discourse of the Priestess Diotima, trans. in B. Jowett, *Works of Plato,* 3:343: "'For he who has been instructed thus far in things of love, and who has learned to see the beautiful in due order and succession, when he comes toward the end will suddenly perceive a nature of wondrous beauty—and this Socrates is that final cause of all our former toils, which in the first place is everlasting: not growing and decaying or waxing and waning; not fair in one point of view and foul in another . . . but beauty only, absolute, simple, separate, and everlasting, which is without diminution and without increase. And the true order of going, or being led by another, to the things of love, is to use the beauties of the earth as steps along which we mount upwards for the sake of that other beauty . . . until we arrive at the essence of beauty. This my dear Socrates,' said the stranger of Mantineia, 'is that life above all others which a man should live, in the contemplation of beauty absolute. . . . In such a communion . . . man could become the friend of God, and be immortal, in so far as lies in the capacity of mortal man.'"
46. *Orat.* 21.2.
47. See R. Gillet, "L'Homme divinisateur cosmique dans la pensée de S. Grégoire de Nysse," *Studia Patristica* 6, Texte und Untersuchungen, 81 (Berlin: Akademie-Verlag, 1962), 62–83.
48. Creatures, Gregory says, can participate in the properties of God but can never attain to identity of nature (τὴν τῆς φύσεως ἰδιότητα). Gregory Nazianzen teaches exactly the same thing. See *Orat.* 45.4, PG 36:628c.
49. Gregory does not posit it so much in terms of power differentiation, as in the fact that the image and its archetype represent changeability and unchangeability. Created being moves and is in flux while the Godhead is perfect and unchanging in the stability of its life. Cf. *Catechetical Oration* 21.1–2.
50. "[The Logos] was transfused throughout our nature, so that our nature, by virtue of this transfusion, might itself become divine." *Catechetical Oration* 25.
51. *Catechetical Oration* 5.
52. *Timaeus* 45bd.
53. *Catechetical Oration* 5.
54. "Discourse on Children," *Gregorii Nysseni Opera,* ed. E. Muhlenberg (Leiden, 1996), 3.2:79.
55. The first two orders of creation were angelicals and materials. The first being wholly spiritual, the second being radically material, and neither having any admixture within their being. The Third Order of Creation (mankind) was, for Gregory, a unique admixture of the spiritual within the material—man's double constitution as an ensouled body is thus the very

basis of his hope to see God, and the plan for salvation that God has constituted to allow that possibility. Gregory Nazianzen understood that as a progressive promotion of the blessed soul to the constitution of the First Order of Creation. Gregory of Nyssa shifted that emphasis on ontological metamorphosis to a complex understanding of the endless "'stretching out" (*epektasis*) of a limited being to participation in the endless being of God.

56. *De Opificio Hominis* 28, PG 45:229b; *De Anima,* PG 45:113b–c.

57. See F. W. Norris, "Apokatastasis," in *Westminster Handbook to Origen,* 59–62.

58. *On the Dead,* PG 46:109.

59. *De Anima* 69; His idea of the eventual restoration of the wicked, including the damned and demons, does not vitiate the fact that he saw this as being accomplished only after the ages of punishment appointed for sins would themselves have been fulfilled. The restoration was proof that the punishments had been effective in transfiguring the wicked to the good; and to this extent the *apokatastasis* does not so much deny the eternal justice of God but fulfills it. See J. Daniélou, *L'Etre et le Temps chez Gregoire de Nysse* (Leiden: Brill, 1970), 223.

60. The purified *nous* of the elect are reconstituted in the first circle of heaven around the Logos, contemplating God with rapt attention. But he still wonders aloud in the *De Principiis* if their attention will again lapse from that attentiveness, resulting in another cosmic fall from true being.

61. Jean Daniélou and Henri de Lubac were among early and important commentators. The concept of participation in God is magisterially studied by D. Balas in his monograph *Μετουσια Θεου:* Man's Participation in God's Perfections according to S. Gregory of Nyssa (Rome: Libreria Herder, 1966).

62. It is central to Balas's thesis, for example, that although the notion of participation in the divine by means of the praxis of the philosophic life was a common motif in much late Platonic theory of the fourth century, Gregory's unique synthesis represents the most thoroughgoing Christianization of the idea attempted since Origen. Cf. Balas, *Μετουσια Θεου,* 164.

63. See *Life of Moses* 1.7–8.

64. *Orat.* 31.

65. Cf. J. A. McGuckin, "Image of God," in *Westminster Handbook to Origen,* 131–34.

66. *De Opificio Hominis* 4.

67. Ibid. 9; Dalmais ("Divinisation," *Dictionnaire de Spiritualité,* vol. 3) notices a parallel to this notion in Plutarch, *De Iside et Osiride* 1.351D. The idea is developed especially in chap. 16 of the *De Opificio Hominis.*

68. "The nature of Man was made precisely in order to be a participant (μέτοχον) in every good." PG 44:184b.

69. *On the Soul and Resurrection,* PG. 46:105a–b; see also Irenaeus, *Adversus Haereses* 4.11.2.

70. *Contra Eunomium* 3.4.22; *De Perfectione Hominis* 8.1.

71. *Catechetical Oration* 8, 26, 35, PG 45:92ab.

Rhetorical Application of *Theosis* in Greek Patristic Theology

Vladimir Kharlamov

WHILE THE CONCEPT OF *THEOSIS* IN THE MODERN WORLD IS OBJECTIONable or controversial to some, when we move to the world of the fourth century, the issue and language of *theosis* is not alien, either for the intellectual elite or the common people. In *Catecheses ad illuminandos,* for example, Cyril of Jerusalem addresses catechumens (people in the process of initiation into the basic principles of Christian teaching) and freely refers to the Holy Spirit as deifier (θεοποιὸν) without giving an explanation of what he means.[1] Such striking use of deification language is a valid historical indication that, by the fourth century, the concept of *theosis* had become a matter of popular Christian theology, perhaps resembling in its practical application the "born again" evangelical theology of today.

However, the enthusiasm with which some Christian writers used the terminology of deification was not unanimously shared. Nor was the gradual emergence of *theosis* as a doctrine in Christian theology and the formation of a specific terminology associated with a systematic process. Further, we must be careful not to exaggerate the popularity of *theosis.* Outside of Alexandria and Cappadocia, very few patristic writers used such terminology. Even in Cappadocia itself, Basil of Caesarea and his younger brother Gregory of Nyssa are very cautious in their application of explicit deification language. It must also be remembered that *theosis,* before Pseudo-Dionysius, was not necessarily an element of mystical theology per se, nor exclusively an aspect of salvation. Moreover, during the fourth and fifth centuries, none of the Fathers, as Jules Gross correctly points out, offered a precise definition for the term or its equivalents.[2] Nevertheless, among those who, like Athanasius and Gregory of Nazianzus, strongly advocated the concept of deification and those who were more cautious about it or did not use this concept at all, we do not have any patristic author who would openly object to the use of this notion until Nestorius.

In my view, the notion of deification during this time was periodically introduced on the margin of theological issues such as immortality and eternal life, creation, the *imago Dei* in the human being, sanctification, redemption, sacramental theology, as well as general and individual eschatology.

These elements of Christian theology, from the time of the ante-Nicene Christian writers, introduced different aspects related to deification but did not precisely explicate the meaning of this concept as such. Thus, the notion of deification, with its tremendously uplifting spiritual attraction, as a marginal concept during the fourth century was often addressed on the periphery of other theological issues and controversies. It was referred to by Christian writers as a sort of appeal to the common knowledge of the Christian community.

While not at the center of theological discussion, it appears that the language of deification in the fourth century was used often as a *rhetorical tool* with a great range of applications to a vast variety of aspects of Christian spirituality, while the concept was not really treated as an independent theological matter. But, when I say that, I by no means want to diminish the theological significance of the concept of deification to rhetoric only and ignore its theological implications. On the contrary, I would like to demonstrate how rhetoric enhanced the notion of deification and made this concept applicable to a broad Christian audience. I would also like to emphasize that, in my view, rhetorical application of the concept of *theosis* is only one facet of this rather multidimensional and complex notion.

Deification as Rhetoric

Plato's standard distinction between rhetoric as persuasion and philosophy as knowledge was not actually operative in the Christian writers of the fourth century. Plato's distinction overall should not be exaggerated, as it rarely appears in pure form during antiquity. Philosophy often implemented rhetorical elements for its own advantage. However, rhetoric was more involved in the matters of political, judicial, and public affairs, while philosophy as an infinite quest for truth and wisdom was not necessarily a public concern but rather a matter of the educated elite. In the Christian theology of the fourth century, these two tendencies became more unified, where theology experienced not only a decisive influence on the minds of both educated and common people but was also a pivotal matter in public life and politics. Theology in the fourth century, perhaps like sports today, appears to have been on the tip of everyone's tongue, to the degree that Gregory of Nazianzus lamented that people would discuss theological issues "after the races, or the theater, or a concert, or a dinner, or still lower employments."[3]

In the Christian writers of the fourth century, rhetoric itself acquires a significant level of development. The church fathers attempt to create not simply impressive speech, although there is no doubt that they would not mind for their message to be impressive, but to construct a meaningful message. As Rosemary Radford Ruether remarks, "This is precisely the reason why sophistic training in the hands of the fourth-century Christians often gives the impression of greater power than among contemporary pagans."[4]

It is not rhetoric for the sake of eloquence as such that points to hidden yet significant and existential meaning, but rhetorically stated affirmations that would play the major role in the popularization of deification. However, as was mentioned earlier, deification is neither the main nor even a controversial or disputed concept at that time. As it was used especially by Athanasius, deification is the vehicle to win the argument against his main adversary, Arius. Thus, the application of deification terminology, without a precise theological explication of the concept, finds its way into the writings of such great rhetoricians of the Christian church as Athanasius and, particularly, Gregory of Nazianzus. It is on these two theologians that we will concentrate our attention.

Deification as Rhetoric in Athanasius

The direct application of deification language in Athanasius is frequent. The main Athanasian word for deification is θεοποιέω and its derivatives,[5] which he uses both in the context of pagan and Christian deification. However, this precedent is unique not only to Athanasius. For example, Cyril of Jerusalem, through the use of similar vocabulary, mentions the Holy Spirit as deifier and yet criticizes pagan divinization in the same homily.[6] Apparently, by the fourth century, even though using identical terminology, the Fathers ascribed a different meaning to the notion of deification in the context of pagan practice and Christian spirituality. This also could be considered an indication that the notion of deification in Christian theology was at that time becoming a component of popular theology despite the fact that it was not yet singled out as an independent theological issue. The noun cognate from θεοποιέω—θεοποίησις (to make into a god, to deify—making divine, deification), Athanasius's personal linguistic invention, is only used in *Contra Arianos* and always in the meaning of Christian deification.[7] However, another noun form, θεοποιία (being made divine), which also occurs in only a single work, *Contra gentes,* is always used in his critique of pagan idolatry.[8] Another Greek word that Athanasius uses, but only twice and always in the context of pagan deification, is ἐκθειάζω (to make into a god, to deify).[9]

Nevertheless, this extensive application of deification language by Athanasius should not be exaggerated. Athanasius indiscriminately, figuratively, and directly applies θεοποιέω to his criticism of non-Christian practices as well as to his fight against Arius and the promotion of Christian deification. Athanasius frequently uses θεοποιέω in *Contra gentes.*[10] Needless to say, the entire work does not have any direct references to Christian deification.

Athanasius uses θεοποιέω three times in various contexts: once he cites Arius's *Thalia,* where Arius uses this word; once it is used in the reference to the council decree on Paul of Samosata; and once figuratively against the Jews.[11] All told, Athanasius uses θεοποιέω in a Christian context only thirty-three times.[12] If we compare these thirty-three direct references to Christian deification with the superabundant references to ὁμοούσιος (cosubstantial), this more than anything else indicates what was the main Athanasian theological concern. The controversy with Arianism provides the content for the development of Athanasian theology and makes Athanasius virtually blind to other heresies.[13] Thus, we may conclude that this dispute with the Arians also significantly shapes his treatment of deification.

Already in *Contra gentes,* especially if we accept the later date of composition, we can see that in this work, which at first glance is not explicitly anti-Arian, Athanasius is slowly building a basis to launch his attack against Arius.[14] He attempts to show the apparent heresy in Arius by ranking Arian theology on the same level with pagan religions. The core falsehood of pagan worship for Athanasius lies in the ontological misplacement of the object of its devotion, namely in the deification and worship of the various elements of creation, products of human art and imagination instead of the Creator.[15] Athanasius notes the immoral behavior of the Olympian gods.[16] And the irony of all this is that "those who hate the adulterer who assaults their own wives are not ashamed to deify (θεοποιοῦντες) the exponents of adultery; and though they do not have intercourse with their sisters, they worship those who do."[17] The impiety of pagan cults for Athanasius is contained in the obvious and self-exclusive contradiction between common and generally accepted morality and the immoral behavior of the gods.

Pagan practices in Athanasian criticism also have two more ironically unreasonable components. The first goes along with the Old Testament argument against idolatry.[18] How could a statue or image made by human hands be god? Athanasius advances this argument a little further by suggesting that if a statue of god is divine, then it is not the statue itself that should be venerated but the artist who produced it.[19] The second aspect of the irrationality of paganism relates to the divinization of human beings.[20] How can mortals make somebody both immortal and divine? And here lies one of the main elements of the Athanasian argument that both disputes the pagan practice of divinization and sets the necessary condition for a Christian understanding of deification, "[T]hose who make gods (θεοποιοῦντας) should themselves be gods, for the maker must be better than what he makes. . . . If then they declare to be gods whomever they wish, they should first be gods themselves. But the remarkable thing is that by dying like men they prove their decree concerning those they deified (θεοποιηθέντων) to be false."[21]

Athanasius is not original in his criticism of the pagan practice of divinization and worship.[22] Even some non-Christian writers would share his sentiment.[23] Nevertheless, Athanasius uses his argumentation against paganism and non-Christian divinization to his advantage and eloquently shifts gears to fight Arius; the notion of deification is only one of the elements that Athanasius employs to pursue his goal. From an Athanasian perspective, for Arius to teach that there was a time when the Logos did not exist would suggest nothing more than that we put our faith in a creature, and in this regard we are no better than pagans who deify and worship creation instead of the Creator.[24] If the Logos is a deity only because of participation in the Father, this would strip him of genuine divinity.[25] And again, even if the Logos is God, but either a lesser God than the Father or in any degree different from the Father in the essence, then the Arians once more could be cited along with paganism for introducing polytheism.[26]

Athanasius's attacks on aspects of the Logos's identity with the Father and the emphasis that Athanasius thereby gave to the deification of human beings might lead to the suggestion that Arius himself used the language of deification,[27] which at the time of the controversy had already acquired certain popularity among Christians of both camps. Mainstream Christianity seems to be adept at engaging in thorough purging. We are told that Arius wrote many works, but except for three letters, some fragments of another letter, and lengthy quotations in Athanasius from *Thalia,* not only do we not have any other surviving works quoted by his supporters or opponents, but we do not even know their names.[28] This makes our assessment of the role of deification in the theology of Arius extremely speculative. However, citing from *Thalia,* Athanasius attributes to Arius a direct reference to deification, where Arius allegedly stated that the Logos was created and, only by participation, was made God.[29] Even if this is an Athanasian interpretation of Arian theology, the whole discourse of anti-Arian polemics and the application of the notion of deification in it serves as strong evidence for assuming that this notion was applied by Arius. If Athanasius uses deification as a tool against the Arians, this suggests that this notion was as popular, or initially even more popular, among early Arians than with anti-Arian writers.

In his polemic against paganism and the Arians, Athanasius very effectively utilizes his rhetorical skills, ridiculing the falsehood of paganism and the heresy of Arius by using a terminology of deification that was common to all parties. By so doing, he tries to sharpen the contrast between the truth of Orthodox Christianity, which he was intending to represent, and the so-called pseudotruth of other religions as well as that of the Arians, or true salvation versus illusory salvation; he does so by opposing pseudodeification with the true one.

In a Christian context, Athanasius uses θεοποιέω thirty-three times in his writings; for him, the process of deification is often analogous with the process of participation. In Athanasius, we can see the general tendency to depict activity flowing from God to humanity in terms of deification language while the movement of human beings toward God is in terms of participation. God deifies, while we participate. Participation also is more often the indicator of the deification process itself, when the deification language signifies either the end result of this process (deified state), or the divine agent (God). A Christian participates in God and is deified by partaking in divine nature. Athanasius uses 2 Peter 1:4 in the context of deification at least six times.[30] Thus, this variety of direct and contextual allusions to deification in his writing significantly increases the theological value of this notion. At the same time, in spite of this abundance of references, Athanasius argues for deification more than he attempts to explain the precise meaning of this concept. Even Gross, who sees in him a doctrinal synthesis for the concept of deification, had to acknowledge that "with Athanasius we would search in vain for a systematic and well-balanced exposition on the matter."[31] Nevertheless, the lack of theological lucidity does not prevent, and perhaps even increases, the popularity of deification.

Athanasius also supplied Christian theology with a determinative statement on deification, where, in paraphrasing Irenaeus, he says, "For he [the Logos] was made man that we might be made god (αὐτὸς γὰρ ἐνηνθρώπησεν, ἵνα ἡμεῖς θεοποιηθῶμεν)."[32] In his writings, with slight modifications, Athanasius repeatedly returns to this statement.[33] This powerful, striking, memorable, and rhetorically well-balanced and eloquent statement is, at the same time, theologically very indefinite. In what sense does a human being become a god?

If we look closely at this statement, we can see that it is more of an affirmation of the incarnation of God than of the deification of human beings. And this is its main purpose: "God was made man." The symmetrical structure of this "exchange formula" by no means assumes a relationship between equal participants. At the same time, as John Cullen points out, "while he [Athanasius] obviously did not mean to suggest that we become God in the sense that God is God, yet his terminology clearly indicates that he did mean something more than 'divine.'"[34] And in spite of all the theological difficulties and uncertainties that can arise from this statement, the rhetorical significance of this formula and the influence it had in the emergence of the notion of deification can hardly be overstated.

If Athanasius is not precisely clear on what it means for a human being to be god, he is very clear about what conditions are necessary for us to be deified. Nobody can be deified by anyone lesser than God himself.[35] Therefore, the Logos must be God to make the deification of human beings even conceivable. If, for Origen, and subsequently for Arius, the Logos was deified in relation to the Father and, in return, became the deifier in relation to humanity, in Athanasius the Logos is the principle of deifying power and, therefore, fully divine and consubstantial with the Father. A created being for Athanasius can only participate in deification but it cannot communicate it further. If we are "deified" by someone who was deified prior to us, our deification is not valid, but merely an illusion.[36] Thus, the Logos, who is God and the deifier, does not require any deification for himself.[37] When we speak about deification in Christ we speak only about the deification of Christ's human nature at the moment of his incarnation.[38]

Deification of a human being is the other side of incarnation.[39] That is, the incarnation of the Logos destroyed the ontological foundation of mortality that was engraved in human nature after the Fall, and reconciled humanity to the Father. In this sense Athanasius is a direct heir of the Irenaean line of theology, where deification is understood as physical immortality and impassibility.[40] Athanasius affirms the general corporeal resurrection, which is the result of Christ's death and resurrection.[41] However, this approach to deification as attainment of immortality and incorruptibility is apparent in Athanasius's early works.[42] There is more to deification in Athanasius than immortality and incorruptibility. Incarnation of the Logos introduced for human beings the possibility of divine filiation. More clearly than any Christian writer before him, Athanasius makes a direct identification between deification and divine sonship (υἱοποιεῖν).[43] In this instance, we can observe the increasing significance of deification terminology in Christian theology that begins to parallel more traditional and biblical concepts.

The process of deification also constitutes a proper knowledge of God. Through the Logos, a human being is able "to see and know realities" by means of assimilation to God; God also reveals to humanity his eternity and restores the power of the human mind to contemplate God.[44] True divine knowledge and contemplation lead to the proper imitation of God. Imitation of God and virtuous life are two concepts that have been, from early on, closely linked together in Christian theology. A moral or virtuous life is only possible when a human being knows God and participates in divine life. Virtuous life is a synergetic result of divine γνῶσις (knowledge) that comes from God and the human effort that is initiated by the individual. This theme receives further and more significant development in the Cappadocians.

For Athanasius, deification of an individual is a dynamic process. A human being first is redeemed from sin; then, in the resurrection, is redeemed from corruption and finally is exalted to heaven.[45] Deification of a human being to some degree parallels the incarnation of the Logos as a gradual and transcending process of revelation and manifestation of God himself in the life of the human individual.[46] As in Christ his humanity transcends its own nature; this is also communicated to people.[47] Norman Russell notes that, in Athanasius, "the renewal of the human race is like a second creation carried out by the Creator, but this time from within."[48] More than once Athanasius notes the superiority of the human redeemed state to the created one.[49] C. R. Strange remarks with reference to Wiles's argument, Athanasius "believed that when the true God became truly man, he did not do so to make it possible for men to become gods in the sense in which he was God, but in order to transform what it means to be a man."[50] A deified human being does not cease to be human just as the Logos did not cease to be consubstantial with the Father after incarnation.[51] It is precisely why the Logos was incarnated; that we can be deified without losing "our own proper substance."[52] "Even in his choice of vocabulary for deification and filiation, Athanasius," as correctly noted by John Cullen, "uses as parallel terms θεοποιέω and υἱοποιέω (to adopt, to make a son), both of which contain the -ποιέω element suggesting agency, something done to or for someone, an act of making by someone, to emphasize the action of God in the progress."[53]

In this regard, Athanasius makes an important distinction between identity and likeness. Identity presupposes the oneness of nature or consubstantiality, while likeness is more like resemblance to some quality of the nature that is not necessarily the predicate of the nature of those who demonstrate such resemblance.[54] Here, Athanasius methodologically makes a distinction between the object of participation and the subject that participates. The subject that participates does not become equal or identical with the object of participation. Thus, we are like God, but not identical with God.[55]

Athanasius frequently speaks about the deification of human beings; however, his references to Christian deification are so sparsely scattered throughout his corpus that even after an attempt to analyze the theological implications of this notion, deification remains a paradoxically volatile concept. Also, Athanasius very rarely speaks about human beings as gods, and when he does so, it is often with the reference of Psalm 81:6 (LXX) or John 10:35.[56] Deification plays a more auxiliary role to his main theological task, which is the defeat of Arianism. Even his exchange formula for deification reflects more the aspect of the full divinity of the Logos rather than the deification of a human being. At the same time, because of his oratorical skills and rather unsophisticated but very reassuring and repetitive style, which would capture the imagination of a popular audience, Athanasius secured a prominent place for the terminology of deification in Christian theology that gradually led to the further development of this concept. In Athanasius, deification not only gains momentum as a convincing force in his fight against the Arians but it also acquires profound significance in Christian spirituality.

Perhaps as the result of the Athanasian influence, deification became a popular notion of Christian theology. Starting with Athanasius we also observe the formation of a certain theological vocabulary where the terminology of deification began to play a more essential role and, at the same time, was reconciled with more traditional and biblical terminology. Eventually, the language of deification, similar to that of trinitarian and Christological terminology, obtained recognition equal only to biblical language, so that when, for instance, Pseudo-Dionysius ventures to imitate the disciple of the apostle Paul and integrates substantially the notion of *theosis* as one of his main concepts, it is not perceived as an anachronistic perplexity.

Gregory of Nazianzus's Rhetoric of Deification

When we come to Gregory of Nazianzus, his references to deification in technical and conceptual language are overwhelmingly rich; however, the theological significance and originality of how Gregory approaches this notion yield to Athanasius. Gregory's vocabulary and rhetorical talent, as well as his ability for creative theological generalization, are what make his contribution significant.

It would not be an exaggeration to place Gregory in the company of the most talented rhetoricians of late antiquity. Gregory would fully conform to the characteristics of the Second Sophists.[57] We only can imagine the effect his preaching would produce on his listeners: the harmony of speech with well-constructed and well-balanced phraseology reinforced by a variety of rhetorical devices, such as rhetorical questions, exclamations, irony, invocations, paradoxes, impersonalizations, and personifications, would persuasively impress and convince his audience. Gregory is fond of classical Attic, poetic words, archaisms and neologisms, which he complements with *koine* Greek. If *koine* Greek would be considered barbaric for traditional Sophists, for Gregory it is a language of Christian scriptures. This is, in a way, an awkward combination, for an exquisite Hellenistic ear prompts Gregory to invent an eclectic, rich, and, at the same time, unique language of his own. His artistic taste protects him against banalities.[58]

Gregory is both more inventive and more explicit than Athanasius when it comes to deification. His vocabulary is somewhat similar to but also somewhat different from that of other Christian writers. It is definitely more diversified, and his urge for eloquence predetermines even his terminological preferences. He uses θεοποιέω only twice, and θεοποιός (making a god) at least as many times.[59] More often for the sake of euphony, Gregory gives preference to an archaism θεὸν ποιέω (to make a god).[60] Gregory also uses extensively, in a variety of contexts, θεὸς εἰμί (to be a god) and θεὸς γίγνομαι (to become a god).[61] In his poetry we encounter such deificational variations as θεὸν τεύχω (to make/produce god), θεὸν τελέω (to complete/accomplish/dedicate god), and τυκτὸς θεὸς (created god).[62]

Overall, Gregory's favorite word for deification is θεόω (to deify), which appears in his writings at least twenty-three times.[63] From this verb, he derives θέωσις, the only noun he uses in the context of deification.[64] This new Greek word, coined by Gregory as a specifically Christian term, eventually acquires the chief position in communicating the concept of deification in

Christian theology. Even though *theosis* becomes the term for deification in Byzantine theology, as Norman Russell notes, "it did not prove immediately popular. It was not taken up again [after Gregory] until Dionysius the Areopagite used it in the fifth century, and only became fully assimilated with Maximus the Confessor in the seventh."[65]

Some indifference to this new term θέωσις at first could be attributed not to a lack of interest in the issue of deification but rather to the linguistic specificity of Gregory himself. The uniqueness of Gregory's language and the peculiarity of his vocabulary confined in a way the application of this term in the writings of other Christian writers of that time. A back formation from the verb θεόω, θέωσις as Norman Russell points out, "is first used when a *homoeoteleuton* is required: ἀναβάσεως καὶ θεώσεως [ascending and deifying].[66] Later it is used for the sake of assonance: ἡ θεότης . . . ἡ θέωσις [divinity . . . deification].[67] On a further occasion Gregory uses the word in order to present a striking oxymoron: τῇ θεώσει θεός [deified god]."[68]

Most of Gregory's direct references to deification are used primarily in the Christian context of human deification; however, his deification language has broader applications than that. For one thing, Gregory occasionally uses the language of *theosis* in a very figurative and metaphorical sense; for another, he uses deification terminology in his criticism of non-Christian divinization. For instance, once he speaks deificationally about parenthood.[69] He parallels the heavenly Father as God uncreated with a biological father as a created god. As the first rules over the whole cosmos and is our universal Parent, so the human "father for his children is also a god."[70] In another instance, Gregory, who in one of his orations is explicitly critical about the imposition of divine status on distinguished people, nevertheless urges earthly rulers to conduct themselves in a godlike manner: "Become gods (θεοὶ γένεσθε) toward your subjects, if I may put it so boldly."[71] Lamenting very analogically about the interruption of his solitude, in one place Gregory calls the desert "mother of the divine ascent and producer of deification in man."[72] However, Gregory more frequently reserves his metaphorical apotheotic imagery for the office of priesthood. The role of the priest, who through his ministry has a deifying effect on others, occupies a significant place in his writings.[73] In these instances the word "god" is applied to parents, rulers, deserts, and priests in a purely analogical and metaphorical sense, which could be attributed more to Gregory's literary and poetic style than to the literal meaning of the word.

Deification language used in a non-Christian context is found significantly less often in Gregory than in Athanasius.[74] Gregory, ironically, in his very rhetorical style in ridiculing non-Christian divinization in Greek antiquity, uses as an example the father of Greek rhetoric himself—Empedocles. Empedocles is notoriously known for proclaiming himself a god. This imposition cost him his life. Attempting to prove his divine rank, Empedocles threw himself into a volcanic crater, which was the end of his divinity.[75] However, theologically, Gregory's main argument against non-Christian divinization and paganism is slightly different from the Athanasian. For Athanasius the basic falsehood of Hellenistic religion lies fundamentally in the ontological disparity between created and uncreated, where the object of pagan worship belongs to the created realm. Gregory of Nazianzus puts more emphasis on the ethical and epistemological aspects. Similar to Basil of Caesarea and Gregory of Nyssa, Gregory of Nazianzus speaks against the "deification" of somebody's belly.[76] And in the twenty-eighth *Oration,* after acknowledging the universal longing of every noetic or rational nature toward God, Gregory points to the failure to contemplate God properly and go beyond visible images. In his view, being too tired to pursue the higher contemplation of God, people often make gods out of things visible, other people, and their worst passions.[77] Thus, the life of a Christian, in its contemplative and deificational propensity, is presented in opposition to the false values of paganism. In his first apologetic oration against the emperor Julian, whom Gregory had known personally at Athens (but safely wrote his apology after the death of the emperor), Gregory contrasts the achievements of pagan Hellenistic thought, virtues, and courage with those of the Christian. Christians not only attained the same level but far surpassed their non-Christian counterpart.[78] In this oration, for the first time, Gregory uses his term *theosis* and sets the main agenda for this concept, which is slightly different than in Athanasius. Gregory points to a very philosophic form of ecstatic deification through contemplation. An Origenistic theme of deification as spiritualization, combined with a Neoplatonic approach to a mystical contemplative ascent to God, and a Philonic theme of ecstasy, constitute one of the *theosis* themes in Gregory's theology.

The virtuous life, as a necessary requirement for the imitation of God in relation to deification, has a prominent place in Gregory. In this sense, a human person becomes "god" by moral purification, for a human being has the natural capability for such purification. The mystical spiritual ascent, accompanied by disembodiment or escape of the soul from the body, and deification go together for Gregory.[79] Love for God, in itself, is "the way to *theosis* (θεώσεως)."[80] Asceticism and celibacy are important practical elements in this process.[81] However, possessing only a natural inclination toward God is not enough to overcome the consequences of the Fall. Thus, deification is a twofold process that goes simultaneously through a human's natural inclination toward God and the salvific activity of God. Along Athanasian lines, Gregory makes a strong connection between the incarnation of Christ and *theosis.*[82] He believes that Christ is the eternal God, and Christ's human nature was deified by the Holy Spirit at the moment of incarnation.[83] In his view, through this union with humanity, Christ is both deifying and deified (θεῶσαν καὶ θεωθὲν).[84] However, Gregory's Christology is more developed and his deificational language is much stronger. In Letter 101, where Gregory refutes the Christology of Apollinarius, he states, "For that which he [Christ] has not assumed, he has not healed; but that which is united to his Godhead is also saved."[85] This Christological affirmation in Gregory reinforces the Athanasian deification "exchange formula." If Athanasius does not strongly advocate a strict parallelism between God becoming fully human in order for human beings to become fully gods, Gregory on the contrary is remarkably more forceful in establishing an egalitarian and symmetrical relationship to this formula: "I might be made god so far as he [Christ] is made man (ἵνα γένωμαι τοσοῦτον θεός, ὅσον ἐκεῖνος ἄνθρωπος)."[86] Or, in another place, Christ is "as much man for your sake as you are made god for his (τοσοῦτον ἄνθρωπον διά σε, ὅσον σὺ γίνῃ δι' ἐκεῖνον θεός)."[87] Similarly strong *theosis* affirmations are scattered throughout Gregory's orations and poetry.[88]

However, as strong as it might sound theologically, we should be aware of the power of his rhetorical style. Rosemary Radford Ruether notes, "Exaggeration was the characteristic of sophistic style, and Gregory uses these techniques so frequently that we must speak of his style as consistently hyperbolic and exclamatory."[89] Besides, in Gregory's reinforced exchange formula, similar to Athanasius, more emphasis is placed on the incarnation of God, and in addition to Athanasius, on the full humanity of Christ, rather than on human deification as such. The deification of a human as being equal with God, for Gregory, often is a matter of speech rather than an actual occurrence. His rhetoric often takes precedence over doctrinal content. It is deification, as he says occasionally, "If I dare to speak in this way."[90] Therefore in Donald Winslow's assessment, " 'deification,' both as a word and as a concept, is, like most theological language, a *metaphor.* It is, in a word, the verbal modality by which the distance between reality and our manifold attempts to describe reality is minimized, but never totally eliminated."[91]

Elsewhere on a theological note, Gregory writes, "For that which has a beginning or a progress or is made perfect, is not God, although the expressions may be used of his gradual manifestation."[92] At the end of his career and perhaps as a result of the frustration he experienced at the Second Ecumenical Council, Gregory becomes surprisingly even more pessimistic about the whole advancement of *theosis.* In his *Last Farewell* oration he says, "For the creature must be called God's, and this is for us a great thing, but God never. Otherwise I shall admit that God is a creature, if I become god, in the strict sense of the term. For this is the truth."[93] As Russell notices, "In spite of our deification through the contemplative life or through baptism, in the last analysis we become gods only by analogy."[94]

If the truth is that a human being does not become God in the ontological sense, nevertheless, because of Christ, humanity could be deified. Gregory constructs a paradoxical term for a created human being to become a created god—τυκτὸς θεὸς.[95] This literary oxymoron directly and conceptually very accurately connotes Gregory's understanding of human deification. It is more deification as assimilation into God.[96] An aspect of divine filiation is present in Gregory of Nazianzus;[97] however, it does not play as significant a role in his understanding of *theosis* as it does with Athanasius. Imitation of Christ finds a more prominent place in Gregory's approach to deification. By imitating Christ, on the one hand, a human's natural inclination toward God becomes realized.[98] On the other hand, by imitating Christ the human nature undergoes an ontological transformation—an eschatological deifying process of dematerialization.[99]

Finally, deification for Gregory is more than merely salvation; it is an ontological, transformative, spiritual process that perfects beyond the salvific restoration of the image of God in a human being.[100] *Theosis* even goes beyond being a dynamic transformation in which human nature is liberated from materiality; it is equated with the full participation in the glorification and the vision of God. The final realization of this process is accomplished in the afterlife when God will be "all in all." On that day "we are no longer what we are now, a multiplicity of impulses and emotions, with little or nothing of God in us, but are fully like God, with room for God and God alone. This is 'maturity' toward which we speed."[101]

Conclusion

For both Athanasius and Gregory, *theosis* is a dynamic transformation, the full significance of which can only be approximated in the power of theological rhetoric. In Athanasius we have a very complex theological environment where such concepts as salvation, deification, divine filiation, and sanctification are often implemented synonymously, interrelationally, and interchangeably in an explicitly trinitarian context. Certain parallelism and the exchangeability of traditional biblical language with technical deification vocabulary becomes a common phenomenon. The technical language of deification becomes established more firmly in Christian theology and receives significant popularity. Starting with Athanasius, this language obtains a specifically Christian expression both conceptually and linguistically.[102] The framework of deification for Athanasius, as well as for Gregory of Nazianzus, is a multidimensional issue, but both fathers argue for deification more than they attempt to explain the concept. At the same time we should not discard the intended shocking effect their deification statements would produce on the audience, striking their imagination with powerful and uplifting images. If during the Middle Ages a similar effect was often provoked by references to the burning flames of hell, in patristic writers the attempt to enhance the devotional zeal for spiritual life and the commitment to Christ was carried out by no less shocking, but significantly more positively oriented, affirmations. Not eternal punishment as retribution for sinful life was emphasized, but rather eternal life in God, divine therapeutic forgiveness, and the restored harmony of the whole creation. Emphasis was placed not on what would happen to people if they did not obey the divine commandments, but rather on what awaits them if they reconcile themselves with God.

In Gregory, his sophistic style, overflowing with the full set of rhetorical devices, tremendously impacts deification language. Gregory follows the pattern established by Athanasius, rhetorically reinforcing the Athanasian deification "exchange formula" and advancing his Christology. Contrary to Athanasius, Gregory puts a stronger emphasis on the spiritualization of human nature and ascent to God in Neoplatonic and Philonic terms. In Gregory, perhaps for the first time, ascetic life is explicitly presented as a prerequisite for deification. But deification of a human being is not confined to the monastic life.

Gregory of Nazianzus, more than Athanasius, demonstrates Hellenistic influences not only in his elaborate style, but also in his thought. He is perfectly aware of this fact and even appears to be proud of his Hellenistic background. At least in one instance he favors his Hellenism, views it as an element of Christian culture, and positions it as being opposite to barbarism.[103] And, at the same time, as Hanson notes, "In any event we cannot believe either that Gregory completely ignored late Greek philosophy nor that he was entirely dominated by it."[104] The Hellenistic influence on Christian theology overall is far more complex than simple borrowing and dependence of the Christian tradition on Greek philosophy. It also does not diminish the originality and distinctiveness of Christian writers, in spite of some similarities, that might reflect a common educational and cultural background with their non-Christian counterparts. Both sides, while operating often with similar concepts, express fundamental differences. They interpret realities of the world often in similar terms but from significantly different angles. Both Christian and non-Christian Greeks are the product of essentially one overarching culture, but their agendas and starting premises are different. This cultural interaction both linguistically and conceptually becomes very apparent when we study the emergence of the Christian concept of deification.

Notes

1. *Catech.* 4.16.

2. Jules Gross, *The Divinization of the Christian according to the Greek Fathers* (Anaheim, CA: A & C Press, 2002), 271–72. Originally published in French as *La divinisation du*

chrétien d'après les Pères grecs: Contribution historique à la doctrine de la grace (Paris: J. Gabalda et Cie., 1938).

3. *Or.* 27.3, PG 36:16, NPNF 2 7:285.

4. Rosemary Radford Ruether, *Gregory of Nazianzus, Rhetor and Philosopher* (Oxford: Clarendon Press, 1969), 56.

5. He uses it throughout his works at least fifty-eight times.

6. θεοποιέω and its derivative θεοποιός; *Catech.* 4.6 and 4.16.

7. Norman Russell, *The Doctrine of Deification in the Greek Patristic Tradition,* Oxford Early Christian Studies (Oxford: Oxford University Press, 2005), 168; *C. Ar.* 1.39, 2.70, 3.53.

8. *C. Gen.* 12, 21, 29.

9. *C. Gen.* 8 and 9.

10. *C. Gen.* 9 (five times), 12 (three times), 13, 18, 20, 21 (twice), 24, 27, 29 (twice), 40, 45, 47. θεοποιέω also used in pagan context in *De Inc.* 49.2 and *Vit. Ant.* 76.

11. *C. Ar.* 1.9, PG 26:29; *Syn.* 26.4, PG 26:729; *Ep. Serap.* 4.18, PG 26:665.

12. *De Inc.* 54.3; *Decr.* 14 (twice); *Syn.* 51 (four times); *C. Ar.* 1.38, 1.39 (three times), 1.42, 1.45, 2.47, 2.70 (four times), 3.23, 3.33, 3.34, 3.38, 3.39, 3.48, 3.53 (twice); *Ep. Serap.* 1.24 (twice), 1.25 (three times); *Ep. Adelph.* 4; *Ep. Max.* 2.

13. B. Otis, "Cappadocian Thought as a Coherent System," *Dumbarton Oaks Papers* 12 (1958): 105.

14. Athanasius, *Contra Gentes; and, De Incarnatione,* ed. Robert W. Thomson, Oxford Early Christian Texts (Oxford: Clarendon Press, 1971), xxi–xxii.

15. *C. Gen.* 8–9.

16. *C. Gen.* 12.

17. *C. Gen.* 12. Thomson, *Contra Gentes; and, De Incarnatione,* 34–37.

18. Is. 44:6–20; Jer. 10:1–16.

19. *C. Gen.* 13, 18, 21.

20. *C. Gen.* 9.

21. *C. Gen.* 9. Thomson, *Contra Gentes; and De Incarnatione,* 26–27.

22. His dependence on Eusebius of Caesarea in this regard was first pointed out by T. Kehrhahn, *De sancti Athanasii quae fertur Contra Gentes oratione* (Berlin, 1913). See also Thomson, *Contra Gentes; and, De Incarnatione,* xxii–xxiii, and footnotes to the text.

23. When Emperor Claudius after his death was consecrated by the Senate as *divus,* Seneca wrote his parody *Apocolocyntosis divi Claudii* [The Pumkinification of Claudius].

24. Cf. *C. Gen.* 8.

25. *Syn.* 51.

26. *C. Ar.* 3.15.

27. See Rowan Williams, *Arius: Heresy and Tradition,* rev. ed. (Grand Rapids, MI: W. B. Eerdmans, 2002), 241.

28. R. P. C. Hanson, *The Search for the Christian Doctrine of God* (Edinburgh: T & T Clark, 1988, repr., 1997), 5–6.

29. *C. Ar.* 1.9.

30. *C. Ar.* 1.16, 3.40; *Ep. Serap.* 1.23, 24; *Vit. Ant.* 74; *Ep. Adelph.* 4. See Kolp, "Partakers of the Divine Nature: The Use of 2 Peter 1:4 by Athanasius," *Studia Patristica* 17 (1982): 1018–23; Russell, "Concept of Deification," 336–37.

31. Gross, *Divinization of the Christian,* 163.

32. *De Inc.* 54.3. Thomson, *Contra Gentes; and, De Incarnatione,* 268; NPNF 2 4:65. Cf. Irenaeus, *Haer.* 5.pref.

33. *De Inc.* 16; *Decr.* 14; *C. Ar.* 1.38, 1.48, 2.61, 3.33, 3.34, 3.40; *Ep. Adelph.* 4; *Ep. Epict.* 6; *Ep. Max.* 2; *Vit. Ant.* 74.

34. John Cullen, "The Patristic Concept of the Deification of Man Examined in the Light of Contemporary Notions of the Transcendence of Man" (PhD diss., Oxford University, 1985), 91.

35. *C. Ar.* 2.69–70.
36. *Ep. Serap.* 1.24.
37. *C. Ar.* 1.38–39, 3.38; cf. *C. Ar.* 1.16; *Syn.* 51.
38. *C. Ar.* 1.45; cf. *C. Ar.* 1.42; *Decr.* 14; *Ep. Adelph.* 4.
39. *C. Ar.* 3.33.
40. *C. Ar.* 2.69, 3.34; *Decr.* 14. However, the emphasis on "physicality" in Athanasius seems to be overstated. His understanding of the final elevation of a human being is more spiritualistic, but is nevertheless different from Origen's.
41. *C. Ar.* 3.48; cf. *C. Ar.* 1.41, 2.74.
42. See Keith Norman, "Deification: The Content of Athanasian Soteriology" (PhD diss., Duke University, 1980), 6. Cf. Gross, *Divinization of the Christian,* 164.
43. Gross, *Divinization of the Christian,* 172. *C. Ar.* 1.38–39; *Ep. Serap.* 1.25.
44. *C. Gen.* 2; cf. *Syn.* 51.
45. *C. Ar.* 1.43; cf. 2.69.
46. Alan Kolp, "Participation: A Unifying Concept in the Theology of Athanasius" (PhD diss., Harvard University, 1976), 304. Cf. *C. Ar.* 3.53.
47. *C. Ar.* 3.53.
48. Russell, *Doctrine of Deification,* 172. Cf. *Ep. Serap.* 1.25.
49. *C. Ar.* 1.44, 2.59, 2.67, 3.53.
50. C. R Strange, "Athanasius on Divinization," *Studia Patristica* 16:6 (1985): 343.
51. *Decr.* 14; cf. *C. Ar.* 3.19–20.
52. *Decr.* 14, PG 25:448, NPNF 2 4:159. Cf. *C. Ar.* 3.19.
53. Cullen, "Patristic Concept of Deification," 95.
54. *Syn.* 53; cf. *Ep. Afr.* 7.
55. *Ep. Afr.* 7; *C. Ar.* 1.9, 1.39, 2.59, 3.19–20; *Ep. Serap.* 2.4; *Syn.* 51, 53.
56. *De Inc.* 4; *C. Ar.* 1.9, 1.39, 3.19–20; *Ep. Serap.* 1.4; *Ep. Afr.* 7. Russell, "Concept of Deification," 332.
57. For the overview of Gregory's style I follow Ruether, *Gregory of Nazianzus,* esp. 55–128, who in turn follows Marcel Guignet, *Saint Grégoire de Nazianze et la rhetorique* (Paris: A. Picard, 1911).
58. Ruether, *Gregory of Nazianzus,* 58.
59. For θεοποιέω, see *Or.* 2.73, 40.39. Migne's edition of Gregory's works has the third instance in *Or.* 31.29, PG 36:168. However, a more recent critical edition, as Russell correctly points out, uses θεοῦν instead of θεοποιοῦν, SC 250:334; "Concept of Deification," 382. Russell himself misses one instance where Gregory applies this word in *Or.* 40.39, SC 358:288. For instances of θεοποιός, see *Or.* 3.1 and *Carm.* 2.2.7.69.
60. *Or.* 2.22, 28.13, 28.14, 30.14, 30.21, 31.4.
61. *Or.* 2.73, 36.5, 43.48 and *Carm.* 1.2.1.210; and *Or.* 1.5, 7.22, 7.23, 14.23, 17.9, 25.2, 29.19, 30.3, 30.21, 36.11, 39.17, 40.45, 42.17.
62. *Carm.* 1.1.3.4; *Carm.* 1.2.14.92; and *Carm.* 1.2.9.132.
63. Or. 31.28, 34.12, 38.11, 38.13 (twice), 40.42, 41.9 (twice), 45.7, 45.9 (twice); *Ep.* 6.3, 101.21, 101.46; *Carm.* 1.2.2.560, 1.2.10.61 (twice), 1.2.10.630, 1.2.10.922, 1.2.17.2, 2.1.34.83, 2.2.7.190.
64. *Or.* 4.71, 4.124, 11.5, 17.9, 21.2, 23.12, 25.2, 25.16, 39.16; *Carm.* 1.2.34.161.
65. Russell, *Doctrine of Deification,* 215.
66. *Or.* 4.71, PG 35:593; cf. *Or.* 21.2, PG 35:1084.
67. *Or.* 25.16, PG 35:1221.
68. *Or.* 39.16, PG 36:353. Russell, *Doctrine of Deification,* 215.
69. *Carm.* 2.2.3.1–6.
70. *Carm.* 2.2.3.6, PG 37:1480.

71. *Or.* 28.14, *Or.* 36.11, SC 318:264, FC 107:228. θεοὶ γένεσθε is translated in FC as "behave like gods." Cf. *Ep.* 140.1.

72. *Or.* 3.1, SC 247:242.

73. *Or.* 2.22, 2.73, 25.2.

74. I was able to locate only six such references: *Or.* 4.59, 28.13, 28.14, 28.15, 40.39; *Carm.* 2.2.7.69–72.

75. *Or.* 4.59, SC 309:166. See also *Carm.* 2.2.7.281–85.

76. *Or.* 40.39. Cf. Basil, *Reg. br.* 63 and *Hom. Ps.* 28.2; Gregory of Nyssa, In *Eccl.* 8, *Gregorii Nysseni Opera,* ed. W. Jaeger (Leiden: E. J. Brill, 1952–), 5:428.

77. *Or.* 28.13–14.

78. *Or.* 4.71.

79. *Or.* 11.5, 21.2, 38.11–45.7; *Carm.* 1.2.2.556–61.

80. *Carm.* 1.2.34.161, PG 37:957.

81. *Carm.* 1.2.10.630, 1.2.10.920–22, 1.2.17.1–2

82. *Or.* 30.3, see also *Or.* 30.14, 30.21, 40.45; *Ep.* 101.46–47; *Carm.* 1.1.10.5–6, 1.2.14.90–92.

83. *Or.* 25.16. Cf. *Or.* 30.3, 40.42; *Or.* 30.21; *Carm.* 1.1.10.56–61.

84. *Carm.* 1.1.10.56–61, PG 37:469. Cf. *Or.* 30.21.

85. *Ep.* 101.32, PG 37:181–84, NPNF 2 7:440.

86. *Or.* 29.19, PG 36:100, NPNF 2 7:308.

87. *Or.* 40.45, SC 358:306, NPNF 2 7:377.

88. *Or.* 7.23, 14.23, 30.14; *Carm.* 1.2.14.90–92.

89. Ruether, *Gregory of Nazianzus,* 70.

90. *Or.* 11.5 (PG 35:837), 14.23 (PG 35:888), 36.11 (SC 318:264). Cf. *Or.* 2.55 (SC 247:164), 38.7 (SC 358:116).

91. Donald Winslow, *The Dynamics of Salvation: A Study in Gregory of Nazianzus* (Cambridge, MA: Philadelphia Patristic Foundation, 1979), 193.

92. *Ep.* 101.24, PG 37:180–81, NPNF 2 7:440.

93. *Or.* 42.17, SC 384:86, NPNF 2 7:391.

94. Russell, *Doctrine of Deification,* 222.

95. *Carm.* 1.2.9.132, PG 37:678.

96. Gross, *Divinization of the Christian,* 197.

97. *Or.* 7.23, 14.23.

98. *Or.* 17.9.

99. *Or.* 7.23.

100. *Or.* 38.4, 16–17.

101. *Or.* 30.6, PG 36:112, *Faith Gives Fullness to Reasoning: The Five Theological Orations of Gregory Nazianzen,* intro. and commentary Frederick W. Norris, trans. Lionel Wickham and Frederick Williams (Leiden: E. J. Brill, 1991), 266. This passage is omitted in NPNF.

102. For instance, Athanasius coins and secures for exclusively Christian usage θεοποίησις, and Gregory introduces the classical Christian designator for deification θέωσις.

103. *Ep.* 62.

104. Hanson, *Christian Doctrine of God,* 868.

Divinization as Perichoretic Embrace in Maximus the Confessor

Elena Vishnevskaya

BY THE END OF THE SIXTH CENTURY, THE IDEA OF DIVINIZATION WAS FAR from a novel concept in the Eastern patristic milieu, where it had gradually evolved into a potent designation for the faith community in the process of spiritual ascent and, in particular, the final state of heavenly beatitude. But it was a masterful mediation of Maximus the Confessor (580–662) that assured the idea of divinization a position of distinction in Eastern Orthodox theology and spirituality.

Maximus's remarkable legacy has drawn much scholarly attention, and this essay is another attempt to grasp the intense complexity and enduring significance of the Confessor's thought, particularly his understanding of divinization. Here I explore the implications of Maximus's Christological *perichoresis,* or coinherence, for religious experience that transfigures human existence. The *perichoresis* of God and the believer, which has its prototype in the *perichoresis* of the hypostatic union in the person of the Logos, can be seen, in Maximus, as an organic relation of human freedom and divine grace, as fulfilled in divinizing union.

The Hypostatic Union in the Person of the Logos

The Chalcedonian Christological postulation of "one hypostasis in two natures" leads Maximus to aver the reciprocity of Christ's natures, which—with the purity of both safeguarded—interpenetrate and exchange their attributes in the person of the Logos.[1] In the Confessor's view, "The ineffable union of the human nature and the divine, whereby God suffers and humanity descends from heaven with the divine, expresses the most excellent communication according to the exchange of properties which naturally belong to each nature of the unique Christ and Son."[2]

For Maximus, the *perichoretic* movement, inherent to divinization of Christ's flesh, is undeniably commenced by the divine nature of the Logos who "united our nature to himself in a single hypostasis, without division and without confusion."[3] However, a one-sided penetration, that is, solely on the part of divine nature, seems inconceivable to Maximus who consistently espouses the dynamic role of human nature in the *perichoretic* process. Maximus affirms the vitality of the response of human nature, which, in virtue of the Godhead's magnanimous giving of itself, is able to penetrate the divine—not just passively reciprocate by surrendering itself to the other—and communicate to it human properties. Thus, the Confessor is able to speak of the "whole power of his humanity, with all its openness to suffering, quite unimpaired by the union,"[4] as subsumed, along with the breadth of divinity, in the Logos. In fact, Maximus stresses the unscathed integrity of both natures, which interpenetrate in the person of Christ: "And what could be more amazing than the fact that, being God by nature, and seeing fit to become man by nature, he did not defy the limits of either one of the natures in relation to the other, but instead remained wholly God while becoming wholly human? Being God did not hinder him from becoming man, nor did becoming man diminish his divinity. He remained wholly one amid both, since he preserved both natures, and was truly existent in both natures at once."[5]

The Confessor rejects any Monophysite implication suggesting that the two natures interact to a radically uneven degree in virtue of the weight of divine will overwhelming the human element. Maximus accepts that the divine and the human penetrations cannot be alike—they differ at a root level, in conformity with the essences of their respective natures. Nonetheless, what Maximus does establish is the active reciprocity on the part of both natures, which are harmonized in the hypostasis of the Logos. Only because each nature eagerly advances through the other, one is able to speak of their exchange of properties as a fruit of mutual disposition and inclination. Thus, in *Opuscula* 9, Maximus insists that one should not see Christ as "either realizing divine doings according to God but by the intermediary of His body, along with the soul and the mind, united to Him in the hypostasis, or realizing human things according to the human being but with an authority and infinite power and without being submitted to the necessity."[6]

Divinization as Mutual Interpenetration of God and Humanity

Similarly, in his soteriological reflection, Maximus appears to approach divinization as a doing of two mutually engaged parties that will to form a consequential union. Considering divinization from the perspective of the *perichoresis* of God and the human being, Maximus carefully explores two corresponding movements, which reflect a somewhat balanced alignment between the two diametrically different orders: as God, in charity, enters the human realm and fulfills his economy, the human being reciprocates by embracing the preordained divine plan and partaking of the Triune life.[7]

The Confessor's idea of the *perichoresis* of Creator and creature confirms that these are relational terms, and each is understood better in the context of the other. The mutual partaking of the other bears witness to, on the one hand, a God who, through the Incarnation, is fully invested in the human being, the recipient of the abundance of divine grace, and, on the other, the believer who is free, by nature, to orient his or her being toward God and become like him in divinization. Accordingly, Maximus celebrates the supralogical reciprocal interpenetration of the ontologically polar: "It is in this blessed and most holy embrace that is accomplished this awesome mystery of a union transcending mind and reason by which God becomes one flesh and one spirit with the Church and thus with the soul, and the soul with God."[8]

The reciprocity between the ontologically distinct God and creature is presented, by the Confessor, as "identity in difference" (ἡ ταὐτότης ἐν ἀμφοτέροις τῃ ὁμοιότητι διάφορος).[9] In fact, Maximus's entire thought—from Christology to cosmology—appears to center on the ideas of the all-encompassing unity and safeguarded identity, that is, for Maximus, unity and difference are mutually predicated. In *Mystagogia* 1, the Confessor asserts that as "cause, beginning, and end" of the created order, "[God] leads all beings to a common and unconfused identity of movement and existence." As their guiding "principle," God, for Maximus, "abolishes and dims all their particular relations considered according to each one's nature, but not by dissolving or destroying them or putting an end to their existence. Rather [he] does so by transcending them and revealing them, as the whole reveals its parts."[10]

The Confessor turns to Christology to explicate the dynamics of unity and distinction within the divine-human relationship. While staunchly maintaining the ontological difference (διαφορά) between the two natures of Christ, that is, contending that divinity and humanity are naturally, or essentially, unlike, Maximus asserts that there is no distance to cause separations within the person of the Logos.[11] Unimpeded, divinity and humanity interpenetrate and exchange that which is particular to each nature. Similarly, God and the human being, the infinite and the finite, join in divinizing union by prevailing over the differences that generally divide and alienate the opposites. With the distance between them safeguarded and yet surmounted, God and the redeemed enjoy a *perichoretic* communion, which exemplifies, for Maximus, both a numinous bridging of the gulf and freedom from any confusion.

Reciprocity of Love in the Divine-Human Relationship

On account of the shared love, which acts as a magnet, drawing them toward union, "God and man are paradigms (παραδείγματα) one of another."[12]

Maximus explains in *Mystagogia* 2: "For it is necessary that things which manifest each other bear a mutual reflection in an altogether true and clear manner and keep their relationship intact."[13] The active reciprocity of love in the divine-human relationship is quintessential for the Confessor: "Love is . . . a great good, and of goods the first and most excellent good, since through it God and man are drawn together in a single embrace (ἔχοντα συνάπτουσα)."[14] Infused with the divine ways of love, the faithful willfully exchange self-love for the love toward God and the created order. Thus, "the interpenetration of love is: to love the Lord God with all the heart and soul and power, and the neighbor as oneself."[15]

For the Confessor, love is the key opening up secret passages through which the *nous* travels to and discovers God, and God, in his turn, gathers the *nous* to himself: "As the light of the sun attracts the healthy eye, so does the knowledge of God draw the pure mind to itself naturally through love."[16] Thus, love, in Maximus's view, is an active force bequeathed to humans from above, lived out and perfected by those seeking their end in God. Hereof, Larchet observes that "participating in the principal quality of God, the believer acquires the divine property par excellence," and since most divine properties are subsumed in love, the Christian partakes of them all.[17] For Maximus, participation in God is always divinizing; hence, the divinizing role of love.[18]

Maximus's reflection on the nature of love in the context of divinization evolves from his conception of ecstasy. The Confessor builds on Pseudo-Dionysius, for whom God, "the lover," gives himself away to his creation, "the beloved." Hence, in ecstasy, God is "carried outside of himself in the loving care he has for everything."[19] Nonetheless, God is also the beloved, who draws the creation, the lover, toward himself.[20] The soul's going out toward the object of its ultimate desire is humanly willed, and the believer's resolve to abandon the self for the sake of the supra-logical union with God is indispensable for the authentic divine-human reciprocity. Hence, the soul, which "dwells entirely in God alone in a loving ecstasy, and has rendered itself by mystical theology totally immobile in God,"[21] emerges as Maximus's ideal of spiritual life. For the Confessor, the stillness of the soul is transforming—unperturbed by the natural order left behind, the soul penetrates and partakes of the divine things and, in the end, is divinized: "The ages of the flesh, in which we now live . . . are characterized by activity, while the future ages in the Spirit, which are to follow the present life, are characterized by the transformation of humanity in passivity. Existing here and now, we arrive at the 'end of the ages' as active agents and reach the end of the exertion of our power and activity. But in the ages to come we shall undergo by grace the transformation unto deification and no longer be active but passive."[22]

Maximus repeatedly underscores the weight of both poles in the divine-human synergy, for each necessitates the other in realizing full reciprocity. For the Confessor, the mutual interpenetration in ecstatic love is inseparable from the concurrence of the divine gift of the image and the human response in appropriation of divine likeness.

Dynamics of Image and Likeness

Maximus appears convinced that the gratuitous gesture of God's giving of the image should be joined by the believer's willful cooperation in the cultivation of goodness, whereby "[the soul] will be beautiful and splendid, having become similar to him as much as it can."[23] Contemplating "the ultimate condition that will one day prevail," Maximus reiterates Gregory of Nazianzus, who spoke of "mingl[ing] our god-formed mind and divine reason to what is properly its own."[24] For Maximus, the final rising of the *nous* to God is humanly willed and divinely realized. Thus, in a reciprocal movement, "the image returns to the archetype (ἡ εἰκὼν ἀνέλθῃ πρὸς τὸ ἀρχέτυπον)," who, in turn, imparts to it the divine life: "The mind is deemed another 'god,' insofar as in its habitude it experiences, by grace, that which God himself does not experience but 'is' in his very essence."[25]

Only a restored image can communicate to the soul divine perfection; realization of likeness to God in fulfillment of divine-human reciprocity becomes, therefore, an existential endeavor. Maximus asserts that the divine image, obscured by the Fall, will once again be pure and radiate the brilliancy of the Archetype, who facilitates the divine-human *perichoresis* by creating space for human freedom to fully realize itself in the movement of nature, that is, in emulating God himself. After all, by "unit[ing] us in himself," Christ "showed us properly and truly to be simply human beings, thoroughly transfigured in accordance with him, and bearing his intact and completely unadulterated image, touched by no trace at all of corruption."[26] In the reciprocity between the Archetype and the divine image, God and the faithful are mutually manifest: "The creator of humankind appears as human, through the undeviating likeness of the deified to God in the good so far as is possible to humankind."[27]

For Maximus, the essence of all ascetic endeavor is "to struggle to attain God alone," that is, to attain the divine likeness and recover the divine image. With a new type of love, cleansed of any attachment to the self, the human being "will embrace God and manifest the one who loves God to be God himself."[28] The Confessor affirms that love for God is evident in the practice of virtues, or intentional progress in divine likeness, and "in accordance with such love the dignity of sonship, the divinely-fitting gift of continual converse with God in his presence, is granted."[29] As an expression of true human freedom, the redeemed bear fruit of the ascetic life graced by the

Spirit and, therefore, fulfill their part in divine-human reciprocity: "[God] gives adoption by giving through the Spirit a supernatural birth from on high in grace, of which divine birth the guardian and preserver is the free will of those who are thus born. By a sincere disposition it cherishes the grace bestowed and by a careful observance of the commandments it adorns the beauty given by grace."[30]

For Maximus, realization of human life in similitude to God, or divinization, subsumes the ideal of divine inhabitation, which manifests the incarnation of Christ in human virtues.[31] The Confessor opines that to open up human existence for Christ's incarnation within, or welcome his interpenetration of one's life, the believer needs to "purify [his or her] mind of anger, resentment, and shameful thoughts," that is, undergo a spiritual cleansing. Only "then you will be able to know the indwelling of Christ."[32] Maximus avers that the soul "becomes united to the God of all in imitating what is immutable and beneficent in his essence and activity by means of its steadfastness in the good and its unalterable habit of choice."[33] Here, the Confessor appears to propose a human initiative, manifesting a natural movement of free will—even though kindled by the divine love—which is readily reciprocated by God.[34]

Maximus appears to speak of a transformed type of human beings—the divinely energized, rising above nature in a new *tropos* of existence that renders them divinized. He writes in *Ad. Thal.* 22:

> The modes of the virtues and the principles of those things that can be known by nature have been established as types and foreshadowings of . . . future benefits. It is through these modes and principles that God, who is ever willing to become human, does so in those who are worthy. And therefore whoever, by the exercise of wisdom, enables God to become incarnate within him or her and, in fulfillment of this mystery, undergoes deification by grace, is truly blessed, because that deification has no end. For he who bestows his grace on those who are worthy of it is himself infinite in essence, and has the infinite and utterly limitless power to deify humanity. Indeed, this divine power is not yet finished with those being created by it; rather, it is forever sustaining those . . . who have received their existence from it. Without it they could not exist.[35]

Hence, for Maximus, the believer crosses the threshold of ordinary existence and penetrates into the divine by cultivating goodness and thereby fostering the embodiment of Christ within. A virtuous human life is a divine mode of being, while Christ's gracious epitomizing of the righteous living is a human mode of being: "The one Word of God is the substance of virtue in each person. For our Lord Jesus Christ himself is the substance of all the virtues. . . . It is evident that every person who participates in virtue as a matter of habit unquestionably participates in God, the substance of virtues."[36] On the one hand, the believer cannot gain a divine standing in any other way but by advancing in a divine mode of being, or adopting likeness to God in operation: "The 'salvation' of which [the Apostle Peter in 1 Pt 4:18] speaks is the fullest grace of deification bestowed on the worthy and utterly attained by one who clings to divine realities at the highest level."[37] On the other hand, God could not—or rather chose not to—penetrate into the human order in any other way but by identifying with the human condition through self-emptying. In *Mystagogia* 24, Maximus writes of this reciprocal participation in the other: "The one who can do good and who does it is truly God by grace and participation because he has taken on in happy imitation the energy and characteristic of his own doing good. And if the poor man is God, it is because of God's condescension in becoming poor for us and in taking upon himself by his own suffering the sufferings of each one and 'until the end of time,' always suffering mystically out of goodness in proportion to each one's suffering."[38]

Without any violation of the principle of nature, the visage of humanity comes to resemble the divine Archetype, who, in turn, appears human anew in those who are divinized. Thus, Maximus asserts, "[God] has granted to you the splendor of virtue, which deifies you by grace, by sublimating your human characteristics. In you virtue also makes God condescend to be human, by your assumption, so far as is possible for humans, of divine properties."[39] This reciprocity of divine embodiment in the virtues and human imitation of the One embodied represents, for Maximus, a coinherent communion par excellence, whereby "God lifts up man to the unknowable as much as man manifests God, invisible by nature, through his virtues."[40]

The Divinizing Sacraments

Sacramental life of the church is another milieu that Maximus considers integral to the divinizing process. In *Mystagogia* 1, the Confessor writes, "The holy Church of God is an image of God because it realizes the same union of the faithful with God. As different as they are by language, places, and customs, they are made one by it through faith."[41] For Maximus, God penetrates the human order by communicating grace through the sacraments; the believing community reciprocates by partaking of the transforming media of the divine plenitude bequeathed in the church. The sacramental grace is conferred upon all; its appropriation, however, is a matter of individual response and, particularly, one's spiritual perspicacity.

Maximus explains that in the Eucharist, "we have grace and familiarity which unites us to God himself. By holy communion of the spotless and life-giving mysteries we are given fellowship and identity with him by participation in likeness, by which man is deemed worthy from man to become God."[42] Thus, through the eucharistic gifts, the Logos inhabits the soul of the believer and spiritually assimilates it to Divinity. In eating Christ's flesh and drinking his blood, the faithful are infused with the divine properties that render them like God, save for the essence of being. For the Confessor, the Eucharist "transforms into itself and renders similar to the causal good by grace and participation those who worthily share in it. To them is there lacking nothing of this good that is possible and attainable for men, so that they also can be and be called gods by adoption through grace because all of God entirely fills them and leaves no part of them empty of his presence."[43]

Maximus's treatment of baptism appears especially replete with the idea of synergy. God bestows the riches of baptismal grace—from liberation from the bondage to sin to spiritual illumination to the gift of participation in the divine beatitude—upon Christian believers, who respond by sustaining and nourishing the conferred grace in their lives.[44] Hence, Maximus writes in *Mystag.* 24: "In making each of us who conducts himself worthily as best he can in Christ, [the holy Church of God] brings to light the grace of adoption which was given through holy baptism in the Holy Spirit and which makes us perfect in Christ. . . . [L]et us with all our strength and zeal render ourselves worthy of the divine gifts in pleasing God by good works."[45]

Larchet observes that, for the Confessor, "the incorruptibility recovered in baptism is potential; its actualization, though accomplished by grace, presupposes the participation of our will in the mortification of passions and the practice of virtues."[46] Hereof, Maximus writes in *Ad Thal.* 6: "The inclination to sin does not disappear as long as [the baptized] will it. For the Spirit does not give birth to an unwilling will . . . but converts the willing will toward deification."[47] Thus, the accord of the wills is paramount for the efficacious mutual interpenetration of the divine and the human in the sacrament of rebirth.

Maximian sacramental reflection shows that "the movement of man and the world towards God, which was begun (or restored) by the incarnation of Christ, continues in the Church."[48] Indeed, the Confessor appears to affirm that the penetrative movement of creature into Creator is real and compelling, and is reciprocated by God in the church, through the sacraments, and also, as we have examined, on a number of other levels. Hence, in an effort to offset any extant Monophysite implications of a narrow conception of *perichoresis* as an exclusively divine activity that pervades and wholly consumes the human realm, Maximus unreservedly maintains the authenticity and balance of the divine-human reciprocity.

Human Response and Resultant Transformation through Participation

Certainly, the divine initiative and its incontestable authority remain, for the Confessor, a solid premise of the divinizingly *perichoretic* relationship between God and the human being: "Confirming the truth of His Incarnation, He has become everything for us and has done everything for us out of His own free will, without distorting His essence, or its perfect and natural properties, even though he divinized them, like the iron made red-hot, having rendered our essence wholly theurgic, having penetrated (περιχωρήσας) it in an utmost manner by virtue of the union, having become one with our essence without confusion, according to the same and sole hypostasis.[49] After all, the created order "is 'called and indeed is' a 'portion of God'" because their *logoi* are enclosed in "the Logos that preexisted in God."[50] Heedful of the absolute divine preeminence, Maximus, nonetheless, establishes and highlights a dynamic response on the part of the believer: "we are active agents," who are kinetically oriented toward God by nature and thereby realize our natural movement in cooperation with divine grace.[51] For the Confessor, "The perfect soul is the one whose affective drive is wholly directed to God."[52] The believer "penetrates (εἰσδὺς) into God, Himself, and [is] wholly made and translated to the whole."[53] The divinized human being "inserts himself [or herself] wholly in God alone (μὲν τῷ Θεῷ μόνῳ δι' ὅλου ἐνθέμενος),"[54] who attends to the faithful along the path of God-becoming. Thus, "by an inclination towards God they might be securely deified by grace."[55]

For Maximus, human penetration into God "takes place on behalf of the whole creation."[56] Since "with us and through us [Christ] encompasses the whole creation,"[57] the human being, once entrusted with the role of the cosmic intermediary, is still called, following the divine lead, to gather the created order and raise it, unified, to the Creator. God incarnate guides the human being in this quest, for "by nature [Christ] is the fashioner and provider of all, and through himself draws into one what is divided, and abolishes war between beings, and binds everything into peaceful friendship and undivided harmony."[58] Thus, in the reciprocity of love, God will permeate the cosmos and munificently introduce it to the divine Pleroma: "God will penetrate (χωρήσαντος τοῦ Θεοῦ) everything in general and each in particular, filling up everything with a measure of His grace."[59]

In asserting the realization of the divinizing union of God and creature, ultimately benefiting the latter, the Confessor takes pains to avoid any implication of a respective *ontological* transformation as a result of the partaking of the other. Time and again Maximus asserts that the redeemed are "divinized by love and made like him by participation in an indivisible identity to the extent that this is possible."[60] Hence, the Confessor avers that God "did not do away with the natural operation of those who will suffer this (deification), . . . but show[ed] the supersubstantial power as alone effective of deification and become (the possession) of the deified by grace."[61] Further, in *Amb.* 20, Maximus writes: "The being and being called god man has neither of nature nor from relation; but he becomes and is named so by institution (θέσις) and grace. For the grace of institution is entirely without relations and has no power whatsoever in nature receptive of it."[62] Thus, for the Confessor, "The whole of the human being is interpenetrated (περιχωρήσας) by the whole of God and becomes all that God is, excluding identity of essence. The human being receives to itself the whole of God and, as a prize for ascending to God, inherits God Himself."[63]

Mutual Movement of Wills

We have seen that in all of his reflections on divinization, Maximus is guided by a double volitional perspective: propelled by their united wills, God and the human being reciprocally move toward each other in a mutual surge of love. Commenting on the type of human will that responds to divine will, the Confessor writes, "And this they wisely call the will, without which the human nature cannot be. For the natural will is 'the power that longs for what is natural' and contains all the properties that are essentially attached to the nature."[64] Living out the natural will, "we are able to have one inclination and one will (μίαν γνώμην καὶ θέλημα) with God and with one another, not having any discord with God or one another."[65] Maximus states that reciprocity of the divine and the human wills allows for the intercommunication of the divine and the human attributes, whereby God and the believer become one and also the other: "So the human being is made God, and God is called and appears as human, because of the one and undeviating wish (in accordance with the will) and movement of both."[66] The *perichoretic* harmonization of the divine and the human wills leads to the oneness of operation, which is pregnant with soteriological implications: "A seal conforms to the stamp against which it was pressed. . . . [I]t lays hold of God's power or rather becomes God by divinization and delights more in the displacement of those things perceived to be naturally its own. Through the abundant grace of the Spirit it will be shown that God alone is at work, and in all things there will be only one activity, that of God and of those worthy of kinship with God. God will be *all in all* wholly penetrating (περιχωρήσαντος) all who are his in a way that is appropriate to each."[67]

If there is anything that may frustrate the reciprocity between God and creature, that is obviously the individual or gnomic will, which leads humans away from the source of their spiritual nourishment toward that which gives immediate gratification. The Confessor insists that sin corrupts one's faculty of willing, rather than a natural order as established by God: "Our Lord and God Jesus Christ, manifesting his love for us, suffered for all mankind and granted to all equally the hope of resurrection, though each one renders himself worthy either of glory or punishment."[68] Maximus affirms the promise, or potentiality, of filial adoption and the ideal of its fulfillment through the actuality of one's spiritual endeavor.[69]

The Confessor appears well aware that any coercion of human powers would render divine-human union, including its fruit of divinization, flawed. Thus, for Maximus, participation in the divine life necessitates "a close cooperation of the believer with the divine grace and presupposes a continuous exercise of the individual freedom of choice."[70] While the *logos* of human nature, along with human potencies, is preordained by God, it is within the free choice of the human being to either conform one's *tropos* to the *logos* of nature or assume a *tropos* contrary to nature. Thus, in *Amb.* 65, Maximus affirms that God will dwell wholly in those "who by choice serve the *logos* of their being according to nature."[71] The Confessor also insists on the submission of free will to the *logos* of nature that results in "the reconciliation of God with nature."[72]

The fruition of the threefold movement from being to well-being to ever-being, epitomizing God's purpose for the created order, is also based on the reciprocity of the divine and the human wills, particularly a proportionate synchronization of a willful human cooperation with the divine intention. The Confessor writes, "I am speaking of a firm and steadfast disposition, a willing surrender, so that from the one from whom we have received being we long to receive being moved as well. It is like the relation between an image and its archetype."[73] Once the faithful are wholly oriented and inclined toward God, he moves and energizes them.[74]

For Maximus, creation participates in God by "essential and habitual fitness (οὐσιώδη καὶ ἑκτικὴν ἐπιτηδειότητα)."[75] Hereof, Tollefsen notes that the "essential fitness" appears to indicate that "a created nature is fit to receive the divine activity to a certain degree," in accordance with the principle of nature. However, "if the creature moves or acts as it is designed to do, it becomes fit to receive the activity of God to a still higher degree according to the *logoi* of well-being and eternal well-being,"[76] that is, the creature acquires the "habitual fitness." Further, Maximus speaks of "graced nature" and "graced activity"; the former, "generally speaking," while the latter, "particularly speaking."[77] Larchet observes that "this distinction allows [Maximus] to maintain the antinomy proper to the synergy."[78]

Conclusion

Everything considered, Maximus's idea of divinization subsumes a genuinely reciprocal relation between the believer and God, or rather the entire Trinity whereby the divine Persons, while three, operate and will as one. Maximus firmly upholds the Trinity, itself a "personal reality of perichoretic activity and supreme union. It is the mystery of love and the mystery of freedom which is the mystery of God, three in one."[79] And it is in keeping with this trinitarian ineffability that God, in the greatest act of self-donation, interpenetrates into human existence and, at the same time, opens himself up for human participation, that is, the trinitarian Godhead creates conditions for mutual indwelling in divinization.[80] The believer reciprocates in love by entering into the life of the divine Persons—even while here on earth—and fulfills the human vocation of divinization as intended by God from eternity.

Maximus's soteriological insights, as embodied in the idea of divinization, illumined complex Christological questions of his day, thereby vindicating the fullness and integrity of both the divine and the human natures in a hypostatic union, as maintained by the Council of Chalcedon. As a result of his ardent struggle to champion Chalcedonian Christology in the face of the imperial opposition, the Confessor underwent degrading trials, torture, mutilation, and the final exile that ended in his death. Accordingly, Maximus's life became a tribute to the Orthodox dogma of the undivided Christ, wholly divine and wholly human, exhibiting two wills and two energies, through which he accomplishes the "fullness of grace of divinization."[81]

Notes

1. *Opusc.* 16, PG 91:189D. The following abbreviations are used in this essay: *Ad Thal.—Quaestiones ad Thalassium; Amb.—Ambiguorum liber; CC—Capita de charitate; CT—Capita theologiae et oeconomiae; Ep.—Epistula; Mystag.—Mystagogia; Opusc.—Opuscula theologica et polemica; Orat. Dom.—Expositio orationis Dominicae.* Where possible, reference to English translations follows original source references.
2. Ibid. 20, PG 91:240A.
3. *Amb.* 7, PG 91:1097B, PPS 70.
4. Ibid. 5, CCSG 48:33, 286–87, *MC* 179.
5. Ibid. 42, PG 91:1320B, PPS 84.
6. *Opusc.* 9, PG 91:120A.
7. Hans Urs von Balthasar, *Cosmic Liturgy: The Universe according to Maximus the Confessor,* trans. Brian E. Daley, 3rd ed. (San Francisco: Ignatius Press, 2003), 281. Cf. Andrew Louth, *Denys the Areopagite,* Outstanding Christian Thinkers (Wilton, CT: Morehouse-Barlow, 1989), 115: "Maximus rarely uses Denys's Neoplatonic language of procession and return, speaking instead of God's movement towards us in incarnation and self-emptying and our movement of return and response as deification."
8. *Mystag.* 5, PG 91:680D–681A; *SW* 194.
9. *S. Maximi scholia in librum de ecclesiastica hierarchia* 4, PG 4:153A, quoted in von Balthasar, *Cosmic Liturgy,* 235.
10. *Mystag.* 1, PG 91:665A, *SW* 186.
11. *Ep.* 12, PG 91:472D; Ibid. 15, PG 91:556A, 561AB; *Opusc.* 20, PG 91:232D.
12. *Amb.* 10, PG 91:1113B, *MC* 101.
13. *Mystag.* 2, PG 91:669D, *SW* 189.
14. *Ep.* 2, PG 91:401C, *MC* 90.
15. Ibid.

16. *CC* 1.32, PG 90:968A, *SW* 38. Cf. ibid. 1.9, PG 90:964A: "If the life of the mind is the illumination of knowledge and this is born of love for God, then it is well said that there is nothing greater than love." *SW* 36.

17. Jean-Claude Larchet, *La divinisation de l'homme selon saint Maxime le Confesseur* (Paris: Cerf, 1996), 481, citing *CC* 2.52.

18. Cf. *Amb.* 20, PG 91:1241B; ibid. 21, PG 91:1249B.

19. *De divinis nominbus* 4.13, PG 3:712AB, cited in Maximus *Amb.* 71, PG 91:1413AB. Pseudo-Dionysius continues in the same place: "He is, as it were, beguiled by goodness, by love, and by yearning and is enticed away from his transcendent dwelling place and comes to abide within all things, and he does so by virtue of his supernatural and ecstatic capacity to remain, nevertheless, within himself." *Pseudo-Dionysius: The Complete Works,* trans. Colm Luibheid, CWS (Mahwah, NJ: Paulist Press, 1987), 82.

20. *Amb.* 23, PG 91:1260C. Cf. Panayotis Christou, "Maximos Confessor on the Infinity of Man," in *Maximus Confessor, Actes du Symposium sur Maxime le Confesseur,* ed. F. Heinzer and C. von Schönborn (Fribourg: Editions Universitaires, 1982), 263: "[The divine] is moved with the aim of causing an inward relation of eros and agape in those who are capable of receiving this activity and moves as naturally attracting the desire of those who are moved for this reason."

21. *CT* 1.39, PG 90:1097C, *SW* 135.

22. *Ad Thal.* 22, CCSG 7:141, 69–79, PPS 117.

23. *Mystag.* 5, PG 91:680A, *SW* 193.

24. *Amb.* 7, PG 91:1077B, PPS 54; *Orat.* 28.17.

25. *Amb.* 7, PG 91:1077AB, PPS 53–54; *Ad Thal.* 6, CCSG 7:69, 32–71, 35, PPS 104.

26. *Amb.* 41, PG 91:1312A, *MC* 160.

27. *Ep.* 2, PG 91:401C, *MC* 90.

28. Ibid., PG 91:397B, *MC* 87.

29. *Amb.* 10, PG 91:1140B, *MC* 116.

30. *Orat. Dom.,* CCSG 23:32, 97–102, *SW* 103.

31. See *CC* 4.70; The Confessor builds on Origen's doctrine of the Logos's manifold incarnations—whether in Scripture, the world, or the virtuous Christian believer.

32. *CC* 4.76, PG 90:1068A, *SW* 84.

33. *Mystag.* 5, PG 91:676A, *SW* 191.

34. See *Ad Thal.* 15, CCSG 7:103, 35–40.

35. *Ad Thal.* 22, CCG 7:143, 101–14, PPS 118.

36. *Amb.* 7, PG 91:1081D, PPS 58.

37. *Ad Thal.* 61, CCSG 22:103, 303–6, PPS 141.

38. *Mystag.* 24, PG 91:713B, *SW* 212. Cf. 2 Cor 8:9; Mt 28:20.

39. *Ep.* 2, PG 91:408B, *MC* 93.

40. Christou, "Infinity of Man," 267, citing *Amb.* 10, PG 91:1113BC.

41. *Mystag.* 1, PG 91:668BC, *SW* 187–88.

42. Ibid. 24, PG 91:704D, *SW* 207.

43. Ibid. 21, PG 91:697A, *SW* 203.

44. Larchet, *La divinisation de l'homme,* 418, citing *Mystag.* 24, PG 91:712B.

45. *Mystag.* 24, PG 91:712B, *SW* 211.

46. Larchet, *La divinisation de l'homme,* 421, citing *Ad Thal.* 6, CCSG 7:69, 9–13. Note an Aristotelian influence.

47. *Ad Thal.* 6, CCSG 7:69, 20–23, PPS 103–4.

48. V. M. Zhivov, "The Mystagogia of Maximus the Confessor and the Development of the Byzantine Theory of the Image," *St. Vladimir's Theological Quarterly* 31, no. 4 (1987): 370.

49. *Opusc.* 4, PG 91:60B.

50. *Amb.* 7, PG 91:1080B, PPS 55. Cf. Pseudo-Dionysius, *De divin. nomin.* 5.5–7; 1 Jn 3:1.

51. *Ad Thal.* 22, CCSG 7:141, 82, PPS 117; Cf. *CC* 3.35, PG 90:1028C: "Impurity of soul means not acting according to nature." *SW* 66.
52. Ibid. 3.98, PG 90:1048A, *SW* 75.
53. *Amb.* 10, PG 91:1141B.
54. Ibid. 7, PG 91:1084C.
55. Ibid. 10, PG 91:1412C, *MC* 166.
56. Lars Thunberg, *Microcosm and Mediator: The Theological Anthropology of Maximus the Confessor,* Acta Seminarii Neotestamentici Upsaliensis, no. 25 (Lund: C.W.K. Gleerup, 1965), 444.
57. *Amb.* 41, PG 91:1312A, *MC* 160.
58. Ibid., PG 91:1313B, *MC* 162.
59. *Opusc.* 1, PG 91:25B.
60. *Mystag.* 13, PG 91:692D, *SW* 200.
61. *Opusc.* 1, PG 91:33C–36A, quoted in Polycarp Sherwood, *The Earlier Ambigua of Saint Maximus the Confessor and His Refutation of Origenism,* Studia Anselmiana, vol. 36 (Rome: Orbis Catholicus, Herder, 1955), 135.
62. *Amb.* 20, PG 91:1237AB, quoted in Sherwood, *Earlier Ambigua,* 132.
63. Ibid. 41, PG 91:1308B.
64. *Opusc.* 3, PG 91:45D, *MC* 193. Cf. *Opusc.* 26, PG 91:276C.
65. *Ep.* 2, PG 91:396CD, *MC* 87.
66. Ibid., PG 91:401B, *MC* 90.
67. Cf. 1 Cor 15:28; *Amb.* 7, PG 91:1076C, PPS 52–53.
68. *CC* 1.71, PG 90:976C, *SW* 43.
69. See *Ad Thal.* 6, CCSG 7:69, 8–13, PPS 103.
70. Larchet, *La divinisation de l'homme,* 658.
71. *Amb.* 65, PG 91:1392D.
72. *Orat. Dom.,* CCSG 23:65, 667, *SW* 115.
73. *Amb.* 7, PG 91:1076B, PPS 52.
74. See *Opusc.* 20, PG 91:233D–236A.
75. *Amb.* 7, PG 91:1080B.
76. Torstein Tollefsen, "Did St. Maximus the Confessor Have a Concept of Participation?" in *Studia Patristica* 37 (2001): 623. Cf. Lars Thunberg, "Spirit, Grace and Human Receptivity in St. Maximus the Confessor," in *Studia Patristica* 37 (2001): 615.
77. *Ad Thal.* 61, CCSG 22:99, 237–40, PPS 139.
78. Larchet, *La divinisation de l'homme,* 422.
79. George C. Berthold, "The Cappadocian Roots of Maximus the Confessor," in *Maximus Confessor, Actes du Symposium sur Maxime le Confesseur,* ed. F. Heinzer and C. von Schönborn (Fribourg: Editions Universitaires, 1982), 56.
80. Jean Mouroux, *The Christian Experience: An Introduction to a Theology,* trans. George Lamb (New York: Sheed and Ward, 1954), 329.
81. *Ad Thal.* 61, PG 90:640A.

Paradise as the Landscape of Salvation in Ephrem the Syrian

Thomas Buchan

Introduction

By the fourth century, the early Christian conception of salvation as deification had come to occupy a profoundly influential place in the theological reflection of the Eastern Greek-speaking churches. The language of deification is present in the writings of earlier Christian theologians—most notably Irenaeus—and faithfully reiterated and developed in the writings of subsequent theologians, including patristic luminaries such as the Cappadocian Fathers and countless others in the Orthodox tradition.[1] The doctrine nonetheless received what may justifiably be regarded as a kind of classic articulation in Athanasius of Alexandria's treatise *On the Incarnation of the Word of God.* Athanasius's succinct and (still) frequently cited assertion that Christ "was made man that we might be made God" remains one of the most compact, incisive, and memorable formulations of the view of human salvation as deifying union with God.[2] For all of his subsequent influence and prominence, however, Athanasius was not the only fourth-century defender of the faith of Nicaea with a talent for concisely and potently expressing this perspective. East of Alexandria, and, if Theodoret of Cyrrhus is to be believed, "unacquainted with the language of the Greeks," Ephrem the Syrian was crafting his own striking expressions of the concept of salvation as the divinization or deification of humanity.[3]

A close contemporary of Athanasius, Ephrem was born in the Mesopotamian city of Nisibis, probably in the latter half of the first decade of the fourth century. He died, according to the sixth-century *Chronicle of Edessa,* on June 9, 373—just over a month after the bishop of Alexandria. No less than Athanasius, Ephrem regarded Christ's Incarnation as the central event of the Christian mystery, the divinely initiated and accomplished bridging of the ontological chasm between the Creator and his fallen creation for the purpose of reconciliation and human salvation. No less than Athanasius, Ephrem conceived of salvation in Christ as the deification of humanity. In contrast to Athanasius, however, Ephrem frequently reiterated the reciprocal relationship between the Incarnation and humanity's deification.

As a result, one may find brief expressions of Ephrem's view of salvation as deification scattered throughout his prose and poetic writings. For all their particularity as expressions of a distinctively Syriac theological context, the strong resemblance these statements bear to the familiar dictum of Athanasius cannot be denied. What is perhaps the most strikingly similar example can be found in the *Hymns on Faith* where Ephrem wrote of Christ: "He gave us divinity / we gave Him humanity."[4] This, however, is by no means the only statement of its kind to be found in Ephrem's work. Concise articulations of the "exchange formula" of deification can also be found in Ephrem's *Hymns on the Nativity* where he asserts that Christ "descended and became one of us that we might become heavenly" and proclaims in praise of Christ, "Blessed is He Who came in what is ours and mingled us into what is His."[5] Elsewhere, in his prose *Homily on Our Lord,* somewhat more extensive statements of the salvific and deifying effect of the Incarnation are in evidence where Ephrem offers "Glory to the One Who took from us in order to give to us, so that we should all the more abundantly receive what is His by means of what is ours,"[6] and in the following passage:

> It is He who was begotten of Divinity,
> according to His nature,
> and of humanity,
> which was not according to His nature,
> and of baptism,
> which was not His habit;
> So that we might be begotten of humanity,
> according to our nature,
> and of divinity,
> which is not according to our nature,
> and of the Spirit,
> which is not our habit.[7]

In addition to such concise statements, one also finds in Ephrem's works an abundance of more elaborate articulations of his conception of human salvation as deification. Very frequently his complex meditations on the pattern of salvation made use of the paradise narrative of Genesis 1–3 in a way that emphasized the unity of God's works of creation and redemption in the economy of human salvation. Ephrem's view of paradise and his theological use of Genesis 1–3 have been the subjects of a significant degree of academic interest and inquiry, and over the course of the last fifty years a number of helpful and illuminating explications of these aspects of the Syrian poet's thought have appeared in scholarly literature.[8] For Ephrem, the importance of the biblical narrative of paradise in theological reflection exceeded a mere reckoning of the events of the creation of the world and humanity, the origins of sin, and the expulsion of Adam and Eve from the Garden of

Eden. Ephrem, of course, would not have denied that the paradise narrative contained an account of these primordial events of the history of divine-human interaction, but he was also the heir to what Sebastian Brock has described as "a much richer understanding of Paradise [that] had grown up within Judaism, finding expression in apocalyptic works such as the First Book of Enoch (perhaps of the second century BC); in these writings Paradise is understood as representing both the primordial and the eschatological state at the end of time, for it has now also become the abode of the righteous."[9] As a result, Ephrem returned again and again to the paradise narrative of Genesis, not only in his commentary on that biblical book and his *Hymns on Paradise,* but also in many places in his other writings including the *Commentary on the Diatessaron,* the *Homily on Our Lord,* and the collections of hymns *On the Nativity, On Virginity, On the Church,* and *On Nisibis.* Throughout these works, Ephrem appropriated and adapted elements of the biblical text of Genesis 1–3 in order to explicate the trajectory of the history of salvation and the shape of the Christian life. In what follows, we will consider Ephrem's theological uses of the paradise narrative as a paradigm of deification, an interpretive framework for the history of redemption, and a spiritual geography for the conceptualization of deifying union with God as the goal of the Christian life.

The Paradise Narrative and the Divine Intent for Humanity's Deification

One important aspect of Ephrem's thought concerning paradise has to do with its location relative to the ordinary space and time of human existence and history. On the one hand, some of Ephrem's discussion of the origins of the Garden in his *Commentary on Genesis* would seem to suggest that paradise is part of the earthly creation, "planted" on the third day along with the rest of the earth.[10] Elsewhere, however, and especially in his *Hymns on Paradise,* Ephrem made it clear that, although it was somehow adjacent to the currently inhabited earth, paradise was not, strictly speaking, merely earthly. According to Ephrem, "the sight of Paradise is far removed / and the eye's range cannot attain to it."[11] The seeming inconsistency of these two perspectives should not be taken as a shortcoming of Ephrem's thought, but seen as an intentionally deployed strategy to describe the simultaneous situation of paradise both in moral and spiritual relation *to* and in temporal and spatial distinction *from* the inhabited earth. In Ephrem's writings, paradise occupies and operates as a liminal space: it is the part of the created cosmos intended to serve as the venue for divine and human communion and as such it is special and set apart in relation to the rest of creation.

Ephrem's view of the special status of paradise relative to ordinary space and time can be seen clearly in light of his conception of paradise as a mountain of cosmic proportion. Though Eden was not depicted as a mountain in the biblical text of Genesis 1–3, other portions of the Hebrew Scriptures that identified Eden and Zion contributed to the emergence of a concept of paradise as a mountain in the Jewish literature of the intertestamental period and, later, in the writings of Ephrem and some other early Syriac-speaking Christians.[12] Ephrem envisioned paradise as dwarfing all other mountains, its summit being higher than every other summit.[13] In Ephrem's thought, the circular base of the paradisiacal mountain encompassed both the land and the sea of the terrestrial earth.[14] Throughout his *Hymns on Paradise,* Ephrem provided diverse depictions of the mountain's topography and altitudinal subdivisions, depicting the peak of paradise as the seat of the Shekinah of God's presence.[15] Taken, not as a description of mundane geography, but as an aspect of his symbolic model of the cosmos, Ephrem's view of paradise indicates the proximity of Eden to all of the terrestrial earth even as it is located "beyond the borders of the phenomenal."[16]

Ephrem's vision of the paradisiacal mountain is significant relative to his conception of the divine intent for communion and fellowship with humanity, providing vivid symbols of vertical distance as a principal metaphor of divine-human communion. Within the Garden, Ephrem imagined that the Tree of Knowledge was planted halfway up the mountain, while the Tree of Life was located, with the Shekinah, at the mountain's peak. The trees were placed in this way, not arbitrarily, but with respect to God's intent toward Adam and Eve, as becomes clear in Ephrem's explication of the narrative of Genesis 1–3. In his *Commentary on Genesis,* Ephrem indicated the special status of Adam within God's created order, calling attention especially to "the dominion that Adam received over the earth and over all that is in it that constitutes the likeness of God who has dominion over the heavenly things and the earthly things."[17] Elsewhere, Ephrem enumerated the "many ways" in which God honored Adam: "first, in that it was said, *God formed him with His own hands and breathed life into him;* God then set him as ruler over Paradise and over all that is outside of Paradise; God clothed Adam in glory; and God gave him reason and thought so that he might perceive the majesty [of God]."[18] Clothed in glory, Adam was given rule over creation, over all within and all outside of paradise.[19] Humanity's original condition was one designed for active participation as, in Ephrem's words, "a second god over Creation."[20] Nevertheless, according to Ephrem, "when God created Adam, He did not make him mortal, nor did He fashion him immortal, so that Adam by either keeping or transgressing the commandment, might acquire from one of the trees, the [life] that he preferred."[21] Humanity was thus created by God in an exalted state reflective of God's own image and glory. Though not perfect, humanity was perfectible, endowed with free will, and charged by God with keeping a single commandment. In Ephrem's thought, the purpose of God's decree was clear:

> Even though God, in His goodness, had given them everything else, He wanted, in His justice, to give them immortal life that was to be conferred by their eating from the tree of life. Therefore, God set down for them a commandment. It was not a great commandment relative to the great reward that He had prepared for them; He withheld from them one tree, only enough for them to be under a commandment. God gave them all of Paradise so that they would be under no constraint to transgress the law.[22]

Originally situated midway up the paradisiacal mountain, Adam and Eve were intended, through their steadfast obedience to God's commandment in the face of temptation, to receive the reward of the fruit of the Tree of Life. Since the Tree was located at the summit of paradise, they would ascend the mountain, moving into closer communion with the divine, drawing near to the Shekinah of God's presence at the paradisiacal peak.[23] Thus, according to Ephrem, paradise was designed and ordered as an environment specifically conducive to humanity's attainment to divine perfection and immortality. It was God's intent that Adam and Eve should be "deified," that, by means of the proper application of their divinely bestowed free will, they should actively seek and freely choose "the immortal life that was to be conferred by their eating from the tree of life."[24] This divine intent for humanity's deification is made abundantly clear in Ephrem's commentary on what would have been conferred on Adam and Eve had they overcome the temptation of the serpent.

> If the serpent had been rejected along with sin, Adam and Eve would have eaten from the tree of life and the tree of knowledge would not have been withheld from them; from the one they would have gained infallible knowledge and from the other they would have received immortal life. They would have acquired divinity with their humanity, and if they had acquired infallible knowledge and immortal life, they would have possessed them in those same bodies. Thus, by its counsel, the serpent brought to naught everything that was soon to have become theirs. . . . Thus, the serpent, through the divinity that he promised them, prevented them [from receiving] divinity.[25]

Through the misapplication of their wills, however, Adam and Eve thwarted the divine purpose for humanity's perfection, transgressing the commandment and falling into sin. Consequently, humanity was exiled from Eden, denied access to the Tree of Life, and prevented from reentering the Garden by God's placement of an angelic sentry described by Ephrem as a "living fence."[26]

The Paradise Narrative as an Interpretive Framework for the History of Redemption

Though expelled from the Garden and barred from reentry in Adam and Eve, humanity was not entirely cut off from paradise and its promise of participation in the divine life. According to Ephrem, humanity remained in relative nearness to paradise, living in the foothills below the mountain.[27] In the time of Noah's flood, when human beings were found "unworthy to be neighbors to Paradise"[28] because of their continuing sin, God more distantly separated humanity from its relative proximity to the Garden of Eden. Yet, despite the dislocation of humanity from the environment intended for their communion with God, Ephrem regarded spiritual access to paradise as remaining available by means of God's grace, made visible in a variety of historical events that served as simultaneous reminders and promises of humanity's divinely intended destiny. On the one hand, Ephrem found assurance of the possibility of human access to paradise in the biblical figures of Enoch and Elijah, both of whom he regarded as examples of the successful human evasion of death and inheritance of the immortal life of divinity by virtue of a righteousness achieved through the proper application and use of God's good gift of free will.[29] Elsewhere, Ephrem identified Noah's ark and God's gift of the law on Sinai as typological representations of paradise of a sort that reached their Old Testament zenith in God's presence to Israel first in the Tabernacle and later in the Temple. Both of these locations reiterated the spiritual topography of paradise and rendered it present on the earth by virtue of the Shekinah's residence between the cherubim of the ark of the covenant.[30] The paradise narrative, granted a paradigmatic status, thus provided Ephrem with an interpretive framework for the events of the history of redemption.

For Ephrem, however, the Incarnation of Christ and his work of redemption represented the fulfillment of all the types and symbols of the Old Testament by which God had revealed aspects of the divine intent for the salvation of humanity. Accordingly, Ephrem's use of the paradise narrative as a hermeneutic of salvation can be clearly seen in his discussion of the redemption and deification of humanity in Christ. Interpreting the events of Christ's Incarnation, life, death, and resurrection by means of terms appropriated from Genesis 1–3, Ephrem viewed salvation in Christ as the recovery of all that was lost in Adam.

In Ephrem's thought, Adam, formed of the dust of the earth and the breath of life, was not only the first man, but also the symbol and source of the whole of humanity. It was Adam's status as the representative of the human race in its impaired potential for perfection and communion with God that provided Ephrem with a potent image for Christ's identification with humanity in his Incarnation and work of salvation. "Clothed" in Adam, according to one of Ephrem's favorite descriptions of the Incarnation, and by extension, "clothed" in fallen humanity, Christ made himself uniquely capable of restoring his fallen creation. Articulating this symbolic relationship, Ephrem wrote:

> All these changes did the Merciful One make,
> stripping off glory and putting on a body;
> for He had devised a way to reclothe Adam
> in that glory which Adam had stripped off.
> Christ was wrapped in swaddling clothes,
> corresponding to Adam's leaves,
> Christ put on clothes, instead of Adam's skins;
> He was baptized for Adam's sin,
> His body was embalmed for Adam's death,
> He rose and raised up Adam in His glory.
> Blessed is He who descended, put on Adam and ascended![31]

The renewal of the image of God in Adam/humanity, begun in Christ's Incarnation, was carried further in the events of his earthly life and ministry. In his baptism, Christ opened the way for Adam's primordial robe of glory, in which he had originally been clothed in paradise, to be restored to humanity.[32] In his temptation and obedience on the mountain in the wilderness, Christ rehearsed the events and reversed the effects of Adam's temptation and disobedience on the mountain of paradise, rehabilitating human free will and reiterating the proper paradigm for its use.[33] However, it was above all in his death on the cross and resurrection from the dead that Christ returned Adam/humanity to the life of Eden. Making recourse to the narrative of Genesis 1–3, Ephrem summarized Christ's restoration of humanity to paradise as follows:

> Adam was heedless as the guardian of Paradise,
> for the crafty thief stealthily entered;
> leaving aside the fruit—which most men would covet—
> he stole instead the Garden's inhabitant!
> Adam's Lord came out to seek him; He entered Sheol and found him there,
> then led and brought him out to set him once more in Paradise.[34]

Ephrem's conception of humanity's return to Eden in Christ entailed not merely a restoration to their primordial perfectibility, but a consummation of God's original salvific and deifying intent. As Sebastian Brock has observed, Ephrem's works testify to his understanding of the restoration of Adam to life in paradise as the achievement of humanity's deification. One example of this is to be found in the sixty-ninth of Ephrem's *Hymns on Nisibis:*

> The Most High knew that Adam wanted to become a god,
> so He sent His Son who put Him on in order to grant him his desire.[35]

Another example of Adam's redemption as deification is provided in Ephrem's *Hymns on Virginity.*

> Freewill succeeded in making Adam's beauty ugly,
> for he, a man, sought to become god.
>
> Grace, however, made beautiful his deformities
> and God came to become a man.
>
> Divinity flew down
> to draw humanity up,
>
> For the Son had made beautiful the deformities of the servant
> and so he has become a god, just as he desired.[36]

The Paradise Narrative as the Spiritual Geography of the Church

In his theological reflection on the salvation of humanity in Christ, Ephrem made use of another element of the paradise narrative of Genesis 1–3, transposing it onto the history of redemption as a point of orientation that would enable Christians to locate themselves and move freely within the spiritual geography of the paradise to which they had been returned in Christ. Identifying the cross of Christ with the Tree of Life, Ephrem wrote:

> Greatly saddened was the Tree of Life
> when it beheld Adam stolen away from it;
> it sank down into the virgin ground and was hidden—
> to burst forth and reappear on Golgotha;
> humanity, like birds that are chased,
> took refuge in it
> so that it might return them to their proper home.
> The chaser was chased away, while the doves
> that had been chased
> now hop with joy in Paradise.[37]

As the Tree of Life, Christ's cross was, for Ephrem, the source of humanity's intended immortality and communion with God. Accordingly, as the body of Christ, the Eucharist was seen as the fruit of the Tree. In his *Hymns on the Nativity* Ephrem wrote concerning Christ:

> For His death is like a root inside the earth,
> His resurrection like the summit in Heaven,
> His words [extend] in every direction like branches,
> and His fruit [is] His body for those who eat it.[38]

Situated at the center of the sacramental life of the church, the Eucharist, understood as the fruit of the Tree of Life, provided the pivotal feature of the spiritual topography of the ecclesiological paradise. Ephrem's vision of the church as Eden was beautifully rendered in his *Hymns on Paradise:*

God planted the fair Garden, He built the pure Church;
upon the Tree of Knowledge He established the injunction.
He gave joy, but they took no delight, He gave admonition, but they were unafraid.
In the Church He implanted the Word
which causes rejoicing with its promises, which causes fear with its warnings:
he who despises the Word, perishes, he who takes warning, lives.
The assembly of saints bears resemblance to Paradise:
in it each day is plucked the fruit of Him who gives life to all;
in it, my brethren, is trodden the cluster of grapes, to be the Medicine of Life.
The serpent is crippled and bound by the curse,
while Eve's mouth is sealed with a silence that is beneficial
—but it also serves once again as a harp to sing the praises of her Creator.

Among the saints none is naked, for they have put on glory,
nor is any clad in those leaves or standing in shame,
for they have found, through our Lord, the robe that belongs to Adam and Eve.
As the Church purges her ears
of the serpent's poison, those who had lost their garments,
having listened to it and become diseased, have now been renewed and whitened.

The effortless power, the arm which never tires,
planted this Paradise, adorned it without effort.
But it is the effort of freewill that adorns the Church with all manner of fruits.
The Creator saw the Church and was pleased;
He resided in that Paradise which she had planted for His honor,
just as He had planted the Garden for her delight.[39]

The radiant image of the church presented in the preceding stanzas of Ephrem's poetry may incline skeptics to regard his vision of the church as paradise as overly optimistic, or worse, an example of naive triumphalism. It is important to remember that Ephrem, as a Christian living in the Roman Empire in the fourth century, was well acquainted with the imperfections of the church. As a promoter of Nicene Orthodoxy Ephrem was keenly aware of challenges posed to Christian unity by doctrinal disputes and factionalism, and he frequently engaged in theological polemics against "Arians" as well as the heresies of Marcion, Bar Daisan, and Mani, which had originated closer to Ephrem's Mesopotamian home.[40] Additionally, as one who viewed the Roman emperor as an important and saintly patron, Ephrem's hopes for the imperial church's preservation and security were repeatedly frustrated, first during the reign of Julian the Apostate (361–63), and later during the reign of Valens (364–78), whose “arianizing” tendencies ran counter to Ephrem’s Nicene convictions.[41] Ephrem’s awareness of the church’s own shortcomings can be clearly seen in his hymn *On the Church,* which now prefaces his *Hymns Against Julian:*

> The kings who used to provide shade, cooled us in the droughts.
> We ate their fruits; we were ungrateful for their branches.
> Our soul luxuriated in the bounties and shadows.
> Our mouth raved and attacked our Creator.
> Battles in the shadows we waged with our investigations.
> He has stripped away our shade to make us mindful of our drought![42]

Ephrem, therefore, did not consider the church in the world to be entirely free from sin or its effects—only in the eschaton would the human susceptibility to evil be fully eradicated. Though it was not yet the eschatological fulfillment of humanity’s salvation, the church was symbolically and sacramentally identified with Eden because it provided the venue for redeemed humanity’s proleptic participation in the eschatological paradise. In Ephrem’s thought, paradise—the environment intended by God for the deification of humanity—had been opened by Christ and made accessible to a humanity for whom the image of God was renewed in baptism, free will was restored in the imitation of Christ, and the life of immortality was accessible in the eucharistic fruit of the Tree of Life. Mapping the life of the church in terms of the story of paradise in Genesis 1–3, Ephrem provided Christians with a narrative context and a spiritual geography by means of which they might conceptualize the process of salvation as deification and participation in the divine life.

Conclusion

Ephrem the Syrian, no less than his better-known Greek-speaking neighbors to the West, was a theologian for whom the mystery of salvation in Christ consisted in humanity’s deification through communion with God.

In a number of brief but clear statements, which strongly resemble the better-known dictum of Athanasius, Ephrem’s conception of deification can be most fully appreciated in light of his interpretation and appropriation of elements from the paradise narrative of Genesis 1–3. For Ephrem, paradise was provided by God as the environment intended to foster and promote human union with the Divine Trinity, not only “in the beginning,” but throughout the course of the history of salvation. Though direct access to the Tree of Life, the source of immortality, was lost as the result of Adam and Eve’s transgression and refusal of the divinity they would have attained through obedience, access to paradise and the Tree of Life was restored through the Second Adam's redeeming passion and resurrection and through Christ's sacramental presence in the church's Eucharist. Though humanity's return to paradise would not be fully realized until the eschaton, Christians could proleptically participate in the life of Eden Regained in the paradise of the church.

Notes

The following translations are used, unless otherwise indicated: HNat, HVirg—K. E. McVey, *Ephrem the Syrian: Hymns,* CWS (Mahwah, NJ: Paulist Press, 1989); CGen, SdDN—K. E. McVey, ed., *St. Ephrem the Syrian: Selected Prose Works; commentary on Genesis, Commentary on Exodus, Homily on Our Lord, Letter to Publius,* trans. E. G. Mathews, Jr. and J. P. Amar, FC 91 (Washington, DC: Catholic University of America Press, 1994); HPar—S. P. Brock, *St. Ephrem the Syrian: Hymns on Paradise* (Crestwood, NY: St. Vladimir's Seminary Press, 1990); HFaith—P. S. Russell, *Ephraem the Syrian: Eighty Hymns on Faith* (unpublished manuscript, 1995); HNis—*Selections Translated Into English From the Hymns and Homilies of Ephraim the Syrian,* trans. J. Gwynn, NPNF 2 13 (repr. Peabody, MA: Hendrickson, 1994). Original language sources are as follows: HNat—E. Beck, ed., *Des Heiligen Ephraem des Syrers Hymnen de Nativitate (Epiphania),* CSCO 186, Scriptores Syri 82 (Louvain: Secrétariat du CorpusSCO, 1959); HVirg—E. Beck, ed., *Des Heiligen Ephraem des Syrers Hymnen de Virginitate,* CSCO 223, Scriptores Syri 94 (Louvain: Secrétariat du CorpusSCO, 1962); CGen—Tonneau, ed., *Sancti Ephraem Syri in Genesim et in Exodum Commentarii,* CSCO 152, Scriptores Syri 71 (Louvain: Imprimeri Orientaliste L. Curbecq, 1955); SdDN—E. Beck, ed., *Des Heiligen Ephraem des Syrers Sermo de Domino Nostro,* CSCO 270, Scriptores Syri 116 (Louvain: Secrétariat du CorpusSCO, 1966); HPar—E. Beck, ed., *Des Heiligen Ephraem des Syrers Hymnen de Paradiso und Contra Julianum,* CSCO 174, Scriptores Syri 78 (Louvain: Secrétariat du CorpusSCO, 1957); HFaith—E. Beck, ed., *Des Heiligen Ephraem des Syrers Hymnen de Fide,* CSCO 154, Scriptores Syri 73 (Louvain: Imprimerie Orientaliste L. Curbecq, 1955); HNis—E. Beck, ed., *Des Heiligen Ephraem des Syrers Carmina Nisibena (Zweiter Teil),* CSCO 240, Scriptores Syri 102 (Louvain: Secrétariat du CorpusSCO, 1963).

1. Irenaeus of Lyons, *Against All Heresies,* in ANF 1:526, 527: "Following the only true and steadfast Teacher, the Word of God, our Lord Jesus Christ, who did, through his transcendent love, become what we are, that He might bring us to be even what He is Himself" (book 5, preface); "the Lord thus has redeemed us through His own blood, giving His soul for our souls, and His flesh for our flesh, and has also poured out the Spirit of the Father for the union and communion of God and man, imparting indeed God to men by means of the Spirit, and on the other hand, attaching man to God by His own incarnation." (book 5.1.1); cf. Irenaeus of Lyons, *On the Apostolic Preaching,* trans. J. Behr (Crestwood, NY: St. Vladimir's Seminary Press, 1997), 65: "[40] Thus, in this way, is the Word of God preeminent in all things, for He is true man and 'Wonderful Counsellor and Mighty God,' calling man back again to communion with God, that by this communion with Him we may receive participation in incorruptibility." Also see Gregory Nazianzen, *Oration II: In Defense of His Flight to Pontus,* in NPNF 2 7:209: "The scope of our art is to provide the soul with wings, to rescue it from the world and give it to God, and to watch over that which is in His image, if it abides, to take it by the hand, if it is in danger, or restore it, if ruined, to make Christ dwell in the heart by the Spirit: and, in short, to deify, and bestow heavenly bliss upon, one who belongs to the

heavenly host" (22); Gregory of Nyssa, *The Great Catechism,* in NPNF 2 5:502: "But the descent into the water, and the triune immersion of the person in it, involves another mystery. For since the method of our salvation was made effectual not so much by His precepts in the way of teaching as by the deeds of Him Who has realized an actual fellowship with man, and has effected life as a living fact, so that by means of the flesh which He assumed, and at the same time deified, everything kindred and related may be saved along with it, it was necessary that some means should be devised by which there might be, in the baptismal process, a kind of affinity and likeness between him who follows and Him Who leads the way" (35).

2. Athansius, *Dei Incarnatione Verbei Dei* 54.3, in NPNF 2 4:65.

3. Brock, *Hymns on Paradise,* 73.

4. HFaith 5.17, P. S. Russell, *Ephraem the Syrian: Eighty Hymns on Faith* (unpublished manuscript, 1995), 20; cf. 22.

5. HNat 3.16; 21.12.

6. SdDN 10.1, McVey, *Selected Prose Works,* 285; cf. Beck, *Sermo de Domino Nostro,* 8.

7. "Homily on Our Lord" 2.1, in McVey, *Selected Prose Works,* 276; cf. Beck, *Sermo de Domino Nostro,* 2.

8. See, for example: G. A. Anderson, "The Cosmic Mountain: Eden and Its Early Interpreters in Syriac Christianity," in *Genesis 1–3 in the History of Exegesis: Intrigue in the Garden,* ed. G. A. Robbins (Lewiston, NY: E. Mellen, 1998), 187–224; G. A. Anderson, *The Genesis of Perfection: Adam and Eve in Jewish and Christian Imagination* (Louisville, KY: Westminster John Knox Press, 2001); T. Bou Mansour, *La Pensée Symbolique de Saint Ephrem le Syrien,* no. XVI (Kaslik, Lebanon: Bibliothèque de l'Université Saint-Esprit, 1988); Brock, *Hymns on Paradise;* J. Daniélou, "Terre et Paradis chez les Pères de l'Eglise," *Eranos-Jahrbuch* 22 (1953): 433–72; T. Kronholm, "The Trees of Paradise in the Hymns of Ephrem Syrus," *Annual of the Swedish Theological Institute* 12 (1978): 48–56; T. Kronholm, *Motifs From Genesis 1–11 in the Genuine Hymns of Ephrem the Syrian with Particular Reference to the Influence of Jewish Exegetical Tradition,* Coniectanea Biblica – Old Testament Series 11 (Lund, Sweden: CWK Gleerup, 1978); R. Murray, "The Lance Which Re-opened Paradise," *Orientalia Christiana Periodica* 39 (1973): 224–34, 401; I. Ortiz de Urbina, "Le Paradis eschatologique d'après Saint Ephrem," *Orientalia Christiana Periodica* 21 (1955): 467–72; N. Sed, "Les hymnes sur Paradis de Saint Ephrem et les traditions juives," *Le Museon* 81 (1968): 455–501; P. Yousif, "Le croix de Jésus et le Paradis d'Éden," *Parole de l'Orient* 6/7 (1975/76): 29–48.

9. Brock, *Hymns on Paradise,* 49.

10. CGen 2.5.1–2. Here, Ephrem wrote, "After Moses spoke of how Adam was so gloriously fashioned, he turned to write about Paradise and Adam's entry therein saying, *The Lord had previously planted Paradise in Eden and there He placed Adam whom He had fashioned.* Eden is the land of Paradise and [Moses] said *previously* because God had [already] planted it on the third day. He explains this by saying, *the Lord caused every tree that is pleasant to the sight and good for food to sprout forth from the earth.* And to show that he was talking about Paradise, [Moses] said, *and the tree of life was in the midst of Paradise, and the tree of the knowledge of good and evil.*"

11. HPar 1:8.

12. See Anderson, "The Cosmic Mountain," 192ff., and Brock, *Hymns on Paradise,* 51–52.

13. HPar 1.4. "With the eye of my mind I gazed upon Paradise; the summit of every mountain is lower than its summit." Cf. Beck, *Hymnen de Paradiso,* 2.

14. HPar 1.8–9.

15. HPar 1.8, 2.6, 3.3–4, 4.1; and 2.11.

16. Mansour, *La Pensée Symbolique,* 155.

17. CGen 1.29.1.

18. CGen 2.4.
19. CGen 2.10.3, 2.14.2, 2.17.2; CGen 2.10; and CGen 2.17.2.
20. CGen 2.10; ibid. 2.26.1.
21. Ibid. 2.17.3.
22. Ibid. 2.17.5.
23. HPar 2.11.
24. Ibid. 12.15–18; CGen 2.17.5.
25. CGen 2.23.1.
26. Ibid. 2.35. It is clear in Ephrem's *Commentary on Genesis* that the expulsion of humanity from paradise was an act of mercy as much as punishment. According to Ephrem, if Adam and Eve had eaten from the Tree of Life after their sin, the pains incurred would have been rendered eternal. Therefore, "God took Adam far away from there lest he also incur loss from the tree of life just as he had been harmed by the tree of knowledge." CGen 2.35.3; also see 2.36.
27. CGen 2.36.
28. CGen 3.5.
29. HPar 1.10.
38. CGen 5.2.1. Ephrem wrote concerning Enoch, "[Moses] wrote about Enoch who was pleasing to God and *was not.* Some say that while Adam was looking at him God transported him to Paradise lest [Adam] think that Enoch was killed as was Abel and so be grieved. This was so that [Adam] might be comforted by this just son of his and that he might know that for all who were like this one, whether before death or after the resurrection, [paradise] would be their meeting-place." CGen 5.2.1. Concerning Elijah, see HNat 14.16–17. Ephrem speaks of Elijah's departure from earthly life for the life of paradise in the following terms: "Since Elijah repressed / the desire of his body, he could withhold the rain / from the adulterers. Since he restrained his body, / he could restrain the dew from the whoremongers / who released and sent forth their streams. / Since the hidden fire, bodily desire, / did not prevail in him, the fire of the high place / obeyed him, and since on earth he conquered / fleshly desire, he went up to [the place] where / holiness dwells and is at peace." HNat 14.16–17. Also see NPNF 2 13:196–97. In the thirty-sixth of his *Hymns on Nisibis,* Ephrem (through the personification of a somewhat perplexed Death) meditates both on Enoch and Elijah's attainment to paradise and the relative rarity of the achievement. "But there were two men (for I do not lie) / whose names are missing in Sheol. / For Enoch and Elijah did not come to me. / I have sought them in all of creation—even where Jonah descended / I descended and searched and they were not there. And though I suppose that into Paradise / they have entered and escaped, a strong cherub guards it. / The ladder that Jacob saw! Perhaps they have entered heaven by it. / Who has measured the sand of the sea / and spilled only two grains? / In this harvest where everyday there labor / diseases as harvesters, I alone carry / the sheaves and heap them up. Those who bind sheaves, in haste / leave behind handfuls. Vintagers overlook clusters / but only two grapes have escaped me / in that great vintage which I alone have plucked." HNis 36.7–8. Cf. Beck. *Carmina Nisibena,* 10–11.
30. HPar 2.10–13 and HPar 3; 15.7, 8.
31. HNat 23.13. S. P. Brock, *The Luminous Eye: The Spiritual World Vision of Saint Ephrem the Syrian,* CS 124 (Kalamazoo, MI: Cistercian Publications, 1992), 85.
32. HVirg 16.9. McVey, *Hymns,* 331. cf. Beck, 57.
33. HNis 35.4, HVirg 12, 13, 14, NPNF 2, 13:193. cf. Beck, ed. *Carmina Nisibena,* 4.; McVey, *Hymns,* 310–24. Cf. Beck, *Hymnen de Virginitate,* 38–51.
34. HPar 8.10.
35. HNis 69.12. Brock, *Luminous Eye,* 152. Cf. Beck, *Carmina Nisibena,* 112.
36. HVirg 48.15–18. Brock, *Luminous Eye,* 152–53. Cf. Beck, *Hymnen de Virginitate,* 157.

37. HVirg 16.10. Brock, *Hymns on Paradise,* 60–61. Cf. Beck, *Hymnen de Virginitate,* 57–58.

38. HNat 26.4.

39. HPar 6.7–10.

40. For more on Ephrem's controversial and polemical writings, see S. H. Griffith, "Setting Right the Church of Syria: St. Ephraem's Hymns against Heresies," in *The Limits of Ancient Christianity: Essays on Late Antique Thought and Culture in Honor of R. A. Markus.* ed. W. E. Klingshirn and M. Vessey, 97–114 (Ann Arbor: University of Michigan Press, 1999); P. S. Russell, *St. Ephraem the Syrian and St. Gregory the Theologian Confront the Arians* (Kottayam, Kerala: St. Ephrem Ecumenical Research Institute, 1994).

41. For more on Ephrem's imperial theology and the challenges posed to it by the ways in which both Julian and Valens failed to conform to the Syrian poet's expectations, see S. H. Griffith, "Ephraem, the Deacon of Edessa, and the Church of the Empire," in *Diakonia: Studies in Honor of Robert T. Meyer,* ed. T. Halton and J. P. Williman, 22–52 (Washington, DC: The Catholic University of America Press, 1986); S. H. Griffith, "Ephraem the Syrian's Hymns 'Against Julian': Meditations on History and Imperial Power," *Vigiliae Christianae* 41 (1987): 238–66; McVey, *Hymns,* 17–23, 34–39; S. H. Griffith, "Images of Ephraem: The Syrian Holy Man and His Church," *Traditio* (1989–90): 7–33, esp. 20–26.

42. "Hymn on the Church" 15. McVey, *Hymns,* 224–25. Cf. Beck, *Hymnen de Paradiso,* 70.

IV

Theosis in Medieval and Reformation Thought

The Copto-Arabic Tradition of *Theosis*: A Eucharistic Reading of John 6:51–57 in Būluṣ al-Būshī's Treatise *On the Incarnation*

Stephen J. Davis

In the Coptic Church, the thirteenth and fourteenth centuries were a "golden age" for the production of theological literature in Arabic. And yet, among modern scholars, especially in the West, this period in the history of Egyptian Christianity has received little attention. Indeed, the Arabic-speaking Christian communities of the Middle East, which have survived for centuries under Islamic rule, have largely been left out of the sacred canons of church history taught in universities and theological seminaries. In this essay, I would like to help redress this oversight by examining how a particular Coptic theologian, Būluṣ al-Būshī (Paul of Būsh), interpreted the Gospel of John in developing a sacramental Christology that emphasized *human participation in the divinized body of the incarnate Word.* More broadly, I also hope to foster an increased awareness of the richness of the Arabic Christian theological tradition as a resource for scholars interested in the history of biblical interpretation, systematic theology, medieval church history, Islamic studies, and comparative religion.

Būluṣ al-Būshī (ca. 1170–1250) was one of a select group of Arabic-speaking Egyptian theologians that helped shape the Coptic "golden age" set in the Ayyubid rule of Egypt. His name reflects the fact that he was from "Būsh," a town located in Middle Egypt (just north of Beni Suef). Much of the early part of his career was spent as a monk, probably at the Monastery of Anba Samuel Qalamun in the Fayūm, a large agricultural oasis located adjacent to the Nile Valley, southwest of Cairo. During the last decade of his life, he served as bishop of Old Cairo, the most prestigious of the local Egyptian bishoprics at the time.[1]

In addition to being a respected church leader, Būluṣ was a prolific theological author whose diverse writings include the following: a treatise on spirituality, a book of confession, biblical commentaries on Revelation and Hebrews, and a series of eight homilies on the life of Christ corresponding to eight major feasts in the Coptic calendar.[2] One of Būluṣ al-Būshī's most important writings, however, is his systematic theology, which is organized in four parts with separate treatises on the unity of God, the Trinity, the Incarnation, and the well-being (or truth) of Christianity.[3]

Būluṣ's treatise *On the Incarnation*—and specifically, his use of the Gospel of John in developing his Christology—will be my focus.

Organization of Būluṣ al-Būshī's Treatise *On the Incarnation*

On the Incarnation is organized into three parts and nine chapters, systematically explaining (1) How God the Word became Incarnate, (2) Why God became Incarnate, and (3) the Fruits of the Incarnation.

In parts 1 and 2, Būluṣ conducts a (fictional) dialogue with an anonymous Muslim interlocutor and responds to the questions of how and why the divine Word became flesh. Then, in the third part, Būluṣ turns to the issue of soteriology: namely, how the incarnation of the Word provided for human salvation by granting us eternal life and participation in the body of Christ. Here Būluṣ specifically relies on the Gospel of John (esp. Jn 6:51–57) in order to develop a sacramental theology of the Incarnation that emphasizes our participation in Christ's divinized body. Būluṣ's Christology and sacramental reading of John can be best understood by examining it in two primary interpretive contexts: first, Christian apologetic within an Islamic religious environment, and second, the hermeneutical tradition of Egyptian patristic writers (especially the influence of Athanasius and Cyril).

Christian Apologetic within an Islamic Religious Environment

Būluṣ al-Būshī's interpretation of the Gospel of John was conditioned by Christian apologetic concerns within an Islamic religious environment. In both form and content, he actually models the structure of his treatise on the Islamic rhetorical and theological convention of *ʿilm al-kalām* (which may be translated "the science of the word" or "the science of discourse"). The rhetoric of *al-kalām* is characterized by a dialogical question-and-answer style. In order to construct an apology for "right belief," Muslim authors would frequently pose (and then answer) a series of theological questions. These questions were placed in the mouth of a hostile, but often anonymous, opponent. As such, the discourse of *al-kalām* functioned as a rationalist, discursive method of defending the theological viewpoints held by the author and the author's community against challenges from other religious perspectives (including Christians, Jews, and other Muslims who differed in viewpoint).[4]

Būluṣ uses the dialogical style of *al-kalām* to structure the body of his treatise *On the Incarnation.* From chapter 2 through chapter 6, he introduces each chapter (and several subheadings within the chapters) with a question posed by a group of anonymous Muslim interlocutors. Several examples of this rhetorical technique include:

On the Incarnation 20–21 (chapter 2, section 1)
If they say, "How does the Divine become incarnate in the human race that He created?" . . .
To them it is said, . . . (analogy of the burning bush)

On the Incarnation 40–41 (chapter 3, section 1)
And if they say, "How is it possible that the incarnation concerns one person of the Trinity without concerning the Father and the Holy Spirit, while (at the same time) you describe Him as not being divided into parts?" . . .
To them, it is said, . . . (explanation of the unity of God: analogy of the sun)

On the Incarnation 64–65 (chapter 4, section 1)
And if they say, "What is the proof that this incarnate one is the creative power for all created things?" . . .
To them, it is said, . . . (argument from Christ's works)

On the Incarnation 84–86 (chapter 5, section 1)
If they say, "What was it that compelled Him to become incarnate?" . . .
To them, it is said, "And who is the one who compelled Him to create Adam and his descendents?"
And if they ask about that,
it is said to them, "His generosity and His favor!"

On the Incarnation 95–96 (chapter 6, section 1)
If they say, "Why does He not send an angel from below him for the salvation of His people?" . . .
To them, it is said . . . (argument that the Creator alone is able to reconcile creation to Himself)

On the Incarnation 98–103 (chapter 6, section 2)
If they are not content with that (answer), and seek the clarification of the evidence concerning it, and [the knowledge] of the trouble that came from humanity and of the illness that made the Incarnation necessary for the human condition. And they imagined how God did not create what He wills by (his) authority, because he is able (to do so), and how he did not send a messenger (*rasūl*), and did not assist him in the salvation of his people,

And if they ask, "What evidence is there for his incarnation especially?" . . .
To them, it is said, . . . (argument concerning the purpose of the Incarnation: the remedy of the human condition).

The presentation of these questions is formulaic: each is introduced with the words, "If they say . . ." (*fa 'in qālū*) or "If they ask . . ." (*fa 'in sa'alū*). Following each question, Būluṣ presents an apologetic response introduced by the words, "To them it is said . . ." (*yuqālu lahum*). This formulaic structure is typical of literary dialogues produced in the *kalām* style.[5]

The content or subject matter of Būluṣ al-Būshī's treatise also resonates with the larger *kalām* tradition. In addition to its consistent rhetorical form, the *kalām* tradition in Islam also reveals a consistent set of theological concerns around which the apologetic dialogue is constructed. The Arabic Jewish writer Maimonides (1135–1204) witnesses four religious beliefs that were fundamental to *al-kalām* literature around the turn of the thirteenth century: 1) the creation of the world, 2) the existence of God, 3) the unity of God, and 4) the incorporeality of God.[6] According to Maimonides, these themes were shared not only by Muslim *mutakallimūn* (that is, writers of *al-kalām*), but also by their Christian and Jewish apologetic precursors.[7] Maimonides, whose life span overlaps with that of Būluṣ al-Būshī, provides valuable contextual evidence for the practice of *al-kalām* in Egypt at the end of the twelfth century.[8] He in fact served as the leader of the Jewish community in Old Cairo (and as the personal physician of the sultan in Egypt) less than half a century before Būluṣ al-Būshī would serve there as bishop.

The specific questions posed by Būluṣ al-Būshī's anonymous interlocutors reflect this context of *al-kalām* theology. For example, the questioners ask how God could become human without compromising God's incorporeal status (chapter 2), how God could become incarnate without sacrificing divine unity and dividing God into parts (chapter 3), how the incarnate one could be considered the source of creation (chapter 4), and how God could be compelled in his essence to become incarnate (chapter 5). In addition, the questions also reflect the type of distinctive theological challenges that the medieval Coptic community would have faced in dialogue with contemporary, every-day Muslim critics. For example, in chapter 6, section 2, the questioner asks, "Why does God not send an angel from below for the salvation of God's people?" and is said to wonder "how God did not send a messenger (*raṣūl*)" to fulfill that same purpose.[9] Here the language used—messenger, or *raṣūl*—reflects the context of Christian-Muslim dialogue over the respective roles of Christ and Muhammad the Prophet (*al-raṣūl*). In this context, it is significant that Būluṣ al-Būshī responds by citing the Koran itself: "It is said to them that *God (may he be greatly praised!) did not create anything without purpose* (Sura 23:115), and that the circumstance of his incarnation was not without purpose as they contend."[10]

Indeed, the status and role of Christ were key issues of debate in Christian-Muslim apologetic and polemic encounter in the *kalām* tradition. A good example of this is a work entitled *The Excellent Refutation of the Divinity of Jesus from the Text of the Gospel* (*Al-Radd al-gamīl li-ilāhīyat ʿIsa bi-ṣarīh al-Ingīl*). This treatise is attributed to the famous eleventh- and twelfth-century Muslim writer al-Ghazali (1059–1111), but in fact it was probably penned by a later unidentified Egyptian author. Evidence in the treatise suggests that the author was likely a medieval Coptic convert to Islam.[11] This Egyptian "pseudo-al-Ghazali" uses a similar question-and-answer rhetorical style that conforms to *al-kalām* tradition. He introduces questions with the phrase, "And if it is said . . . ," and then responds with either "we say . . ." or "the response is . . ." This dialogical formula is used on at least thirteen occasions in the treatise to introduce themes and arguments, and of these thirteen occurrences, almost half of them (six) are concentrated in the section of the work on the "Divinity and Humanity of Jesus."[12] Thus, in light of the evidence from Maimonides and this pseudo-al-Ghazali, Būluṣ al-Būshī's use of dialogical forms and themes in his treatise *On the Incarnation* is best understood within the context of Christian-Muslim debate in medieval Egypt where the tradition of *al-kalām* was often employed for apologetic or polemic ends.

The Hermeneutical Tradition of Egyptian Patristic Writers

In part 3 of his treatise *On the Incarnation,* Būluṣ al-Būshī discusses the "Fruits of the Incarnation," beginning with the subject of eternal life in chapter 7. Then, in chapter 8 he begins to construct a sacramental theology of the Incarnation. His aim here is to show how humans are made able to participate in the body of Christ, first through baptism and then through the Eucharist. In the rest of this essay, I will be focusing on how Būluṣ interprets John 6:51–57 in developing his eucharistic Christology.

Būluṣ presents his interpretation of John 6 sequentially (for a translation of the Arabic text, see the appendix at the end of this chapter). He begins with verse 51 and proceeds step-by-step to verse 57, first quoting a passage from John and then offering an interpretation of the quoted passage in the fashion of a formal commentary. His purpose here is to draw his readers through an inexorable series of logical steps, starting with the presupposition that Christ's "life-giving body" is the tangible sign of God's grace. Indeed, he introduces his commentary by observing that Christ "added to us in grace with regard to the state Adam was in before his error, and he gave us his life-giving body."[13]

Būluṣ begins his commentary proper by quoting John 6:51 where he connects this "life-giving body" with the "life-giving bread . . . from heaven."[14] Then, in commenting on John 6:53,[15] he links that body further to the theme of eternal life (a theme he had introduced in the previous chapter as the First Fruit of the Incarnation). In quoting from John 6, verses 55 and

56 (lines 171–73), Būluṣ focuses on the statement, "My body is true food," and uses it to link Christ's body and the eucharistic bread to Christ's divinity. He does so by effectively reading the word "true" as a cipher for the Word's divinization of Christ's body.[16] Finally, Būluṣ interprets John 6:57 ("whoever eats me") as a witness to the truth of the Incarnation, in which there is no differentiation between Christ's humanity and divinity in the body.[17] Once again, he draws this conclusion through a series of word associations: first, "me" (for Christ) means his body; second, his body is identifiable with "the living bread" (from 6:51); third, that bread was "*truly* his body," that is, "divinely" his body, and therefore a witness to the fact that he is God incarnate—a witness to his identity with God the Father even in the body. From this, Būluṣ derives his conclusion that the act of partaking in the eucharistic bread grants us a participation in the life-giving, divine body of Christ.[18] Finally, he quotes the apostle Paul (*al-rasūl Būluṣ*) and the Nicene Creed as further intertexts to prove his point.[19]

In this line of Christological reasoning, Būluṣ al-Būshī situates himself within a long mystagogical tradition in the ancient Egyptian Church, an Eastern patristic tradition of sacramental realism in which typological interpretations of the Eucharist were held in tension with interpretations that assert "a complete physical identity between the bread and the body of Christ (on the one hand) and between the wine and the blood of Christ (on the other)."[20] Several well-known examples of mystagogical catechesis in the early church appear in the writings of fourth-century church fathers like John Chrysostom, Theodore of Mopsuestia, and Cyril of Jerusalem. However, in the Egyptian tradition, elements of this mystagogical approach are already evident in the late second-century writings of Clement of Alexandria.

In his treatise entitled *The Instructor* (*Paedagogus*), Clement cites John 6:53 in developing a physicist or realist position on the Eucharist,[21] which he then juxtaposes to more figurative readings of the sacrament. Already in Clement, one finds the notion that by partaking of "the drink and of the Word," the believer experiences "growth" (sanctification) and shares in the Lord's immortality. Similar readings of John 6 appear in Origen as well.[22] In fact, on one occasion in his *Commentary on John,* Origen quotes John 6:53–56, applying the text to a eucharistic identification of "true food," "the flesh of Christ," and the Word that has become flesh (cf. Jn 1).[23]

Būluṣ al-Būshī's sacramental interpretation of John has much in common with this early Egyptian hermeneutical tradition; however, the details of his Christology seem to have been shaped even more determinately by later developments in the Egyptian tradition—especially the writings of Athanasius and Cyril of Alexandria as they were forged by the theological controversies of the fourth and fifth centuries. In Athanasius, one sees a more systematic attempt to connect the Incarnation with soteriology, especially the Word's perfecting of humankind and granting of eternal life.[24] Recently, an Egyptian scholar named Joseph Faltas, in his doctoral dissertation written for the University of Athens (written in modern Greek), has traced the specific lines of continuity between Athanasius's Christology and that of Būluṣ al-Būshī.[25]

Two examples of this may be noted with regard to the following passage from Athanasius's treatise *Against the Arians:*

> The human race is perfected in him and restored, as it was made at the beginning, but with even greater grace. For, having risen from the dead, we shall no longer fear death, but shall reign forever in Christ in the heavens. And this has been done, since the Word of God himself, the very one who is also from the Father, has put on the flesh, and has become a human being. For if he were a creature and had become human, humankind would have no less remained just as it was, not joined to God; for how would it, being a work, have been joined to the Creator by another work? . . . And how, if the Word were a creature, would he have power to undo God's judgment, and to forgive sin, even though it is written in the prophets, that this work belongs to God?[26]

Clearly, Būluṣ al-Būshī was indebted to Athanasius in his conception of how, through the Incarnation, humankind was restored to something resembling its original state at creation, only with even "greater grace." It is interesting to compare this to Būluṣ's statement in his treatise *On the Incarnation,* where he says that the incarnate Word has "added to us in grace with regard to the state Adam was in before his error."[27]

Būluṣ also adopts Athanasius's concern to distinguish the divine state of the Incarnate One from that of creatures. For Athanasius, in his ongoing polemic against the Arians, the divinity of the Word had profound implications for human salvation. He writes, "For if he were a creature and had become human, humankind would have no less remained just as it was, not joined to God."[28] A similar point is pressed home by Būluṣ al-Būshī in chapter 6 of his treatise *On the Incarnation.* However, in the case of Būluṣ, this Athanasian soteriological argument is applied to the context of Christian-Muslim apologetic (in particular, the importance of distinguishing Christ's role from that of the prophets, and from the prophet Muhammad).

And yet, Būluṣ al-Būshī's indebtedness to Athanasius was not an exclusive one. While Athanasius, on occasion, espouses a physicist or realist view of the eucharistic elements and their transformation into the body and blood of Jesus Christ, he does not systematically or consistently link this eucharistic theory to his Christological reflection on the Incarnation. Such a link, more fully expressed, is found in the writings of Cyril of Alexandria. Indeed, in Cyril's *Third Letter to Nestorius,* one observes a confluence of themes and logical steps remarkably similar to that which is found in Būluṣ's Christological treatise.

> And thus we perform in the churches an unbloody worship, and in this way approach mystical blessings and are sanctified, becoming participants in the holy flesh and the precious blood of Christ the Saviour of us all. We do not receive this as ordinary flesh, God forbid, or as the flesh of a man sanctified and conjoined to the Word in a unity of dignity, or as the flesh of someone who enjoys a divine indwelling. No, we receive it as truly the lifegiving and very-flesh of the Word himself. As God he is by nature life and since he became one with his own flesh he revealed it as life-giving. So even if he should say to us: "Amen, Amen, I say to you, If you do not eat the flesh of the Son of Man, and drink his blood" (John 6:53), we must not consider this as if it were the flesh of any man like us (for how could the flesh of a man be life-giving from its own nature?) but rather that it has truly become the personal flesh of him who for our sakes became, and was called, the Son of Man.[29]

In this text, Cyril first identifies the bread and wine as the "holy flesh . . . and precious blood of Christ," and argues that participation in this flesh and blood brings sanctification. Second, Cyril says that the flesh of Christ is "truly" life-giving, and seems to associate this language with the divinity of the Word ("As God he is by nature life"). Third, like Athanasius before him, Cyril emphasizes the distinction between the divine flesh of Christ and "the flesh of any man like us," saying, "If it were human flesh it would not be life-giving." Fourth, it is significant that Cyril makes these points in the context of interpreting John 6:53. This use of John 6 for such ends is not an isolated case in Cyril's writing. In his *Explanation* of his scathing *Twelve Chapters* against Nestorius, Cyril uses John 6:57 to support a similar line of Christological logic.[30] In his *Synodical Deposition of Nestorius,* Cyril offers a sequential commentary on John 6, verses 56, 57, and 58, and uses the Johannine text to argue for the Eucharist reality of the incarnate flesh of Christ.[31] Finally, in his *Commentary on the Gospel of John,* Cyril offers another sequence of interpretation, focusing on John 6:53–56, where he dwells at length on the life-giving nature of the body united with the Word and manifest in the Eucharist, and on the nature of our union with that body (and, by extension, with the divine) through participation in the sacrament.[32]

Given this evidence from Athanasius and Cyril, I would argue here that Būluṣ al-Būshī, in developing his own sacramental theology of the Incarnation, was redeploying this Egyptian hermeneutical tradition—a tradition that continued to view the Nicene Creed as foundational—within a new cultural context.

Conclusion

Early Christian apologetic literature often purported to be a dialogue or appeal directed to authority figures in the larger (non-Christian) society. Rather than being directed to a Muslim audience, as some scholars assert,[33] such literature functioned primarily to mark boundaries and shape group identity *within* Christian communities. In the case of Būluṣ al-Būshī, it is noteworthy that a number of the apologetic elements in his treatise *On the Incarnation* were taken—borrowed—from his eight earlier homilies on the life of Christ, homilies that would originally have been preached to Copts on a series of feast days within the annual cycle of the Coptic liturgy. The social function of Būluṣ's treatise in marking out discursive boundaries for the Coptic community is especially evident in his final reflections on the sacraments. Immediately after his commentary on John 6, he writes: "And whoever does not have this portion of faith in him, nor has received baptism, nor has communion in his living thrones, also does not truly have a portion or a share in the inheritance of eternal life, but is completely alien to it altogether."[34] In denying those outside the sacraments access to eternal life, Būluṣ's words effectively delimit the boundaries of the community that, in fact, celebrates those sacraments and lays claim to that eternal life—an eternal life made available through the sacramental partaking of Christ's divinized body.

This internal, sociological function of Būluṣ al-Būshī's apologetic is also reflected in the two main organizational genres of his treatise: first, in his use of the *kalām* dialogical tradition; and second, in his commentary on John. On the one hand, in his employment of *kalām* conventions, Būluṣ sought to answer characteristic Muslim objections to the Incarnation and to defend (and thereby reinforce) the Coptic Church's understanding and sacramental enactment of its own Christological doctrine. In the process, as I have shown, he framed his Christology and overall systematic theology within the larger concerns of Christian-Muslim encounter. On the other hand, by reading the Gospel of John through the lens of his own Egyptian interpretive tradition, Būluṣ was also shaping the historical identity of his Arabic-speaking Christian readers as theological heirs to the ancient church of Athanasius and Cyril. It is perhaps fitting that this thirteenth-century Coptic bishop would have sought inspiration in these two figures, for like Athanasius and Cyril in the fourth and fifth centuries, Būluṣ al-Būshī composed his Christology in the midst of larger theological debates that had profound implications for the self-identity of the Egyptian Church and the social and religious landscape of Egypt.

Appendix: An Excerpt from Būluṣ al-Būshī's Treatise *On the Incarnation*

Būluṣ al-Būshī, On the Incarnation, excerpt from chapter 8.

(165) Then, after that, (God) added to us favor in relation to the state Adam

was in before his error, and he gave us his life-giving body, (166) just as he said, "I am the life-giving bread, which came down from heaven. (167) Whoever eats of this bread will live forever!" (John 6:51). (168) Then, he told us what the bread is when he said, "The bread that I give is my body, which I offer up for the life of the world" (John 6:51). (169) Indeed, he even added to that an announcement, saying, "If you have not eaten the body of the Son of Man, nor drunk his blood, there is no eternal life in you" (John 6:53). (170) His statement, "in you," means that it (eternal life) comes to existence in your essential nature (essence). It is not external to you, nor is it alien to you. (171) He settled that matter when he said, "Because my body is true food, (172) and my blood is true drink whoever has eaten my body and has drunk my blood remains in me, and I in him" (John 6:55–56). (173) As for his statement "true food," (he said) that because his divinity is united with his body. He has been united with the holy bread and has transformed it into his body, in truth and not (merely) in likeness. (174) Then he said the greatest thing when he made the statement, "Just as the living Father sent me, and I have life on account of the Father, so too whoever eats me lives on account of me" (John 6:57). (175) He did not need to say here, "whoever eats my body," because he already had established that in the preceding statement. (176) He said first, "the living bread" (John 6:51), and informed us that that bread was truly his body. (177) Then, he said third, "whoever eats me" (John 6:57). He means (here) that he is God incarnate, and his divinity is not differentiated from his humanity. (178) Whoever partakes (of the Eucharist) in a worthy manner and with faith, (God) resides in him and gives him the life that he gave to the body united to him. (179) The apostle said, "He is ready to change the body of our weakness and transform it into something resembling the body of his glory, as the act of his powerful hand, to which everything is devoted in worship!" (180) As for his statement, "the Father lives, and I live on account of the Father" (John 6:57), (its meaning is), just as was introduced earlier in the first part of this book, that he is perfection from perfection, (181) and "light from light, life from life, (182) true God from true God, begotten not made, equal to the Father in essence" (Nicene Creed).

Notes

1. On Būluṣ al-Būshī's life, see Samir Khalil Samir, ed., *Traité de Paul de Búš sur l'Unité et la Trinité l'Incarnation, et la Vérité du Christianisme* (*Maqālah fī al-Tathlīth wa-al-Tagassud wa-Ṣiḥḥat al-Masīḥiyyah), Patrimoine Arabe Chrétien* 4 (Zouk Mikhail: al-Turāth al-[c]Arabī al-Mesīhī, 1983), 15–27; Aziz S. Atiya, "Būluṣ al-Būshī," *Coptic Encyclopedia,* vol. 2 (New York: Macmillan, 1991), 423–24; Joseph Moris Faltas, "Ho megas Athanasios hôs pêgê tês theologias tou Būlūs al Būši," PhD diss., University of Athens, 1994, 11–17.

2. For a complete listing of his works, see Samir, *Traite de Paul de Būš,* 29–40; also Faltas, "Būlūs al Būši," 18–25.

3. A critical edition of the Arabic text has been produced by Samir, *Traite de Paul de Būš,* 129–258. The treatise *On the Incarnation* appears on pages 187–227. This Arabic text has been reproduced with a modern Greek translation in Faltas, "Būlūs al Būši," 29–52 (modern Greek translation).

4. On the tradition of *ᶜilm al-Kalam,* see Harry Austryn Wolfson, *The Philosophy of the Kalam* (Cambridge, MA: Harvard University Press, 1976); L. Gardet, "ᶜIlm al-Kalām," in *The Encyclopedia of Islam,* New Edition, vol. 3 (Leiden: E. J. Brill; London: Luzac & Co., 1971), 1141–50; Georges C. Anawati, "Kalām," trans. R. J. Scott, *The Encyclopedia of Religion,* ed. Mircea Eliade, vol. 8 (New York: Macmillan, 1987), 231–42. Finally, for a detailed treatment of the dialectical logic of *kalām* in the Islamic theological tradition, see the following two articles by Josef van Ess: "The Logical Structure of Islamic Theology," in *Logic in Classical Islamic Culture,* ed. G. E. von Grunebaum, 21–50 (Wiesbaden: Otto Harrassowitz, 1970); and "Disputationspraxis in der Islamischen Theologie: Eine vorläufige Skizze," *Revue des etudes islamiques* 44 (1976): 23–60.

5. Van Ess, "Structure of Islamic Theology," 23; and "Disputationspraxis in der Islamischen Theologie," 25.

6. Moses Maimonides, *Dalālat al-Ḥa'irīn* 1.71, ed. Hussein Atay (Cairo: Maktabat al-thaqāfa al-dīnīa, 1980), 182–86; Wolfson, *Philosophy of the Kalam,* 45.

7. On the late antique antecedents of Islamic *kalām* literature, see also van Ess, "Structure of Islamic Theology," 24; and "Disputationspraxis in der Islamischen Theologie," 24–25.

8. For examples of earlier Muslim *mutakallimūn* in Egypt (ninth and tenth century CE), see van Ess, *Theologie und Gesellschaft im 2. und 3. Jahrhundert Hidschra: Eine Geschichte des religiösen Denkens im frühen Islam,* Band II (Berlin: Walter de Gruyter, 1992), 729–42.

9. Būluṣ al-Būshī, *On the Incarnation* 95, 101, in *Traite de Paul de Būš,* 208–9.

10. Ibid., 103, in *Traite de Paul de Būš,* 210.

11. The text of the work has been edited by Muhammad ᶜAbdullah al-Sharqawi, *Al-Radd al-gamīl li-ilāhīyat ᶜIsa bi-sarīh al-Ingīl,* 3rd ed. (Beirut: Maktabat al-Zahrā', 1990). For an English summary of the work, see J. Windrow Sweetman, *Islam and Christian Theology: A Study of the Interpretation of Theological Ideas in the Two Religions* (London: Lutterworth Press, 1955), 262–309. On the question of authorship, see Jean Marie Gaudeul, *Encounters and Clashes,* vol. 1 (Rome: Pontificio Istituto di Studi Arabi e Islamici, 1984), 95–98; and more recently, Gabriel Said Reynolds, "The Ends of *Al-Radd al-Jamīl* and Its Portrayal of Christian Sects," *Islamochristiana* 25 (1999): 45–65.

12. Ps. al-Ghazali, *Al-Radd al-gamīl li-ilāhīyat ᶜIsa bi-sarīh al-Ingīl,* ed. Muhammad ᶜAbdullah al-Sharqawi, 95, 99, 104, 113, 126–27, 129, 131–32, 133, 135, 153, 154, 168. The section of the work on the "Divinity and Humanity of Jesus" appears on pages 125–36.

13. Būluṣ, *On the Incarnation,* 165, in *Traite de Paul de Būš,* 221.

14. Ibid., 166–68, in *Traite de Paul de Būš,* 221–22.

15. Ibid., 169–70, in *Traite de Paul de Būš,* 222.

16. Ibid., 171–73, in *Traite de Paul de Būš,* 222–23.

17. Ibid., 174–77, in *Traite de Paul de Būš,* 223–24.

18. Ibid., 178, in *Traite de Paul de Būš,* 224.

19. Ibid., 179–82, in *Traite de Paul de Būš,* 224.

20. Enrico Mazza, *The Celebration of the Eucharist: The Origin of the Rite and the Development of Its Interpretation* (Collegeville, MN: Liturgical Press, 1999), 147–48.

21. Clement of Alexandria, *Paed.* 1.6.42.3ff.; 2.2.19.4–20.1.

22. Origen, *Contra Celsum* 8.33; *In Num. hom* 16.9.

23. Origen, *Commentary on John* 10.17.99.1–19.

24. See, for example, Athanasius, *Against the Arians* 2.21.67: "We shall ever reign in Christ in the heavens. And this has been done since the own Word of God Himself, who is from the Father, has put on the flesh and become man."

25. Faltas, "Būlūs al Būši," esp. 86–191.
26. Athanasius, *Against the Arians* 2.21.67, PG 26:289.
27. Būluṣ, *On the Incarnation* 165, in *Traite de Paul de Būš,* 221.
28. Athanasius, *Against the Arians* 2.21.67, PG 26:289.
29. Cyril of Alexandria, "Third Letter to Nestorius 7," in *St. Cyril of Alexandria: The Christological Controversy: Its History, Theology, and Text,* trans. John A. McGuckin (Leiden: E. J. Brill, 1994), 270–71.
30. Cyril of Alexandria, "Explanation of the Twelve Chapters 29," in McGuckin, *Christological Controversy,* 292.
31. Cyril of Alexandria, "The Synodical Deposition of Nestorius," in *Nestoriana die Fragmente des Nestorius,* ed. Friedrich Loofs (Halle: Niemeyer, 1905), 228.4–16. Translated in McGuckin, *Christological Controversy,* 376.
32. Cyril of Alexandria, *Commentary on the Gospel according to St. John 4:2,* ed. Philip Edward Pusey, vol. 1 (Oxford: J. Parker, 1874), 528.12–536.18. Translated in Norman Russell, *Cyril of Alexandria* (London: Routledge, 2000), 114–19.
33. Joseph Faltas has suggested that Būluṣ directed his treatise to a Muslimn audience, a viewpoint with which I respectfully disagree. See Faltas, "Būlūs al Būši," esp. 55–58.
34. Būluṣ, *On the Incarnation,* 183–84, in *Traite de Paul de Būš,* 225.

St. Anselm: *Theoria* and the Doctrinal Logic of Perfection

Nathan R. Kerr

What is really at stake in retrieving the doctrine of *theosis*/deification in the West is the very task of theology itself, or in other words, the possibility of having anything theological to say at all. Insofar as Western theology, on the whole, has obscured the idea of deification as a dogma (i.e., an official teaching of the church), it has done so on the basis of its own reluctance to concede that some notion of creaturely perfection could provide a doctrinal starting point for articulating the idea that all theology as such is an exercise in *theoria*—of coming to "see" or "know" God by way of contemplative ascent to the transcendental attributes of divine being. As a result, where the doctrine of deification does appear in the West, it often arises as a peripheral notion or doctrinal addendum to the assumed task of theology, which might have something significant to say about who we are as redeemed creatures but offers very little by way of insight into who God is as such and *in se*.

The Western Theological Crisis of Intellection

The Western reticence to deal with the possibility of human perfection as deification is understandable, for it seems the height of hubris to suggest that our own perfection should condition the appearance of divine perfection to us. Indeed, is it not the case that God's perfection stands over-against our own finite creaturely imperfections, the indictment of which only then makes possible the suggestion that we might someday be "deified"? Does not theology-as-*theoria* have ultimately to speak of the being of *God,* the final ascent to which marks the *exitus* of "natural" creaturely finitude? If deification truly signifies our "becoming divine," should it not be the case that such "divinity" cannot in any sense be dependent upon or explained in terms of who we are as creatures, but is explicable only in consequence of the divine will, inaccessible to us in its *potentia absoluta?*

If debates between East and West over the proper "place" for deification as a doctrine in theology have encouraged such questions,[1] the result has often been that they are not resolved, but only recast and proliferated in various forms. Perhaps it is not the case that the West has failed to articulate a doctrine of deification, but that it has failed to understand the nature and function of theology, and to put the vision of deification properly to work. If so, Western theology ironically has neglected its own most important point: deification *is* doctrinally a constituent of the doctrine of God; and not fully to grasp the implications of this is to forestall and deactivate the fundamental task of *theoria*—redemptive insight into the perfection of divine *esse.*

To say this is to say that theology in the West has suffered from a basic misapprehension of what it has (since Augustine) taken to be its primary theological task. And if this bold assessment is at all accurate, then the neglect of deification in the Western theological landscape is not so much a doctrinal crisis as it is a crisis of intellection. To seek to rehabilitate the doctrine in the West, then, is rather to ask again what it means for theology to make recourse to *theoria,* in which God alone is the proper "object" of theology. For this reason, my aim is to re-employ the idiom of *theoria* not for the sake of "constructing" a new doctrine of deification for the West, but as a therapeutic means of identifying what has always been there, never far beneath the surface, as an ulterior doctrinal locus for its conceived theological task. In short, to posit the church's doctrine of God as the doctrinal "object" of theology-as-*theoria,* as the West has done since Augustine, *already* is to presuppose a full-fledged doctrine of creaturely deification (the implications of which presupposition theology in the West has never quite owned up to).[2]

It is precisely as an exercise in *theoria* that Anselm's *Proslogion* illustrates the kind of "therapy" that Western theology needs to overcome its present crisis of intellection.[3] A theology that opts for a notion of deification as the consummate doctrinal site for *theoria* uncovers the key ulterior (but lost) motive for the West's deepest doctrinal longings. For as we shall see, there runs straight through Anselm's text a unique "logic of perfection" that reveals a certain doctrine of deification, or participated perfections in God, to be an ineluctable trademark of a theology that would claim to "see" God; and this "logic" is central to who Anselm is as a *Western* theologian. That is to say, humanity comes fully to *see* the believed perfect existence of God through the perfection of its own human nature. And it is in light of such a perfection that we shall finally be called "gods" (P 25).

Analogia Perfectioni: Deification as Constituent of the Doctrine of God

Let me begin with the *de profundis* of Anselm's text, his "ontological" argument for the existence of God, for it is here that Anselm sets out the parameters for his "logic of perfection," according to which God is "perfect" existence only as that *esse* that *perfects* all of creaturely being. Only in this light can deification be seen as constituent of the doctrine of God.

I would like to make a suggestion concerning Anselm's proof, and in so doing delineate a line of interpretation that is congruous with the best scholarly exegesis of Anselm's argument, as well as what Anselm explicitly and implicitly declares.[4] The suggestion is this: the formula according to which Anselm's proof proceeds—God as *aliquid quo maius nihil cogitari posit* (that than which nothing greater can be conceived)—is meant to reclaim for God a certain perfect reality, in such a way as to reclaim for the believer a whole new perception of all finite creaturely reality in its eminent relation to God. The critical move that Anselm makes is in allowing the predicate "greater" (*maius*), when applied to God, to redefine what it means truly to exist. The proof does not stop short with the delineation of God's "general" existence, but rather moves on to argue that, by definition, God alone exists "in a strict and absolute sense" (P 22). As Karl Barth explains it, God "exists as the reality of existence itself, as the criterion of all existence and non-existence which is always presupposed in all thinking of the existence and non-existence of other beings."[5] This occurs by way of Anselm's specification of "that than which nothing *greater* can be thought" as "whatever it is *better* (*melius*) to be than not to be" (P 5).

To put it negatively, driven by an urge to think existence in its imperishable purity, unalloyed by its attachment to the *nihil,* one cannot gain a foothold in what it is possible to imagine as *not* existing.[6] It is reason, of course, mediated by experience, that compels us to conclude thus: as long as thought retains a stringent attachment to the accidental predicaments of *ens commune,* thought cannot properly think *esse,* and so can only think its own destruction. For even if one experiences the existence of a thing in finite reality, one can on the very basis of this finitude think its non-existence, and so is forced to think its non-existence *in re.* Only that One who dwells in "light inaccessible," whose nongeneric *esse* makes possible the perfect coincidence of existence *in intellectu et in re,* cannot be thought as not existing (P 3),[7] and so is able to grant to reality a mode of existence that forbids this oscillation.

In thus qualifying the divine *maius* with this *melius,*[8] Anselm's argument occurs as a kind of quasi-Thomistic reversal of the generic *analogia entis:* it is not by starting from the question of finite existence in general that we are able to reason to the perfect, because quantitatively "greater" (*maius*), existence of God; rather, it is on the basis of God's qualitatively "better" (*melius*), and thus genuinely true, existence that the being of the world apprehends its essence solely in light of what is believed concerning the perfect being of God.

The point I particularly want to stress here is that to think of God's perfect existence still requires thinking of creaturely finitude (in toto) in its subordination to God. This reflects Anselm's keen awareness from the outset that a line of thought that seeks primarily to do with "whatever we believe about the Divine Being" (pref.), ipso facto can only mean also dealing with the world that God has created. What is at stake, then, in the proof proper, is a true and legitimate knowledge of God as *Creator* (P 3) and all that follows from this first article of the church's *Credo.*

The acknowledgment of who God is, is equally rooted in a clear and distinct perception of who we are as creatures in light of that end for which God has created us—the beatific vision of God's own perfection, the possession of which constitutes the beatification of our own created existence. In this way, the analogical dimension of Anselm's argument makes created being itself the "proof" of God's perfect existence, for to grasp created *ens* in its finite measure is already to "see" the infinite shining through it, calling it beyond itself. Creaturely finitude (*ens commune*) "is" not as a "thing" that we grasp, but as an opening onto that which gives it "to be" at all, which means that finite existence is only truly realized insofar as it is somehow analogically "evacuated" from the outset in favor of divine *esse.* In this way, Anselm opens a path down which all genuine existence leads, namely, to the perfect existence of God.

Consequently, the inverted *analogia entis* according to which Anselm's proof proceeds is mediated by a more fundamental *analogia perfectionis.* This is the theological starting point of a doctrine of God that is also, at the same time, a doctrine of deification, of creaturely perfection. As Anselm puts it in a sermon on the beatific vision: "[T]he Father has joined us to his almighty Son as his body and as co-heirs with him, and made us who are called in his name to be gods. But God is the one who divinises; you on the contrary will be the one who is divinised."[9]

The voice of an Athanasius, or a Gregory of Nyssa, is as readily apparent in these words as is the voice of an Augustine: the logic of perfection compels us to apprehend God in God's perfection as the one who deifies (perfects), and concomitantly ourselves as those creatures deified (perfected) by God. Here we encounter what is by far the most profound implication of Anselm's "logic of perfection": if we are to be deified, we will be deified as creatures, and if we are to "see" God fully, it will be a matter of seeing ourselves more completely in our creaturely concordance (*concordantia*) with God.

Analogia Gratiae: Is Anselm Really a Western Theologian?

We have seen that the definition of God by which Anselm's famous "proof" proceeds is derivative of the first article of the church's *Credo,* such that to say "we believe (*credimus*) that [God is] something than which nothing greater can be thought" (P 2), is of a piece with saying "we believe in God the Father almighty, creator of heaven and earth." The logic of perfection according to which the believer names God entails nothing less than a whole new perception of reality, of the created world in its concordant relation to the creator. Here we are led to a crucial observation: there is not a single aspect of our lives, or of the created world as a whole, that is not now bound up with the existence of God, and the logic of perfection that God's *esse* evinces. The universal demand of the Christian *intelligere fidem,* therefore, is to see God by seeing all finite things in the light of that perfection for which they were originally created—namely, ontological participation in the divine *intellectus* (a demand that is carried over from the *Monologion* [see M 34–36, 67–69 and passim]).

Yet if Anselm does put to work here a doctrine of deification in the service of his doctrine of God, he does so in a particularly Western way, namely, in a manner that takes seriously the question of original sin. The primacy of divine grace is nowhere subverted but it is accorded the fullest weight possible. While we acknowledge in Anselm's grammar a logic of perfection that structurally coincides with a certain "Eastern" logic of deification, we must grant that Anselm's "dialect" is scarcely "Greek," and actually cuts for us an epochal figure that is identifiably a distinctive product of "Western" Augustinianism. But what is interesting is that at the same time that Anselm employs the classically Augustinian distinction of "sin" and "grace," he does so in a way that problematizes the use to which the sin-grace dialectic would be put in the Western theological method of later centuries. For these peculiarly "Western" characteristics of Anselm's discourse emerge solely as a function of what he sees as methodologically most important for theology undertaken as *theoria:* a doctrine of God that is also a doctrine of one who deifies—perfects—the created world.

The limitations of this essay hardly allow me to explicate this point in full, which would require a sustained rereading of some of Anselm's more straightforwardly "dogmatic" treatises, such as *Cur Deus Homo* and *De Processione Sancti Spiritus.* However, already within the *Proslogion* itself, Anselm goes some way toward reemploying the Western tropes of "sin" and "grace" as a means of stressing the idea that we cannot even think theologically except by way of a faith that believes that the perfect God is *perfecting* our own creaturely life in order that we might live as an everlasting analogical "performance" of the perfection of God.[10] Anselm deploys these doctrinal tropes heuristically in order to remind us that, precisely *because* we are creatures, our creaturely existence must itself be deified if we are indeed to "see" God.

This first becomes clear with regard to what Hans Urs von Balthasar has called the "deeply broken" structure of Anselm's text,[11] wherein Anselm realizes that his own vision has failed to attain the insight that his argument had apparently made accessible to the believing intellect. Having wondrously been granted access to the transcendental conditions of God's perfect being—"life itself, light, wisdom, goodness, eternal blessedness and blessed eternity," whose nature it is to "exist everywhere and always"—Anselm finds that he is lacking the felt experience of that which he has "found" by way of ontological "proof" (P 14). At the heart of this "felt inexperience" lies Anselm's own recognition of the full import of the existence of "perfect reality." If the God who is always *maius* than whatever can be thought is to be seen, this God can *only* be "seen" *by God* (P 14). The logical implication of this recognition should be obvious: where our own insight into the divine *maius* is concerned, only full creaturely participation in the divine *esse* will suffice for such illumination.

This means that our being creatures in distinction from the creator must somehow carry with it our participation in the divine *esse.* A *fides quaerens intellectum* that presupposes the belief that God is perfect existence, the truth of being itself, must ultimately assert on some level its own creaturely participation in God's perfect mode of being. Apart from this belief in participation, God is inevitably brought down to the level of being-in-general and "seen" as a banal thing that can be approached from the outside and conceptually "grasped." Contrariwise, for Anselm we believe *in* the supreme essence, so that faith seeks understanding by "staying inside" (M 76), coming to a knowledge of who we are "in God," and so "knowing" God only on that basis.[12] Indeed, for us genuinely to ascertain our creaturely distance from God is for us to come to an awareness of our first having been seen by God, and to recognize in this divine gaze the *esse* in which we move and have our very own being.[13] The light that is God's being is that very light by which we "see" at all (P 16), so that to see God is properly to contemplate who we are as creatures created to participate in the "ever greater" and "always more" of the perfect divine reality.

All of this is to say that our desire for the fulfillment of *theoria* is mediated by a certain perception of created reality, and is to be measured against it. In this way, Anselm's textual *aporia* simply extends the point to which we were led by Anselm's proof, namely: if the discourse of *theoria* unfolds as a faith seeking insight into God's perfect existence, it unfolds equally as an inquiry into what it means to be a creature, and to *be perfected* as a creature who exists only by way of a certain deferential relation to the divine *esse.* Because God's life is what it is in its perfect existence, we are what we are, namely, creatures being perfected as creatures by God. Subsequently, who we are as finite creatures must be capable of being received in such a way as to mark out for us our journey into the life and being of God. Here again Anselm rehearses a key point from the *Monologion.* There, in elucidating what it means to be rational creatures conscious of supreme being, Anselm asserts that "the efficacy of the mind's ascent to knowledge of the supreme nature is in direct proportion to the enthusiasm of its intent to learn about itself" (M 66), such that to think God is finally to think of one's finitude as it "mirrors" or "images" the "supreme essence" (M 67). Therefore, if the vision of God that we are created for, and have yet to attain, is to occur, it will happen via the distension of our creaturely alterity *into* God—*tendere in deum* (see M 76).[14] The life of *theoria*—the true life of a theologian—is a mode of life in which our creatureliness persists and perdures for us in such a manner as to continually draw us further into the infinitely plenitudinous *esse* of God.

This is an extremely important point, for only in understanding how our own creaturely existence is called from the outset to participate in the divine logic of perfection are we then able to grasp how it is that sin is not simply an offense against an alien perfection that belongs to God alone, but is preeminently a matter of refusing to apprehend participation in this perfection as that end for which we were fashioned. So it is that in chapters 17 and 18 of *Proslogion,* Anselm recasts the question of original sin in precisely these terms, namely, as that which prevents our becoming the creatures we were created to be, and so precludes our *becoming* (in a mode of being proscribed by our creatureliness) what God is in God's own "ineffable manner." By allowing ourselves to be "enclosed within" (*involutum in*) our creaturely finitude, we "involve" ourselves with its realities and goods in such a way as to take them as ends-in-themselves, and consider it sufficient to dwell in our "darkness and misery" as the basis of our own true existence (P 17–18). In so doing, we merely repeat the logic of the Fall, taking as real and true a portion of the created world in self-sufficient disjunction from its creator. To continue to seek "to know" and "to see" God on this scheme, as a "thing" that we can continually progress toward through the self-transcendence of our own finitude, is simply to play "the fool," for it is to elevate the creature above the Creator, by taking creaturely finitude as the limit-case of existence (see P 3–4).[15]

That the "harmony, fragrance, sweetness, softness, and beauty" of the created order fails to give way to a felt experience of God's own harmony, beauty, and so on, is not a failure of created being so much as it is our own failure to receive the harmony and beauty of the earth as given (as *gifts*) by God, and so as continually pointing beyond themselves to the ineffable beauty and perfection of God (P 17). Sin, then, is the failure to receive our own creaturely existence *as* the harmony and beauty of the divine *esse, as* that harmony and beauty that we shall enjoy in inexhaustible fullness in heaven, where we in fact "will be called 'sons of God' and indeed 'gods,'" being fully divinized as creatures in relation to our Creator (P 25).

Apropos to this reconceived doctrine of sin, the reparative grace of redemption is not for Anselm an automatic reaction to the loss of an alien glory, but is the work of God to restore to creation a nature deprived of its original beauty and dignity. While this sense of redemptive grace comes to the fore most conspicuously in *Cur Deus Homo* (in a way that undoubtedly problematizes the idea that this text straightforwardly adumbrates the "forensic" account of atonement taken up by later Western theologians),[16] it is seminally articulated in the *Proslogion,* where God's perfect existence occurs to us as a grace without which we would not *be* at all. For Anselm, God is "something-than-which-nothing-greater-can-be-thought" on account of a "grace-than-which-one-cannot-come-earlier."[17] Just as it is by the grace of God that we begin to seek insight (P 1), through the divine "free gift" (*donare*) that allows us even to believe in the first place, so it is through God's illumination (*illuminare*) alone that we come to "see" and to "know" (P 4). And because such "seeing" and "knowing" are just what we were created for, the divine light of grace is that very first light by which we are able to see at all (P 16); by this grace, we apprehend our creatureliness *as* it was created. Thus, via grace, we know God *through* knowing ourselves as creatures, and this because true creaturehood "is" by referring beyond itself to an eternally present Creator God.

What this means is that God's redemptive grace does not and cannot stand in dialectical disjunction to an inherently sinful human nature. Rather, if we are to be restored to our first vocation of *theoria*—of seeing God as creatures, and so of becoming divine by way of creaturely *concordantia* with God's own perfect reality—then such restoration will occur by way of God's own creating and re-creating us as human beings naturally graced from the outset for just such a vocation (P 1). And this fully adheres to the doctrinal logic of perfection as adumbrated throughout the *Proslogion:* the very essence of God is to exist as one who makes and remakes us as creatures in God's own image.

If redemptive grace is that grace that restores to creation its original vocation and again puts creation upon its path of perfection, then it follows that the grace given in God's work of redemption is not merely imputational. For this is a grace that perfects our very being, such that an account of the arrival of grace must mean also an account of our own created nature's ability to enact its own perfection, by overcoming sin through the performance of its own creatureliness. As Eadmer, Anselm's biographer, tells us: "[Anselm] was in the habit of saying . . . which perhaps appeared to some people remarkable, that he would prefer to be free from sin and go to hell innocently, than to go to the kingdom of heaven polluted with the stain of sin."[18] This is by no means to circumvent the force and prevenience of divine grace, but to radicalize it. For God's grace does not simply belong to God alone vis-à-vis who we are as creatures, but, precisely as grace, is given to us from the outset in order that we might truly be who we are: creatures who are perfected through the *epektatic* referral of creaturely goodness back to its uncreated source. The primacy of grace in one respect depends upon this creaturely "giving-back," even as the first procession outward of divine grace conditions our return.

It is according to this primacy of grace that Anselm makes recourse to analogical attribution, inasmuch as no transcendental good is predicated of creatures as what is "proper" to them alone, but as that which "is" only by the referring of its term wholesale to God. As Anselm relates near the end of chapter 24, true goodness is to be found not in the life that is created good, but in the Good Life that creates; authentic joy is to be found not in the salvation that the creature experiences, but in the Joyous salvific will that brings about this redeeming work; true knowledge is inherent not to the wisdom of creaturely conjecture, but to the Wisdom whose act of *creatio ex nihilo* is the source of all knowledge. It is in this way alone that sin for Anselm is genuinely "overcome" by grace: *not* via a "supernatural" grace that must be given *in addition to* our "natural" created reality, but rather through a grace that maximizes one's references to the goods of created reality so that they can be seen for what they really are, not as ends in themselves that provide a means of advance toward the quantitatively greater, but as pure gifts that are good only through their receptive self-transcendence to the eternal giver. Thus, we find Anselm describing our *delectatio* of God's perfect attributes as the perfection of our strength, health, peace, wisdom, desire, and so on (P 25), insofar as we are made to be so perfected in our dependence upon God as creatures that we are now capable of receiving God's own strength, health, peace, wisdom, and desire as *pure gifts* appropriate for us as creatures. In redemptive grace, God simply gives us again the gifts to be the creatures that we are, gives to us again our created nature as that means through which we shall enter into God's own perfect *beatitudo* (P 27).

What this reworked conception of the sin-grace relation does is problematize the idea that Anselm's peculiar brand of methodological "theocentrism" leads inevitably to the (typically Protestant) view that what theology solely has to speak about is God's alien glory, wherein sin is what it is as an original and enduring affront to that glory, and redemption is spoken of primarily as a restoration of that glory (with our own salvation as creatures being something of an adjunct to that restoration, imputed to us as an "addition" to who we simply "are" as fallen beings). Obviously, Anselm is a thoroughly Western theologian in that his conscious decision to do theology in the Augustinian tradition provides him with a certain "Western" grammar—that of the language of "creaturely sin" (darkness) and "divine grace" (light). But his theology provides a doctrinal logic that at the same time subverts the polarities of that grammar, and in fact seems to reorient it entirely. His conscious decision to do theology-as-*theoria* turns out to be a conscious decision for a doctrine of God that is also a doctrine of creaturely deification, and for a doctrine of grace that can only be said to overcome sin *through* this deification.

THE "PLACE" OF DEIFICATION IN THE WEST: RETRIEVING *THEOLOGIA* AS *THEORIA*

Herein lies the point upon which my whole thesis turns: if Western theology, as it has developed in the Augustinian tradition, has led to the neglect of the doctrine of deification and has been unable to free itself from the sin-grace dialectic, it is because it has fundamentally perverted its own account of the theological task; namely, insight into the being and nature of God. Once *theoria* for the West became a matter of apprehending who God is vis-à-vis who we are as creatures, it could not but perpetuate a dual dialectic of sin/grace and nature/supernature. Perforce, the doctrine of *theosis*/deification quickly assumed an adjunctive position. For Anselm, however, this was not and could not be the case. Rather, what Anselm is ultimately pursuing in his extended discursus upon the existence and nature of God is the portrait of a life established by God's perfection and conditioned upon it—a life that is being perfected through its discovery of and insight into the perfection of God. Indeed for Anselm a faith that would believe in order to understand God is, from beginning to end, a faith that would seek to *believe into God—credere in Deum* (M 76). Further, it would seek preeminently to live its life and practice its theology on this very supposition,[19] namely, that one's progress toward the beatific vision in this life is always to be conceived as progress *in* the supreme essence—albeit in a manner that retains our creaturely distinction from and concordance with the Creator.

Such is the theological vocation of *theoria* for Anselm. And such a conception of the theological task fully depends upon the doctrinal inversion that this essay has sought to propound: the doctrine of God that faith presupposes, and that the *Proslogion* seeks tirelessly to understand, itself entirely presupposes a doctrine of creaturely perfection or deification without which a *fides quaerens intellectum* on pilgrimage in this world is unable finally to proceed.

But the point I would like to stress is that this doctrinal inversion occurs not by way of Anselm's making a conscious decision to emphasize a particularly "Eastern" doctrinal development (*theosis*) over a "Western" one (original sin, or the sin-grace dialectic), but rather simply as a matter of methodological rigor, as an outgrowth of his desire, in line with the church fathers, to do *theologia*-as-*theoria,* to contemplate nothing less than the transcendental attributes of perfect Being itself. If there is a doctrinal "logic" to this method, it is that doctrine cannot but be the means by which we are educated into the life that would "see" God as this perfect Being, and ourselves in participatory concordance with it. Deification/*theosis* is in this sense for Anselm no mere doctrinal addendum, and this because our own perfected participation in the divine *esse* is bound up with the church's doctrine of God and is an integral part of that which we believe in from the outset as the presupposition of the faith that seeks understanding.

This is why I think it would be wrong to mistake Anselm's precise doctrinal formulations—of sin, grace, the Trinity, the atonement, and so on—as defining solely what it means for him to be a "Western" theologian, as if this could account for why he never explicitly "systematized" a doctrine of sanctification-as-deification, per se. For this would be to miss the fact that already in the *Proslogion* Anselm is putting to work peculiarly "Western" notions of sin, creaturely finitude, redemptive grace, and the eschaton precisely in service of this text's logic of perfection, which sets the parameters for his theological vocation. Always the good Benedictine, Anselm deploys these doctrines catechetically[20] so as to proffer his text as a pedagogy in the art of creaturely existence: as creatures, we must learn what it means to see *God's* perfection *in our very creatureliness.*

That being said, I would like very much for this essay to be taken as a commendation of Anselm as an alternative source for reevaluating the "place" of the doctrine of deification in Western theology. What I am suggesting is that our many attempts to search for an explicit formulation of the *doctrine* of deification in certain "Western" thinkers (without attention to method) is highly misdirected and is the wrong way of approaching the doctrinal impasse between East and West. Indeed, if that is how theology must be done, Anselm is and will remain a paradigmatically Western thinker and any attempt to ascertain a doctrine of deification in his writings will inevitably retain the marks of the East-West divide.[21] What Anselm may show us, however, is that deification is not a doctrine to be "formulated" or "constructed" as such, but rather that our being perfected into participation in the divine *esse* as creatures lies at the very heart of the theological enterprise. In this sense it need not be alarming that Anselm's oeuvre is without a sustained treatise on *theosis* or the "divinization of the creature," for it allows us to commend to the theological West (and East, for that matter) not Anselm's *doctrine* of *theosis,* but rather Anselm's way of doing theology as *theoria,* which, without its peculiar "logic of perfection" (which is fully translatable as a "logic of deification") leaves the theologian who seeks insight into the life and being of God with nothing, manifestly, to do or say.

Notes

1. On the importance of where one "places" deification in theology, see Andrew Louth's essay, "The Place of *Theosis* in Orthodox Theology," in this volume.

2. As John McGuckin has put it with regard to the Cappadocians in the East, "*theoria* is the engine that drives *theosis*" (see "The Strategic Adaptation of Deification in the Cappadocians," in this volume). It is precisely this perspicuous observation that Western theologians

seem never to have made with much consistency, though Anselm alone is perhaps closest to the Cappadocians in making this observation the very foundation of his theological work.

3. I take *Proslogion* to be a prototypical exercise in *theoria* insofar as it is written "from the point of view of one trying to raise his mind to contemplate God" (pref.). In line with the Great Tradition of philosophical theology, Anselm seeks to contemplate the transcendental attributes of Being itself: Beauty, Truth, Goodness, and so on—all of which together issue forth in the "pure joy" (*delectatio*) or "blessedness" (*beatitudo*) of having "seen" God. In this essay, all references to the *Monologion* and *Proslogion* are made parenthetically, and are marked as "M" and "P," respectively, followed by the corresponding chapter number. Unless otherwise noted, all quotations are taken from Anselm of Canterbury, *The Major Works,* ed. Brian Davies and G. R. Evans (Oxford: Oxford University Press, 1998), 3–81; 82–104. Where recourse is made to the Latin editions of Anselm's texts, I have consulted Anselmus Cantuariensis, *L'Oeuvre d'Anselme de Cantorbéry,* ed. M. Corbin (Paris, 1986).

4. Of the vast number of scholarly studies that the last century has produced, a few, to my mind, stand out as paramount and have been consulted intermittently throughout the composition of this essay. See Karl Barth, *Anselm: Fides Quaerens Intellectum; Anselm's Proof of the Existence of God in the Context of His Theological Scheme,* trans. Ian W. Robertson (Richmond: John Knox, 1960); Charles Hartshorne, *Anselm's Discovery: A Re-examination of the Ontological Proof for God's Existence* (LaSalle: Open Court, 1965); Aidan Nichols, OP, "Anselm of Canterbury and the Language of Perfection," *Downside Review* 103 (July 1985): 204–17; Jean-Luc Marion, "Is the Ontological Argument Ontological? The Argument according to Anselm and Its Metaphysical Interpretation according to Kant," in *Flight of the Gods: Philosophical Perspectives in Negative Theology,* ed. Ilse N. Bulhof and Laurens ten Kate, 78–99 (New York: Fordham University Press, 2000). Both Hartshorne and Nichols have alluded to the "logic" or "language" of perfection according to which the present essay is attempting to proceed; I am especially indebted to the work of the latter. For a rather helpful critical assessment of Anselmian scholarship in the last half century or so, see Colin Grant, "Anselm's Argument Today," *Journal of the American Academy of Religion* 57, no. 4 (1989): 791–806; cf. Jeffrey C. Pugh, "*Fides Quaerens Intellectum:* Anselm as Contemporary," *Theology Today* 55, no. 1 (April 1998): 35–45.

5. Barth, *Anselm,* 142.

6. "Something-than-which-a-greater-cannot-be-thought exists so truly then, that it cannot even be thought not to exist. And You, Lord our God, are this being. You exist so truly, Lord my God, that You cannot even be thought not to exist. . . . In fact, everything there is, except You alone, can be thought of as not existing. You alone, then, of all things most truly exist (*solus igitur verissime omnium*) and therefore of all things possess existence to the highest degree; for anything else does not exist as truly, and so possesses existence to a lesser degree" (P 3).

7. On the basis of this claim, Anselm replies to Gaunilo (chap. 4) that God's existence alone can be proven, for it is the one "distinguishing characteristic of God that He cannot be thought of as not existing." Anselm, *Reply to Gaunilo,* in *Major Works,* 115–16. Furthermore, it is precisely on this score that Anselm can proceed to "prove" the rational truth of faith's claims upon the Divine Being while bracketing their authoritative foundation, namely, Scripture. For as reason itself tells us, that which we seek to understand is that by which our very existence is upheld, such that in the journey of *theoria* the divine existence occurs to us not as an ontic reality over-against our own self-substantive facticity, but as the very condition of our existence, a condition to which we must already have been granted access to in order to be able to seek, or to *see,* at all (P pref., 1). It is for this reason that Anselm can insist upon the absolute legitimacy of the content of the church's faith, and aver that, quite apart from any appeals to scriptural authority, whatever in reason contradicts with this faith is to be acknowledged as false. For it is not that the human *ratio* seeks autonomously (and apologetically) to

establish the reasonableness of faith's claims, but rather that it is initiated into a journey upon which it is educated in faith's reason, which is the *ratio* of God, the only genuinely true *ratio,* in relation to which our *ratio* functions as similitude or image (M 32). Thus, for Anselm, all rational "proofs" for God's existence can by definition never "psychologize" or "rationalize" the deity, insofar as by uncovering the ontological structures of *ratio* itself, they reveal that there can *only* be a supreme *ratio,* and that finite reason is always already participatory in it.

8. See Marion, "Is the Ontological Argument Ontological?" 93–97. Marion argues that the proof itself only becomes operative with this elision, where the orienting formula *aliquid quo maius nihil cogitari potest* becomes *quo nihil melius cogitari potest* in chapter 14, foreshadowed by the *deus sit quidquid melius est esse quam non esse* in chapter 5.

9. Quoted in Hans Urs von Balthasar, *Glory of the Lord: A Theological Aesthetics,* ed. Joseph Fessio and John Riches, vol. 2, *Studies in Theological Style: Clerical Styles,* trans. Andrew Louth et al. (San Francisco: Ignatius Press, 1984), 238.

10. For the language of "performance" here I am indebted to A. J. Vanderjagt, "The Performative Heart of Anselm's *Proslogion,*" in *Anselm: Aosta, Bec, and Canterbury; Papers in Commemoration of the Nine-Hundredth Anniversary of Anselm's Enthronement as Archbishop, 25 September 1093,* ed. D. E. Luscombe and G. R. Evans, 229–37 (Sheffield: Sheffield Academic Press, 1996).

11. Von Balthasar, *Glory of the Lord,* 2:235.

12. Another point made in the *Monologion* that is carried over into the *Proslogion,* there orienting Anselm's explication of the divine nature: God, for example, is that which is in no finite thing but contains all things (P 19); God is "before and beyond" all things as the end of all things (P 20); God is "that one thing necessary in which is every good," and on this basis alone is "uniquely and completely and solely good" (P 23).

13. "O supreme and inaccessible light; O whole and blessed truth, how far You are from me who am so close to You! How distant you are from my sight while I am so present to Your sight! You are wholly present everywhere and I do not see You. In You I move and in You I have my being and I cannot come near to You. You are within me and around me and I do not have any experience of You" (P 16).

14. In chapter 76 of the *Monologion,* Anselm employs the Latin *tendere* in much the same manner as Gregory of Nyssa uses the Greek *epektasis,* as a way of describing our "progress in" the supreme being of God. If one considers that the Nyssen famously redefined perfection as perpetual progress in the divine life, we may not at all be remiss to suggest that Anselm's own "logic of perfection" is (conceptually, at least) fully "Greek."

15. In this vein, Karl Barth has noted that the key point of distinction between the believer and the *insipiens* is that between "two radically different modes of human existence determined by a fundamentally different attitude of man to God" (Barth, *Anselm,* 105). The believer, that is, speaks by grace in faith, from the perspective of one who as a creature is being redeemed; the "fool" is such insofar as she takes her creaturely situation to be the limit-case of existence (see 159–61).

16. On this, see the insightful article of D. Bentley Hart, "A Gift Exceeding Every Debt: An Eastern Orthodox Appreciation of Anselm's *Cur Deus Homo,*" *Pro Ecclesia* 7 (1993): 333–49.

17. I owe the gloss to Professor Craig Keen, who suggested the phrase to me (with only passing reference to Anselm) as a way of articulating my own nascent understanding of grace-as-gift (a view that owes as much to Wesley's notion of "preventing grace" as it does to Augustine's).

18. Eadmer, *The Life of St Anselm: Archbishop of Canterbury,* trans. R. W. Southern (New York: Thomas Nelson, 1962), 84. Eadmer continues, "Hence he always strove with all his might to avoid being infected by sin," and it was in this way that he "pressed forward to attain

everlasting life" (84–85; cf. 69–71, 93–98). This performance-by-grace of the perfection of existence is just what Anselm seems to mean, throughout his oeuvre, by the life of "works." This, in biographical form, enacts the theological import for Anselm's life of what we are given in "doctrinal" form in *Monologion,* chaps. 69–75, thus affirming Eadmer's confession "that it would be unthinkable to suppose that [Anselm's] life differed from his teaching" (80).

19. In this sense, as David Moss has pointed out, Anselm carries out "the ancient and orthodox demand of the Fathers of the Church . . . that it is only when one is perfected in *praktike* that one can undertake *theoria.*" David Moss, "Friendship: St. Anselm, *Theoria* and the Convolution of Sense," in *Radical Orthodoxy: A New Theology,* ed. John Milbank, Catherine Pickstock, and Graham Ward (London: Routledge, 1999), 128. As Anselm himself says in commending *Cur Deus Homo* to Pope Urban II, between faith and the beatific vision comes the journey of life, and it is just this pilgrimage that "mediates understanding" (*inter fidem et speciem intellectum esse medium intelligo*). Anselm, *Why God Became Man,* in *Major Works,* 260. Moss's essay masterfully explores the ethical dimensions, with reference to Anselm's personal letters, of what I am here investigating the doctrinal dimensions of, with reference to Anselm's treatises.

20. On Anselm as an example of one who does theology as catechesis, see Ellen T. Charry, *By the Renewing of Your Minds: The Pastoral Function of Christian Doctrine* (New York: Oxford University Press, 1997), 155–75.

21. As it does, for example, in Vladimir Lossky's reading of Anselm in "Redemption and Deification," in Lossky, *In the Image and Likeness of God,* ed. John H. Erickson and Thomas E. Bird (Crestwood, NY: St. Vladimir's Seminary Press, 1974), 97–110.

Martin Luther: "Little Christs for the World"; Faith and Sacraments as Means to *Theosis*

Jonathan Linman

Introduction

ALTHOUGH DEIFICATION OR *THEOSIS* AS A THEOLOGICAL THEME HAS A scriptural foundation and historical Christian proponents, it is not until the contemporary period, particularly with the emergence of the new Finnish school of Luther interpretation, that Lutherans have begun to dialogue with others and articulate an understanding of *theosis* consistent with the tenets of their theological and spiritual tradition. By an examination of selected writings of Martin Luther and a summary of pertinent Finnish Luther scholarship, this essay explores a Lutheran understanding of *theosis* as the unitive or participatory state between the person of faith and Christ where faith itself functions as the source of deification. Such an interpretation may be regarded as the gift of the Finns to current Lutheran spiritual theology.

By paying particular attention to the crucial role of the proclamation of the Word and the administration of the sacraments in the creation and nurturing of faith, a Lutheran understanding of *theosis* upholds the centrality of baptism and the Eucharist in the soteriological dynamics leading to *theosis*. A concluding reflection begins to explore the implications of a distinctive Lutheran view of deification for ecumenical witness, dialogue, and ethics.

Typical Lutheran Attitudes toward *Theosis*

The union of Christ with Christians certainly is suggested in the Scriptures, and 2 Peter 1:3–4 is often cited as the foundation for this view. In the patristic age, the theological category of *theosis*—that through Christ humans can share in the divine nature—was developed by such luminaries as Irenaeus of Lyon and Athanasius of Alexandria, who wrote: first Irenaeus, "Our Lord Jesus Christ . . . did, through His transcendent love, become what we are, that He might bring us to be even what He is Himself," and then Athanasius, "[Christ], indeed, assumed humanity that we might become God."[1]

At first blush, the notion that depraved, fallen humanity could in any way participate in the divine life, that humans could become divine, seems ludicrous and theologically untenable for Lutherans and their theology. According to the *Formula of Concord,* one of the major Lutheran confessional documents, justification by faith is related to objective, external righteousness; the sinner is declared forgiven by God as in a court of law, but the sinner's being (*esse*) remains corrupt and as such does not share directly in the divine life.[2]

This understanding has been reinforced since the late nineteenth century in Germany and elsewhere by neo-Kantian philosophical influences on Lutheran theology in which God's being is separated from God's effects.[3] Suffice it to say that a Lutheran understanding of mystical union or *theosis* has largely been untenable, and justification by faith has been reductionistically interpreted in terms of the forensic, objective, external, and imputed forgiveness of sins without significant regard for the transformation of the sinner.

The Finnish School

However, since the 1970s, a new school of Luther interpretation has emerged in Finland that is much more favorably disposed to a Lutheran understanding of mystical union and *theosis.* Motivated by the bilateral dialogues between the Church of Finland and the Russian Orthodox Church, Finnish scholars have reread Luther with an eye toward viewing justification as involving deification and have opened up new hermeneutical vistas with rather surprising and convincing results. In short, the new Finnish school asserts that union with Christ is made possible by faith, such that justification by faith is no longer understood simply as the forgiveness of sins but also as the means to our participation in the divine life (*theosis*). Tuomo Mannermaa is the "father" of the Finnish school, and he writes:

> Central in Luther's theology is that in faith the human being *really* participates by faith in the person of Christ and in the divine life and the victory that is in it. Or, to say it the other way around: Christ gives his person to the human being through the faith by which we grasp it. . . . According to the Reformer, justifying faith does not merely signify a reception of the forgiveness imputed to a human being for the sake of the merit of Christ, which is the aspect emphasized by the Formula of Concord. Being a real sharing (participation) in Christ, "faith" stands also for participation in the institution of "blessing, righteousness and life" that has taken place in Christ. . . . Therefore, justifying faith means participation in God in Christ's person.[4]

Another Finnish scholar, Simo Peura, reinforces Mannermaa's views and further states that "justification is not only a change in self-understanding, a new relation to God, or a new ethos of love. God changes the sinner ontologically in the sense that he or she participates in God and in his divine nature, being made righteous and 'a god.'"[5] Moreover, Peura writes, "All of this is possible only if Christ is united with the sinner through the sinner's faith. So, the crucial point of this interpretation rests in the notion of *unio cum Christo.*"[6] And, quoting Peura yet again, "The self-giving of God is realized when Christ indwells the sinner through faith and thus unites himself with the sinner. This means that the Christian receives salvation *per Christum* only under the condition of *unio cum Christo.* Luther's conviction on this point leads to the conclusion that a Christian becomes a partaker of Christ and that a Christian is in this sense also deified."[7]

Scholars from the Finnish school offer convincing arguments for a Lutheran understanding of *theosis* and seem to have won over two of Lutheranism's major, traditional theologians in the United States: Carl Braaten and Robert Jenson. It is noteworthy to witness how a new set of hermeneutic lenses can make a significant difference when reexamining texts that have been read for centuries through traditional eyes of faith. With alternate hermeneutical strategies, very familiar texts suddenly reveal radically new understandings as if these meanings were "hidden in plain sight" all along. For example, Luther himself presents a bold understanding of the Christ event which points to *theosis,* as seen in his Christmas sermon of 1514:

> Just as the word of God became flesh, so it is certainly also necessary that the flesh may become word. In others words: God becomes man so that man may become God. Thus power becomes powerless so that weakness may become powerful. The Logos puts on our form and pattern, our image and likeness, so that it may clothe us with its image, its pattern, and its likeness. Thus wisdom becomes foolish so that foolishness may become wisdom, and so it is in all other things that are in God and in us, to the extent that in all these things he takes what is ours to himself in order to impart what is his to us.[8]

It is obvious from this homiletical excerpt that Luther was very familiar indeed with Irenaeus and Athanasius, and that *theosis,* as they articulated it, is not a foreign category in his thinking.

In the very extensively studied treatise "Freedom of a Christian," Luther again points to themes of *theosis* by employing the bridal imagery commonly seen in the writings of the medieval mystics when they talk about mystical union, and he offers this imagery in the context of a discussion of the marriage of grace and faith:

> [Another] incomparable benefit of faith is that it unites the soul with Christ as a bride is united with her bridegroom. By this mystery, as the Apostle teaches, Christ and the soul become one flesh [Eph 5:31–32]. And if they are one flesh and there is between them a true marriage . . . it follows that everything they have

> they hold in common, the good as well as the evil. Accordingly the believing soul can boast of and glory in whatever Christ has as though it were its own, and whatever the soul has Christ claims as his own. . . . By the wedding ring of faith [Christ] shares in the sins, death, and pains of hell which are his bride's. . . . [T]he believing soul by means of the pledge of its faith is free in Christ, its bridegroom, free from all sins, secure against death and hell, and is endowed with the eternal righteousness, life, and salvation of Christ its bridegroom. Who then can fully appreciate what this royal marriage means? Who can understand the riches of the glory of this grace?[9]

If grace is the source of the marriage between Christ and the Christian, mystical union between the believer and Christ is consummated through faith, and as faith makes the person of Christ present to the Christian, *theosis* can be seen as the end result of the life of faith. Thus, the believer shares in the divine life and is deified, if you will.

Luther's View of Faith and Its Relation to *Theosis*

How is this mystical union of grace through faith accomplished? Such a question raises the issue of "what is faith?" from a Lutheran perspective. In its most profound sense, faith is not finally the intellectual assent to a set of doctrines (despite a long history of Lutheran proclivity for doctrinal accuracy and purity). At its deepest level, faith is trust, specifically trust in Christ to accomplish human salvation. Or as Luther himself writes, "Faith is a living, daring confidence in God's grace, so sure and certain that the believer would stake his life on it a thousand times."[10] Sin, in Luther's theology, is understood as misplaced trust, driving us away from Christ toward those idols in which we would otherwise trust, rely, bet, and bank on. Such misdirected trust drives a wedge between God and humanity. The posture of trust in Christ for salvation, on the other hand, drives us into the Savior's loving arms and embrace. And there we find a home and are united with Christ. Such faith, such a posture of trust, compels us to Christ himself even as Christ draws us to himself. This process of entrusting ourselves to Christ is a complex exchange, but is central to Lutheran theology.

The Holy Spirit Creates Faith through Means

In classical Lutheran understanding, faith is not a work that we accomplish by our own effort, but is the result of the activity of the Holy Spirit mediated through the proclamation of the Word, the administration of the sacraments, in short, through the ministry of the church. As Luther asserts in his explanation to the Third Article of the Apostles' Creed in his Small Catechism, "I believe that by my own reason or strength I cannot believe in Jesus Christ, my Lord, or come to him. But the Holy Spirit has called me through the Gospel, enlightened me with his gifts, and sanctified and preserved me in true faith, just as he calls, gathers, enlightens, and sanctifies the whole Christian church on earth and preserves it in union with Jesus Christ in one true faith."[11] The centrality of the Holy Spirit's work of faith mediated through the church is reinforced in Article Five of the Augsburg Confession: "To obtain . . . faith God instituted the office of the ministry, that is, provided the Gospel and the sacraments. Through these, as through means, he gives the Holy Spirit, who works faith, when and where he pleases, in those who hear the Gospel."[12]

The sacraments of baptism and the Eucharist in particular are intended to awaken and strengthen faith, even as the sacraments are received in faith. Again, in the Augsburg Confession, Article Thirteen: "It is taught among us that the sacraments were instituted not only to be signs by which people might be identified outwardly as Christians, but that they are signs and testimonies of God's will toward us for the purpose of awakening and strengthening our faith. For this reason they require faith, and they are rightly used when they are received in faith and for the purpose of strengthening faith."[13]

Luther reinforces the intimate and inseparable connections among the Spirit's activity, the proclamation of the Word, and the celebration of the sacraments in uniting us with Christ by justifying faith when he writes in a lecture on Jacob's dream of the ladder:

> In this way we ascend into Him and are carried along through the Word and the Holy Spirit. And through faith we cling to Him, since we become one body with Him and He with us. He is the Head; we are the members. On the other hand, He descends to us through the Word and the sacraments by teaching and by exercising us in the knowledge of Him. The first union, then, is that of the Father and the Son in the divinity. The second is that of the divinity and the humanity in Christ. The third is that of the church and Christ.[14]

Again, and in short, for Luther, faith as a means to our union with Christ is not simply an act of the will but a gift of the Holy Spirit mediated through Word and sacraments. While faith comes primarily through the hearing of the Word of the gospel (Rom 10:17), the significance of baptism and the Eucharist for faith, and thus for union with Christ, must not be overlooked.

The Role of Baptism in *Theosis*

In baptism we are baptized into Christ's death and resurrection. As such we are baptized into Christ's person and united with him. According to Simo Peura, "The essential idea in Luther's theology of baptism is that baptism is a merciful and consoling union in which God joins himself with the sinner and becomes one with him or her. Thus, baptism is not just a covenant or an agreement between two partners bound together to function or act for the same purpose, the salvation of the baptized. It is much more: through the sacramental act of baptism God binds himself ontologically to a sinner and is one with him through his whole earthly life, if he adheres to Christ in faith."[15] Such union is reliant on divine presence in the sacrament. Or as Luther suggests in a sermon on Matthew 3:13–17, "We should not doubt at all that wherever one is being baptized the heavens are assuredly open and the entire Trinity is present and through its own presence sanctifies and blesses the person being baptized."[16]

Though baptism is an objective, external act with its own efficacy and validity through the presence of the whole Trinity, the meaning of this event needs to be apprehended by faith. Luther writes in the Large Catechism:

> God's works . . . are salutary and necessary for salvation, and they do not exclude but rather demand faith, for without faith they could not be grasped. Just by allowing the water to be poured over you, you do not receive Baptism in such a manner that it does you any good. But it becomes beneficial to you if you accept it as God's command and ordinance, so that, baptized in the name of God, you may receive in the water the promised salvation. This the hand cannot do, nor the body, but the heart must believe it.
>
> Thus you see plainly that Baptism is not a work which we do but is a treasure which God gives us and faith grasps, just as the Lord Christ upon the cross is not a work but a treasure comprehended and offered to us in the Word and received by faith.[17]

Luther suggests that faith in the efficacy of the work of God in baptism is itself God's work, and that faith begins at baptism, even in an infant's or child's inability to rationally grasp the meaning of what is occurring in the sacrament. Luther writes, "To be sure, children are brought to Baptism by the faith and work of others; but when they get there and the pastor or baptizer deals with them in Christ's stead, it is [Christ] who blesses them and grants them faith and the kingdom of heaven. For the word and act of the pastor are the Word and work of Christ himself."[18] And furthermore, because faith does not depend on the operation of reason, Luther concludes, "In baptism children themselves believe and have faith of their own. God works this within them through the intercession of the sponsors who bring the child to the font in the faith of the Christian Church. And this is what we mean by the power of a foreign faith. We do not mean that anyone can be saved by it, but that by it, that is, through its intercession and help, he may, from God himself, obtain a faith of his own, through which he is saved."[19]

Thus *theosis* as a theme in Luther is rooted in faith and begins in baptism. The act of baptism itself creates nascent faith in the baptized as a gift of God, mediated through the Spirit's work in sponsors and in the whole church acting on behalf of the baptized. The same mechanics of faith are present in the Eucharist.

The Role of the Eucharist in *Theosis*

The sacrament of the altar, the Eucharist, is also for Luther a concrete means to an expression of our union with Christ and our sharing in the divine life. In his 1519 treatise on the Blessed Sacrament, he writes:

> Christ appointed these two forms of bread and wine, rather than any other, as a further indication of the very union and fellowship which is in this sacrament. For there is no more intimate, deep, and indivisible union than the union of the food with him who is fed. For the food enters into and is assimilated by his very nature and becomes one substance with the person who is fed. Other unions, achieved by such things as nails, glue, cords, and the like, do not make one indivisible substance of the objects joined together. Thus in the sacrament we become united with Christ, and are made one body with all the saints, so that Christ cares for us and acts on our behalf.[20]

As in baptism, the Eucharist objectively has its own efficacy and validity, but it likewise must be apprehended in faith for one to be aware of its benefits. Luther writes in a sermon preached on March 14, 1522:

> It is very necessary here that your hearts and consciences be well instructed and that you make a big distinction between outward reception and inner and spiritual reception. Bodily and outward reception is that in which a man receives with his mouth the body of Christ and his blood, and doubtless any man can receive the sacrament in this way, without faith and love. But this does not make a man a Christian, for if it did, even a mouse would be a Christian, for it, too, can eat the bread and perchance even drink out of the cup. It is such a simple thing to do. But the true, inner, spiritual reception is a very different thing, for it consists in the right use of the sacrament and its fruits.[21]

Faith as spiritual apprehension of the sacrament's meaning and the physical eating and drinking of the bread and wine results in union with Christ in the Eucharist. Luther elaborates on this point in arguing for the real presence of Christ in the Eucharist in 1527:

> The mouth eats the body of Christ physically, for it cannot grasp or eat the words, nor does it know what it is eating. As far as taste is concerned the mouth surely seems to be eating something other than Christ's body. But the heart grasps the words in faith and eats spiritually precisely the same body as the mouth eats physically, for the heart sees very well what the uncomprehending mouth eats

> physically. But how does it see this? Not by looking at the bread or at the mouth's eating, but at the word which is there, "Eat, this is my body." Yet, there is only one body of Christ, which both mouth and heart eat, each in its own mode and manner. The heart cannot eat it physically nor can the mouth eat it spiritually. So God arranges that the mouth eats physically for the heart and the heart eats spiritually for the mouth, and thus both are satisfied and saved by one and the same food. . . .
>
> Perishable food is transformed into the body which eats it; this food, however, transforms the person who eats it into what it is itself and makes him like itself, spiritual, alive, and eternal. . . .
>
> So, when we eat Christ's flesh physically and spiritually, the food is so powerful that it transforms us into itself and out of fleshly, sinful, mortal men makes spiritual, holy, living men. This we are already, though in a hidden manner in faith and hope; the fact is not yet manifest, but we shall experience it on the Last Day.[22]

Conclusions and Implications

In the preceding discussions about the nature of justifying faith and the process of faith in relation to the sacraments of baptism and the Eucharist, I have attempted to explore the mechanics of how justifying faith functions as the source of mystical union and *theosis* in the thought of Martin Luther and in confessional Lutheran theology. One cannot simply assert without qualification or theological exploration that a believer's faith automatically unites the believer to Christ and thereby deifies the believer. However, it is evident from the preceding discussions that faith, or trust in Christ, is intimately and inseparably linked to the deifying work of Christ and the Holy Spirit, as expressed in the proclamation of the Word of God, the role of the sacraments, and the ministry of the church as the community of all believers. If the faith of believers unites them to Christ in such a way that there is an ontological participation in the divine life, this process must be understood in the context of mediation through the proclamation of the Word ("for faith comes through the Spirit in the hearing of the Word") and the administration of the sacraments of baptism and the Eucharist (which awaken and strengthen faith). In short, it is by means of sharing in the mission and ministry of the whole Church that the believer is deified.

Faith does not come about ex nihilo, but through the concrete embodiment of the church and its activity. Faith does not effect some kind of magical, unmediated, ontological transformation. Rather, one can biblically, historically, and empirically trace the emergence of faith as the uniting of souls with Christ, or if you will our *theosis,* in the particular expressions of the church's ministry of Word and sacraments. The gift of the Spirit serves to create, nurture, and sustain faith, even as the gift of faith empowers believers to apprehend the meaning and significance of the church's mission and ministry in Word and sacraments. Through these empirical means and the power of the Holy Spirit, we come to entrust ourselves to Christ and to share in his divine life. Justification by faith is the complex constellation of these concrete gifts of grace such that we are not only forgiven but are made "partakers of the divine nature" through our faith—a new creation initiated by God in Christ and sustained by the Spirit working in Word and sacraments. Such are the mechanics of justification by faith as the basis for *theosis* in Martin Luther.

The importance of the Finnish school's interpretation of Luther for future theological dialogue is great. There are a number of implications brought about by the conclusions stated above, but we will mention only a few.

The Importance of the Finnish School for Lutheran Theology and Witness in the Twenty-First Century

In his discussion of the future of Christian spirituality, Karl Rahner predicted that "the Christian of the future will be a mystic or he or she will not exist at all."[23] If the current interest in spirituality in general and the Christian mystics in particular is any indication, Rahner's prediction seems to be coming to pass. Traditional and common Lutheran preoccupation with forensic justification, with a focus on imputed righteousness by the forgiveness of sins, no longer speaks with immediate intelligibility in the current milieu. The challenge of our age is not individual sin but isolation, alienation, and broken, if not nonexistent, community life. A renewed focus on justification by faith as a means to a deeper and more intimate relationship with Christ via the community of faith can allow Lutheranism to engage with others and speak distinctively about *theosis* in the current age. The Finnish school of Luther interpretation is to be credited for providing a new, fresh voice of Lutheran theology and witness.

The Importance of the Finnish School for Lutheran–Roman Catholic Dialogue

In addition to advancing Lutheran-Russian Orthodox dialogue in Finland, the Finnish school also has much to offer Lutheran–Roman Catholic dialogue throughout the world. The Joint Declaration on Justification signed by the Vatican and representatives of the Lutheran World Federation has taken Lutheran–Roman Catholic ecumenical relationships to a new level. But the Finnish school could take this bilateral dialogue further. As Simo Peura suggests:

> Because of Luther's view of the real union with Christ, we can connect the effective aspect of justification to the forensic aspect. But this argument has not informed

> the method of the Joint Declaration. That document lacks totally the idea of union with Christ. According to the document the forensic aspect seems to characterize especially the Lutheran way of understanding justification, and the effective aspect explains specifically the Catholic point of view. The document indicates that the two aspects describe two different sides of the same thing. But actually the two aspects are connected to each other so that we might properly say that they coexist side by side.[24]

In such a light it would be productive to return to an examination of Luther in relation to the medieval mystics, work begun years ago by the late Lutheran ethicist Bengt Hoffman in his book *Luther and the Mystics* that was panned by mainstream Lutheranism of the time, but that is regaining favor as a result of the Finnish School.

The Importance of the Finnish School for Lutheran Ethics

Finally, a field of particular importance for our time, especially in response to the social injustices that give rise to terror and war, is theological ethics. Historically, Lutherans have been conspicuously quiet when it comes to articulating a distinctive Lutheran approach to ethics. However, a Lutheran social ethic can be built on the understanding of justification by faith as a means to *theosis*. Our participation in the divine life of Christ in a Lutheran social ethic would link mystical union with social action. Luther himself, in a sermon on Matthew 8:1–13, suggests such an intimate connection between our union with Christ and the life lived ethically in the world for the other:

> Faith makes us lords, love makes us servants; aye, through faith we become gods and partakers of the divine nature and name, as Psalm 82:6 says: "I have said, Ye are gods; and all of you are children of the Most High." But through love we become the equals of the very lowliest. According to faith we are in need of nothing but have a sufficiency of everything; according to love we serve everybody. Through faith we receive gifts from above, from God; through love we dispense them downwards to our neighbor. Just so Christ was in need of nothing according to His divinity, but according to His humanity He served everybody who was in need of Him.
>
> We have often enough said that we, too, must, through faith, in this way be born God's children and gods, lords, and kings, just as Christ is born true God of the Father in eternity; and again we must break forth in love to help our neighbor with well-doing, just as Christ became man in order to help all of us.[25]

As faith unites us to Christ through the proclamation of the Word and administration of the sacraments in the church's ministry, we, as Luther suggests, "become as it were a Christ to the other that we may be Christs to one another and Christ may be the same in all."[26] As we engage our ethically faithful and courageous mission to and for the sake of a broken world, we function as "little Christs" growing up into full divinity for those in desperate need of God's love and transforming embrace.

Notes

1. Irenaeus, *Adversus Haereses* 5.praef, ANF 1:526; Athanasius, *On the Incarnation* (Crestwood, NY: St. Vladimir's Seminary Press, 1982; repr., 1989), 93.
2. Simo Peura, "Christ as Favor and Gift (*donum*): The Challenge of Luther's Understanding of Justification," in *Union with Christ: The New Finnish Interpretation of Luther,* ed. Carl E. Braaten and Robert W. Jenson (Grand Rapids, MI: William B. Eerdmans, 1998), 45.
3. Ibid., 46.
4. Tuomo Mannermaa, "Justification and *Theosis* in Lutheran-Orthodox Perspective," in *Union with Christ,* 32.
5. Peura, "Christ as Favor and Gift," 48.
6. Ibid.
7. Ibid., 51.
8. Quoted in Tuomo Mannermaa, "Why is Luther So Fascinating? Modern Finnish Luther Research," in *Union with Christ,* 11.
9. Martin Luther, "Freedom of a Christian," trans. W. A. Lambert, rev. Harold J. Grimm, in *Selected Writings of Martin Luther: 1520–1523,* ed. Theodore G. Tappert (Philadelphia: Fortress Press, 1967), 27–28.
10. *Word and Sacrament I,* trans. Charles M. Jacobs, ed. and rev. E. Theodore Bachmann, vol. 35, *Luther's Works,* ed. Helmut T. Lehmann (Philadelphia: Muhlenberg Press, 1960), 370.
11. "The Small Catechism of Dr. Martin Luther for Ordinary Pastors and Preachers," in *The Book of Concord,* ed. and trans. Theodore G. Tappert (Philadelphia: Fortress Press, 1959), 345.
12. Martin Luther, "The Augsburg Confession," in *The Book of Concord,* 31.
13. Ibid., 35–36.
14. *Lectures on Genesis Chapters 26–30,* in *Luther's Works,* Jaroslav Pelikan, assoc. ed. Walter A. Hansen, vol. 5 (St. Louis: Concordia, 1968), 223.
15. Peura, "Christ as Favor and Gift," 53–54.
16. W 37:649, trans. in *What Luther Says: An Anthology,* ed. Ewald M. Plass (St. Louis: Concordia Publishing House, 1957), 1:47.
17. "The Large Catechism of Martin Luther," in *The Book of Concord,* 441.
18. W 17 2:84, trans. in *What Luther Says,* 1:51.
19. W 17 2:82, trans. in *What Luther Says,* 1:53.
20. "The Blessed Sacrament of the Holy and True Body of Christ and the Brotherhood, 1519," in *Word and Sacrament I,* trans. Jeremiah J. Scheindel, rev. E. Theodore Bachmann, vol. 35, *Luther's Works,* (Philadelphia: Muhlenberg Press, 1960), 59.
21. *Sermons I,* ed. and trans. John W. Doberstein, vol. 51, *Luther's Works,* (Philadelphia: Muhlenberg Press, 1959), 92.
22. "That These Words of Christ, 'This Is My Body,' etc., Still Stand Firm against the Fanatics, 1527," in *Word and Sacrament III,* ed. and trans. Robert H. Fischer, *Luther's Works,* vol. 37 (Philadelphia: Muhlenberg Press, 1961), 93, 100, 101.
23. Karl Rahner, *The Practice of Faith: A Handbook of Contemporary Spirituality* [*Praxis des Glaubens*] (New York: Crossroads, 1983), 22.
24. Peura, "Christ as Favor and Gift," 64.
25. W 17 2:74–75, trans. in *What Luther Says,* 1:502–3.
26. "Freedom of a Christian," in *Martin Luther: Selections from His Writings,* ed. John Dillenberger (Garden City, NY: Anchor Books: 1961), 76.

John Calvin: United to God through Christ

J. Todd Billings

"We shall at length be really and fully united to Thee [Almighty God] through Christ our Lord."
—Calvin, Lecture 123

FOR SOME, THE ONLY SURE THING THAT CAN BE SAID ABOUT CALVIN AND deification is that he did not believe in it.[1] How could someone who so emphasized the majesty of God and the sinfulness of humanity—and hence the separation between the two—affirm deification?[2] Moreover, some of the notions associated with Calvin—the bondage of the will to sin, an alleged tension between nature and grace—are cited as precisely the notions that a theology of deification allows one to escape.[3] The problem is made worse by the fact that recent studies tend to look to late Byzantine theologians such as Gregory Palamas as the standard for deification, even when comparing Western theologians who were unfamiliar with Palamas.[4] However valuable this may be for ecumenical discussion, this approach tends to underestimate the possibility that there may be different, yet legitimate, conceptions of deification in the West, arising from the common sources for theologies of deification: Scripture and the church fathers. If late Byzantine theology is the paradigm for theologies of deification, there is a danger not only of making Western theology look too much like late Byzantine theology, but also of dismissing Western theology when it fails to meet the late Byzantine "standard." Thus, while scholars like Eric Perl are right to guard against attempts to make Thomas Aquinas functionally affirm the late Byzantine distinctions of "essence" and "energies," he is misguided in implying that the absence of this distinction is fatal to any theology of salvation as deification.[5]

Drawing upon the language of participation, ingrafting, and adoption in select Pauline and Johannine passages, Calvin teaches a particular model of deification as the qualified participation of humanity in the Triune God, affirming the differentiated union of humanity with God in redemption through an eclectic use of Augustine, Irenaeus, and Cyril of Alexandria.[6] Yet, in distinction from alternative theologies that teach deification, Calvin teaches that the uniting of believers with God through Christ is only properly understood when the imputation of Christ's righteousness is affirmed and "partitive," synergistic understandings of the Spirit's work are rejected. Moreover, for Calvin "participation in Christ" is inseparable from ecclesial *koinonia* and social acts of compassion. Thus, while Calvin's vision is distinct from late Byzantine conceptions of deification, his theology nonetheless offers an instructive account of the possible consequences of affirming that the fullest manifestation and final end of humanity are found in union with God through Christ.

The central objection to the claim that Calvin "could" teach deification is that he systematically opposes humanity and divinity such that a transformative union between the two is unthinkable.[7] In his anthropology, Calvin emphasizes the sinfulness of human nature; the role and contribution of humans in the appropriation of salvation and sanctification seems practically nil. This post-Augustinian anthropology appears to emphasize the powerlessness of the human to move toward the good telos of creation. Calvin not only repudiates theologies of synergism and cooperative grace, but seems to speak of humanity becoming "nothing," even to the point of "obliteration" in the process of redemption.[8] A doctrine of deification normally provides an anthropology from within a trinitarian doctrine of God—such that divinity and humanity are in fundamental concordance. In contrast, Calvin's view of sinful humanity in relation to an all-powerful divine will may give the impression that the human side of the divine-human relationship has virtually vanished.

The Unity of Divinity and Humanity in Calvin's Theology of Redemption

Calvin faced criticisms related to his allegedly "negative" anthropology in his own day. In reaction to Calvin's theology of grace and providence presented in the 1539 *Institutes,* Roman Catholic theologian Albert Pighius wrote *Ten Books on Human Free Choice and Divine Grace* in 1542. The central argument was that the church fathers speak in one voice against Calvin's claim that the will is in bondage to sin apart from the effectual work of the Spirit. Calvin's strong doctrine of sin is said to distort his account of grace and regeneration. Offended by the idea that humans contribute "nothing" in salvation, Pighius defends an approach that aims to "balance" the work of salvation in order to preserve human responsibility. Calvin responds in 1543 with *The Bondage and Liberation of the Will.* This work of Calvin is important to consult regarding the allegations of his "negative" anthropology for two reasons: First, in contrast to the earlier sixteenth-century debate between Erasmus and Luther on free choice, Calvin meets Pighius on his own terms and argues his case from the church fathers rather than primarily from Scripture.[9] Second, in responding to these Roman Catholic objections, Calvin makes important distinctions and qualifications to his position (partly through concessions to patristic concerns) that are not included in the later *Institutes.*[10]

In response to Pighius's objection to his "negative" language concerning humanity in redemption, Calvin claims these negative statements speak of "prideful," fallen humanity, not humanity as it was created in Adam or fulfilled in Christ. It is fallen humanity that sees itself as essentially independent from God—claiming that it has power "in itself" rather than "in" or "united to" God. Thus, when Calvin says that "whatever is ours" is obliterated in regeneration, Calvin is not being "negative" about humanity but "negative" about sin. His language is indebted to the Pauline notion that believers die to the "old self," not living "according to the flesh" but "according to the Spirit." Calvin writes, "By 'whatever is ours' I understand that which belongs to us. Moreover, I define this as what we have in ourselves apart from God's creation."[11] In Pauline terms, one "dies" to the "flesh" in regeneration, but this is not the death of God's good creation, but a vivification by the Spirit.[12] In a similar way, Calvin uses the image of the vine and the branches in John 15 to draw out the contrast between the branch "in itself," which is useless apart from the nourishment and strength of the vine, and the branch "in the vine." The emphasis of this Johannine passage is that the human will "in itself" does not cooperate with God—as if it could act and cooperate on its own power apart from God—yet when the human is ingrafted onto God as the vine, God produces fruit through those human faculties.[13] Humanity at its fullest is humanity united to God. Yet, as in John, this positive principle has a negative corollary: "without me you can do nothing" (Jn 15:5).

Calvin's principle is, in fact, a deeply Christological one: full humanity must not be thought of as essentially independent or autonomous from divinity, but the two must be thought together in a manner of *interpenetration.* Although Calvin quotes a variety of biblical, patristic, and conciliar sources for this view, one of the most important is Augustine in his anti-Pelagian writings.[14] While the Pelagian controversy may appear to some as distant from Christological concerns, for both Augustine and Calvin (in his appropriation of Augustine), the Incarnation is the supreme example of an anti-Pelagian theology of grace.[15] For Augustine, grace is displayed through the priority of the Spirit in the virgin birth. In contrast to adoptionistic Christologies, Augustine taught that there was no humanity "prior" to the union of divinity and humanity in Christ that could "will" the union from an autonomous space. Indeed, although Augustine's anti-Pelagian work preceded the debate between Nestorius and Cyril of Alexandria, his concern to affirm the presence of God the Word in the womb of Mary has certain parallels with Cyril's later defense of the Theotokos.[16] In terms of his reception of Augustine's theology of grace, Calvin highlights the importance of the Incarnation,[17] thus complementing his larger claim that full humanity is naturally and fundamentally in union with God.

In order to portray this union of humanity with God in the original creation,

Calvin utilizes Aristotelian categories in *Bondage and Liberation of the Will.*[18] Humanity is not naturally at odds with God, but only opposed to God because of the Fall: the *substance* of human nature as created by God, Calvin says, is good. Indeed (as he later expounds in the *Institutes*) before the Fall of Adam, human nature is "united" to God.[19] Yet, after the Fall, human nature has been corrupted through the disease of sin. This corruption—as real as it is for Calvin—is *accidental* to human nature. Thus, when salvation comes to a person, the bond of this accidental characteristic of sinning is gradually diminished, although this process will be far from complete in this life.

While this Aristotelian language is not incorporated into the *Institutes,* it does provide a clarification of potentially misleading language in Calvin's theology and piety. Calvin often speaks of believers becoming "nothing" so that God's new creation can come forth. This is an aspect of participation in Christ's death such that one dies to the "old self" where one lives by the "flesh" in order for the "new self" to live by the Spirit in Christ.[20] Using this Pauline language about being crucified to the "old self" that is enslaved to sin, Calvin emphasizes the need to "die" to sin. Yet, Pighius has misunderstood this language when he sees human participation in Christ's death as a "death" to the good creation in Adam. For Calvin, this "death" is a mortification of the sinful desires that corrupt the good creation in Adam. Moreover, participation in Christ's death is always followed by a participation in Christ's resurrection,[21] which involves a fulfillment of the original telos of creation, the good "substance" of human nature.

Thus, citing Irenaeus in his favor, Calvin affirms that redemption heals and restores the original "good will" and "good nature" of Adam.[22] The created nature is good, and the created nature is restored in redemption. This is not a nature conceived of as an autonomous possession apart from God. Rather, as with Adam—and even more fully with Christ—this "good nature" is activated in the human only when the human is united to God by the Spirit. Thus, it is Calvin's strong insistence that God and humanity *are* naturally united in a fundamental way that requires him to oppose Pighius who seeks to honor human effort by dividing the agency and credit between God and humanity.[23] For Calvin, since God is the fountain of all life and goodness, Pighius's partitive solution is unacceptable. In sanctification, all of the human faculties are, in fact, utilized—but if one views humanity as *fundamentally* related to God, indeed as truly flourishing only *in union* with God, then one must not speak of a good human action in separation from God's action.[24]

For Calvin, the fundamental unity of divinity and humanity is not only apparent in the Spirit's prevenient work, but in God's "gift" of faith to believers. Although the reception of faith involves the voluntary assent of believers, and the assent "is properly called ours," it does not "derive from us" in exclusion from God, but is a work of the Spirit.[25] Moreover, when believers act in love, it is not "as if constrained by a necessity of the law," but voluntarily.[26] So, how can Calvin speak positively of the human acts of "assent" and "voluntary" actions of love? For Calvin, the free action of a human being is not in competition with the action of the Spirit. The Spirit empowers these actions—and deserves the praise for these actions—but these actions are still "properly called ours." As a part of this account, Calvin denies the popular medieval doctrine of "infused habits," along with the distinction between "natural" and "supernatural" virtues. Instead, Christian acts of love emerge directly from the indwelling activity of the Holy Spirit.[27] Yet, in Calvin's account, the human faculties are not bypassed in this process, but activated by the Spirit. Moreover, the divine will is not coercive toward the human person. Rather, God "renews a right spirit in their inner nature" so that the will voluntarily obeys God, consenting to faith through the work of the Spirit.[28]

From this exposition, both in *Bondage and Liberation of the Will* and in the *Institutes,* Calvin develops a theology of redemption that has much in common with many patristic writers. Calvin's debt to Augustine is immense, as shown through his extensive appropriation of Augustine's anti-Pelagian theology of grace. Calvin also shows his deep concern to stay with Irenaeus in the unequivocal affirmation of the goodness of creation, and the restoration of creation in Christ.[29] Although Calvin utilizes Aristotelian categories to do this, these categories clarify for Calvin the Irenaean motif that the original union of God and humanity in Adam is restored and fulfilled in Christ, reuniting humanity to God.[30] Moreover, concerning unredeemed humanity Calvin expands his theology of *imago Dei* in the *Institutes,* calling it a "participation in God."[31]

While Calvin develops this soteriological account in dialogue with Augustine and Irenaeus, his central sources are scriptural. In addition to the Johannine language of indwelling and ingrafting mentioned above, another key influence on Calvin is the language of participation in the book of Romans. For Calvin, Romans provides "an open door to all the most profound treasures of scripture."[32] Thus, just as the book of Romans becomes crucial for the development of the *Institutes* and the *Commentaries,* so the themes of participation, adoption, and ingrafting in Romans become crucial for Calvin's theology.[33] From Romans 6:1–11, Calvin emphasizes union with Christ in his death and resurrection, and the life of the Christian as participation in Christ. From Romans 8:12–17 and 26–27, Calvin emphasizes our adoption as the children of God, given access to the Father through the Spirit who prays through the believer. In Romans 11:17–19, Calvin finds his well-loved image of the ingrafting of believer by faith.[34] In the commentaries, the content of these three passages—involving union with Christ, participation in Christ by the Spirit, adoption, and ingrafting—are used together as mutually illuminating images.[35]

Frequently, even if only one image is used in the biblical passage, Calvin will link it to another image from Romans. Likewise, partly through the influence of Romans, the language of participation has a far-reaching influence on the doctrinal loci of the *Institutes.* The *Institutes* uses this language to speak of justification, baptism, the Lord's Supper, the resurrection, the Incarnation, the Trinity, the atonement, the *imago Dei,* and "participation in God."[36] Through the use of Romans as a "door" to the rest of Scripture and as a lens to reread the doctrinal loci, the themes of participation, adoption, and ingrafting become prominent in Calvin's theology.

Calvin's development of the biblical themes of union, adoption, ingrafting, and participation gives a strongly "Catholic" character to his theology of deification. Relying upon interpretations of John and Paul as well as Irenaeus and Augustine, Calvin teaches that the final end and goal for humanity is a trinitarian union of humanity with God. The oneness and unity of the Trinity extends to incorporate the believer: "Just as he [Christ] is one with the Father, so we become one with him."[37] In their union with Christ, believers are "participants not only in all his benefits but also in himself." Indeed, "day by day, he grows more and more into one body with us, until he becomes completely one with us."[38] Moreover, believers are "fully and firmly joined with God only when Christ joins us with him."[39] Yet, this union with Christ is impossible without a participation in the Spirit, who unites the believer to Christ.[40] Indeed, through the Spirit we "become participants in God (*in Dei participationem venimus*)."[41] Through Christ and the Spirit, believers are gathered "into participation in the Father."[42] As the "perfection of human happiness is to be united to God," this union takes place in redemption.[43] Yet, while this union does not make us "consubstantial with God" like a fourth member of the Godhead, it is always in Christ, through "the grace and power of the Spirit."[44] Calvin also speaks of a coming beatific vision, a "direct vision" of the Godhead, "when as partakers in heavenly glory we shall see God as he is."[45] This final, temporal end is in fact that "end of the Gospel" that is "to render us eventually conformable to God, and, if we may so speak, to deify us."[46] While Calvin does not go into detailed speculation on this final, eschatological end, his language concerning a trinitarian incorporation of humanity into union with God is remarkably clear and emphatic.

Calvin's Differences with Osiander on Participation

In claiming that Calvin has a doctrine of deification, I am not simply asserting that his theology contains the themes of union, participation, and adoption. A theology containing the themes typically associated with deification would not necessarily result in a *doctrine* of deification.[47]These themes are, after all, biblical ones that can be found in nearly any Christian theology. A doctrine of deification involves the development of these biblical themes and a differentiation among various theological alternatives connected with them. For Calvin, some of this differentiation comes through his appropriation of patristic developments relating to deification such as the goodness of creation, the union of divinity and humanity, and the beatific vision. In the process of this development, Calvin usually prefers to stay with biblical language to describe this process in redemption, though at times he makes positive and negative use of *deificari* and *apotheosis* to differentiate his position from various theological alternatives.[48] However, it was various disputes about the significance of the language of "participation" that led Calvin to most clearly differentiate his position from other sixteenth-century alternatives.

The controversy about "participation" that is most pertinent to deification is Calvin's dispute with Osiander.[49] Calvin does not start writing against Osiander until after he is accused of being Osiandrian in his theology by his Lutheran opponents.[50] Indeed, Osiander had some common concerns with Calvin: he appropriated the Johannine language of indwelling; he emphasized the importance of a growth in holiness as one received the gift of faith; and he wanted to appropriate Augustine's theology of grace.[51]

Like Calvin, Osiander was fond of the language of "participation," seeing justification as participation in Christ's righteousness. But for Osiander, this meant that justification could not be forensic. For Osiander, a person is called righteous when Christ, as God's righteousness, indwells the believer. Thus, the divine nature of Christ is possessed by the believer—Osiander's notion of "essential righteousness." The original goodness of humanity is restored through this union with Christ, partaking of Christ's divine nature. Justification does not mean forensic pardon of a sinner by grace, but the possession of Jesus Christ's divine righteousness by the infusion of the divine to the believer. On this decisive point, Osiander was condemned by his Lutheran colleagues. And, holding so much in common with Osiander, Calvin was condemned by some of the same Lutherans as being "Osiandrian."

Concerning the decisive issue of justification, Calvin was clearly not Osiandrian. For Calvin, justification and sanctification are distinguishable but inseparable, for "Christ contains both of them inseparably in himself." "You cannot possess him [Christ] without being made partaker in his sanctification, because he cannot be divided into pieces."[52] While justification always and necessarily leads to real sanctification, the former is forensic and the latter involves a moral transformation of the believer by the Spirit. As opposed to Osiander, forensic notions of pardon are not opposed to the themes of indwelling and participation in Calvin. Rather, Calvin has two main reasons why these two must be held together.

First, if salvation is to be truly a gift from God—and sanctification a life of gratitude—a forensic notion of pardon is the necessary prerequisite for such a life of sanctification. In the late medieval model of the believer as pilgrim (*viator*), the "assurance" of salvation cannot be emphasized since it is dependent upon the continuing acts of sanctification by the believer.[53] Calvin criticizes this soteriology as keeping the conscience in fear and anxiety, thus unable to fulfill the law of love with gratitude. Rather than being in "perpetual dread" as to whether one has fulfilled God's law, with imputation the believer is moved to "eager readiness to obey God" in properly receiving this pardon from God.[54] When "forensic" pardon is received, the adoption of the believer is realized, for believers are freed from the "severe requirements" of the law so that they can act like children: believers "hear themselves called with fatherly gentleness by God" and "will cheerfully and with great eagerness answer and follow his leading."[55] Calvin is clear that this grateful following of God's leading is, in fact, a "participation" in God through Christ, by the indwelling of the Holy Spirit. Yet, theological emphasis upon the indwelling presence of God is not enough. For Calvin, if this indwelling presence is to be in concordance with a truly human gratitude, one must oppose Osiander's denial of the forensic character of justification.

A second significant difference between Calvin and Osiander relates to the trinitarian dynamics of Osiander's claim that believers share the deity of Christ in justification. For Calvin, the bond of our union with Christ—and the manner of divine indwelling—is not through the "infusion" of the "essence" of God into the believer. Rather, Osiander "does not observe the bond of this unity," which denotes that believers are "united with Christ by the secret power of the Spirit."[56] By the Spirit, believers participate not just in the divine nature of Christ, but in the whole person of Christ.[57] Through this participation in Christ, believers participate in the Trinity.[58]

In emphasizing that the Spirit is the bond for our union with God in Christ, Calvin has several concerns. First, he wants to keep a Nicene trinitarian theology; Calvin fears that Osiander's account of "participation in Christ" leaves out the essential role of the Spirit.[59] But Calvin is also expressing a concern to maintain a creature-Creator distinction amid our union with Christ. Because Osiander denies a role to the human nature of Christ in justification, Christ's own human nature becomes dangerously de-emphasized.[60] Not only does this raise concerns related to Chalcedonian orthodoxy (with a "union" without "confusion" between divinity and humanity), but if believers participate solely in the divine nature, their perfected humanity in redemption seems to disappear. Just as the communication of idioms for Calvin is applied to the person of Christ *in concreto,*[61] so also believers participate in the person of Christ, the focal point of the union (without confusion) of divinity and humanity. Likewise, in his debate with Osiander, believers are united with God through Christ so as to be "completely one" with Christ, participating in God. Yet, the creature is not identical to the Creator.

Through his debate with Osiander, Calvin affirms what he teaches elsewhere about 2 Peter 1:4: that in the union of Creator and creature in redemption, the former does not "swallow up" the latter.[62]

While Calvin's emphasis upon the forensic character of justification is distinct to Calvin's concerns as a Reformer, his insistence upon a union without "confusion" of the divine and human holds much in common with his conciliar and patristic sources. Calvin was not seeking to be "unique" in this latter emphasis, but to uphold the concerns of the broader Catholic tradition. On the one hand, Calvin sought to be "orthodox" on justification in the terms of the Reformation in response to the criticisms of his Lutheran opponents. On the other hand, he sought to be "orthodox" on trinitarian and Christological issues in broader Catholic terms, refuting Roman Catholic accusations that the Reformation is a "new" movement leaving behind the church fathers and counsels. Thus, Calvin's doctrine of deification retains broadly a Catholic character in affirming the union of divinity and humanity in Christology and in the final redemption of believers in Christ. Yet Calvin's distinctive concerns as a Reformer also shape his doctrine of deification.

Calvin's Distinctive Doctrine of Deification

In terms of contemporary theological discussion, perhaps the greatest current danger in claiming that Calvin teaches "deification" is that his view could be too quickly assimilated into late Byzantine notions of *theosis,* from which he retains distance. As noted above, Palamite theology is frequently used as the "standard" by which to judge other theologies of deification. As a result, theologies of deification in the West end up looking like more or less truncated versions of a late Byzantine theology with which they never explicitly engaged. Scholarship on Calvin is no exception to this trend. In an account emerging from Orthodox-Reformed dialogues in the 1960s, Joseph McLelland makes some strange claims regarding Calvin and deification.[63] As part of a comparison of Calvin with Palamas, he draws upon Calvin's theme of "participation in Christ," such that we "participate" in Christ's righteousness in justification and sanctification. After noting that this theme takes place in the context of the "mystical union" between Christ and the believer, McLelland claims that "on this decisive point Calvin is one with our Orthodox brethren in their idea of *theosis.*"[64] After this, however, McLelland laments how this "mystical" dimension in Calvin's thought is greatly diminished in later Calvinism, such that "justification has become legal, forensic."[65]

While I believe that McLelland is correct in ascertaining that Calvin taught deification in some sense, his analysis actually undermines some of Calvin's distinctive concerns. Let us examine a passage in which Calvin discusses justification in the first edition of the *Institutes* (1536), an account that was retained and greatly expanded in later editions.

> We experience such participation in him that, although we are still foolish in ourselves, he is our wisdom before God; while we are sinners, he is our righteousness; while we are unclean, he is our purity; while we are weak, while we are unarmed and exposed to Satan, yet ours is that power which has been given him in heaven and on earth to crush Satan for us and shatter the gates of hell; while we still bear about with us the body of death, he is yet our life. In brief, because all things are ours and we have all things in him, in us there is nothing. Upon this foundation we must be built if we would grow into a holy temple to the Lord.[66]

Is this passage "legal" (like the "Calvinists") or "mystical," as McLelland would have it? The passage certainly makes it clear that the doctrine of justification is not a detached, "judicial" doctrine wherein an impersonal transaction takes place: it is about union with Christ and the wondrous exchange that takes place in this union. In addition, Calvin makes it clear that the believer grows in real holiness in sanctification, such that we "grow into a holy temple to the Lord." Yet, contra McLelland, the passage is deeply "forensic" and "legal" in asserting that by participation in Christ, Christ's righteousness is *imputed* to the believer ("While we are sinners, he is our righteousness; while we are unclean, he is our purity"). In Calvin, the "forensic" imputation of Christ's righteousness and the mystical union with Christ are held in the closest possible relationship—one is unthinkable without the other. For Calvin, "forensic" pardon is not an opposing category to the more "organic" images of union, adoption, and ingrafting to speak of participation in Christ. The two belong together. Indeed, as noted above, the believer can participate in her adoption only when she has come to realize the Father's kindness in freely pardoning the sinner. Without imputation, Calvin's ethics of "participation in Christ" become impossible, as the conscience is never given the rest that true gratitude requires.[67] In a word, according to Calvin, a participation in Christ without a participation in his righteousness (through imputation) is no participation at all.

In addition, McLelland speaks of the "mysticism" of Calvin (in common with other accounts of deification) in a way that does not recognize Calvin's distinctive approach to mystical participation in Christ. For Calvin, participation in Christ is inseparable from the active participation in the love and unity of the Body of Christ, the church. A key passage for Calvin on this point is 1 Corinthians 10:17. From it he argues that just as believers have a vertical participation in the body and blood of Christ, they simultaneously have a horizontal participation in the church as Body. In receiving the Lord's Supper, we must have *koinonia* in both directions.

> What is the source of the *koinonia* or communion, which exists among us, but the fact that we are united to Christ so that "we are flesh of His flesh and bone of His bones"? For it is necessary for us to be incorporated, as it were, into Christ in order to be united to each other. Besides, Paul is discussing here not a mere human fellowship, but the spiritual union between Christ and believers, in order to make it plain from that, that it is an intolerable sacrilege for them to be contaminated by communion with idols. Therefore from the context of this verse we can conclude that *koinonia* or communion of the blood is the alliance which we have with the blood of Christ when he ingrafts all of us into His body, so that He may live in us, and we in Him.[68]

This *koinonia* wherein Christ lives in us and we in him is, in fact, the source of the *koinonia* among members of the church. The "ingrafting" into the Body of Christ is both mystical and horizontal or social. Indeed, when late sixteenth-century English Puritans stubbornly refuse the practice of a "private" Eucharist, they are in deep accord with Calvin here.[69] It is impossible to participate in Christ through the Lord's Supper in an exclusively "vertical" direction. Participation in Christ simply must involve the horizontal activity of *koinonia* and love.

While participation in Christ in the Lord's Supper is inseparably connected with ecclesial *koinonia* and the broader duties of charity,[70] this does not stop Calvin from emphasizing the significance of the vertical *communicatio* that takes place in the sacrament. The Lord's Supper involves a "true participation in Christ himself. For those benefits would not come to us unless Christ first made himself ours." Thus, in the Supper believers "grow into one body" with Christ and become "partakers of his [Christ's] substance, that we may also feel his power in partaking of all his benefits."[71] Indeed, Calvin appropriates the notion in Cyril's theology that the flesh of Christ is "life-giving," "pervaded with the fullness of life," and then "transmitted to us" in the Lord's Supper.[72] In one of his many summaries of Cyril, Calvin says, "the flesh of Christ is made vivifying by the agency of the Spirit, so that Christ is in us because the Spirit of God dwells in us."[73] This language of vivification is included in Calvin's liturgy for the Lord's Supper in Geneva. Through the Supper the souls of the faithful are "nourished and vivified with his [Jesus Christ's] substance." This is followed by a participation of the believer in the ascension of Christ, wherein believers are "raised above all terrestrial objects, and carried as high as heaven, to enter the kingdom of God where he dwells."[74] Through the power of the Spirit, believers participate in the ascent of Christ.[75]

As Calvin developed his theology of participation and union between God and humanity in Christ, he was not always sure what words were most appropriate for this union. In the 1545 French edition of the *Institutes,* Calvin wrote that in union with Christ, believers are "made of one substance with him." Calvin goes on to say that "daily he [Christ] more and more unites himself to us in one and the same substance (*une mesme substance*)."[76] Although these additions of *substance* language in the 1545 *Institutes* are later deleted, Calvin continues to speak of the believer and Christ uniting into "one substance" in several commentaries, keeping this language through the final editions of these works.[77] As noted above, Calvin is clear that he does not advocate a union in which humanity is "swallowed up" or completely assimilated into divinity.[78] Nevertheless, Calvin pushes the limits of biblical language in seeking to express the closeness of the union between the believer, Christ, and God. In explaining the image of ingrafting into Christ in his comments on Romans 6, Calvin finds it necessary to move to the language of 2 Peter 1:4: "In the grafting of trees, the graft draws its nourishment from the root, but retains its own natural quality in the fruit which is eaten. In spiritual ingrafting, however, we not only derive the strength and sap of the life which flows from Christ, but we also pass from our own nature into his (*sed in eius naturam ex nostra demigramus*)."[79]

Conclusion

In sum, I believe it is fair to say that Calvin does have a doctrine of deification of his own sort. Although he mentions Plato positively on the theme of deification,[80] Calvin's main sources are biblical and patristic: the language of participation, union, adoption, and ingrafting in Paul, abiding and indwelling in John, as well as various theological developments borrowed and adapted from church fathers such as Augustine, Irenaeus, and Cyril. Calvin's appropriation of these sources gives a broadly Catholic character to Calvin's doctrine of deification. Redemption involves the restoration and fulfillment of the original union of God with human beings in creation, which has been disrupted by the Fall. The life of the Christian involves a participation in Christ through the Spirit as the believer grows to be "conformable" to God; this process is culminated in the participation in Christ's resurrection and glorification, and a beatific vision. In addition to adopting this soteriological structure wherein the culmination of the Christian life of sanctification is in deification, Calvin spreads the language of "participation," "union," and "adoption" through a wide variety of doctrinal loci in his *Institutes* and commentaries.

The Catholic dimensions of Calvin's doctrine of deification are robust and strongly stated. Yet, his doctrine of deification is distinctive.[81] It cannot be assimilated into late Byzantine notions of *theosis*. Although there may be ways to find hints of distinctions in Calvin paralleling the Palamite usage of "essence" and "energy,"[82] I have generally avoided making distinctions foreign to Calvin's own tradition. Calvin has his own way of insisting on the Creator-creature distinction. On the other hand, Calvin is also quite distinct from theologies of deification found in figures such as Aquinas, even though he holds in common many of the Western sources for deification. The genuinely Catholic elements of Calvin's doctrine of deification should not blind us to his distinctive claims: participation in Christ is impossible without receiving the imputation of Christ's righteousness; participation in the life-giving *substantia* of Christ is inseparably linked with ecclesial unity and love; full humanity as humanity united with God means that partitive, synergistic understandings of grace and the Spirit must be rejected. These features are not just "additions" to the "Catholic" passages in Calvin, which teach that the end of the Gospel is "to deify us." Rather, they are constitutive to Calvin's distinctive doctrine of deification.

Notes

The epigraph is taken from Calvin's prayer at the end of Lecture 123 on Jeremiah 31, CTS. I am grateful to Sarah Coakley, Tony Lane and Benjamin King for their feedback on earlier drafts of this work. An extended version of this essay appears in *The Harvard Theological Review* 98:3 (2005): 315–34. Quotations from the *Institutes* are from John Calvin, *Institutes of the Christian Religion,* ed. John T. McNeill, trans. Ford Lewis Battles, Library of Christian Classics (Philadelphia: Westminster Press, 1960).

1. According to Francois Wendel, Calvin fears "anything that might have led to the admission of any deification of man, even by way of Jesus Christ, and even in his person." *Calvin: Origins and Development of His Religious Thought,* trans. Philip Mairet (Durham, NC: Labyrinth Press, 1987), 258–60. In addition, Roland Bainton claims that in Calvin God is "so high and lifted up, so unspeakably holy, and man so utterly unworthy, that no union between God and man could be thinkable." *Hunted Heretic: The Life and Death of Michael Servetus, 1511–1553* (Boston: Beacon Press, 1960), 46–47.

2. For a summary of the claims concerning the "sharp separation" of God and humanity in Calvin, see Philip Walker Butin, *Revelation, Redemption, and Response: Calvin's Trinitarian Understanding of the Divine-Human Relationship* (New York: Oxford University Press, 1995), chapter 1.

3. Vladimir Lossky, *The Mystical Theology of the Eastern Church* (Crestwood, NY: St. Vladimir's Seminary Press, 1976), 130–34, 196–216. Also, see a similar account in Joseph C. McLelland, "Sailing to Byzantium," in *The New Man: An Orthodox and Reformed Dialogue,* ed. John Meyendorff and Joseph C. McLelland, 10–25 (New Brunswick, NJ: Agora Books, 1973).

4. See Carl E. Braaten and Robert W. Jenson, *Union with Christ: The New Finnish Interpretation of Luther* (Grand Rapids, MI: Eerdmans, 1998); Tuomo Mannermaa, *Der Im Glauben Gegenwärtige Christus: Rechtfertigung Und Vergottung Zum Ökumenischen Dialog* (Hannover: Lutherisches Verlagshaus, 1989); Michael J. McClymond, "Salvation as Divinization: Jonathan Edwards, Gregory Palamas and the Theological Uses of Neoplatonism," in *Jonathan Edwards: Philosophical Theologian,* ed. Paul Helm and Oliver Crisp, 139–60 (Aldershot, Hants, England: Ashgate, 2003); A. N. Williams, *The Ground of Union: Deification in Aquinas and Palamas* (New York: Oxford University Press, 1999). For a comparison of Luther with Palamas that affirms that Luther teaches deification, yet also indicates Luther's distance from Palamas, see Reinhard Flogaus, *Theosis Bei Palamas Und Luther: Ein Beitrag Zum Ökumenischen Gespräch* (Göttingen: Vandenhoeck & Ruprecht, 1997).

5. Perl is entering into an older debate about the relation between Thomism and Palamism. See Eric D. Perl, "St. Gregory Palamas and the Metaphysics of Creation," *Dionysius* 14 (1990): 105–30. There is a similar problem in Joseph Farrell's comparison of Calvin and Maximus the Confessor in the appendix of Joseph P. Farrell, *Free Choice in St. Maximus the Confessor* (South Canan, PA: St. Tikhon's Seminary Press, 1989). Farrell is right in recognizing a certain amount of distance between Calvin and Maximus, displayed largely through a technical schema and vocabulary on the part of both authors that was unavailable to the other. Yet, he is wrong in inferring that because Calvin does not use Maximus's language, he is subject to the criticism of Maximus's opponents.

6. In speaking about the "union" of believers with God through Christ, I do not mean an "indistinct union" wherein the creature is assimilated into the divine. The "union" of God and human beings in Calvin's theology is a *differentiated* union that does not annihilate the distinction between Creator and creature.

7. See notes 1 and 2.

8. In summarizing a passage from the 1539 *Institutes* Calvin writes that "everything which is ours should be obliterated when we are regenerated by the Lord." *The Bondage and Liberation of the Will: A Defence of the Orthodox Doctrine of Human Choice against Pighius,* ed. A. N. S. Lane, trans. Graham I. Davies (Grand Rapids, MI: Baker Books, 1996), 212. The original passage that Calvin was summarizing is an exposition of Ez 36:26–27, where the "heart of stone" is removed by God to be replaced by "a heart of flesh" by the Spirit. Calvin writes "If therefore, a stone is transformed into flesh when God converts us to zeal for the right, whatever is of our own will is effaced. What takes its place is wholly from God." *Institutes* 2.3.6, OS 3:279–80.

9. Thus, perhaps not surprisingly, *Bondage and Liberation of the Will* has more patristic citations than any work of Calvin besides the *Institutes.*

10. Certain aspects of Calvin's developments are included in later editions of the *Institutes.* Yet, other crucial features of *Bondage and Liberation of the Will,* such as Calvin's Aristotelian distinctions, are not included in the *Institutes.* On Calvin's development through *Bondage and Liberation of the Will,* see A. N. S. Lane, *John Calvin: Student of the Church Fathers* (Edinburgh: T & T Clark, 1999), 179–91.

11. Calvin, *Bondage and Liberation of the Will,* 212.

12. Although the original passage in 1536 was an exposition of Ez 36:26–27, it is significant that Calvin moves to Pauline sources when he further explains the meaning of his statement in the 1559 edition of the *Institutes.* I have chosen the Pauline language of dying to the "old self" and the contrast between "flesh" and "spirit" because of its significance in the book of Romans, which was so influential on Calvin, as well as its similarity with Calvin's language that "whatever is ours" is "annihilated" in regeneration. OS 3:279–80.

13. Calvin, *Bondage and Liberation of the Will,* 229–31.

14. R. J. Mooi lists 1708 explicit citations of Augustine in Calvin's writings. The anti-Pelagian writings, in particular, were central for Calvin. See Remko Jan Mooi, *Het Kerk, En Dogmahistorisch Element in De Werken Van Johannes Calvijn* (Wageningen: H. Veenman, 1965), 369; Richard A. Muller, "Augustinianism in the Reformation," in *Augustine through the Ages: An Encyclopedia,* ed. Allan Fitzgerald (Grand Rapids, MI: W. B. Eerdmans, 1999).

15. For example, *The Predestination of the Saints* (15:30–31), *The Gift of Perseverance* (9:21), *Enchiridion* (sections 36, 40). For Calvin's appropriation of Augustine on this theme, see Calvin, *Bondage and Liberation of the Will,* 129–30.

16. See the letters between Cyril and Nestorius in Richard A. Norris, *The Christological Controversy: Sources of Early Christian Thought* (Philadelphia: Fortress Press, 1980).

17. See Calvin, *Bondage and Liberation of the Will,* 129–30.

18. The Aristotelian categories of substance, accident, and habit are used repeatedly in the

work. See Lane's introduction for a listing of citations. See Lane, *Bondage and Liberation of the Will,* xxv, xxvi.

19. "It was the spiritual life of Adam to remain united and bound to his Maker." *Institutes* 2.1.5.

20. *Institutes* 3.3.5–9.

21. Calvin is very insistent on this point, following Rom 6:5–6 that we will not simply be united with Christ in his death, but also in his resurrection. "Both things happen to us by participation in Christ." See *Institutes* 3.3.9.

22. On the issue of freedom, Calvin claims that Irenaeus is in basic agreement with him in seeking to affirm the goodness of the original creation (and the restoration that follows). See Calvin, *Bondage and Liberation of the Will,* 71–72. For Calvin, the nature is not only restored to the Adamic state, but is transformed to a superior state. "The condition which we obtain through Christ is far superior to the lot of the first man." See Calvin's comments on 1 Cor 15:46, CTS. For more on this transformation, see Richard Prins, "The Image of God in Adam and the Restoration of Man in Jesus Christ: A Study in John Calvin," *Scottish Journal of Theology* 25 (Fall 1972): 32–44.

23. In speaking about how God and humanity are "naturally" united, I am referring to the primal, prefallen state of divine-human relations. This state of being united does not blur the distinctions between Creator and creature, but it is a state of differentiated unity and communion between God and humanity. Calvin does not accept the language of "cooperative grace" as used in medieval scholasticism precisely because he thinks it divides the agency and credit between God and humanity in a partitive manner. While Calvin is more sympathetic to Augustine's use of the language, he does not retrieve the phrase because of its possible misleading connotations. See *Institutes* 2.3.7.

24. See Calvin, *Bondage and Liberation of the Will,* 193–200.

25. Ibid., 119–20.

26. *Institutes* 2.8.49.

27. Concerning the issue of whether love is an "infused habit," Calvin is relatively close to Lombard in book 1.17 of the *Sentences.* The majority of medieval scholastics disagreed with Lombard on this point. In his *Sentences* commentary of 1510/11, Luther made his own agreement with Lombard on this point explicit. See Steven E. Ozment, *The Age of Reform (1250–1550): An Intellectual and Religious History of Late Medieval and Reformation Europe* (New Haven: Yale University Press, 1980), 31–32.

28. Calvin denies that God would "coerce anyone by violence." Instead, "so that he may have willing [*voluntarios*] servants who follow of their own accord and obey, he creates a new heart in them and renews a right spirit in their inner nature." *Bondage and Liberation of the Will,* 193–94, 232.

29. Although Calvin cites Ireneaus and shows a concern to have continuity with Irenaeus at points, it should be recognized that Calvin is using Ireneaus—and other patristic writers—for his own distinct purposes. Thus, the Ireneaus that Calvin draws upon is not the Ireneaus of contemporary scholarship, but one adapted and recontextualized by Calvin. With this said, one should avoid overstating the fact that Calvin makes a polemical use of patristic writings. Calvin's humanist training serves him well when he returns to the original sources (*ad fontes*). Moreover, the fact that Calvin's interaction with patristic writings in *The Bondage and Liberation of the Will* leads him to make distinctions that are absent from his other works indicates that his engagement with the church fathers *influences* his theology.

30. Although Calvin does not use the term *recapitulatio,* he has a great deal in common with Irenaeus's doctrine of creation, recapitulation, and Second Adam Christology. See Johannes Van Oort, "John Calvin and the Church Fathers," in *The Reception of the Church Fathers in the West: From the Carolingians to the Maurists,* ed. Irena Dorota Backus (Leiden: E. J. Brill, 1997), 685–86.

31. *Institutes* 1.2.1.

32. At the beginning of *Romans* Calvin writes that "if we have gained a true understanding of this Epistle, we have an open door to all the most profound treasures of Scripture." CC 8:5.

33. While the influence of Romans upon the *Institutes* is frequently affirmed in Calvin scholarship, Richard Muller has shown the extent to which Romans is crucial for Calvin's development of the doctrinal loci beginning in 1539. In addition, it is in 1539/40 that Calvin outlines his project for the commentaries. It is during this crucial time of development that Calvin makes his statement about Romans being an "open door" to the rest of Scripture. See Muller, *The Unaccommodated Calvin: Studies in the Foundation of a Theological Tradition* (New York: Oxford University, 2000), chapters 7 and 8.

34. Calvin sometimes speaks of the believer being ingrafted into the community of God's people—the subject of Rom 11—but he also speaks of being ingrafted into Christ, which develops imagery from Jn 15:1–11. Although Calvin sometimes refers to one or the other sense, he makes no separation between the two. Theologically speaking, being ingrafted into Christ and adopted by the Father is necessarily connected with being ingrafted into the family of God's children. See, for example, *Institutes* 4.1.2–4.

35. On the *Institutes,* see the following note. Examples of this clustering in the commentaries, without the warrant of the immediate biblical context, include passages on the following verses. Each passage speaks of participation in God, Christ, or the Spirit, linked with the language of adoption and/or ingrafting: Gen 17:8, participation and adoption; Is 40:8, participation and adoption; Is 60:2, participation and adoption; Lk 23:43, participation and ingrafting; Jn 3:29, participation and adoption; Acts 10:4, participation and ingrafting; Eph 2:4, participation and ingrafting; Phil 1:7, participation and adoption; 1 Thess 4:14, participation and ingrafting; 1 Thess 5:10, participation and ingrafting; 2 Tim 1:9, participation and ingrafting; Tit 3:5–6, participation, ingrafting, and adoption; Heb 6:4, participation and adoption; Heb 10:22, participation and adoption; 1 Jn 1:3, participation and adoption; in addition, there are multiple occurrences of this cluster of images in *Romans.*

36. There are many examples of participation language applied to a variety of loci. Here are a few examples from the topics listed above: justification (3.17.11), baptism (4.16.2), the Lord's Supper (4.17.10), the resurrection (3.3.9), the Incarnation (2.12.5), the Trinity (4.1.3), the atonement (2.16.12), the *imago Dei* (2.2.1) and "participation in God" (1.13.14).

37. My own translation of *et quemadmodum unus est in patre, ita nos unum in ipso fiamus.* Note the parallel of "oneness" and mutual indwelling between the trinitarian oneness (Father and Son) and economic oneness (Christ and the believer). Sermon on 1 Sam 2:27–36, John Calvin, *Ioannis Calvini Opera Quae Supersunt Omnia,* ed. Eduardus Cunitz Guilielmus Baum and Eduardus Reuss, *Corpus Reformatorum* (Brunsvigae: Apud C.A. Schwetschke et filium, 1863), 29:353.

38. *Institutes* 3.2.24.

39. *Institutes* 2.16.3.

40. *Institutes* 3.1.2. For an account of the crucial role of the Spirit in Calvin's trinitarian doctrine of participation, see Julie Canlis, "Calvin, Osiander and Participation in God," *International Journal of Systematic Theology* 6, no. 2 (April 2004): 169–84.

41. A literal translation. Beveridge renders the overall passage "By means of him [the Spirit] we become partakers of the divine nature (*in Dei participationem venimus*), so as in a manner to feel his quickening energy within us. Our justification is his work; from him is power, sanctification, truth, grace, and every good thought, since it is from the Spirit alone that all good gifts proceed." *Institutes* 1.13.14. John Calvin, *Institutes of the Christian Religion,* ed. Henry Beveridge and Robert Pitcairn (Edinburgh: Calvin Translation Society, 1845). OS 3:128.

42. *Institutes* 1.8.26.

43. *Institutes* 1.15.6.

44. *Institutes* 1.15.5.

45. *Institutes* 2.14.3.

46. CTS, Calvin's comments on 2 Pt 1:4.

47. For the distinction between a "theme" of deification and a "doctrine" of deification, I am indebted to Gösta Hallonsten's essay, "*Theosis* in Recent Research: A Renewal of Interest and a Need for Clarity," which appears in the present volume.

48. On Calvin's use of these terms, see Carl Mosser, "The Greatest Possible Blessing: Calvin and Deification," *Scottish Journal of Theology* 55, no. 1 (2002): 41, 53–55.

49. Other relevant controversies include Calvin's eucharistic dispute with the Lutherans Westphal and Heshusius, and Calvin's opposition to Servetus's interpretation of Ps 82. With the eucharistic dispute, the central issue is how one partakes of the "substance" of Christ in the Eucharist. Calvin gives a strongly pneumatological account of this participation, claiming that his opponents fail to give sufficient weight to the Spirit as the mode by which believers partake of the flesh of Christ. See Thomas J. Davis, *The Clearest Promises of God: The Development of Calvin's Eucharistic Teaching* (New York: AMS Press, 1995), chapters 5 and 6. With Servetus, the central dispute seems to be the exegetical interpretation of Ps 82, as well as the affirmation of "deity in believers" in a non-Chalcedonian, non-eschatological way. See Mosser, "The Greatest Possible Blessing," 50–53.

50. Although it is frequently pointed out that Calvin has a negative response to Osiander as early as the Colloquy of Worms, Calvin's main polemic against Osiander's theology does not come until the 1559 edition of the *Institutes.* In Calvin's debate with both Westphal and Heshusius, he was accused of being Osiandrian. See David Steinmetz, *Reformers in the Wings* (Philadelphia: Fortress Press, 1971), 91; James Weis, "Calvin Versus Osiander on Justification," *Springfielder* 29 (1965): 42–43.

51. For a sympathetic account of Osiander's appropriation of Augustine's theology of grace and participation, see Patricia Wilson-Kastner, "Andreas Osiander's Theology of Grace in the Perspective of the Influence of Augustine of Hippo," *Sixteenth Century Journal* 10, no. 2 (1979): 72–91. Unfortunately, Wilson-Kastner misinterprets Calvin's reasons for opposing Osiander, claiming that it is due to a "separation of the divine from the human" in Calvin (88).

52. *Institutes* 3.16.1.

53. See Heiko Augustinus Oberman and Paul L. Nyhus, *Forerunners of the Reformation: The Shape of Late Medieval Thought,* 1st ed. (New York: Holt Rinehart and Winston, 1966), 131–33.

54. *Institutes* 3.19.4.

55. *Institutes* 3.19.5.

56. *Institutes* 3.11.5.

57. *Institutes* 3.11.8.

58. *Institutes* 3.11.5.

59. Canlis gives a helpful account of the crucial role of the Spirit in Calvin's debate with Osiander. Unfortunately, her account tends to underestimate the decisive importance of imputation for Calvin in the Osiander controversy, downplaying Calvin's "forensic" dimensions in an effort to retrieve his theology of participation. See Canlis, "Calvin, Osiander and Participation in God."

60. *Institutes* 3.11.8–9.

61. See Richard A. Muller, *After Calvin: Studies in the Development of a Theological Tradition* (New York: Oxford University Press, 2003), 13.

62. "The Manicheans formerly dreamt that we are a part of God, and that, after having run the race of life we shall at length revert to our original. There are also at this day fanatics who imagine that we thus pass over into the nature of God, so that his swallows up our nature. Thus they explain what Paul says, that God will be all in all (1 Cor 15:28), and in the same

sense they take this passage. But such a delirium as this never entered the minds of the holy apostles; they only intended to say that when divested of all the vices of the flesh, we shall be partakers of divine and blessed immortality and glory, so as to be as it were one with God as far as our capacities will allow." CTS, Calvin's comments on 2 Pt 1:4.

63. This dialogue, from 1968–70, was between representatives of the Standing Conference of Canonical Orthodox Bishops in America and the World Alliance of Reformed Churches, North America Area.

64. McLelland, "Sailing to Byzantium," 16.

65. Ibid., 17. In this section, McLelland also claims that Calvin puts justification "*within* the context of sanctification"—a point showing significant conceptual confusion on the part of McLelland. Against Roman Catholic theologians and also Osiander, Calvin is at pains to emphasize that justification is distinct from sanctification—providing the only proper starting point for sanctification—even though justification is ultimately inseparable from sanctification. See Calvin's account of this "double grace" in the *Institutes* 3.11.

66. John Calvin, *Institutes of the Christian Religion, 1536 Edition,* trans. Ford Lewis Battles (Grand Rapids, MI: Eerdmans, 1986), 36.

67. In his work on Calvin's ethics, Guenther H. Haas writes, "Calvin bases his view of the Christian life upon our participation in Christ. Every action of the Christian is to be an expression of this participation." *The Concept of Equity in Calvin's Ethics* (Waterloo, ON: Wilfrid Laurier University Press, 1997), 49. While Haas gives a good account of how love is involved in this participation, the notion of gratitude is key also. On the necessity of freeing the conscience for gratitude and love, see David Little, "The Law of Supererogation," in *The Love Commandments: Essays in Christian Ethics and Moral Philosophy,* ed. Edmund N. Santurri and William Werpehowski, 157–81 (Washington, DC: Georgetown University Press, 1992).

68. Comments on 1 Cor 10:17 from CC.

69. See David Little, *Religion, Order, and Law: A Study in Pre-Revolutionary England* (Chicago: University of Chicago Press, 1984), 154.

70. For an account of the connection between the Lord's Supper and almsgiving in Calvin, see Elsie Anne McKee, *John Calvin on the Diaconate and Liturgical Almsgiving* (Genève: Librairie Droz, 1984).

71. *Institutes* 4.17.11.

72. *Institutes* 4.17.9.

73. John Calvin, *Tracts and Treatises,* trans. Henry Beveridge, vol. 2 (Grand Rapids, MI: Eerdmans, 1958), 541. One of Calvin's affirming quotations of Cyril is particularly revealing on how far Calvin was willing to go with Cyril on the subject of indwelling: "Just as a man by pouring other wax upon melted wax completely mixes both together, so it is necessary, if one receives flesh and blood of the Lord, for him to be joined with Christ, so that Christ may be found in him and he in us." *Institutes* 4.17.35.

74. Ibid., 122.

75. On the participation of believers in the ascent and glorification of Christ, see *Institutes* 4.17.29, 4.17.31; *Commentary* on 2 Thess 1:10, 12; Mosser, "The Greatest Possible Blessing," 45–46.

76. OS 4:35. See David Willis-Watkins, "The Unio Mystica and the Assurance of Faith according to Calvin," in *Calvin: Erbe Und Auftrag,* ed. Willem van't Spijker (Kampen, Netherlands: J H Kok, 1991), 90.

77. Although much is made of this omission by Mosser and Willis-Watkins, Calvin uses the same language of union into "one substance" in his commentaries. For example, in speaking of the believer's incorporation into Christ in the Supper while commenting on 1 Cor 11:24, Calvin speaks of being united into "one life and substance" with Christ. Calvin uses "substance" in a similar sense in his commentary on Eph 5:31. A third example of "one substance"

language is in Calvin's sermon on Gal 3:26–29. Both of the commentaries are written after the *Institutes* of 1545, and these passages are kept through the revisions of the Epistle commentaries in 1551 and 1556.

78. See pages 8–9, 12.

79. CC 8:124.

80. See *Institutes* 3.25.2 and Calvin's *Commentary* on 2 Pt 1:4.

81. In claiming that Calvin's doctrine of deification is distinctive, I do not mean that it is unique. Although a full-length comparison would be necessary to make an assessment, other early Reformers with sympathies for the fathers (such as Martin Bucer) seem to have a great deal in common with Calvin's "distinctive" doctrine of deification. My point is that Calvin's doctrine is "distinctive" in relation to theologies that are commonly known as "theologies of deification": namely, late Byzantine theologies in the East, and in some discussions, Aquinas's theology in the West.

82. For an attempt to find a parallel to the "essence" and "energy" distinction in Calvin, see Mosser, "The Greatest Possible Blessing," 54–55.

John Wesley: Christian Perfection as Faith Filled with the Energy of Love

Michael J. Christensen

Eastern Orthodoxy and Wesleyan theology are natural conversation partners because they drink from the same stream, and both are returning to the sources of their respective traditions.[1] As a Wesleyan theologian, I seek to articulate a distinctively Wesleyan understanding of the doctrine of Christian perfection in relation to *theosis* and its possible theological antecedents in Greek patristic Christianity. My focus is on the question: to what extent does John Wesley's doctrine of perfection or "entire sanctification" represent a *direct* channel of influence from Greek patristic conceptions of *theosis* (as Albert Outler was first to assert); and to what extent does the similarity of ideas between Wesleyan perfection and patristic deification simply reflect Wesley's reading of selected writers of the East as well as certain seventeenth- and eighteenth-century divines "whose thought the window to the East remains open" (as Richard Heitzenrater argues)?[2]

Theosis and Sanctification

Living in a transitional time between the premodern and modern periods, John Wesley (1703–91) was a child of both classical theology and Enlightenment rationalism. He drank from both wells and appropriated a vision from the East—notably from Clement, Origen, Marcarius, and Ephrem—and reformulated it in the West in the programmatic interest of what seemed practically attainable "by grace through faith" *in this life.* Subsequently, a distinctively Wesleyan spirituality characterized as "faith filled with the energy of love" emerged in the early Methodist movement in continuity with the older patristic tradition of deification. Reclaiming an authentic Wesleyan heritage in the twenty-first century requires not simply understanding Wesley's eighteenth-century doctrine of Christian perfection, but in knowing his patristic sources and theological antecedents as well as the contemporary existential situation.

Theosis in its various theological expressions within the Greek patristic tradition is a fascinating, controversial, and often objectionable religious idea, as well as a bold vision of human potential for spiritual perfection. Originating in ancient Greece, and developed and refined by patristic theologians of the first five centuries, it survived the fourth-century purges of heresy and persists in Eastern Christianity as a challenge to Western soteriology. According to one of the leading interpreters of the Eastern tradition, Vladimir Lossky, Christianity teaches that we are creatures "called to *attain* to union with God, to *become* god by grace but in no way god by virtue of his origin," which sheds some light on what Athanasius (293–373) famously said of the Incarnation: "God became man so that man might become God."[3]

Entire sanctification (holiness, perfection) in the Wesleyan tradition refers to John and Charles Wesley's doctrine of spiritual transformation and Christian perfection, which is available by grace through faith in this life. It is understood by many Wesleyan theologians as a religious experience and transformation occurring subsequent to justification, with the effect that the Holy Spirit takes full possession of the spirit, cleanses the soul, sanctifies the heart, and empowers the will so that one can love God and others perfectly and blamelessly in this life.[4] As creatures set apart for a holy purpose, the holiness of God (along with other divine attributes) is believed to be actually *imparted* and not just *imputed* to the believer's life on the basis of what Christ accomplished on the cross. The power of sin in one's life is rendered inoperative as one participates in the higher life of the divine.[5]

The doctrine of entire sanctification admits to at least two models of interpretation: (1) instantaneous perfection, involving an "eradication" of sin and a "blameless" walk with God; and (2) progressive sanctification, or gradually "going on to perfection."[6] The variations are not the present concern of this essay, only the more broadly defined doctrine of Christian perfection as full redemption from sin and mortality through what John Wesley described as a heart "habitually filled with the love of God and neighbor."[7] This longing for perfect love is most beautifully embodied in the last verse of Charles Wesley's famous hymn "Love Divine All Loves Excelling":

Finish then, thy new creation;
Pure and spotless let us be.
Let us see thy great salvation
Perfectly restored in thee;
Changed from glory into glory,
Till in heaven we take our place,
Till we cast our crowns before thee,
Lost in wonder, love, and praise.[8]

John Wesley's Reformulation of a Patristic Doctrine

Are these two concepts—entire sanctification and *theosis*—theologically distinct or merely similar in thought? Historically, is entire sanctification as a doctrine derived from the older idea of *theosis?* If so, what were Wesley's primary sources and how was the one derived from the other? Theologically, are Wesleyan perfection and patristic deification radically distinct doctrines, functionally equivalent, or similar in comparison? In posing these questions of similarity and derivation, I invoke the scholarly company of Albert Outler, Ted Campbell, Randy Maddox, and Richard Heitzenrater in order to apply the problem of *theosis* as a test case for their assertions regarding Wesley's use of patristic sources.[9]

Albert Outler first alerted Wesleyan scholars to the influence of the church fathers, especially the "Eastern, Greek" patristic writers, on Wesley. It was his suspicion that Wesley's doctrine of sanctification was directly influenced by his exposure to the *Spiritual Homilies* attributed to Macarius of Egypt but actually written by a fifth-century Syrian monk under the theological influence of Gregory of Nyssa.[10] Orthodox theologian Charles Ashanin also has pointed out that the classical Methodist doctrine of entire sanctification "is probably Wesley's adaptation of the Patristic doctrine of *Theosis.*"[11] Wesleyan theologian Randy Maddox is more nuanced in his assertions, but essentially concurs: Understanding the doctrine of entire sanctification in its therapeutic, soteriological context, he says, "has significant parallels with the Eastern Orthodox theme of deification (*theosis*)."[12] What are some of these parallels and possible adaptations?

In his 1756 "Address to Clergy," Wesley commends the church fathers, as the most reliable commentators on Scripture, "being both nearest the fountain, and eminently endued with that Spirit by whom all Scripture was given." Among the ante-Nicene theologians he commends are Clement of Alexandria, Origen, Tertullian, and Cyprian as particularly worthy guardians of "the religion of the primitive church." He also insists that his preachers have "some acquaintance" with such post-Nicene writers as Chrysostom, Basil, Jerome, Augustine "and, above all, the man of a broken heart, Ephraem Syrus." In other references to his favorite authors, Wesley dropped Jerome and Augustine (who he came to disfavor) and added "Makarios the Egyptian."[13]

The issue of patristic influences, however, is not simply a matter of Wesley appreciating and importing theological concepts from the second- to the fifth-century Orthodox East and applying them in the eighteenth-century Protestant West. As Ted Campbell documents in his *John Wesley and Christian Antiquity,* Wesley's use of patristic sources was "programmatic"—by which he means that Wesley revised and edited his sources rather than preserved their original meaning, and did so with a pastoral motivation and agenda of church reform. Wesley was not a historian but a practical theologian whose mission was to reform a nation. His particular "vision" of Christian antiquity, more than the historical accuracy of his conceptualization, formed his sense of the tradition. Thus Wesley's "programmatic" (pastoral and polemical) use of patristic sources can be distinguished from what his sources historically meant or taught.[14]

One striking example of Wesley's reformulation of a patristic source is his use of Clement of Alexandria. Wesley learned from Clement that there are three kinds of people: the unconverted, the converted but immature, and the mature or perfect Christian. Each required spiritual instruction appropriate to their state.[15]

Wesley included a poem, "On Clemens Alexandrinus's Description of a Perfect Christian," in *Hymns and Sacred Poems* (1739), which describes the spiritual pilgrimage of a human being toward the state of perfection and how the "mystic powers of love" can perfect the soul intent to cross over into the "simple life Divine."[16] For Clement, the ascent of the soul to God is by means of contemplative knowledge and wisdom.[17] In Wesley's appropriation of Clement, "perfect love" replaces *gnosis* as the way of salvation and sanctification. Despite its Gnostic context, Wesley makes Clement sound like a good Methodist.

Likewise, in response to queries about the meaning of the term "Methodist," Wesley, in 1742, published a tract entitled "On the Character of a Methodist." According to Campbell, Wesley later acknowledged that his description was based on "the character of a perfect Christian drawn by Clemens Alexandrinus."[18] For Clement, we pass from paganism to Christianity through faith. From faith we rise to God through *gnosis.* From *gnosis* we see God face-to-face, and we are deified: "Being baptized, we are illuminated; illuminated, we become sons (i.e., children or heirs); being made . . . (heirs), we are made perfect; being made perfect, we are made immortal, as the Scripture says 'Ye are gods.'"[19] For Wesley, we are justified and sanctified by "faith filled with the energy of love" neither by works nor by *gnosis.* We enjoy *communion* with God as creatures, but not *union* with God as equals. We may become *like* God, Wesley hopes and prays, but we do not become divine![20]

Albert Outler concludes: "It is almost as if Wesley had read 'agape' in the place of the Clementine 'gnosis.'"[21] When Wesley appropriates Clement's vision, he "corrects" the assertion of *gnosis* as the means to perfection, resulting in the reformulation of an ancient Christian vision of *theosis.* Perfection in Wesley is a less esoteric experience and more practically focused on what he deemed possible in this life. This reconstruction may constitute a refinement to the patristic tradition, and it may be in continuity with the tradition, but Christian perfection is not the same as the ancient vision of *theosis.*[22]

As much as one may prefer Wesleyan perfection to patristic *theosis,* the historical issue remains: Did John Wesley intentionally substitute the eighteenth-century concept of "Christian perfection" for that of an earlier vision of *theosis,* or was he simply inspired to develop a similar but more tenable doctrine? If the former, by whose authority and by what criterion did he amend his sources, "correct" previous visions, and reformulate patristic conceptions of *theosis?*[23] If the latter, then Wesley's distinctive doctrine of entire sanctification has some striking parallels with patristic *theosis.*

In my judgment, what John Wesley taught as Christian perfection, holiness, or entire sanctification is both historically and theologically *derivative* and *dependent* on the more ancient doctrines of deification as taught by theologians in the Greek patristic tradition of the first four centuries. The eighteenth century saw the dawning of a new age with new problems to address theologically, and Wesley made an appropriate shift in doctrinal formulation. The effect of Wesley's reconstruction of *gnosis* and *theosis* was the turning of the Gnostic ladder of human ascent on its side to make perfection in love more reasonable and more accessible in this life. By replacing the Platonic notion of assimilation and union ("becoming god according to grace") with the less esoteric and ambitious notion of imitation and communion (becoming *like* God by grace through faith), Wesley promoted a vision and a movement of "going on to perfection." Nonetheless, and despite the positive qualities of Wesley's theological innovation, it is hard to avoid the conclusion that compared to the high and lofty patristic visions of *theosis,* Wesleyan sanctification appears as a domesticated (or democratized) version of the more ancient doctrine.

In light of Wesley's reformulation of Christian antiquity, I suggest that Wesleyan scholars today accept Campbell's historical critique and follow Outler's theological lead to read Wesley *with his sources,* and not simply read back into his ancient sources Wesley's distinctive eighteenth-century vision of perfection or programmatic agenda of reform.[24]

Charles Wesley's Forgotten Strand

In his hymn "Love Divine All Loves Excelling" quoted above, Charles Wesley envisions perfection as human beings being "changed from glory into glory."[25] Did Charles share John's vision of Christian perfection or did he hold an older view of deification (perhaps similar to that of Gregory of Nazianzus who employs the same language)? The brothers Wesley certainly critically engaged and theologically disagreed about the nature, time, manner, and extent of perfection in this life and the next. According to A. M. Allchin's insightful study, *Participation in God: A Forgotten Strand in Anglican*

Tradition, Charles Wesley was committed to an earlier model of patristic *theosis.*[26] As a poet-theologian in the tradition of St. Ephrem,[27] Charles expressed in hymns what is difficult to state in doctrine:

> 5. He deigns in flesh to appear,
> Widest extremes to join,
> To bring our vileness near,
> *And make us all divine;*
> And we the life of God shall know,
> For God is manifest below.
>
> 6. Made perfect first in love,
> And sanctified by grace,
> We shall from earth remove,
> And see his glorious face;
> His love shall then be fully showed,
> And man shall all be lost in God.[28]

In the Advent hymn above, the truth embodied in the doctrines of Incarnation, sanctification, glorification, and deification are all brought together in one cosmic vision that must be sung to be appreciated. But suppose we tried to analyze the thought. In the line "And make us all divine," does the word "all" qualify "us" or qualify "divine"? If the former, then Charles is a Universalist (And make *all of us* divine). If the latter, he blurs the final distinction between Creator and creation and risks being pantheistic (And make us *divine in every part*). According to Allchin, Charles means neither or both! Admittedly, such language may be "dangerously pantheistic," involving the objectionable notion of ontological absorption of humanity into God. However, says Allchin, Charles Wesley's intention "is to simply point in song to what cannot be categorized in discursive doctrine."[29] We must retreat into the mystery of *theosis* in order to affirm the doctrine of perfection. Charles remains a mystic speaking "ec-statically" (in the original meaning of "standing outside oneself"). Caught up in the rapture of cosmic vision and praise, the poet seeks only to use language worthy of the experience. Charles's poetic vision is of a mystical union in which the Christian soul is divinized and "lost in God." At journey's end, Charles wrote in *Hymns and Sacred Poems* (1739), the sanctified soul will be

> Plunged in the Godhead's deepest sea,
> And lost in thine immensity![30]

The finest Charles Wesley hymn that points to the mystery of *theosis,* according to Allchin, is found in the 1750 *Hymn Book* under the section "Seeking for Full Redemption."

Heavenly Adam, life divine,
Change my nature into Thine;
Move and spread throughout my soul,
Actuate and fill the whole;
Be it I no longer now
Living in the flesh, but Thou.
Holy Ghost, no more delay;
Come, and in thy temple stay;
Now thine inward witness bear,
Strong, and permanent and clear;
Spring of life, thyself impart,
Rise eternal in my heart.[31]

Not all of Charles's hymns that yearn for full redemption made it into John's published collections. Characteristically, John edited, revised, or deleted Charles's hymns according to his own standards and sensibilities for Methodist audiences. This reflects, among other differences between the two brothers, John and Charles at variance on the nature and extent of perfection in this life. According to John Tyson's study, *Charles Wesley: A Reader,* John expected to go on to perfection in this life, Charles at the threshold of death or in the next life.[32] John affirmed a perfection of the will, a cleansing of the heart, and a divine possession of the soul in this life. Charles would settle for nothing less than sinless perfection, the full recovery of the *imago Dei,* the achievement of divine *likeness,* and humanity's restoration to the angelic nature and beyond—the same vision of perfection John and Charles *both* shared during their Oxford years.[33] This same theological tension is evident in the letters of John to his brother Charles as represented in Tyson's study. For example:

> *June 27, 1766:* Concerning setting perfection too high. That perfection which I believe, I can boldly preach; because I think I see five hundred witnesses of it. Of that perfection which you preach, you think you do not see any witnesses at all. . . . I verily believe there are none upon the earth; none dwelling in the body. . . . Therefore I still think, to set perfection so high is effectively to renounce it.[34]
>
> *February 12, 1767:* The whole comes to one point: Is there, or is there not, any instantaneous sanctification between justification and death? I say, Yes. You (often seem to) say, No. What arguments brought you to think so? Perhaps they may convince me too.[35]
>
> *June 14, 1768:* I think it is high time that you and I, at least, should come to a point. Shall we go on asserting perfection against all the world? Or shall we quietly let it drop? We really must do one or the other. . . . What shall we jointly and explicitly maintain, (and recommend to all our Preachers,) concerning the nature, the time, (now or by and by?) and the manner of it? instantaneous, or not? I am

weary of intestine war; of Preachers quoting one of us against the other. At length, let us fix something for good and all.[36]

A Postmodern Wesleyan Agenda

In this study, I have explored Wesley's concept of entire sanctification or Christian perfection by looking for points of similarity to and derivation from the Greek patristic sources he may have used. Building on the insights of Albert Outler and Randy Maddox, and attempting to apply Ted Campbell's thesis, my own evaluation supports the notion that what Wesley envisioned as Christian perfection, holiness, or entire sanctification is theologically dependent upon earlier versions of *theosis.* I have further explored how Wesley selectively accessed the patristic tradition (principally in the writings of Clement), and how he may have reformulated the doctrine of deification "programmatically" according to his own vision of antiquity in light of contemporary concerns of what seemed practical and attainable *in this life.* I also have considered how Charles Wesley, as poet and hymnist, guarded the native strands of *theosis* and perfection within the Anglican tradition.

Further, I have suggested that the Wesleyan doctrine of entire sanctification may have developed over time from the dialectic of the brothers Wesley as they engaged their critics and employed their sources to promote a transformative vision of salvation and perfection in a revival movement for a particular age.

Since the time of the Wesleys, other paradigm shifts have occurred, and a distinctively modern, perfectionist, Wesleyan-Holiness pietism and theology has emerged in the American Holiness tradition—with both positive and negative results—which now may be in need of refinement or reformulation. It may be time to reassess and reconstruct the Wesleyan inheritance and vision of perfection for a new, postmodern age. However, reclaiming a Wesleyan heritage today requires not only understanding Wesley's developed doctrine of Christian perfection, but in knowing and appreciating those who taught before him. As Outler first suggested, "Wesley must be read in light of his sources—and therefore within the larger ecumenical perspectives of historic Christianity."[37]

In reading Wesley with his sources, I find him in continuity with the patristic tradition, yet distinctive and limited in his understanding of both the promise and the process of what the patristic writers meant by becoming "partakers of the divine nature." Therefore, I find it fruitful to go behind and beyond John Wesley: affirming his ancient sources *and* appreciating his positive contributions to the tradition; invoking the early Wesley (as well as his steadfast brother Charles) to correct the middle Wesley; and then standing with the mature Wesley in his openness to new light of revelation within the tradition. When John Wesley is read in tandem with Charles, and both brothers in conjunction with their sources, Charles's poetic vision of perfection can be reconsidered and reincorporated into the Wesleyan tradition. Wesleyan theologians can then go back to Charles and beyond John (and back to the Scriptures to exegete anew the passages allegedly pointing to deification) in order to construct a more biblical, global, Wesleyan spirituality for the Third Millennium of Christendom.[38]

Such a reformulation would incorporate the best of John Wesley's theological refinements and improvements on the ancient doctrine of *theosis* (i.e., appropriation by faith not by works or knowledge, inward assurance over perpetual seeking, accessibility in this earthly life), while fully appreciating the Eastern emphasis on "therapeutic" soteriology with its biblical affirmation of original humanity and original blessing. In so doing, we may arrive at a progressive Wesleyan Orthodox vision of *theosis* as part of the essential quest for human wholeness and completion of the new creation in Christ.

Notes

1. S T Kimbrough, ed., *Orthodox and Wesleyan Spirituality* (Crestwood, NY: St. Vladimir's Seminary Press, 2002), 7.

2. Albert Outler, *John Wesley* (New York: Oxford University Press, 1964). See also Randy Maddox, *Responsible Grace: John Wesley's Practical Theology* (Nashville, TN: Kingswood Books, 1994); and Ted Campbell, *John Wesley and Christian Antiquity* (Nashville, TN: Kingswood Books, 1991); and Richard Heitzenrater, "John Wesley's Reading of and References to the Early Church Fathers," in *Orthodox and Wesleyan Spirituality,* 25ff.

3. Vladimir Lossky, *The Mystical Theology of the Eastern Church* (Crestwood, NY: St. Vladimir's Seminary Press, 1998), 117; Athanasius, *On the Incarnation* 54.

4. See esp. Paul Basset, *Exploring Christian Holiness,* vol. 2, *The Historical Development* (Kansas City, MO: Beacon Hill Press of Kansas City, 1985), 208–9.

5. See John Wesley's sermon, "The One Thing Needful," in *The Bicentennial Edition of the Works of John Wesley,* ed. Frank Bakers (Nashville, TN: Abingdon, 1984), 4:351–59; and in *John Wesley's Sermons: An Anthology,* ed. Albert Outler and Richard Heitzenrater (Nashville, TN: Abingdon Press, 1991), 33–38.

6. Nineteenth-century holiness theologians generally adopted the instantaneous sanctification model. American Wesleyan and Nazarene theologians have tended to adopt the progressive model of Wesley's doctrine of entire sanctification. See Basset, *Exploring Christian Holiness,* 208–9. United Methodists have tended to adopt this model of Wesley's doctrine of perfection. See *The Book of Discipline of The United Methodist Church* (Nashville, TN: UM Publishing House, 2000), 47.

7. See "A Plain Account of Christian Perfection" and "Farther Thoughts on Entire Sanctification" for Wesley's most mature conception of the doctrine.

8. "Love Divine All Loves Excelling," in *A Collection of Hymns for the Use of the People Called Methodists* (1780), Hymn #374, *Bicentennial Edition,* 7:547. See also *The Poetical Works of John and Charles Wesley,* collected and arranged by G. Osborn, 13 vols. (London: Wesleyan-Methodist Conference Office, 1868), 4:220.

9. Albert Outler, *John Wesley* (1964); Ted Campbell, *John Wesley and Christian Antiquity: Religious Vision and Cultural Change* (Nashville, TN: Kingswood Books, 1991). Randy

Maddox says that understanding the doctrine of sanctification in its therapeutic, soteriological context, "has significant parallels with the Eastern Orthodox theme of deification (*theosis*)," in *Responsible Grace,* 122. Heitzenrater argues that John Wesley is just name-dropping and not really deriving a doctrine from church fathers. The similarity of ideas between Wesley and Eastern Christianity are simply the result of Wesley's reading of certain seventeenth- and eighteenth-century divines "whose thought the window to the East remains open," in "John Wesley's Reading," in *Orthodox and Wesleyan Spirituality,* 30. Building primarily on the insights of Outler and Maddox, and attempting to apply Campbell's thesis of how Wesley appropriated his patristic sources, my article, "*Theosis* and Sanctification: John Wesley's Reformulation of a Patristic Doctrine" (*Wesleyan Theological Journal* 31, no. 2 [Fall 1996]: 71–94), explores the theological parallels between *theosis* and sanctification and probable historical derivations.

10. Outler, *John Wesley,* viii.

11. Charles Ashanin, *Essays on Orthodox Christianity and Church History* (Indianapolis: Broad Ripple, 1990), 90.

12. Maddox, *Responsible Grace,* 122.

13. "An Address to Clergy," in *The Works of John Wesley,* Jackson Edition, vol. 10 (Grand Rapids, MI: Baker Books, 1996), 484–92; see also Campbell's discussion in *Wesley and Christian Antiquity,* 41–51.

14. Campbell, *Wesley and Christian Antiquity,* 20.

15. Clement's three principal works (*Protreptikos, Paidagogos,* and *Stromateis*) addressed these three classes of people: 1. *Protreptikos* (Exhortation to the Greeks) addresses the unconverted and unenlightened pagan; 2. *Paidagogos* (Instructor) addresses catechumens and simpleminded believers in need of recovery, moral instruction, and the milk of Christ; and 3. *Stromateis* (Miscellanies) addresses the true Gnostic in need of the meat of esoteric initiation into the Christian mysteries and ancient (possibly Hermetic) wisdom.

16. *Poetical Works,* 1:35.

17. Russian Orthodox theologian Vladimir Lossky compares Clement's Gnostic content to certain passages in *Poimandres*—the collection of Hermetic texts originating in Egypt "in which contemplative knowledge is presented as a deifying formula by which one is raised to the sphere of the fixed stars [*Corpus Hermeticum,* Treatise X, *Bude's collection,* 1:112f.]." Lossky says that "Clement mentions the writings of Hermes Trismegistus [see *Strom.* 4.4 (PG 9:253)], but he never quotes them." *The Vision of God,* trans. Ashleigh Moorhouse, 2nd ed. (Crestwood, NY: St. Vladimir's Seminary Press, 1973), 54.

18. Clement's description of the "true Gnostic" is in book 7 of his *Stromateis.* Wesley's "entirely sanctified Methodist" and Clement's "perfect Christian gnostic" share common elements, according to Campbell: "Both stress prayer without ceasing, love of neighbor, obedience to God's commandments, freedom from worldly desires and hope of immortality as characteristics of the ideal Christian (Gnostic or Methodist!)." *Wesley and Christian Antiquity,* 42.

19. *Stromateis* 6. Clement's exhortation in chapter 12 of *Paidagogos* is representative of the Alexandrian vision of *theosis:* "But let us, O children of the good Father—nurslings of the good Instructor—fulfill the Father's will, listen to the Word, and take on the impress of the truly saving life of the Savior; and meditating on the heavenly mode of life according to which we have been deified, let us anoint ourselves with the perennial immortal bloom of gladness."

20. For a discussion on Wesley's appropriation of Clement and others, see Campbell, *Wesley and Christian Antiquity,* 41–44.

21. Outler, *John Wesley,* 31.

22. In interpreting Wesley's appropriation of Clement, Paul Basset admits that Clement "does speak of man's becoming God . . . in the language of the mystery of the Incarnation, of

God having become man, not in the philosophical or everyday languages of metaphysics, logic, or sense-experience." But Bassett seems unwilling to call Clement a Gnostic or to say that Wesley either misunderstood Clement's intended meaning or simply corrected his source on the doctrine of *theosis.* See Basset, *Exploring Christian Holiness,* 57.

23. According to Campbell, Wesley both learned from his sources and amended his sources on points he believed did not conform to the teachings of Scripture and the revealed order of salvation as he understood them. Wesley, in other contexts, found that the church fathers required editing, earlier proponents of perfection needed correcting, and even ecumenical councils merited selective approval. The Apostolic Tradition, for Wesley, was open to improvement and required amendment according to the tests of Scripture, reason, and experience. However justified this view may be theologically, from a historical viewpoint, Campbell concludes, "Wesley's notions of early Christianity were frequently incorrect both in detail . . . and in general," and his programmatic use of his sources required deliberate manipulation of the early texts. Campbell, *Wesley and Christian Antiquity,* 4. For specific examples of how Wesley "corrected" the church fathers, see Campbell, *Wesley and Christian Antiquity,* 39–40, 64.

24. Much "holiness" doctrine today has elements of theological eisegesis—the uncritical and unhistorical reading back into both the biblical texts and the patristic tradition, eighteenth- or nineteenth-century Wesleyan conceptions of perfection or sanctification and presenting this vision of holiness as scriptural and patristic (e.g., Bassett, *Exploring Christian Holiness,* 50–67).

25. Hymn #374, *Bicentennial Edition,* 7:547. See also *Poetical Works,* 4:220.

26. A. M. Allchin, *Participation in God: A Forgotten Strand in Anglican Tradition* (Wilton, CT: Morehouse-Barlow, 1988).

27. John refers to Ephrem as the "most awakened of all the ancient writers," whose poetry is preserved in current Armenian hymns. Kathleen McVey, "Ephrem the Syrian: A Theologian of the Presence of God," in *Orthodox and Wesleyan Spirituality,* 241.

28. Charles Wesley, *Hymns for the Nativity of Our Lord* (1745), Hymn #5 (Madison, NJ: Charles Wesley Society, 1991), 14; emphasis mine.

29. Allchin, *Participation in God,* 25.

30. "Hymn to the Holy Ghost," Hymn #363, *Bicentennial Edition,* 7:532; see also *Poetical Works,* 1:164.

31. Hymn #379, *Bicentennial Edition,* 7:552, emphasis mine.

32. John Tyson, *Charles Wesley: A Reader* (New York: Oxford University Press, 1989), 360.

33. Ibid., 360. See also Wesley's sermon, "The One Thing Needful" (1734), which he never published, perhaps because it did not reflect his mature views on the subject, but which was preserved by Charles (who retained this earlier view of perfection).

34. Ibid., 131.

35. Ibid., 132.

36. Ibid., 136.

37. Albert Outler, "A New Future for Wesley Studies: An Agenda for Phase III," in *The Wesleyan Theological Heritage: Essays of Albert C. Outler,* ed. Thomas Oden and Leicester Longden (Grand Rapids, MI: Zondervan, 1991), 138.

38. See Ps 82:6; Jn 10:34–35; 2 Cor 3:18; 2 Pt 1:4; and 1 Jn 3:1–2.

V
Theosis in Modern Thought

Neo-Palamism, Divinizing Grace, and the Breach between East and West

Jeffrey D. Finch

FROM THE USURPATION OF ECCLESIAL GOVERNANCE BY THE PAPACY TO THE interpolation of the *filioque* into the Creed, from the abuses of the Fourth Crusade to the cultural incubation of Marxism and modernism, tears were shed, ink spilled, and blood extracted over the real and/or perceived offenses of Western Christendom against the Christian East. In the twentieth century at least one new obstacle to East-West unity has arisen—this one apparently of purely doctrinal origin—focused on the distinctive Eastern vision of *theosis.*

It apparently began with a polemical 1925 article on St. Gregory Palamas, the fourteenth-century monk of Mount Athos and Eastern apologist, which appeared in the *Dictionnaire de théologie catholique* and was authored by the Augustinian friar, Martin Jugie, who accused Palamas therein of teaching a "veritable heresy" with his "real distinction" between the divine essence and the divine energies.[1] This prompted Vladimir Lossky, whose own Parisian teacher, Etienne Gilson, had instructed him in the importance of St. Thomas's "real distinction" within creatures between *esse* and *essentia,* to begin a spirited and protracted defense of Palamas's theology—one that would come quickly, with the help of John Meyendorff and many other Orthodox theologians. This defense made the Palamite essence-energies distinction a touchstone of Orthodox identity in the West for most of the remainder of the twentieth century, even until the present time.[2] For this reason, Lossky is generally regarded as the founder of the neo-Palamite school of thought, which is properly called *neo*-Palamism because Palamas had been almost forgotten within Eastern Orthodoxy until Lossky and Meyendorff revived interest in his thought.[3]

What I propose to do in this essay is to demonstrate that the divisive issue that was framed by Jugie and his neo-Palamite respondents concerning the nature and simplicity of God is more fundamentally a dispute over the authentically Christian meaning of "participation in the divine nature," or deification; and moreover, that the neo-Palamite critique of Western theology is grounded in a false alternative.

Neo-Palamite Logic of Essence-Energies Distinction

Vladimir Lossky implies the truth of this correlation between the doctrine of God and soteriology when he reasons, typically of his school, that if the biblical promise of 2 Peter 1:4 that the redeemed will be "partakers of the divine nature" is to be construed as anything more than an "illusion" or a "rhetorical expression or metaphor" and if the Pauline/Johannine language of living "in Christ" refers to a union in any sense real, then we will be

> compelled to recognize in God an ineffable distinction, other than that between his essence and his persons, according to which he is, under different aspects, both totally inaccessible and at the same time accessible. This distinction is that between the essence of God, or his nature, properly so-called, which is inaccessible, unknowable and incommunicable; and the energies or divine operations, forces proper to and inseparable from God's essence, in which he goes forth from himself, manifests, communicates, and gives himself.[4]

The essence or nature of God must be considered absolutely incommunicable, unknowable, and imparticipable to creatures even *after* the Father's self-disclosure through the incarnation of the Son and the insufflation of the Holy Spirit (indeed, for all eternity) because, as the neo-Palamite logic requires, if it were possible to know or to participate in the essence of God "even in the very least degree, we should not at that moment be what we are, we should be God by nature" and God "would have as many hypostases as there would be persons participating in his essence."[5] If it were true, therefore, as the historic opponents of Palamas are said to have claimed, that there exists metaphysically nothing other than God in his absolutely simple, immutable, fully actuated, trihypostatic essence and created effects of God's essence, then the uncreated operations or agency of God in the world "must be either identified with the essence or separated from it completely as actions which are external to it," thereby rendering a creaturely participation in the divine life possible only at the expense of God's transcendent integrity.[6] Hence, the Western doctrine that "whatever is not essence does not belong to God," Christos Yannaras complains, renders "any external manifestation" of God's activity in the world "necessarily 'heteroessential,' i.e., a created result of the divine cause," which in turn "means that, in the final analysis, the *theosis* of man, his participation in the divine life, is impossible, since even grace, the 'sanctifier' of the saints, is itself an effect, a result of the divine essence."[7]

The neo-Palamite logic of the essence-energies distinction very briefly outlined here reveals and assumes a particular understanding of God's operations or energies, his essence, the precise nature of whatever distinction there may exist between the two, and, indeed, the meaning of human participation in God, which all are agreed is tantamount to grace.

Historically, St. Gregory Palamas himself initially applied the term *energeia* to the "uncreated light," which he believed that he and his fellow fourteenth-century hesychasts on Mount Athos beheld in contemplative prayer, the very light that perfused Christ's body at his transfiguration on Mount Tabor, the uncreated splendor with which "the righteous will shine like the sun" (Mt 13:43). It is identical to "divinizing grace" and is responsible for the theophanies of Hebrew Scripture.[8] For this interpretation of his mystical experience, Barlaam, a Western nominalist tutored by William of Occam, accused Palamas of Messalianism, a heresy of the fourth through the seventh centuries, which taught that by the practice of continual prayer, one could come to see God with corporeal eyes. If on nothing else, Jugie, Lossky, and Meyendorff agree that it was this allegation that prompted Palamas to have recourse to the essence-energies distinction in the first place.[9] More than the radiant brilliance with which God enables himself to be encountered mystically in prayer, however, the energies came to be identified by the Palamite tradition with divine virtues or attributes, God's will, and with the ideas or *logoi* with which God planned eternally the temporal creation, similar to the manner in which Thomas Aquinas characterized the divine energies or operations.[10]

In defense of the Palamite position, Vladimir Lossky boasts that Scripture's "anthropomorphic expressions do not trouble Palamas at all" because he understood that God's attributes or names are "living and personal forces—not in the sense of individual beings, as Palamas' opponents wanted to define them, accusing him of polytheism, but precisely in the sense of manifestations of a personal God."[11] Dumitru Stăniloae likewise defines the uncreated energies as "nothing other than the attributes of God in motion."[12]

Following Palamas, who drew an "equation" between the divine will, grace, and energies and "claimed that his own theology was only a development of the decisions of [the Third Council of Constantinople in 680] about the two 'energies' or wills of Christ," it has also become a commonplace among theologians of the neo-Palamite school to locate God's will among his *energeiai*.[13] Yannaras, in fact, contends that the real, historic issue in dispute between Palamas and Barlaam was whether or in what sense God's will is distinct from his nature.[14] Lossky, as expected, draws a sharp distinction between the two, maintaining that God's "temporal missions" in the world are "a work of the will common to the three hypostases," for which the Greek Fathers customarily used verbs προΐημι and προχέομαι, whereas "the eternal procession of the Persons" is an act of "the very being of the Trinity," to which the same Fathers carefully reserved the use of the verb ἐκπορεύομαι.[15]

According to most neo-Palamite authors, the energies of God are as fully akin to the divine ideas or *logoi* as they are to God's will. A distinctively Eastern Christian "doctrine of divine ideas" holds that God's "volitional thoughts (θελητικὴ ἔννοια)" constitute the intention with which God predestined all things to be created in their manifold diversity, although, as Lossky is careful to specify, they are not "the eternal reasons of creatures contained within the very being of God, determinations of the essence to which created things refer as to their exemplary cause, as in the thought of St. Augustine which later became the common teaching of the whole Western tradition and was more precisely formulated by St. Thomas Aquinas."[16] Instead, the Greek Fathers are said to have located the divine ideas outside the essence of God, making them more "dynamic" and "intentional," "to be identified with the will" and thus not subject to the "necessity" to which the essential generation of the Son and spiration of the Spirit are subject. If the divine ideas or models or *logoi* of creation were part of the essence of God (which, Lossky complains, is all that Augustine recognizes in God), then "either the created world will be disparaged, and deprived of its original character as the unconditioned work of the creative Wisdom, or else creation will be introduced into the inner life of the Godhead"; Augustine falls prey to the first error, wherein "the divine ideas remain static—unmoving perfections of God," while certain Eastern sophiologists are susceptible to the latter.[17]

Thus, whereas *energeia* is most literally rendered "activity" or "operation," the term came to signify within the Palamite tradition everything that God revealed of himself in the economy of salvation—his attributes or names and his will or thoughts—as well as the innumerable acts whereby God and the divine nature and qualities are disclosed, consummately in the uncreated light of Christ's transfiguration, which every true Christian is also destined to receive.

The precise meaning of the term "essence" or *ousia* as the Fathers employed it is as vital as, and, unfortunately, more difficult to discern than the identity of the energies in understanding and evaluating the neo-Palamite proposal. Above all, however ambiguous or "antinomial" their language about the relationship between God's uncreated energies and essence, the neo-Palamites are clear about what they believe the essence of God is *not* and cannot be, namely, what Meyendorff calls "the philosophical notion of essence" or "simple essence," with which he believes "the West" uncritically identified God "on the basis of Greek philosophical presuppositions."[18] The doctrine of divine simplicity as taught in neoscholastic "manuals of theology," Lossky complains, "originates in human philosophy rather than in the divine revelation," inasmuch as the manuals "base the divine simplicity upon the concept of simple essence," for the philosophical concept of "God as pure act cannot admit anything to be God that is not the very essence of God," thus requiring either a communicable essence or a God who cannot be encountered by creatures except through created intermediaries.[19] Meyendorff hypothesizes that the doctrine of deification would not be "suspected in the West of being a single transposition of neo-Platonic pantheism," if the West only shared the Eastern fathers' conception that God is more than his essence. He further suggests that the reason why Protestants cannot come to see the truth of the Eastern Orthodox cult of the saints or their sacramentalism is because the former are still beholden to the "Augustinian tradition" from which "comes the idea that God, being identical with his essence, cannot be participated otherwise than in his essence," thus causing Protestants to believe that God's glory is a zero-sum equation; to the extent that it is attributed to humans, it is deprived from God.[20]

The essence or *ousia* of God, Palamas and his followers propose in the alternative, does not properly denote the full, incomprehensible measure of who God is—God's fully actuated, infinite quiddity, as it were—but refers only to a particular "mode" or dimension of God's being. "The essence is necessarily being, but being is not necessarily essence": this principle, writes Meyendorff, "is the real significance of what is called 'Palamism.'"[21] God transcends God's self, his essence surpassing his being or existence and his being surpassing his essence.

The language and logic of divine supraessentiality can seem tautological at times, inasmuch as its authors appear to contain their conclusions in their presuppositions by assuming in an a priori fashion that in order for God to be transcendent of creation, a distinct mode or aspect of the divine nature must necessarily remain eternally inaccessible to creatures. In this way, Lossky comes close to defining what he and the neo-Palamite school mean by *ousia* in the first place (i.e., apart from its inapproachability) when he calls Aristotle's δεύτεραι οὐσίαι "essences, in the realistic sense of the word," as opposed to Aristotle's primary substances, which Lossky describes as "individual subsistences" and applies not to God's essence, but only to the Persons or *hypostases* of the Trinity.[22] "That is principally, primarily and properly called *ousia* which is stated of no subject and which is in no subject," or, in other words, "those species wherein the 'first ousias' exist." *Ousia,* according to this notion, is a kind of genus like "human" or "animal."[23]

With respect to the precise nature of the neo-Palamite distinction between essence and energy, Aidan Nichols, I think, has neatly and helpfully cut to the heart of the issue with this question: "Is the language of 'energies' nominal or adverbial?"[24] In other words, do the names of God denote multiple, uncreated realities external to or effluent from the simple divine essence, or are they creaturely ways of characterizing the activity of the one, fully essential God?

Only very rarely do the neo-Palamite critics contend explicitly that what theologians, East and West alike, acknowledge to be at least a phenomenological or "adverbial" distinction between God's attributes and God's essence is also necessarily ontological or "nominal," meaning that the energies are subsistent, divine realities external to the divine essence. More commonly, an ontological distinction is suggested only indirectly by one of two oppositions or "antinomies" the neo-Palamites find between the essence and energies, those of freedom vs. necessity, and immanent transcendence vs. economic agency.

Lossky and Meyendorff, first and most conspicuously, oppose the freedom and dynamism of the energies with what they characterize as the necessity of God's inner trinitarian life. The Greek Fathers located the divine ideas outside the essence of God and made them more "dynamic" and "intentional," according to Lossky, because they had "to be identified with the will" and thus not subject to the "necessity" to which he assumes the generation of the Son and spiration of the Spirit are subject.[25] Romanides also denies freedom to the immanent Trinity and to the Father when he claims that, in response to the Arian and Eunomian attribution of the begetting of the Son to the will of the Father, "the Church insisted that the will does not generate," for "only the hypostasis of the Father can be considered the cause and source of the other hypostases."[26] Meyendorff likewise reasons that in order for God's relation to the world of creatures to remain free and personal (presumably unlike the trinitarian relations!), his eternal plans or *logoi* for the creation must be truly distinct from his nature or essence. Otherwise, creation would be as necessary as generation or spiration, from which acts Meyendorff wants to exclude the will and freedom of God: the "thoughts" or "divine ideas" with which God planned the creation of the universe from all eternity "are the expressions . . . of divine will, not of divine nature," and "represent the unlimited potentiality of divine freedom."[27] In other words, in order for God to have been directly responsible for the act of creation, he avers, some latent potentiality within God had to have been actuated when the created world began. Since it is axiomatic that the simple essence of God cannot be altered by its relation to creatures, whatever of God did change must therefore lie outside his essence.

The "essentialist philosophy," which Meyendorff attributes to Augustine and other Latin authors, then, would culminate either in pantheism or Arianism. As Meyendorff sees it, the reason for this is that if there is no ontological basis within God upon which to differentiate between the free act of creation and adoption on the one hand and the necessary act of generation and spiration on the other hand, then neither is there any truly theological reason why creation should not be considered co-essential with God, or the Son and Spirit not be considered creatures.[28] If nothing else, this particular line of argumentation seems to undermine the common neo-Palamite defense that their distinctions involve no separation; if the will of the Father is not at all involved in the generation of the Son and if his thoughts are expressions of his will only, but not of his nature, then it is difficult to see how they are not separate as well as distinct. Moreover, if the will/energies are not involved in the inner life of the Trinity, then how can anything be predicated of that life, since the neo-Palamites insist that only the energies of God are knowable or communicable? If the generation of the Son and the spiration of the Holy Spirit are acts of the essence only, absent the will or energies, how can Meyendorff say anything about them at all and remain within the limitations established by his own gnoseology? However, when one takes fully into account that the triune God, for whom there is no yesterday or today, transcends time, this neo-Palamite either/or between the divine freedom and nature proves to be a false alternative.

A False Alternative

Athanasius, when addressing the question of whether the Father begets the Son by will (freely) or by nature (necessarily), answered his Arians opponents that only from an unacceptably anthropomorphized view of God can such a question arise, for the act of purposive deliberation requires a creaturely interval between being and acting: "And there is this difference [from the Son], that the creatures are made upon the beginning, and have a beginning of existence connected with an interval (διαστηματικὴν ἀρχὴν)."[29] Against those Arians who "dare to apply human contrarities in the instance of God,"[30] Athanasius here simply asserts the irreducible mystery that the God who transcends all temporality acts at once with absolute freedom and in perfect accordance with his own nature. God wills to be what he is essentially and immutably, without any possibility that he could be otherwise, namely, generative, good, and merciful.

Confronted by the Arians with the stark alternative between a God who is required by nature to generate a Son or a God whose will is detached from his nature, thus making him arbitrary, Athanasius offered the solution that there is no true antinomy between the divine nature and the divine will, or, in other words, between the being and acting of God; the Father chooses freely to be "generative by nature," as he chooses to be everything else that he is immutably.[31]

But the primary élan behind the neo-Palamite insistence upon a real distinction within God, as indicated earlier, is their common understanding of participation, one that is reductively entitative, having no analogical or causal dimension, thus requiring that an aspect or dimension of the divine nature be protected from involvement with creation in order to protect God's transcendence.

When, in relation to the biblical promise of 2 Peter 1:4 that the redeemed will become "partakers of the divine nature (θείας κοινωνοὶ φύσεως)," Lossky admonishes that the uncreated nature to which this sublime hope attaches cannot refer even in the most strictly qualified, delimited manner to God's essence, for "if we could at a given moment participate to some degree in the essence, we would not in that moment be what we are, but gods by nature,"[32] he appears to have relied upon Palamas himself. A "part of the substance, even the smallest, contains all of its powers," Palamas reasons, "if indeed we participate in that undisclosed substance of God, whether in all or part of it, we will be all powerful," from which rationale he is able to extrapolate this further principle: "A substance has as many hypostases as it has participants."[33] To participate in an ontologically simple God, as Palamas and his school understand it, would necessarily entail becoming a divine person.

Hence, the neo-Palamite school's understanding of grace and participation is most clearly demarcated from the Western view by its decision not to recognize as grace any created or re-creative effects of God's presence and activity in the world, nor to include as an aspect of participation in the divine nature any newly acquired likeness to God on the order of supernatural human virtue.

In contrast to the West, which attempts to express the transcendent communicability of God by distinguishing between God's uncreated agency in the soul and its created fruits, between "the gifts of the Holy Spirit, the infused virtues, and habitual and actual grace," Eastern Orthodoxy recognizes no such thing as a "created supernatural" in the economy of salvation, that is, no acquisition or perfection of human faculties, according to Lossky.[34] The great soteriological difference between East and West therefore "consists in the fact that the Western conception of grace implies the idea of causality, grace being represented as an effect of the divine Cause, exactly as in the act of creation," whereas the Eastern Orthodox believe that "it is in creation alone that God acts as cause"; grace, on the other hand, "is the presence of the uncreated and eternal light, the real omnipresence of God in all things."[35]

Meyendorff thus posits an either/or opposition between discipleship to Christ and deification in Christ: "The Christian is called not to an 'imitation' of Jesus—a purely extrinsic and moral act," but to "life *in* Christ," which is "a 'communication' (*perichōrēsis—circumincessio*) of the 'energies' divine and human."[36] He is able to say, therefore, that the "miraculous power of the Saints, which in potentiality belongs to all the baptized, is an *uncreated* power."[37] The gifts of the Holy Spirit of which Paul writes in 1 Corinthians 12 and 14—wisdom, knowledge, faith, gifts of healing, working of miracles, prophecy, the discernment of spirits, various tongues, the interpretation of tongues, and so on—are not the created effects of the uncreated operations of God received through the believer's faith and cooperation, but are the uncreated operations themselves.[38] Hence, to participate by grace in God's wisdom, according to this conception, is to become an instantiation of divine wisdom, rather than to acquire a created likeness of the same.

Lot-Borodine also boasts that the Eastern Church, contrary to the Western tradition "under the influence of Augustine," has constantly maintained "the *uncreated nature* of the variety of charisms or gifts of the Spirit—modes of human participation in divine life."[39] To be grafted into Christ, to be united to God, and to be saved is to become "uncreated through grace," for "in Christ and in the baptized there is *one sole* indivisible Spirit and, in him, all distinction between created and uncreated is inadmissible."[40] God's eternal plan of salvation as seen by Athanasius and the Cappadocians was to "restore in man the divine element, which was in danger of getting lost or forsaken, and invite the creature to a real participation, not merely intentional (*in voto*), in the inner life of the divine persons."[41]

To those who would count Augustine and Aquinas among the doctors of the Church, however, the entitative or distributive concept of participation implied by neo-Palamism's refusal to include causality in its doctrine of grace is a truncation of the Eastern patristic teaching at best. Indeed, Orthodox theologian David Bentley Hart boldly wrote that "the anti-Western passion (or, frankly, paranoia) of Lossky and his followers has on occasion led to rather severe distortions of Eastern theology," specifically in his "division of the *ordines* of the economic and immanent Trinities from one another."[42] As G. Podskalsky reads him, Palamas needed recourse to and indeed did propose a real distinction only because he first mistakenly gave a Neoplatonic, emanationist construction to Pseudo-Dionysius, who in fact had "emphasized repeatedly that the differentiation of God's powers from his unknowable essence did not mean that truth, life, light, etc., were something other than being," but only represents "the attempt on our part to put into words the incomprehensible relationship between Creator and creature."[43] Rowan Williams likewise warns that it was the Neoplatonists who first perpetrated an "ontologizing" of Aristotle's logic by reifying the terms (like substance and quality), which he intended merely to govern the laws of logic, and by assigning to each of them different degrees of being. Only within this ontologically hierarchical framework would it make any sense at all to say, as the neo-Palamites do, that the uncreated, natural energies of God are objectively outside his *ousia*. Apart from an emanationist doctrine of God, however, the *ousia* cannot be construed as the irreducibly unified, intrinsically unknowable, and imparticipable core reality lurking behind God's three hypostasis, relations, and activities, but simply "Whatever-it-is-to-be-God."[44]

Similarly, the threefold ontology of the imparticipable (ἀμέθεκτον), the participated (μεθεκτόν), and the participating (μετέχον) proposed by Palamas is taken almost directly from Proclus, according to Flogaus, who believes that it was "Palamas' understanding of participation as necessarily introducing a division in that which is participated" that caused him to reject Augustine's teaching that uncreated grace is the very Person of the Holy Spirit in the soul.[45] Garrigues also argues that Palamas effected a kind of "reduction of the idea of participation to that of entitative participation," which he defines as "being made part of another" and calls a "neo-platonic conception."[46] Palamas ignores two other "modes" of participation: "participation in the causality of the act of being and the volitional participation proper to spiritual beings," which together "dispense with the need to postulate participable intermediate entities in order to safeguard the transcendence of the divine essence."[47] Because the West grounds the difference between the generation of the Son and the adoptive filiation of the redeemed in the infinite, immutable eternity of the former and the finite, created temporality of the latter, unlike neo-Palamism, "they would have recourse to a theory of participation which is not a parceling out."[48]

Hans Urs von Balthasar, who claims that the fathers who influenced him the most were all Easterners (namely, Irenaeus, Origen, Gregory of Nyssa, and Maximus the Confessor), regards the Palamite essence-energies distinction as a reversion both to Middle Platonism and to the Hellenized, cabalistic doctrine of late antique Judaism, which "hypostasized the utterances and attributes" of God and distinguished them from his essence in order to secure God's transcendence.[49] More specifically, like Flogaus, he locates the origin of the real distinction between participable and imparticipable in Proclus, whose language was introduced into the Christian lexicon by Pseudo-Dionysius, but "radicalized and systematized" by Palamas, particularly in the latter's claim that the creature can never encounter the essence of God even through all eternity.[50] The tradition that is expressed most clearly by Maximus the Confessor and Aquinas, on the other hand, understands human participation in God to involve the acquisition of "a likeness of God's perfections of being . . . through the efficient causality which confers existence."[51]

Such Western formulations of the traditional Christian usage of the language of participation for sanctifying or divinizing grace seem to be vindicated by the best patristic scholarship on the topic. In perhaps the most comprehensive study to date on the concept of participation in the patristic era, Friedrich Normann writes that the language of participation employed by the fathers was grounded in a "sharp differentiation between participation and identification," such that "the individuation of either party is not compromised." According to this latter conception, "participation can never be misconstrued as mixture," since the fathers intended their affirmations of human participation in the divine nature to be taken "only in an analogical sense," even though they would widely prefer the more startling formulas like "God became man so that man might become God" over the biblical language of 2 Peter 1:4.[52]

Theodorou likewise characterizes the patristic doctrine of divinization in terms of fully differentiated assimilation: the "ontological cleft" that underlies their understanding of participation protects the fathers' doctrine of divinization from any and all objections that it might lead to pantheism, since the finite being of the divinized creature remains forever finite and the infinite being of God remains utterly unchanged.[53] And in response to Harnack's allegation that the fathers taught a crudely physical or magical soteriology,

Martin George calls the "ethical way of divinization through the praxis of the good" an "essential" and "the most striking component" of the Eastern patristic teaching on participation in the divine nature.[54]

Another, more irenic, modern school of thought, however, one which includes Orthodox theologian and bishop Kallistos Ware,[55] recognizes and seeks to demonstrate that the alternative between entitative participation and analogical participation, or between the indwelling of uncreated grace and its equally gratuitous created effects, is a false one. Congar, for instance, believes that neo-Palamites tend to reject the scholastic or Thomistic doctrine of created grace only because they fail to grasp "the depth and realism" of "the intentional union of the Thomists."[56] The truth, he explains, is that Thomas Aquinas and his fellow high scholastics never reduced the effusive light of glory to the created yet gratuitous means by which the human soul is made capable of receiving it, nor did they reduce the indwelling of God to the created effects of which he is the cause, for "Western theologians knew that there is no created grace without uncreated grace, since grace is that gift with which God himself is given or rather, it is what God gives when he gives himself."[57] Moreover, Podskalsky, Flogaus, and others notwithstanding, several Western scholars contend that the teaching of St. Gregory Palamas himself is compatible with Roman Catholic thought on the matter. G. Philips, for example, argues that Palamas taught no objective distinction at all: because Palamas also "declares that the energies are really identical to the essence" of God, his antinomial distinction is merely "*another way* of approaching an ineffable mystery" and "a typical example of perfectly admissible theological pluralism."[58] The essence-energies distinction of contemporary Palamism could be "comparable to the *formalis-ex-natura-rei* distinction dear to Duns Scotus," Philips suggests, which is a distinction between the inseparable attributes of God's simple essence—neither ontological nor merely conceptual—and therefore finally compatible with the Roman Catholic magisterium.[59]

Jürgen Kuhlmann also takes a remarkably friendly posture toward Palamism from a Western perspective. The Palamite *energeia,* according to Kuhlmann (who devotes the second part of his book to demonstrating that Palamism was never judged to be heretical by the Roman Catholic Church—not by the Council of Florence, nor by Pope Benedict XII's encyclical, *Benedictus Deus*), "is not God in himself, but God for us, in so far as he is the being of creatures. Since the essence of God neither can be this nor is this, the operation is obviously in some way truly different from the essence."[60] Palamas, he continues, repeatedly refuses to conceive of a composite God, and "wishes only to say with his teaching that God does not remain within himself alone, but wills to exist also for us and that both are not simply identical."[61]

The most recent comparative study on his thought also suggests that Palamas proposed no real distinction, but it does so with less than decisive conviction. A. N. Williams observes that only in two loci does Palamas state explicitly that the energies are as constitutively and ontologically distinct from the essence as are the three Hypostases and only once does he clearly insist that the essence and energies are not the same thing, although he repeatedly implies as much by speaking of the imparticipable essence and the divinizing energies.[62] But Williams believes that even here an ontological or fully real distinction need not be understood, since Palamas's purpose in making these statements was merely to affirm emphatically that the operations of God in the world are fully God, rather than some created intermediary. Indeed, she contends, Palamas never sets out to construct a new doctrine of God, one that would develop or augment the Cappadocian definition of one nature and three persons. Neither does Palamas ever seem concerned to defend or justify or even to define and clarify the essence-energies distinction, but prescinds altogether from the question of whether the language he simply adopted from the fathers is to be understood in an ontological or modal or conceptual fashion. The only purpose for which Palamas uses the distinction is to affirm that God is infinitely knowable and communicable and at once infinitely transcendent and incomprehensible. This, Williams maintains, is identical to the constant faith and dogma of the Western Christian tradition, which expresses the mystery of the communicability of the ever transcendent God in different language.[63] She further argues that Palamas's doctrine is to be distinguished from that of his unnamed modern disciples whose often polemical, tendentious approach has been obstructive to a proper and accurate understanding of the doctrine of Palamas on the part of Westerners. In particular, it is not obvious "whether the (essence-energies) distinction is real or nominal in his work."[64]

Whatever the case with the claims of St. Gregory Palamas, however, we can conclude at least that there is no necessary opposition between the uncreated operations or energies of divine grace and the elevation of human nature that they effect synergetically, nor any incompatibility between following or imitating Christ, as he commanded us to do, and being mystically united to Christ in the adoption of sons through the Holy Spirit. The uncreated self-gift of God is always primary in the whole Christian economy of salvation, both East and West agree, but God's initiative is not complete without effecting what St. Paul referred to as bearing the "image of the man of heaven" (1 Cor 15:39), becoming "a new creation" (2 Cor 5:17), being "conformed to the image of the Son" (Rom 8:29), and similar promised creaturely changes.

Despite many remaining obstructions, therefore, the future of East-West rapprochement appears to be overcoming the modern polemics of neo-scholasticism and neo-Palamism, thanks in large part to the otherwise helpful research of Lossky, Meyendorff, and company. The great advances in neopatristic scholarship provided by the orientophilic, self-styled *ressourcement* school of the twentieth century, notably represented by Henri de Lubac,

Jean Daniélou, Hans Urs von Balthasar, Yves Congar, and Thomas Oden, among others, continues to make the literature and thought of the church fathers ever more accessible. Let us hope that these developments will lead to the realization of John Paul II's oft-repeated prayer that the church begin once again to "breathe with both lungs."

Notes

1. Martin Jugie, "Palamas Grégoire," in *Dictionnaire de théologie catholique,* 11:1735–76, quotation from 1764. Cf. idem, "Palamite (controverse)," in *Dictionnaire de théologie catholique,* 11:1777–1818.

2. Georges A. Barrois, "Palamism Revisited," *St. Vladimir's Seminary Quarterly* 19 (1975): 213. According to Georges Barrois, the "fundamental thesis" of John Meyendorff's *Introduction à l'étude de Grégoire Palamas* is that "the patristic doctrine of the Christian's divinization implies the Palamite dogma of a real distinction, in God, of the essence and the energies."

3. Yves Congar, *I Believe in the Holy Spirit,* trans. David Smith, vol. 3 (New York: Crossroad, 1983), 61, citing as evidence T. de Regnon's failure to mention Palamas in connection with the question of divine energies in his 1898 tome on trinitarian theology, *Etudes de theologie positive sur la Sainte Trinite,* 4 vols. (Paris, 1892–98), which set out to demonstrate both the differences and complementarity between Eastern and Western conceptions. See also the editorial comments in *Istina* 19 (1974): 257, which cite as additional evidence of Palamas's gradually acquired obscurity, Russia's mid-eighteenth-century discontinuance of the practice of reading at each Sunday of Orthodoxy (the second Sunday of Lent and St. Gregory's feast day) the anathemas pronounced against Palamas's adversaries at the Synodikon of 1351.

4. Vladimir Lossky, *The Mystical Theology of the Eastern Church* (London: James Clarke, 1957; repr., Crestwood, NY: St. Vladimir's Seminary Press, 1998), 67, 70.

5. Ibid., 69–70. Lossky continues on 73–74 that if we do not hold an ontological distinction between God's essence and energies then "we cannot fix any very clear borderline between the procession of the divine persons and the creation of the world; both the one and the other will be equally acts of the divine nature." A second but related consequence of this failure to find a real distinction in God is that the economic or *ad extra* life of the Trinity in relation to the created world would be as fully subject to necessity as is the inner life of the Trinity.

6. Lossky, *The Vision of God,* 2nd ed., trans. Ashleigh Moorhouse (Crestwood, NY: St. Vladimir's Seminary Press, 1973), 158. Lossky continues in regard to Palamas's critics: "either they must admit the distinction between essence and operation, but then their philosophical notion of simplicity would oblige them to reject the existence of the glory of God, grace and the light of the Transfiguration among creatures; or else they must categorically deny this distinction, which would oblige them to identify that which cannot be known with what can be known, the incommunicable with the communicable, essence and grace. In both cases, the deification of created being and therefore also all actual communion with God would be impossible." Cf. P. Krivosheine, as quoted by E. von Ivánka, "Palamismus und Vätertradition," in *L'Église et les églises: Neuf siècles de douloureuse séparation entre l'Orient et l'Occident; Études et travaux sur l'unité chrétienne offerts à Dom Lambert Beauduin,* 2:29–46 (Chevetogne: Éditions de Chevetogne, 1955), 30, who also believes that unless one distinguishes between God's essence and energy, one cannot affirm a true human communion with God "sans tomber dans une confusion pantheiste de la creature avec la Divinite" [without falling into a

pantheistic conflation of the creature with the Deity]. Michael Azkoul, *The Influence of Augustine of Hippo on the Orthodox Church* (Lewiston, NY: Edwin Mellen Press, 1990), 50, further claims that "failure to distinguish between God's Essence and his uncreated Energies implies an ontological dualism between God and the world and, consequently, the impossibility of deification." See also Clement Lialine, "The Theological Teaching of Gregory Palamas on Divine Simplicity: Its Experimental Origin and Practical Issue," *Eastern Churches Quarterly* 6 (1945–46): 277.

7. Christos Yannaras, "The Distinction between Essence and Energies and Its Importance for Theology," *St. Vladimir's Theological Quarterly* 19 (1975): 242–43.

8. *St. Gregory Palamas: The One Hundred and Fifty Chapters; A Critical Edition, Translation, and Study (Capita),* trans. and ed. Robert E. Sinkewicz (Toronto: Pontifical Institute of Medieval Studies, 1988), no. 92; Lossky, *Mystical Theology,* 76, citing Hab 3:3–4: "His glory covered the heavens and the earth was full of his praise. His brightness was like the rays flashed from his hand; and there he veiled his power."

9. Lossky, *Vision of God,* 154; Meyendorff, *A Study of Gregory Palamas,* trans. George Lawrence (London: Faith Press, 1964), 46; and Jugie, "Palamas Grégoire," 11:1755.

10. Cf. Thomas Aquinas, *Summa Theologica* 1.2, where Aquinas identifies God's "knowledge, will and power" as among "whatever concerns His operations," which in turn belong to "whatever concerns the Divine Essence."

11. Lossky, *In the Image and Likeness of God,* ed. Thomas E. Bird and John Erickson (Crestwood, NY: St. Vladimir's Seminary Press, 1974), 57. See also Lialine, "The Theological Teaching of Gregory Palamas on Divine Simplicity," 270: "the anthropomorphic expressions of (Scripture) do not cause Palamas the slightest embarrassment." The attention given to God's virtues or attributes by advocates of the essence-energies distinction is a sequela from the doctrine's historic roots in the Arian controversy, when the Cappadocians sought to confound Eunomius's claim that the attribute of unbegottenness belongs to the divine essence, thus obviating the very possibility of coessential sonship. Cf. André de Halleux, "Palamisme et Tradition," *Irénikon* 48 (1975): 482.

12. *The Experience of God,* trans. Joan Ioanita and Robert Barringer (Brookline, MA: Holy Cross Orthodox Press, 1994), 125.

13. *Contra Akindynos* 3.6.1, quoted in L. C. Contos, "The Essence-Energies Structure of St. Gregory Palamas," *Greek Orthodox Theological Review* 12 (1967): 286; Meyendorff, *Gregory Palamas,* 95; and Meyendorff, *Byzantine Theology* (New York: Fordham University Press, 1974), 153.

14. Yannaras, "The Distinction between Essence and Energies and Its Importance for Theology," 235–36. From Palamism's Western critics, Garrigues, "L'énergie divine et la grâce chez Maxime le Confesseur," *Istina* 19 (1974): 278, seems to agree with this assessment.

15. Lossky, *Mystical Theology,* 158.

16. Ibid., 95, citing no text from Augustine or Thomas.

17. Ibid., 96. Lossky takes this doctrine of divine ideas almost entirely from Pseudo-Dionysius, who calls them "models (παραδείγματα)," "predestinations (προορισμοί)," and "providences (προνοίαι)" (*De divin. nom.* 5.2, 5.8. PG 3:817, 824).

18. Meyendorff, *Byzantine Theology,* 188.

19. Lossky, *Mystical Theology,* 77–78, citing Sebastien Guichardan, *Le problème de la simplicite divine en Orient et en Occident aux XIVe et XVe siècles: Grégoire Palamas, Duns Scot, Georges Scholarios* (Lyon, 1933), which he characterizes as "a striking example of this theological insensibility before the fundamental mysteries of faith."

20. John Meyendorff, *Orthodoxy and Catholicity* (New York: Sheed and Ward, 1966), 132.

21. *Gregory Palamas,* 213, quoting Palamas, *Against Akindynos* 2.10.

22. Lossky, *Mystical Theology,* 50.

23. Ibid., quoting Aristotle, *Categories* 5. Yet, Lossky immediately confuses the matter

when, in the same paragraph, he also defines *ousia* as "all that subsists by itself and which has not its being in another," in which case, as he admits, "*ousia* and *hypostasis* are the same thing," each term being equally capable of denoting both "an individual substance" and "the essence common to many individuals."

24. Review of *Maxime le Confesseur: Essence et énergies de Dieu,* by Vasilios Karayiannis (Paris: Beauchesne, 1993), in *The Journal of Ecclesiastical History* 46 (1995): 494. Nichols argues that the answer to this question given by St. Maximus is "adverbial." Note of caution: what Nichols means by "nominal" here is not "conceptual," as when the same appellation is used to provide an alternative to "real" or "ontological."

25. Lossky, *Mystical Theology,* 95.

26. Romanides, "Notes on the Palamite Controversy and Related Topics," *Greek Orthodox Theological Review* 9 (1963–64): 269.

27. Meyendorff, *Byzantine Theology,* 131, citing Gregory of Nazianzus, *Carm theol IV de mundo* 5.67–68; John Damascene, *DFO* 1.9; 2.2; Maximus the Confessor, *Schol,* PG 4:317. Cf. ibid., 132, where Meyendorff cites Maximus, *Amb.* 7, PG 91:1081 and Lars Thunberg, *Microcosm and Mediator: The Theological Anthropology of Maximus the Confessor* (Chicago: Open Court, 1995), 76–84 (esp. 81) to argue that Maximus also located the diversity of creation in the *logoi* or plan or will of God, which existed eternally *in potentia* in God's mind and were actuated at the beginning of time. These *logoi* can mediate between the timeless God and a temporal creation because they are ontologically differentiated both from God's imparticipable essence as well as from the creation. The Logos in whom they reside remains "super-essential and above participation."

28. *Gregory Palamas,* 221–22.

29. *Contra Arianos* 2.57. Cf. Robert C. Gregg and Dennis E. Groh, *Early Arianism: A View of Salvation* (Philadelphia: Fortress Press, 1981), 172n67, who also insist that Athanasius claims no interval (διαστημα) between the divine will and the divine nature.

30. *C. Ar.* 3.62.

31. *C. Ar.* 3.66; Cf. Rowan Williams, *Arius: Heresy and Tradition* (London: Darton, Longman and Todd, 1986), 215–29.

32. Lossky, *Image and Likeness,* 56.

33. *Capita* 108; 109.

34. Lossky, *Mystical Theology,* 88.

35. Ibid., 89.

36. Meyendorff, *Byzantine Theology,* 164, emphasis his. Cf. M. Lot-Borodine, *La déification de l'homme* (Paris: Éditions du Cerf 1970), 63; reprint from "La doctrine de la déification dans l'Église grecque jusqu'au XIe siècle," *Revue de l'Histoire des Religions* 105 (1932): 5–43; 106 (1932): 525–74; 107 (1933): 8–55.

37. *Gregory Palamas,* 176, emphasis his.

38. Ibid., 167, citing *Triads* 2.2.11; *Against Akindynos* 3.6; *Hom.* 24.

39. *La déification de l'homme,* 36n16, emphasis hers.

40. *Gregory Palamas,* 177, emphasis his.

41. Georges A. Barrois, "Two Styles of Theology and Spirituality," *St. Vladimir's Theological Quarterly* 26 (1982): 95, 99.

42. "The Bright Morning of the Soul: John of the Cross on *Theosis,*" *Pro Ecclesia* 12.3 (Summer 2003): 325.

43. G. Podskalsky, "Gottesschau und Inkarnation, Zur Bedeutung der Heilsgeschichte bei Gregorios Palamas," *Orientalia Christiana Periodica* 35 (1969): 36–37, citing Pseudo-Dionysius, PG 3:816d; 953c-65a. Cf. 8–9, where Podskalsky asks rhetorically of the Palamite doctrine: "Did Palamas take into account an authentically Christian concept of the vision (= faith), which affirms both the inexorable creatureliness of man and the necessity of a supernatural redemption in the historical Christ . . . or did he mix in with this some Neoplatonic

elements which are incompatible with Christian dogma—namely, the fall from the One to the many and return to union?" In other words, he continues, "Does the category of the historical (as salvation history) and its related emphasis on personal freedom and encounter in relationship to God have decisive importance in his system, or does he work finally with impersonally material (*neutraldinglichen*) conceptions: light-illumination-becoming light?"

44. Rowan Williams, "The Philosophical Structures of Palamism," *Eastern Churches Review* 9 (1977): 32–33, citing *The Cambridge History of Later Greek and Early Medieval Philosophy,* ed. by A. H. Armstrong (Cambridge: Cambridge University Press, 1970), 319ff. See also Jugie, "Palamas Grégoire," 1753, who finds some of the later hesychast methods and conceptions to be naively physical, many speaking of grace as though the Spirit of God were as palpable as the air we breathe and teaching that the position of the body is decisive in prayer. It was only this extremely "mecanique" form of hesychasm that provoked Barlaam's opposition, Jugie maintains.

45. Reinhard Flogaus, "Palamas and Barlaam Revisited: A Reassessment of East and West in the Hesychast Controversy of 14th Century Byzantium," *St. Vladimir's Theological Quarterly* 42, no. 1 (1998): 9, citing Palamas, *Capita* 89, 93, and 110; Proclus, *Inst. Theol.* 23f. Flogaus, "Palamas and Barlaam," 15, citing Augustine, *De trinitate* 15.19.36; Palamas, *Capita* 75, 93; *Triads* 3.1.8, 3.1.27; 3.1.34. Cf. Lison, *L'Esprit répandu,* 79f, 99f.

46. J.-M. Garrigues, "Maxime le Confesseur," 275–76. Cf. Friedrich Normann, *Teilhabe: Ein Schlüsselwort der Vätertheologie,* Munsterische Beitrage zur Theologie 42 (Munster: Aschendorff, 1978), 8, who characterizes the transition between the Judaic and Hellenic contexts this way: "The Greek philosophical way of thinking tends more toward mixing the divine and the human together, whereas the Judaic theological method turns toward the unique grandeur of Jahweh."

47. Ibid.

48. G. Philips, "La grâce chez les Orientaux," *Ephemerides Theologicae Lovanienses* 48 (1972): 45.

49. Hans Urs von Balthasar, *Unser Auftrag: Bericht und Entwurf* (Einsiedeln: Johannes Verlag, 1984), 33–36; *Theodramatik,* 5 vols. (Einsiedeln: Johannes Verlag, 1973–), 2.1:11–12; and *Herrlichkeit: Eine theologische Ästhetik,* 3 vols. (Einsiedeln: Johannes Verlag, 1961–), 3.1:52. Cf. Dorothea Wendebourg, *Geist oder Energie: Zur Frage der innergöttlichen Verankerung des christlichen Lebens in der byzantinischen Theologie,* Munchener Universitats-Schriften, Bd. 4, Munchener Monographien zur historischen und systematischen Theologie (Munich: Kaiser Verlag, 1980), 8; C. Journet, "Palamisme et Thomisme," *Revue Thomiste* 60 (1940): 443.

50. Hans Urs von Balthasar, *Theologik,* 3 vols. (Einsiedeln: Johannes Verlag, 1985–87), 3:117.

51. Congar, *Holy Spirit,* 3:65–66. Concurring is G. Philips, *L'union personnelle avec le Dieu vivant: Essai sur l'origine et le sens de la grâce créée,* 2nd ed. (Louvain: Leuven University Press, 1989), 253.

52. *Ein Schlüsselwort der Vätertheologie,* 73–74.

53. A. Theodorou, "Die Lehre von der Vergottung des Menschen bei den griechischen Kirchenvätern," *Kerygma und Dogma* 7 (1961): 290, citing Ignatius, Romans 8.2; Magn. 8.2; Justin, PG 6:340c, 464b; Irenaeus, PG 7:1035a; Basil, PG 32:69b; Nyssa, PG 44:161c, 377a; Nazianzen, PG 35:1084c, 1164.

54. Martin George, "Vergöttlichung des Menschen: Von der platonischen Philosophie zur Soteriologie der griechischen Kirchenvater," in *Die Weltlichkeit des Glaubens in der Alten Kirche: Festschrift für Ulrich Wickert zum siebzigsten Geburtstag,* ed. Dietmar Wyrwa et al. (Berlin: de Gruyter, 1997), 137n122.

55. Kallistos Ware, "The Debate about Palamism," *Eastern Churches Review* 9 (1977): 60.

56. Congar, *Holy Spirit,* 3:62.

57. Ibid., 2:84.

58. G. Philips, "La grâce chez les Orientaux," *Ephemerides Theologicae Lovanienses* 48 (1972): 43, emphasis his, citing Palamas, *Capita* 34.

59. Ibid., 38.

60. Jürgen Kuhlmann, *Die Taten des einfachen Gottes: Eine romisch-katholische Stellungsnahme zum Palamismus* (Wurzburg: Augustinus-Verlag, 1968): 107–35, 56. The first half of this work (3–104) consists of a comparison between Aquinas's and Palamas's respective interpretations of Pseudo-Dionysius.

61. Ibid., 56. But for a critique of Kuhlmann's efforts at *détente,* see P. B. Schultze, "Die Taten des einfachen Gottes," *Orientalia Christiana Periodica* 36 (1970): 135–42.

62. A. N. Williams, *The Ground of Union: Deification in Aquinas and Palamas* (Oxford: Oxford University Press, 1999), 148, citing *Capita* 75 ("There are three realities [τριῶν ὄντων] in God, namely, substance, energy and a Trinity of divine hypostases.") and *Triads* 3.2.10.

63. Ibid., 150–56.

64. Ibid., 138.

Sergius Bulgakov: Russian *Theosis*

Boris Jakim

What is offered in this brief essay is a Russian Orthodox perspective on *theosis,* drawing primarily from the writings of Sergius Bulgakov (1871–1944), and including other well-respected Russian saints as well. Though the general perspective is mine, I write as one who has tried to assimilate the essential teachings of the Russian theologians for whom I have translated their work into English.[1]

The purpose of the Christian life (perhaps of all human life), according to St. Seraphim of Sarov, is the acquisition of the Holy Spirit. As a human being empties himself or herself of ego and sinful, fallen nature, the vessel that remains is filled with divinity. Another way of understanding it is that through *theosis* our fallenness is overcome. The royal road to deification is *ascesis* (in Russian: *podvig*); divinity cannot reside in what is corrupt. Indeed, deification is achieved in proportion to the purification of the human nature. This cleansing of the human nature is the precondition for the sanctification, glorification, transfiguration, and deification (the terms are almost synonymous) of the creature by the Creator.

Deification is a mystical, supernatural state. It raises us above this world and its concerns. When we experience it, we are like the Apostle Paul, who encountered divinity on the way to Damascus. Deification is a powerful force that comes to us from outside; it is a gift of God's grace, the reception of which results in the transformation of the creature into a new creation—a Divine-humanity.

The concept of Divine-humanity is rooted in the Creed of Chalcedon, which reads in part: "We . . . teach men to confess one and the same Son, our Lord Jesus Christ, the same perfect in Divinity and also perfect in humanity; truly God and truly man . . . consubstantial with the Father according to the Divinity, and consubstantial with us according to the Humanity."[2] Here, Christ is understood as the head of the renewed or transfigured humanity. In the person of Christ, Divinity united itself not only with a particular man, Jesus, but with the entire human race; and that is why those redeemed by Christ can attain a glory similar to his.

The concept of Divine-humanity in Eastern Christianity was adumbrated by Pseudo-Dionysius, and has been developed more recently by Vladimir

Solovyov and Sergius Bulgakov.[3] Divine-humanity is the subject of Bulgakov's "great trilogy" consisting of *The Lamb of God, The Comforter,* and *The Bride of the Lamb.* What Bulgakov has in mind here, is nothing less than the deification of humanity and, indeed, of the entire world or created order. I shall attempt to trace the flow of his thought regarding deification as we encounter it in his great trilogy, specifically in the terms "Divine-humanity," "sophianization," and "glorification," all of which he uses to describe this process. I will try also to clarify what Bulgakov means by these concepts and how they are related to *theosis.* I will end this discussion with three accounts of *theosis,* all from the modern period and all pertaining to the domain of Russian Orthodox spirituality.

Divine-Humanity and *Theosis*

In his great Christological work *The Lamb of God,* Bulgakov states:

> Through his spirit, man communes with the divine essence and is capable of being deified. Man is not only man but also potentially a god-man. Man desires to become a son of God and enter into the glory of creation, and he is predestined to this. Out of natural man, he is called to become a god-man; he is called to surpass himself in the true God-Man, Christ. Man bears within himself the coming Christ, and prior to Christ's coming, man does not have the power to realize in himself that new spiritual birth which is not of flesh and of blood, but of God.[4]

The human being is the ready form for the birth of Divine-humanity through a process of *theosis. Theosis* is the gift for which we are created and to which we are called. According to Bulgakov, the Incarnation of God is not a catastrophe for the human essence, not a violence done to it. Rather, the Incarnation is the fulfillment of human essence. Consequently, Christ, being a perfect man, is also true humanity; and thus all human beings can potentially be deified in Christ. All can become divinely human, god-persons, in the same fashion that Christ is divinely human, the God-Man.[5]

The Divine-humanity is a particular form of the Divinity's consciousness of itself through humanity; the Divine-humanity likewise is a particular form of humanity's consciousness of itself through the Divinity. It is the fusion of the Creator and creation, a fusion that is simultaneously the *kenosis* of the Divinity and the *theosis* of the humanity, which concludes with the perfect glorification of the God-Man.[6] In human beings, *theosis* and *kenosis* are intimately linked: the more a human being empties himself and lets go of his ego, the closer he can come to divinity. A "god by grace" is one who no longer has himself in himself, but is more conscious of God in himself. Or as the Apostle Paul writes, "I am crucified with Christ, nevertheless I live; yet not I, but Christ liveth in me" (Gal 2:20).

Bulgakov defines deification as "the action of the divine nature on the human essence."[7] This principle is applied not only to Christ in and of himself, but also to all of Christ's humanity. Deification does not consist in the external, physical action of one natural force on another. Rather, it is a *spiritual* penetration, united with the inner reception of this action. The possibility of deification is based on the fact that humanity bears the divine image in the human image, and is therefore called to receive the divine life into its own life.[8]

In *The Comforter,* Bulgakov writes:

> So great is God's love for creation that, in calling creation to being, he gives it the Divine Sophia as the foundation of its being, in order, further, to give himself as well, uniting creation with his own divine life. This is precisely the foundation of the divine-human process. Humanity, the center of the world, is the image of the divine humanity. And humanity is thus called to approach the divine image, and this convergence can go so far as to become a living identification with the divine image. This identification is the task and goal of creation. God creates future "gods by grace" for inclusion in the multihypostatic unity of the Holy Trinity and in the unity of divine life.[9]

Sophiology and *Theosis*

Sophia is the Wisdom of God. Humanity contains within its creaturely nature both the Word (*logos*) and Wisdom (*sophia*) of God. In this sense, humanity is a *creaturely sophianic hypostasis.*[10] Humanity's sophianicity signifies the universal fullness of its being, whereas its creatureliness signifies this fullness only in a state of potentiality. This is akin to the Eastern distinction between image and likeness: image is the fullness, likeness is the realization of the image. In relation to the Divine Sophia, the creaturely sophia is a "receptacle" in which the divine image is reflected. Creaturely sophianicity presupposes the possibility of unlimited sophianization, the approximation of the creature's image to the divine image. The Divine Sophia and the creaturely sophia converge forever without coinciding; and this convergence is "infinite life." Accordingly, the process of individual deification is unceasing: the individual can unceasingly approach divinity by receiving more and more grace; but humanity never reaches full divinity, except in the case of Christ, who is the grace of God.

In *The Bride of the Lamb,* Bulgakov writes, "This reception of grace, or sophianization, follows the path of deification: the union with God that has already been accomplished for all of creation through the union of the two natures, divine and human, in Christ, according to the Chalcedonian dogma, and through the descent of the Holy Spirit upon the apostles and all of humankind, according to the dogma of the Pentecost."[11]

SOPHIANIZATION BY GRACE

In this context, Bulgakov examines the distinction between natural and supernatural grace. Creation awaits the fullness of its protoimage, its "glory," which is given in the action of grace. The distinction between natural and supernatural grace thus expresses the relation between the Divine Sophia and the creaturely sophia, between Divinity and the world in the process of its deification. In its different forms, grace is precisely this deification, or glorification, of creation; its sophianization. Natural grace is the divine image and likeness in humanity. By virtue of this inner image and likeness, human beings are called to Divine-humanity, which is the union of the two natures in Christ. "Divine-humanity extends to all humankind, which possesses 'natural grace' or sophianicity by its creation, and which also receives the divine life in Christ by the Holy Spirit."[12]

Through the Incarnation and Pentecost, grace creates the Divine-humanity. By virtue of sophianicity, that is, the potential for human conformity with God, it is possible for a human being to receive the Holy Spirit and be deified. Sophianicity is the ontological precondition for this reception of which humanity is capable and to which humanity is summoned.[13]

Through God's grace, a person receives the power to become fully himself or herself; through grace one's true self is revealed. One's entire life is actualized on the pathway to deification. As Bulgakov writes, "There is no limit to grace, for it is deification, actualized Divine-humanity, life in God, which is infinitely deep and will never end, not in this age, nor in the age to come. Man is an intermediary, communicating the power of grace (and of deification) to the whole world."[14]

GLORIFICATION AND *THEOSIS*

Besides the ascension of Christ, which is already accomplished, there is also the ascension that is in the process of being accomplished: the glorification of the creature, earthly humanity, which is identical to the humanity of Christ. God "has raised us up together, and made us sit together in heavenly places in Christ Jesus" (Eph 2:6). Through Christ, we "have access by one Spirit unto the Father" (Eph 2:18). The definitive and final ascension is the final glorification when "God will be all in all" (1 Cor 15:28).

This human ascension and glorification is now beyond the limits of what is known to us, but it has already been preaccomplished in the person of the Most Holy Mother of God (the Theotokos), according to Orthodox teaching. Raised up by her son, she has already entered the "mansion" prepared for her (see Jn 14:2–3), that is, Mary has achieved perfect *theosis.*[15]

In the Divine-humanity, through the Incarnation of the Son and the descent of the Holy Spirit, humanity and the world have received the fullness of sophianization. The Divine Sophia has united with the creaturely sophia; creation has been completely deified in the union of the two natures in Christ by the Holy Spirit. In part, this takes place through the glorification, accomplished in a series of events: the resurrection, the ascension, Pentecost, and the Second Coming, this time in glory, in which Christ brings glory to the world and deifies it by the energy of the Holy Spirit.[16] The Second Coming will complete creation; humanity will be given the power to manifest the image of God not only in anticipation but also in the fullness of life, by becoming a "god by grace." Bulgakov writes that "this is accessible only to man resurrected in incorruptibility, immortality, and glory."[17]

Bulgakov's Vision of *Theosis*

In *The Lamb of God,* Bulgakov reminds us that the preface to the liturgy of St. John Chrysostom says that "Thou hast led us from nothingness to being; and Thou hast regenerated us, who are fallen. Thou hast even raised us to heaven and given us Thy kingdom to come."[18] In the same work, he also notes that,

> through the ascension, Christ's humanity appears in heaven, in the depths of the divine life of the Holy Trinity. Initially deified in the Incarnation and undergoing continuous deification in the course of Christ's entire earthly ministry, his humanity now becomes perfectly and definitively deified to the point of fully receiving *the glory of God.* With the completion of the *kenosis,* not only does the Son of God receive from the Father the glory that belonged to him before the creation of the world, but the Son of Man is also glorified in the God-Man. And this glorification of his *humanity* is not the return of the glory; the creature receives it for the first time here. The God-Man's earthly humanity follows his ascension to heaven, first the Most Holy Mother of God, and then the entire Church (Eph 2:6) in the age to come. This is the deification of humanity.[19]

Theosis for Bulgakov is universal. The Holy Spirit abides in the world by the power of the Pentecost, which, by the hypostatic descent of the Spirit, lays the foundation not only for the world's being but also for the world's deification; this through the penetration of the creaturely sophia by the Divine Sophia. Pentecost lays the foundation for the deification of the world when, at the end of time, "God will be all in all."[20] The descent of the Spirit signifies the fulfillment of the work of the Divine Incarnation in the world and in humanity. During Pentecost the Holy Spirit descends not upon the Virgin Mary, as at the Annunciation, and not upon Jesus, as at the Epiphany, but upon all of humanity and all of nature. Thus, the deification of all creation occurs in the eschaton, as Bulgakov anticipates in his description of the conjunction of the Incarnation and Pentecost: "The Incarnation of Christ and the descent of the Holy Spirit are two aspects of one and the same act: the act of Divine-humanity. Heavenly Divine-humanity, Sophia, uniting itself with creaturely Divine-humanity and being ontologically joined with the latter in the God-Man, reveals itself as the supreme meaning and goal of creation."[21]

Theosis: Three Illustrations

Finally, I conclude this brief presentation of Russian *theosis* with three phenomenological accounts of human transfiguration that may point to the process of deification in this lifetime. I hope they will serve as concrete testimonies to the existential reality of deification by grace, and to the Russian contribution to the study of *theosis.*

The Vision of St. Seraphim of Sarov in the Snow

The first account is an example of visible *theosis,* where the transfiguration or glorification (or sophianization, as Bulgakov might call it) of a human being is observed by others. In the Russian mystical tradition, the spiritual quality of Shekinah, the glory, always accompanies those who, like Seraphim, have attained a state of extreme holiness. In the winter of 1831, Fr. Seraphim explained to Motovilov, a landowner, that the entire goal of Christian activity was in the acquisition of the Holy Spirit. Motovilov did not understand how one could be certain of possessing the Holy Spirit. Here is Motovilov's account:

> Father Seraphim took me very firmly by the shoulders and said: "We are now both in God's Spirit! Why don't you look at me?"
>
> I answered: "I can't, father, because lightning is streaming from your eyes. Your face has become brighter than the sun, and my eyes are splitting with pain."
>
> Father Seraphim said: "Don't be afraid. You too have now become as bright as I. You too are now in the fullness of God's Spirit. Otherwise you could not see me as I am now."
>
> As their conversation continued, Motovilov reported that when he looked at Seraphim he saw nothing except a blinding light, which illuminated with its brilliance the snow-covered meadow and the snowflakes that were falling.
>
> Seraphim asked Motovilov what he felt then, and the latter answered: "I feel extraordinarily good. . . . I feel such serenity and peace in my soul that I can find no words to express it."[22]

Sergius Bulgakov's Death-Bed Transfiguration

A second example comes from the eye-witnesses to the death-bed transfiguration of Sergius Bulgakov himself. In June of 1944, Bulgakov suffered a stroke and lay dying. The women who attended him at this time witnessed an astonishing event: Bulgakov's transfiguration (which may be considered an example of *theosis* as witnessed by others). Here is the account of one of these witnesses, Sister Joanna Reitlinger:[23]

> Not only did his face keep changing, but it was becoming more luminous and joyous. The expressions of agonizing concentration that would previously occur from time to time were now completely replaced by a childlike expression. I did not at once notice a new phenomenon on his face: an amazing illuminatedness. But when I turned to one of the others standing around him in order to share some impression of mine, one of the others suddenly said: "Look, look!"
>
> We were witnesses to an amazing spectacle: Father Sergius' face had become completely illuminated. It was a single mass of real light.
>
> One would not have been able to say what the features of his face were like at this time: his face was a mass of light. But, at the same time, this light did not erase or obliterate the features of his face.
>
> This phenomenon was so extraordinary and joyous that we nearly cried from inner happiness. This lasted for about two hours, as Mother Theodosia, who looked at her watch, later noted. That surprised us, for if someone had told us that the experience had lasted but a single instant, we would have agreed with that too.[24]

The "Pentecost" at the Prerov Conference of the Russian Student Christian Movement

A third example of what I would call "communal *theosis*" occurred at a conference of the Russian Student Christian Movement held in Prerov near Prague, on October 1–7, 1923. The following account is taken from an article written by one of the participants—Vasily Zenkovsy—an eminent Russian philosopher and historian of Russian philosophy.[25] After listening to a number of inspired lectures (delivered by such figures as Bulgakov and Berdyaev) and attending a number of joyous liturgies, the attendees (mostly young men and women) began to realize that they were participants in an extraordinary phenomenon. Zenkovksy called this event a "Pentecost" in which the descent of the Holy Spirit was palpable. He writes:

> Everything seemed to be happening in a dream. The excitement which had been growing for such a long time and which had reached its mystical zenith in the confession and in the communion [at the liturgy on the last day of the conference]—

this excitement now burst outward. All present experienced the feeling of a renewal come from above—the birth into a new life, as it were. The whole significance of the Prerov conference in the history of the Russian Student Christian Movement consisted precisely in the fact that there was nothing purely psychological in the rapture and joy experienced by all. All the participants of the conference, both the older and younger ones, became brothers and sisters. Not only did the relations among the participants become easy and joyous, but there was the consciousness of a gracious joy given from above. . . .

In Prerov, the theme "We and the Church" disappeared, and was replaced by the joyous and responsible consciousness of "We in the Church." We touched the mystery of the Church; we absorbed this mystery into ourselves, and we promised to ourselves that we would carry into the world this mystery concerning the Church, this annunciation concerning her power and fullness, her life and joy. In Prerov, we were all born in the spirit—this strange and perhaps imprecise expression nevertheless gives a hint of that profound convulsion experienced by all present at the conference, a hint of that great change which inaugurated for all a new path of life. This change represented not something external and compulsory, but burned in the soul with a flame of radiant and fortifying inspiration.[26]

Transfiguration, sanctification, glorification, deification, and sophianization (the terms are almost synonymous) all point to a spiritual quality and eschatological reality that varies by degrees but not in substance. What is meant by the terms is that human beings may become divine by grace—both individually and corporately in the life of the church—the end result of which, according to Bulgakov and other Russian theologians, can be called the Divine-humanity.

Notes

1. See Vladimir Solovyov, *Lectures on Divine Humanity,* ed. Boris Jakim (Hudson, NY: Lindisfarne Books, 1995); Sergius Bulgakov, *The Lamb of God,* trans. Boris Jakim (Grand Rapids, MI: Eerdmans, forthcoming); Bulgakov, *The Comforter,* trans. Boris Jakim (Grand Rapids, MI: Eerdmans, 2004); Bulgakov, *The Bride of the Lamb,* trans. Boris Jakim (Grand Rapids, MI: Eerdmans, 2002).
2. "Creed of Chalcedon," in *The Greek and Latin Creeds with Translations,* vol. 2, *The Creeds of Christendom with a History and Critical Notes,* ed. Philip Schaff, rev. David S. Schaff, 6th ed. (New York: Harper and Row, 1931; repr., Grand Rapids, MI: Baker Books, 1998), 62.
3. See in particular Solovyov's *Lectures on Divine Humanity.*
4. Bulgakov, *Lamb of God,* 256–57.
5. Ibid., 260.
6. Ibid., 333.
7. Ibid., 342.
8. Ibid.
9. Bulgakov, *Comforter,* 356.
10. There is no secondary literature in English (or for that matter in Russian) on Bulgakov's

doctrine of *theosis*. The following works are of interest in clarifying his doctrine of Sophia, which is related to *theosis:* Paul Valliere, "Sophiology as the Dialogue of Orthodoxy with Modern Civilization," in *Russian Religious Thought,* ed. Judith Kornblatt and Richard Gustafson, 176–94 (Madison: University of Wisconsin Press, 1996); Paul Valliere, *Modern Russian Theology: Bukharev, Soloviev, Bulgakov; Orthodox Theology in a New Key* (Grand Rapids, MI: Eerdmans, 2000), esp. 227–404; Rowan Williams, ed., *Sergii Bulgakov* (Edinburgh: T & T Clark, 1999), esp. 113–228; Andrew Louth, "Wisdom and the Russians: The Sophiology of Fr. Sergei Bulgakov," in *Where Shall Wisdom Be Found,* ed. Stephen Barton, 169–81 (Edinburgh: T & T Clark, 1999); Boris Jakim, addendum on Sophiology to the article on Sergius Bulgakov in the revised edition of the *Macmillan Encylopedia of Philosophy,* forthcoming.

11. Bulgakov, *Bride of the Lamb,* 202–3.
12. Ibid., 296.
13. Ibid., 300.
14. Ibid., 301.
15. *Lamb of God,* 552.
16. *Bride of the Lamb,* 403.
17. Ibid., 451–52.
18. *Liturgy of St. John Chrysostom,* pref., cited in Bulgakov, *Lamb of God,* 557.
19. *Lamb of God,* 557–58.
20. Ibid., 425.
21. *Comforter,* 278.
22. This account is contained in N. A. Motovilov's memoir: "The Spirit of God clearly resting on Father Seraphim of Sarov during his conversation about the goal of Christian life with the Simbirsk landowner Nikolai Aleksandrovich Motovilov." This memoir was first published by S. Nilus in *Velikoe v malom* [The Great in the Small], 2nd ed. (Tsarskoye Selo, 1905); it has been reprinted in Pavel Florensky's *The Pillar and Ground of the Truth,* trans. Boris Jakim (Princeton: Princeton University Press, 1997), 76–77.
23. Taken from *Sergius Bulgakov: Apoctastasis and Transfiguration,* ed. Boris Jakim (New Haven: Variable Press, 1995).
24. Ibid., 45–46.
25. V. V. Zenkovksy, from "Zarozhdenie R.S.Kh.D. v emigratsii" [The Birth of the Russian Student Christian Movement in the Emigration], *Vestnik Russkogo Khristianskogo Dvizheniia,* no. 168 (1993): 21–40.
26. Ibid., 30–31. It is significant that, in a sense, this was the founding conference of the movement and certainly gave it great spiritual impetus.

Karl Rahner: Divinization in Roman Catholicism

Francis J. Caponi, OSA

Introduction

THE THEOLOGICAL VISION OF KARL RAHNER, THE GERMAN JESUIT WHOSE thought has been so influential in the Roman Catholic Church and beyond over the last fifty years, has at its very core the symbol of *theopoiesis*. The process of human divinization is the center of gravity around which move Rahner's understanding of creation, anthropology, Christology, ecclesiology, liturgy, and eschatology. The importance of this process for Rahner is such that we are justified in describing his overall theological project to be largely a matter of giving a coherent and contemporary account of divinization. Rahner's vision of divinization is a comprehensive one, and is most profitably explored within the overarching Roman Catholic vision of the relationship between nature and grace. In this light, there are three key questions to be asked: (a) What is the structure of divinization? (b) What is the essence of divinization? and (c) What are the means of divinization? That is, what are the conditions of the possibility of divinization within the human; what does it mean to actualize those conditions; and how is this actualization accomplished? For Rahner, the answer to all three questions, mutatis mutandis, is participation in the divine nature.

Following St. Thomas Aquinas, Rahner employs the concept of participation in both a philosophical and a theological sense in order to distinguish between God's efficient presence in all created things, and his "quasi-formal" presence as grace in humanity;[1] this latter mode of divine presence takes place through the church, the sacraments, and the theological virtues, in all of which God's self-communication is actualized in the human person as a creature of history and transcendence. Thus, the reflections that follow will focus on Rahner's philosophical understanding of creation as metaphysical participation, his theological understanding of grace as divinizing participation, and his anthropological-ecclesiological understanding of human life as sharing in the divine life of the Triune God.

The Structure of Divinization: Metaphysical Participation in God

Rahner's answer to the first question, on the condition of the possibility of divinization, is articulated in the course of his involvement with the debate within Roman Catholic theology on the relationship between nature and grace. The essence of the Catholic position is expressed with lapidary incisiveness by St. Thomas Aquinas: *gratia non tollit naturam sed perficit* (grace does not destroy but perfects nature).[2] Further, in his *Summa Theologiae,* the Dominican teaches that grace, as the divine movement that justifies, sanctifies, and ultimately divinizes the human person, is "a certain participation in the divine nature," and "a special love, by which God draws the rational creature above its natural condition to have a part in the divine goodness."[3] In line with this, St. Thomas famously taught, "Every intellect naturally desires the vision of the divine substance, but natural desire cannot be incapable of fulfillment."[4] However, the saint did not explain how it was possible both to have a natural desire for the beatific vision (a desire whose lack of fulfillment must logically mean the perpetual incompleteness of the human person), and yet also to maintain that grace is freely given by God. Neither of the alternatives is attractive: Either we must be given grace, thereby destroying its gratuity, or we face the prospect of intrinsically, naturally, longing for a proper fulfillment that God alone can give and yet may withhold.

Saint Thomas's commentators struggled to resolve this paradox, and in the twentieth century the debate entered an especially active phase, with many Roman Catholic theologians pondering the question of nature, grace, and divinization within a dual context: (1) the European movement of *ressourcement,* which focused renewed theological attention on the rich resources offered by the church fathers and a revitalized reading of Thomas Aquinas; and (2) the neoscholastic Roman Catholic theology of the nineteenth century's end and the twentieth century's first half.[5] The latter, following Cajetan and Suárez, solved the puzzle left by Thomas by rejecting the idea of a natural desire for beatific vision. Instead, neo-scholasticism posited a double finality: Human nature possessed sufficient powers of intellect and will for its natural goals, and upon this self-sufficient nature the gift of grace was laid like a superstructure, thus bestowing on human nature a second, supernatural finality.[6] Reacting against this perspective, Rahner proposed an alternate model: Grace is the "innermost heart" of the world, so that, far from being an extrinsic imposition, it is the proper fulfillment of human nature. This contention—that we are by nature intended to be sharers of the divine nature—is Rahner's central theological contention, and requires careful exposition.

Rahner's first step is the adoption of the Irenaean perspective in which God created humanity "not as if He stood in need of man, but that He might have [someone] upon whom to confer His benefits."[7] The primary decision of

God for grace involves the correlative decision for creation, a decision that calls humanity into existence.[8] From the outset God freely wills to give himself away, and so must create a nondivine "nature" to whom he can impart himself. Therefore, the creation is the first movement in the process of divinization; or, as Rahner puts it, "Nature is, because grace has to be."[9]

Rahner draws out the metaphysical implications of this assertion. The divine will for Self-bestowal conditions the structure of the other, which is thereby brought into being; that is, because creation takes place for the sake of grace, the creation that comes about is, at some level, open to the divine *self*-bestowal, the personal self-communication of God. Working firmly within the Thomistic tradition, Rahner specifies the structure of created being in terms of causal participation. For both Aquinas and Rahner, God efficiently causes existence in creatures not through the impartation of a common form, but by participation: "God is being by his own essence, because he is the very act of being [*esse*]. Every other being [*ens*], however, is a being by participation. . . . God, therefore, is the cause of being [*essendi*] to all other things."[10]

Developing this metaphysical vision from within an anthropological framework,[11] Rahner teaches that all human knowing is a matter of both the unthematic, transcendental affirmation of Absolute Being (*Esse*) and the thematic, categorical affirmation of the limited being (*esse*) possessed by a finite object. Take the example, "This tree is green." Such a judgment is the assertion of limited existence (this object exists in the mode of treeness, it possesses greenness), and such an assertion is logically possible only if the human intellect already possesses an anticipation of unrestricted existence, against which is made the judgment that this tree is a limited instance of existence. Thus, every act of human knowing is the intellectual grasp of the participatory structure of created reality.[12] Knowing is always the grasp of a concrete existent *as* a limited realization of being (*ens*), as the unlimited act of existence (*esse*) here limited by a particular form.[13]

Rahner alternately calls the intellectual power that accomplishes this by its Thomistic name (agent intellect), and by his own term (*Vorgriff auf esse*), but in both cases he makes it clear that it is fundamentally the capacity to know a world that metaphysically participates in the divine. Knowledge attains to being,[14] and so every judgment *critiques* the object, measures its degree of existence, affirms it as a partial realization—a participant—in the unlimited *esse* against which it is known. "The agent intellect is the 'light' that permeates the sense object, i.e., puts it within the domain of being as such, thus revealing how it participates in being as such."[15] From what the human intellect is actually able to do, Rahner deduces that the agent intellect must be "pure openness for absolutely everything, for being as such."[16] The intellect's openness has no intrinsic finite limit, it never meets an object that completely fills its scope, but is of infinite breadth. Thus, the transcendental affirmation of Absolute Being is an a priori, unthematic, and necessary dimension of all categorical knowledge.[17]

From this, we see that at the heart of Rahner's metaphysical anthropology is the unity-in-difference of the transcendental and the categorical aspects of knowledge. The transcendental refers to human spirit as *Vorgriff auf esse,* unthematically open to the horizon of all being. Rahner describes it thus: "[T]he subjective, unthematic, necessary and unfailing consciousness of the knowing subject that is co-present in every spiritual act of knowledge, and the subject's openness to the unlimited expanse of all possible reality."[18] The categorical is the realm of the concrete, the historical, the communal, the a posteriori. Throughout his works, Rahner holds that the relationship between the transcendental and categorical elements is mutual, necessary, and intrinsic. Each is the condition of the other, such that there is a "relationship of *mutual* conditioning in human existence between what is transcendentally necessary and what is concretely and contingently historical. It is a relationship of such a kind that both elements in man's historical existence can only appear together and mutually condition each other: the transcendental element is always an intrinsic condition of the historical element in the historical itself, and, in spite of its being freely posited, the historical element co-determines existence in an absolute sense."[19] In our knowing (and willing), we are always already beyond the objects of our knowledge and will; and since this transcendence is limitless, we are creatures "open for a possible revelation of God" within the categorical, historical realm.[20] Further, because of the structure of human spirit, if such a revelation occurs, it will necessarily take place in history. (The importance of this claim for Rahner's understanding of divinization will become clearer below, when the roles of Jesus Christ and the church in God's self-communication are considered.)

We may conclude that humanity is that part of material creation that participates in the divine existence at the level of intellect (and freedom). We are perpetually being (efficiently) caused by God to exist in an intellectual mode that is so structured that our knowledge of the sensible, categorical world is made possible by our transcendental anticipation of the Absolute; and our knowledge of God is always a matter of our grasp of the categorical realm, that is, of analogical apprehension of the Absolute through the limited.[21] This form of intellectual participation in the divine being constitutes the human openness to divinizing grace.

Created for partnership with the divine, humanity in its created aspect participates in the divine by existing as a hypaethral race, a creature of *spirit,* a being whose essence is "obediential potency," a natural receptivity to grace. As a matter of philosophical analysis, it cannot be concluded that this openness has been met by the actual offer of God's personal self-communication in grace; all that can be concluded is that, because of our categorically mediated openness to the absolutely transcendent, we are able to listen for such an offer, that, as Rahner writes, "we always and naturally hear the word or the silence of the free absolute God."[22] Human knowing demands an openness to unlimited existence as the condition of its possibility, for we would not be spirit otherwise. Yet, human knowing does not require for its own existence that the mysterious and limitless horizon of existence become personally manifest in the self-communication called "grace" by the Christian tradition.[23] If God chooses to offer us grace, our natures are so structured that the reception of this offer will be a truly human event, a gift that does not violate the Thomistic axiom, *gratia non tollit naturam sed perficit.* As spirit, "a supernatural end can be set for man without annulling his nature."[24] If no such end is set, then human knowing is not destroyed, but rather must be seen as the transcendental awareness of God's silence.[25]

The Essence of Divinization: Saving Participation in God through Christ

We learn from divine revelation, however, that our natural obediential potency has been met by God's will to divinize humanity. As Rahner puts it, the Absolute Being present to all human knowing and willing as distant horizon and source offers himself to us as our truly proper, supernatural end. In the light of Rahner's understanding of creation, this means that we are offered divinizing participation in God through Jesus Christ,[26] as distinct from (yet "building upon," perfecting) the created, or metaphysical, participation in the divine, which characterizes all existing things in their *diversi modi existendi* (diverse modes of existence).

Rahner articulates this understanding of divinization through three interlocking concepts: (1) divine self-communication, (2) supernatural existential, and (3) "quasi-formal" causality. He offers this outline of his perspective:

> God does not bestow merely a certain kind of saving love and intimacy, or a certain kind of saving presence. . . . God does not confer on man merely created gifts as a token of his love. God communicates *himself* by what is no longer simply efficient causality. He makes man share in the very nature of God. He constitutes man as co-heir with the Son himself, called to the eternal life of God face to face, called to receive the direct vision of God, called therefore to receive God's own life. Here we really reach the heart of the Christian conception of reality.[27]

Rahner consistently describes grace as God's self-communication, which accomplishes in humanity a divinizing participation in God's being.[28] For instance, he speaks of the Holy Spirit as "the gift in which God imparts himself to man."[29] The meaning of this assertion is illuminated by a consideration of the distinction between uncreated and created grace. From early in his career, Rahner asserted that the primary meaning of grace is uncreated grace, "God's self-communication in love."[30] Post-Tridentine and neo-scholastic theologies, responding to Protestant positions, emphasized the realism of grace, and thus tended to emphasize created grace to such a point that it was posited as the presupposition for the indwelling of the Holy Spirit.[31] Rahner, however, avers that in the Scriptures, especially St. Paul, and in the patristic authors, especially St. Irenaeus, we find grace portrayed as first and foremost a communication of the Holy Spirit (which Rahner also calls "the self-communication of God in Christ").[32] Grace is "the innermost and enduring deification of the world" and "the ground of an ultimate unity of mankind in itself and with God," because grace is first and foremost God's personal presence: "God communicates himself to man in his own proper reality. That is the mystery and the fullness of grace."[33] Like Thomas Aquinas, Rahner does not neglect the therapuetic impact of grace on sin,[40] but insists that divinization is the primary result of grace, corresponding to the primacy of God's will to self-bestowal: "[G]race is not just pardon for the poor sinner but 'participation in the divine nature.' . . . Grace is God himself, the communication in which he gives himself to man as the divinizing favour which he is himself. Here his work is really *himself,* since it is he who is imparted."[34]

Two important points must be made in connection with this understanding of grace as God's self-communication. First, Rahner's metaphysics of participation hinges upon the absolute ontological distinction between Creator and creation,[35] a distinction absent from all classical Greek and Hellenistic reflection on the divine, but central to the Christian understanding of grace. This distinction serves as an ineluctable element of Rahner's theology of divinization.[36] Because God's transcendence of his creation is complete, divinization is not meaningless or destructive. God can become human, and God can make men and women divine, and neither God nor humanity is destroyed in the process precisely because of both the complete transcendence of Creator to creation, and the intimate causal presence to creation this transcendence makes possible. God's *efficient* causal immanence in creation means that there is a true difference between creation and grace (which will be shown below to be a matter of *formal* immanence). And this efficient causal immanence results, in the case of humanity, in a participation in the divine *Esse,* which is, in intellect and freedom, open to the possibility of grace.[37] Thus, Rahner's view of our gracious participation in God is integrally connected to his view of our metaphysical participation in God.

Second, created grace is still a valid and necessary category for understanding God's relationship to humanity.[38] Rahner consistently upholds the traditional Roman Catholic teaching that justifying grace inheres in the justified, constituting them temples of the Holy Spirit,[39] and giving rise to personal virtue and communal charism. However, the panorama of personal and ecclesial effects in which God's presence becomes concretely incarnate must be understood as the effects of "quasi-formally" communicated uncreated grace, which is essentially "a participation in the reality which in itself is solely that of God himself."[40]

So far, we have traced Rahner's vision from the divine side: God's will for self-bestowal brings about a world that exists for the reception of grace. All creation exists in participation of God's existence and evolves to that level of participating existence that is human spirit.[41] As distinct from God, humanity still receives grace as a gift, not an entitlement intrinsic to its nature; however, humanity's existence as obediential potency for grace means that the gift of God's self-communication is not experienced as superfluous or destructive. Grace, although we are not owed it, is experienced as our fulfillment.

However, on the human side, there is more that must be considered. If the human person possesses no more than an openness to grace, an intrinsic "nonrepugnance" to God's self-gift, then God's call to become a sharer in his nature would remain a decree external to self-contained human nature (prior to justification). Therefore, "a free being at least could always reject such a good without thereby having *inwardly* the experience of losing its end," since the human person so understood does not possess "in his very nature, a disposition which under pain of losing its own meaning finds uniquely in this gift its unique end and its only possible fulfillment."[42] Rahner rejects such a neutral humanity, holding along with St. Thomas that the human person's true (if not "natural," *stricte dicta*) fulfillment is sharing in the divine nature.

Roman Catholic teaching about divinizing grace asserts that it is doubly gratuitous: gratuitous in its offer to created nature, and gratuitous in its acceptance by the human person. This means that (1) the free gratuity of creation must be conceptually distinguished from the free gratuity of God's self-communication;[43] and (2) the obediential potency of transcendent spirit cannot account for the actual acceptance of grace, unless we wish to renew the errors of the school of Pelagius. Rahner recognizes that the complete theological portrait of divinization, if it is to be faithful to Christian tradition and experience regarding the gratuity of both the offer and acceptance of grace, requires more than an analysis of humanity as open in intellect and freedom to the self-communication of God.[44] Consequently, in describing the human person as the subject of God's divinizing grace, Rahner develops the concept of the "supernatural existential."[45] His argument runs so: God's desire that "all might be saved" (1 Tim 2:4) requires that we posit a free offer of grace to all human beings. This universal offer is both gratuitous and intrinsic. It is gratuitous inasmuch as God as personal is free to offer or withhold himself, and inasmuch as the human person, as both created and sinful, can lay absolutely no claim upon the divine self-communication. Yet, this gratuitous offer is also intrinsic: this is the key assertion in Rahner's effort to demonstrate the theological cohesiveness of divinization as "essential" to the human person, and he puts the matter so:

> [M]ust not what God decrees for man be *eo ipso* an interior ontological constituent of his "nature"? For an ontology which grasps the truth that man's concrete quiddity depends utterly on God, is not his binding disposition *eo ipso* not just a juridical decree of God but precisely what man *is,* hence not just an imperative proceeding from God but man's most inward depths? If God gives creation and man above all a supernatural end and this end is first "*in intentione,*" then man (and the world) *is* by that very fact always and everywhere inwardly other in structure than he would be if he did not have this end, and hence other as well before he has reached this end partially (the grace which justifies) or wholly (the beatific vision).[46]

In this account, human *nature* would have lacked nothing if God had not met our obediential potency with the offer of grace; but having been (always) offered, grace is not to be thought of like height, weight, spatial location, skin color, or age, all of which vary without really changing "pure" human nature. Rather, grace is the free gift that forms an abiding dimension or "existential" of the person. Grace is really present within humanity in the form of offer, "becoming" (though we have never been without it) a constitutive part of what it is to be human, not as a matter of nature but as a matter of mode.[47] The transcendence of the human subject in unthematic openness to the whole scope of created being, seen earlier to be the obediential potency for grace, is in every person modified by God. The whole of humanity has always existed in this elevated mode, and so has existed with the offer of grace as a constitutive element of its concrete reality. This constant and free divine self-offer bestows upon the human person, already open to infinity as a matter of natural constitution,[48] a single, supernatural finality, a positive drive for beatific vision.

This idea of a "supernatural existential" entails the idea of "pure nature," which Rahner defends as a theological necessity. Despite the fact that we cannot find and study a human nature untouched by grace, so that we cannot say exactly what humanity possesses strictly as created and what accrues to us through grace in addition to creation, the idea of human nature outside of grace is a crucial one precisely because it permits theology to think about human divinization in a way that does not collapse the distinct gratuities of creation and grace,[49] and so enables theology to interpret correctly Christian experience. Grace is not gratuitous merely in relationship to a hypothetical humanity not called to share in the divine nature, but is abidingly gratuitous for every actual person.[50] "Supernatural existential" and "pure nature" form the conceptual framework within which Rahner gives a theological account of this experience, one which enables the believer to think about the difference between creation and grace while also forbidding this difference to be conceived as an ontological separation.

With grace understood as the divine self-communication that prepares for its own reception by permanently "supernaturalizing" the naturally transcendent human person, Rahner holds that the effect of the actual free, grace-enabled acceptance of this divine self-communication is that the Holy Spirit becomes an internal, constitutive principle of the human person,[51] through what Rahner initially calls a "quasi-formal" causality. Rahner holds that God's capacity to act both efficiently and quasi-formally is the ultimate basis of the distinction between the orders of creation and grace. "Supernatural reality and reality brought about by a divine self-communication of quasi-formal, not efficient, type are identical concepts."[52] Whereas efficient causality is characterized by the production of an effect that is different from its cause,

> we are also familiar with formal causality: a particular existent, a principle of being is a constitutive element in another subject by the fact that it communicates itself to the subject, and does not just cause something different from itself, which is then an intrinsic, constitutive principle in that which experiences this efficient causality. We can reflect on this kind of formal causality in order to clarify what we want to say here. In what we call grace and the immediate vision of God, God is really an intrinsic, constitutive principle of man as existing in the situation of salvation and fulfillment.[53]

As noted above, the particular level of created participation that marks human existence, a material-spiritual level of participation, constitutes our openness to saving participation through grace. This created participation is brought about through God's efficient causality in creation, establishing, in the case of human being, a creature other than God, in the sense of being completely dependent upon God yet possessed of the relative autonomy characteristic of spirit, and expressed through the spiritual activities of knowledge and freedom.[54] In grace, however, that which is other than God is divinized through a sort of formal causality in which, Rahner claims, God's own being is given to humanity as its fulfillment. Without ceasing to be God, God makes himself a constitutive principle of the created existent. This capacity belongs to God alone, since only Absolute Being can establish that which is completely other and communicate itself to this creation without becoming subject to the created order.

In grace, the "natural" divine indwelling of metaphysical participation is supernaturally elevated, so that we are sharers in the divine being in the mode of partners as well as creatures. The essence of divinization is that God "communicates his own divine reality and makes it a constitutive element in the fulfillment of the creature" so that grace, understood as God's self-communication, is "an ultimate and radicalizing modification of that very transcendentality of ours by which we are subjects."[55] This elevation of human nature by God to God through the quasi-formal divine self-communication of grace is a participation in the reality that in itself is God.[56]

Rahner completes his presentation by articulating the constitutive role of Jesus Christ in human divinization. Grace as self-communication is essentially, not incidentally, tied to Jesus Christ—not because God has decreed such a union, though it might have been otherwise; rather, Incarnation and grace are the two inseperable acts of divine self-communication.[57] For Rahner, grace and Jesus Christ are each causally related to the other: Christ is the cause, the "prospective entelechy," of history, and Christ is the absolute fulfillment—the result, as it were—of God's self-communication in grace to spiritual, historical reality.[58] Thus, Incarnation and the divinization of the world by grace are interdependent elements, "two correlative factors of God's one free self-communication to the creature."[59]

Rahner's perspective on the essence of deification can be summarized in six points. First, he advocates the theological perspective in which God's will for self-communication is the final cause of creation. Second, the material creation this brings about is one that evolves into grades of causal participation of the divine *Esse*.[60] Third, in humanity, this causal participation "breaks through" to the spiritual grade of being, in which human intellect and freedom form the obediential potency for grace. Fourth, the humanity that so evolves reaches its own high point in the Incarnation of Jesus Christ, understood as the unique event of God's complete self-communication to human transcendence.[61]

Fifth, his understanding of the hypostatic union as the highest realization of graced human reality leads Rahner to assert that grace and Incarnation are analogous instances of God's self-communication.[62] On the one hand, he explains, the Incarnation is the utterly unique cosmic and historical event of the absolute self-transcendence of the human spirit into God. On the other hand, theology has traditionally held that the effect of the hypostatic union for the created soul of Christ is beatific vision; and this is the goal that theology also presents for all of saved humanity in its eschatological state. Thus, the uniqueness of the hypostatic union need not be construed as that of an absolutely new event of God's self-communication that has nothing in common with his relationship to the rest of spiritual creation. Rather, the assumption by God of a human nature is just what grace means: God's self-communication elevates the recipient to the divine nature. The hypostatic union, therefore, is what occurs when the "assumptive dynamism" of grace reaches its completion in a divine self-communication, which effects an *elevation into identity* of God and human nature.[63]

Sixth, grace as divine self-communication to that which is other than God must take place in history, both as offer and fulfillment, since the humanity to whom this offer is directed is not just created but is intrinsically historical (as a created but irrational animal is not). God's self-communication *can* take place historically because the will-for-Christ brings about a hypaethral humanity; and it *must* take place historically because God's self-communication is addressed to historical creatures, and so must have "a permanent [historical] beginning and must find in this a permanent guarantee of its reality so that it can rightly demand a free decision for the acceptance of this divine self-communication."[64] It is not just a matter of grace building upon nature, but of grace building upon *human* nature, and so needing to take historical form, and this in Jesus Christ.[65]

Together, these summary points support Rahner's claim that the "Incarnation cannot be understood as the end and goal of the world's reality without having recourse to the theory that the Incarnation itself is already an intrinsic moment and a condition for the universal bestowal of grace to spiritual creatures."[66] Grace, "despite the fact that in essence it concerns all men always at all times everywhere and is indispensable to them, is dependent on the 'event' of Jesus Christ. Consequently it possesses an incarnational, sacramental and ecclesiological character and unites man in grace with the life and death of Christ."[67]

The Means of Divinization

In speaking of the historical reality of the Incarnation of God in Jesus Christ, we have already begun to discuss the means of divinization. The intrinsic relationship of grace and Christ gives rise to, and is the result of, the incarnational character of God's self-communication.[68] Grace takes concrete form, as both Old and New Testaments attest;[69] and what makes Rahner's theology of divinization a comprehensive proposal is the attention he gives to the forms whereby human beings participate in the divine life prior to entering their final consummation.

For Rahner, in keeping with his dynamic anthropology in which the human person develops and grows through the exercise of freedom and intellect within concrete historical and communal contexts, these means are essential to the accomplishment of divinization. Rahner's analysis of human spirit stresses the necessity of the categorical dimension in human knowing and willing. Transcendental experience always has a history that is mediated through the categorical, through appearance, history, and community. Though God's self-communication in grace is transcendent, "it has its proper being in the history of salvation and revelation (individual and collective) and this is the medium through which it is accomplished and comes to us."[70] This historical reality is intrinsic to the divinizing capacity of God's self-communication, since it is historical beings whom the Lord seeks to divinize. Thus, grace "has a dynamism towards its own objectification, since it is the principle of divinization of the creature in all its dimensions."[71]

Within this anthropological context, Rahner affirms the Roman Catholic theological teaching on the nature and role of the church in the historical process of divinization. The irrevocable offer of salvation made in Jesus Christ is embodied in the church "as the historical tangibility of the presence of God in his self-communication."[72] The church is an essential element in divinization because in the church there occurs both the authoritative proclamation of the gospel (as the salvation of the whole human person, who is constitutively interpersonal), and the acceptance of the gospel through faith, sacrament, and love of neighbor:

> Obviously a Christian is a Christian in the innermost depths of his divinized essence. Nor would he ever be or ever become a Christian if he were not to live out of the innermost center of his essence as divinized by grace. But the very thing he is in his innermost depths and in the origins of his most individual existence, and is by the grace of God whose domain he cannot leave, this very thing comes from the concrete history of salvation to meet him in the concrete as his very own: it comes in the profession of faith of Christians, in the cult of Christians, in the community life of Christians, in word, it comes in the Church. An absolutely individual Christianity in the most personal experience of grace and ecclesial Christianity are no more radically opposed than are body and soul, than are man's transcendental essence and his historical constitution, or than are individuality and intercommunication. The two condition each other mutually. The very thing which we are from God is mediated in the concreteness of history by what we call church. And it is only through this mediation that it becomes our own reality and our own salvation in full measure. For this reason church exists and has to exist.[73]

Gracious participation in the divine is most especially, but not exclusively, enacted through the sacramental life of the church.[74] Each sacrament "really effects what it expresses: the self-communication of the Holy Spirit in grace," because these sacraments are the self-enactments of the church, which is the primal sacrament of grace (*Ursakrament*), the perpetual sacramental presence of Christ.[75] "The Church is the abiding presence of that primal sacramental word of definitive grace, which Christ is in the world, effecting what is uttered by uttering it in sign. By the very fact of being in that way the enduring presence of Christ in the world, the Church is truly the fundamental sacrament, the well-spring of the sacraments in the strict sense. From Christ the Church has an intrinsically sacramental nature."[76] In line with his understanding that grace is not as an intervention of God at a specific point in space and time into an otherwise secular world, but that "the secular world from the outset is always encompassed and permeated with the grace of the divine self-communication,"[77] Rahner holds that the sacraments are not incursions of God into a secular world, the privileged points of access to a reality that is available but as nowhere else, but are rather "outbursts" into history of God's constant, gracious self-endowment to the world.

Understood as the historically tangible and efficacious sign of the victory of God's grace, the sacraments of the church are the means whereby this victory is made present and God's people are able to participate in it. For instance, Rahner speaks of marriage as a sacrament "which is performed by two baptized Christians who were empowered by baptism for active participation in the church's self-actualization."[78] In short, since the church is *the* sacrament, *the* historical presence of grace, "the ongoing presence of Jesus Christ in time and space . . . the means of salvation by which God offers his salvation to an individual in a tangible way and in the historical and social dimension," then the individual sacraments, most especially the Eucharist, are the means by which the church realizes its essence, and, therefore by which the faithful participate in that essence.[79]

Although much more could be said on the issue of the sacramental means of divinization, I will confine myself to one last aspect of Rahner's thought: his reflections on theological virtues. For Rahner, the virtues are the "living dynamism" of justification and the concrete shape of sanctifying grace.[80] When God quasi-formally communicates himself to a person, the acceptance of this justifying/divinizing self-communication elevates human nature to the capacity for supernatural acts:

> Since supernatural grace (as God's self-communication) radically orders the whole being of the human person in knowledge and freedom to the triune God of eternal life, thus enabling him to tend towards this goal—through acts that have been elevated by grace—by accepting this self-communication, we speak of supernatural ("infused") virtues, that is, virtues bestowed by God in justification as the dynamism of sanctifying grace. They order man's moral and religious acts to direct participation in the life of the triune God. . . . In and through them God in his self-communication effects both the capacity for and actual participation in the life of God himself.[81]

Three observations may be made in connection with this perspective. First, in keeping with his understanding of the assumptive relationship of grace to nature, Rahner emphasizes that the theological virtues bestowed by grace are not new, ex nihilo principles of human action (which would amount to the bestowal of a second nature and finality on the justified, which is just the extrinsicist view of nature and grace Rahner seeks to overcome); rather, they are the elevation of humanity's natural virtues. When human nature, understood as *potenia obedientialis,* is raised by the bestowal of grace, the concrete fruit of that elevation is the capacity of human nature (intellect and will) to give rise to acts of supernatural knowing and willing, namely, acts of faith, hope, and love. Rahner emphasizes that this is precisely what is meant by being in "right relationship" with God: faith, hope, and love "make up the concrete content of [our] justification to the extent that this can be conceived of as the power to produce acts which are directly salvific."[82]

Second, these theological virtues are supernatural capacities bestowed in justification. They are developed into habitual facilities through concrete exercise, through existential engagement of elevated nature with the whole scope of human life.

Third, the theological virtues give rise to meritorious works on the part of the justified. Hence, we can see that the true meaning of merit is precisely the ordering by grace of our natural capacities to those supernatural acts by which we participate in the life of God. Such supernatural acts are works done in the Spirit, and Rahner holds them to be intrinsic to the process of divinization: "they are based on our 'participation in the divine nature,' actualize this participation, and so are acts of eternal life . . . intrinsically proportionate to eternal life itself in its glory."[83]

Conclusion

In summary, Rahner distinguishes between the order of creation, the realm of that which is other than God and is brought about by God's efficient causality, and the order of grace, which involves God's self-communication in quasi-formal causality. The integration of these two orders consists in the divine will for self-communication to a personal, human creature. The divine will results in the distinct actions of creation and divinization, both of which are the effects of the Incarnation of Jesus Christ understood as the final cause and complete realization of God's formal self-communication to humanity. Thus, Rahner's metaphysics finds its ground and completion in the claim that human beings are raised in Christ "by grace to a participation in the life of God in Trinity."[84]

Christ is the reason for a universe structured through metaphysical participation, a universe that, in humanity, becomes open to divinizing grace. God creates a universe that existentially participates in the divine being, so that creatures may arise capable of a personal, gracious participation, which makes them truly divine.[85] Jesus Christ is the event of absolute acceptance and complete realization of that divinizing grace. The church and her sacraments, as "similar in structure to the Incarnation,"[86] are the indispensable tangible embodiments of God's self-offer to historical persons. When this grace is accepted the theological virtues arise, which are nothing less than participation in the divine nature through the grace-enabled exercise of our own elevated humanity. Human activity-in-grace—through the celebration of the sacraments, prayer, the moral life—is not incidental to divinization, not simply a consequence, but an integral part of the process by which God makes intelligent, free, historical, social creatures into participants of the divine nature.

Notes

1. See J. P. Kenny, SJ, *The Supernatural* (New York: Alba House, 1972), 50–56; also, among others, see *Summa Theologiae,* 1.43.3; 1–2.110.1, and 110.2, ad 2; *In II Cor,* 6.3.

2. *Summa Theologiae,* 60 vols. (New York: McGraw Hill and London: Eyre and Spottiswoode, 1964ff.), 1.1.8, ad 2. These two are dynamically related within the Thomistic vision of the coming forth (*exitus*) of all things from God in creation, and the return of spiritual creatures to their source through grace (e.g., *In I Sent.,* 14.2.2).

3. 1–2.112.1 and 1–2.110.1.

4. *Summa contra Gentiles,* 4 vols. (Notre Dame, IN: University of Notre Dame Press, 1975), 3.57.4. See also *Summa Theologiae,* 1–2.3.8 and 62.1, ad 3; *De Malo,* 5.1.1. Rahner writes, "It is not quite certain what Thomas meant by this expression. Every theologian who has written about it seems to have an interpretation." *Hearer of the Word: Laying the Foundation for a Philosophy of Religion,* trans. J. Donceel, SJ (New York: Continuum, 1994), 63.

5. See Gerald McCool, SJ, *From Unity to Pluralism* (New York: Fordham University Press, 1989), 1–38; "Neo-Scholasticism," in *The New Dictionary of Theology,* ed. Komonchak, et al. (Wilmington: Glazier, 1987), 714–15; *The Neo-Thomists* (Milwaukee: Marquette University Press, 1994), 25–42.

6. "Concerning the Relationship between Nature and Grace," *Theological Investigations,* trans. C. Ernst, vol. 1 (Baltimore: Helicon Press, 1961), 298–303. Henri de Lubac, Rahner's colleague in dialogue, and occasional sparring partner, offers a similar assessment of the neoscholastic perspective in *The Mystery of the Supernatural,* trans. R. Sheed (New York: Crossroad, 1998), 37. See also Gerald McCool, *Nineteenth-Century Scholasticism* (New York: Fordham University Press, 1989), 221–22; McCool, *From Unity to Pluralism,* 200–202. Although Saint Thomas's language appears, in a few places (*Summa Theologiae,* 1–2.62.1) to support such a double finality, his distinction between nature and grace is never portrayed as a duality; rather, "nature" is concrete human nature integrated within the context of grace. Louis Dupré, *Passage to Modernity: An Essay in the Hermeneutics of Nature and Grace* (New Haven: Yale University Press, 1993), 171.

7. *Adversus Haereses,* 4.14.1.

8. *Karl Rahner in Dialogue: Conversations and Interviews, 1965–1982,* ed. P. Imhof and H. Biallowons, trans. and ed. H. D. Egan (New York: Crossroad, 1986), 128.

9. "On the Theology of Worship," in *Theological Investigations,* trans. E. Quinn, vol. 11 (New York: Crossroad, 1983), 143. The theological perspective that "nature is, because grace was to be." "Beatific Vision," in *Sacramentum Mundi: An Encyclopedia of Theology,* ed. K. Rahner, et al. (New York: Herder and Herder, 1968), 1:152, col. 2, is utterly foundational to Rahner's theology. See, among others, "Christology within an Evolutionary View of the World," in *Theological Investigations,* trans. K. Kruger, vol. 5 (New York: Crossroad, 1983), 177–78, 185–86; "Concerning the Relationship between Nature and Grace," 310–11; *Foundations of Christian Faith,* trans. W. V. Dych (New York: Seabury Press, 1978), 122–23, 190, 197, 261, 419–20; "Order: III, Supernatural Order," *Sacramentum Mundi,* 4:298, col. 1; "Questions of Controversial Theology on Justification," in *Theological Investigations,* trans. K. Smyth, vol. 4 (New York: Crossroad, 1982), 213–14; "Revelation/II: God's Self-Communication," *Sacramentum Mundi,* 5:354, col. 2 and 355, col. 1; "Thoughts on the Theology of Christmas," in *Theological Investigations,* trans. K. and B. Kruger, vol. 3 (New York: Crossroad,

1982), 32–33. As will be seen below, Rahner gives this a constitutive Christological specification: "[T]he *possibility* of creation rests on that of the Incarnation." "Nature and Grace," *Theological Investigations,* 4:176.

10. *Summa Contra Gentiles,* 1.29.5; see also, 1.80.5; 2.15.4–5; *Summa Theologiae,* 1.8.1; 1.61.1. Saint Thomas explains this idea of causal participation through a brilliant synthesis of the Neoplatonic doctrine of participation and the Aristotelian metaphysics of act and potency. Essence receives and limits existence as potency receives and limits act. *Commentary on the Book of Causes,* trans. V. A. Guagliardo, OP, et al. (Washington, DC: Catholic University of America Press, 1996), 9:64. Thus, each finite thing (*ens*) is a composite unity, a synthesis of essence and the act of existence (*On Being and Essence,* trans. A. Maurer, CSB [Toronto: Pontifical Institute of Mediaeval Studies, 1949], chap. 4, p. 62), wherein existence is "contracted" into "a certain diminished participation" (*Summa Contra Gentiles,* 1.29.5) by this receiving essence (*On Spiritual Creatures,* trans. M. C. Fitzpatrick and J. J. Wellmuth, SJ [Milwaukee: Marquette University Press, 1949], a.I, corp., 23; *Summa Contra Gentiles,* 1.18.2; *On the Power of God,* trans. L. Shapcote [Westminster, MA: Newman Press, 1952], 7:3; *Light of Faith: The Compendium of Theology,* trans. C. Vollert [Manchester, NH: Sophia Institute, 1993], 212; *Quaestiones Quodlibetales,* in *Opera Omnia,* tomus IX [Parma: Petrus Fiaccadorus, 1859], 3.8.20). Therefore, the metaphysical center of every finite existent is, in Etienne Gilson's phrase, "a participated image of the pure Act of Being." Etienne Gilson, *Elements of Christian Philosophy* (New York: Doubleday, 1960), 133. Thomas posits a participated, efficiently caused likeness of the divine *esse* within every finite being. Every finite existent's *actus essendi* is efficiently caused by God and stands as a likeness to the divine in virtue of its caused existence.

11. Rahner transposes the language of metaphysical ontology into the language of knowledge and freedom (*Hearer of the Word: Laying the Foundation for a Philosophy of Religion,* trans. J. Donceel [New York: Continuum, 1994], 104, 124), "an ontology of the transcendental subject," which can theologically deploy the difference between human being and the ontic being addressed by the natural sciences. He argues that this turning from a cosmocentric objectivist philosophy to an anthropocentric transcendental philosophy is implicit in, and faithful to, the most fundamental insights of Saint Thomas. See "Current Problems in Christology," in *Theological Investigations,* 1:168–69; *Foundations,* 68–71; *Hearer,* 51; *Spirit in the World,* trans. W. V. Dych (New York: Continuum, 1994), 181–82; "An Investigation into the Incomprehensibility of God in St. Thomas Aquinas," *Theological Investigations,* trans. D. Morland, vol. 16 (New York: Crossroad, 1983), 247–48; "Man (Anthropology)," *Sacramentum Mundi,* 3:366ff.

12. Here is a key text: "[T]he judgment which ascribes certain quidditative determinations to something which exists in itself, to the exclusion of other possible determinations, is implicitly and precisely a judgment that *esse* does not belong in all its fullness to this thing which exists in itself. But this also means that the real objects of our judgments are not distinguished perhaps merely by their quidditative determinations, but precisely by their *esse* as the ground of these latter. Thus, every judgment is precisely a *critique* of the object, an evaluation of *the measure of esse* which belongs to what is judged. In the essential judgment, the thing-which-exists-in-itself which is meant in the subject of the proposition is limited by the quiddity of the predicate which, as form, already expresses limit in itself; it is partially deprived of the fullness which *esse* expresses in itself. Therefore, the objects of possible judgments are distinguished in their *esse* as such: *esse* can be affirmed of them only analogously insofar as the determinations in each of them are related in the same way to the ground of their reality, that is, to the *esse* proper to each, and insofar as the *esse* of each of these objects as *limited by its essence* must be understood as a *partial realization* of *esse* in itself." *Spirit in the World,* 178–79; see also *Hearer,* 53, 123–24.

13. "The concrete essence of something which exists in itself, expressed in the concretizing

as such, is thus the expression of the extent to which, in a definite existent, *esse,* the ground of reality for an existent, can let such an existent really exist." *Spirit in the World,* 174.

14. Rahner writes that, "as opposed to Kant, there is always question of a noetic hylomorphism, to which there corresponds an *ontological* hylomorphism in the objects, in the sense of a thoroughgoing determination of knowing by being." *Spirit in the* World, liii–liv. On this point, Rahner and Saint Thomas are in complete agreement. Both insist that any discussion of intellect must ultimately be a metaphysical discussion: "Metaphysics dominates noetic as it dominates the rest of philosophy." Gilson, *The Christian Philosophy of St. Thomas Aquinas* (Notre Dame, IN: University of Notre Dame Press, 1994), 232.

15. *Hearer,* 53.

16. *Foundations,* 20.

17. *Spirit in the World,* 165.

18. *Foundations,* 20–21. See *Spirit in the World,* 183, 405–6; "The Development of Dogma," in *Theological Investigations,* 1:64–65.

19. Ibid., 208.

20. Rahner analyzes human freedom in the same terms, since "in every activity, we reach for being as such." *Hearer of the Word,* 140. Also see 45 and *Foundations,* 123.

21. Rahner's writings display a rather quick transition from the language of the human spirit's orientation to *Absolute Being,* to talk about *God* as the term of our transcendence. For example, "We may express our thesis thus: the ultimate condition of the possibility of rationality is the transcendental reference of man to the unfathomable mystery we call God." "Faith, rationality and emotion," in *Theological Investigations,* 16:67; see also *Foundations,* 454. For an interpretation of this transition from within the context of Rahner's metaphysics of participation, see Francis J. Caponi, OSA, "Rahner and the Metaphysics of Participation," *The Thomist* 67/3 (July 2003): 400–408. Also see *Spirit in the World,* 181: "This Absolute Being is not apprehended as a represented object. For the *esse* apprehended in the pre-apprehension, as only implicitly and simultaneously in the pre-apprehension, was known implicitly and simultaneously as able to be limited by quidditative determinations, and as already limited, since the pre-apprehension, if it is not to be a 'grasp,' can only be realized in a simultaneous conversion to a definite form limiting *esse* and in the conversion to the phantasm. The fullness of being which *esse* expresses is therefore never given objectively. If *esse* is made objective in reflection in order to be known itself (not merely implicitly and simultaneously known in the pre-apprehension), then that can only be done insofar as it is itself concretized again by a form."

22. "A metaphysical anthropology has reached its end when it has understood itself as the metaphysics of an obediential potency for the revelation of the supramundane God." *Hearer,* 142; also 150–51; 72.

23. Ibid., 62–63.

24. "Concerning the Relationship between Nature and Grace," 317.

25. *Hearer,* 151; "Concerning the Relationship between Nature and Grace," 315–16.

26. In this, Rahner is again following Saint Thomas, who consistently addresses grace through the conceptuality of participation, speaking of "the light of grace, which is a participation in the divine nature" (*Summa Theologiae,* 1–2.110.3), "that participation in the divine goodness which constitutes grace" (ibid., 1–2.110.2, ad 2), and holding that "it is necessary that God alone make godlike, by communicating a share in his divine nature by participation and assimilation" (ibid., 1–2.112.2).

27. "Grace," *Sacramentum Mundi,* 2:415, col. 2; see "*Theos* in the New Testament," *Theological Investigations,* 1:124–25.

28. *Foundations,* 120.

29. "Experience of the Holy Spirit," in *Theological Investigations,* trans. E. Quinn, vol. 18 (New York: Crossroad, 1983), 189. See *Summa Theologiae,* 1.43.3.

30. "Concerning the Relationship between Nature and Grace," 307.

31. "Nature and Grace," 172. Rahner regards the inversion of this relationship to be a hallmark of scholastic theology as well ("Some Implications of the Scholastic Concept of Created Grace," *Theological Investigations,* 1:324). See David Coffey, "The Gift of the Holy Spirit," *The Irish Theological Quarterly* 38, no. 3 (July 1971): 202; and Vladmir Lossky, *The Mystical Theology of the Eastern Church* (Crestwood, NY: St. Vladmir's Seminary Press, 1976), 70–87.

32. "Questions of Controversial Theology on Justification," 216.

33. "On the Theology of Worship," 143, 147. This is the official teaching of the Roman Catholic Church, as expressed at Vatican II: "In his goodness and wisdom God chose to reveal himself and to make known to us the hidden purpose of his will (see Eph 1:9) by which through Christ, the Word made flesh, man might in the Holy Spirit have access to the Father and come to share in the divine nature (see Eph 2:18; 2 Pet 1:4). Through this revelation, therefore, the invisible God (see Col 1:15; 1 Tim 1:17) out of the abundance of His love speaks to men as friends (see Ex 33:11; Jn 15:14–15) and lives among them (see Bar 3:38), so that He may invite and take them into fellowship with Himself." *Dei Verbum,* 1.2. Also see "Nature and Grace," 175.

34. Indeed, he endorses the Thomistic idea (*Summa Theologiae,* 1–2.50.22) that grace heals precisely by elevating human nature to the capacity of salutary acts. See *Foundations,* 118; "Grace," *Sacramentum Mundi,* 2:420–42; "Justification," in Karl Rahner and Herbert Vorgrimler, *Concise Theological Dictionary,* ed. Cornelius Ernst, trans. Richard Strachan (New York: Herder and Herder, 1965), 247; "Salvation/IV: Theology," in *Sacramentum Mundi,* 4:427, cols. 1 and 2; "Sanctifying Grace," *Concise Theological Dictionary,* 422; "Self-Communication of God," in *Concise Theological Dictionary,* 429–30. This aspect of Rahner's thought will be seen again below, in connection with the meaning of virtue. Also see "Nature and Grace," 177 and see "Gnade," in *Lexikon für Theologie und Kirche,* ed. J. Höfer and K. Rahner (Freiburg: Herder, 1959), 4:992.

35. As Colin Gunton observes, for Orthodox Christianity this distinction is not a dualism or a division; rather, it is a "duality-in-relation." *The Christian Faith* (Oxford: Blackwell, 2002), 11. Rahner insists that "we ourselves never cease being creatures even when we become partakers of the Godhead." "The Eternal Significance of the Humanity of Jesus for Our Relationship with God," in *Theological Investigations,* 3:46; see "Christology within an Evolutionary View of the World," 165; "Man (Anthropology)," *Sacramentum Mundi,* 3:366, col. 2; "Jesus Christ/IV: History of Dogma and Theology," in *Sacramentum Mundi,* 3:203, col. 2.

36. *Foundations,* 119, 121. For a good account of the importance of this distinction for the whole of Christian theology, see Robert Sokolowski, *The God of Faith and Reason* (Notre Dame, IN: University of Notre Dame Press, 1982).

37. When St. Thomas teaches that created things "partake existence," he explicitly states that he does not mean that creation is a matter of formal participation in *Esse Divinum* (*Summa contra gentiles,* 1.26; *Summa Theologiae,* 1.3.4 ad 1; *De Potentia,* 7.2 ad 6). Rather, as he writes in *Summa Theologiae,* "God exists in everything; not indeed as part of their substance or as an accident, but as an agent is present to that in which its action is taking place. . . . The perfection of his nature places God above everything, and yet as causing their existence he also exists in everything." 1.8.1 and ad 1. Rahner is faithful to this insight: "God himself is his difference from his creature." "Revelation/II: God's Self-Communication," in *Sacramentum Mundi,* 5:354, col. 2; see also *Foundations,* 119–20. Human knowing is, at its very heart, the assertion that objects are not merely material veils for the *Esse Ipsum Subsistens.* See *Hearer,* 123–24; "The Eternal Significance of the Humanity of Jesus," 40.

38. *Foundations,* 120; see Karl-Heinz Weger, *Karl Rahner: An Introduction to His Theology,* trans. D. Smith (New York: Seabury, 1980), 110.

39. "Grace," *Sacramentum Mundi,* 2:418, cols. 1–2. He sounds a caution against understanding grace as "a self-communication of God which is reified and understood entirely after the manner of a thing." *Foundations,* 116.

40. Ibid., 417, col. 2; *Foundations,* 120.
41. See below, on Christology and evolution.
42. "Concerning the Relationship between Nature and Grace," 298 and 307.
43. Rahner's thinking here is complex. "[I]f the ordination cannot be detached from the nature, the fulfillment of the ordination, from *God's* point of view precisely, is exacted. . . . In other words, it follows from the innermost essence of grace that a disposition for grace belonging to man's nature is impossible, or it follows that such a disposition, in case it is needed, itself belongs to this supernatural order already; but it does not follow that as natural it would permit the unexactedness of grace to subsist." "Concerning the Relationship between Nature and Grace," 306, 308. But can we not say that God, having freely pledged himself to humanity as its proper end in the very act of freely *creating* human nature with an intrinsic supernatural ordination, is here subjected to no necessity outside that of his own divine will, thus making his offer of grace to humanity a perfectly free gift, and one that he was perfectly free to have withheld by creating humanity with no such supernatural ordination? In this light, the complexities of the "supernatural existential" would also be superfluities, since God's free creation ex nihilo of a creature intrinsically ordained to divinization secures the "subsequent" freedom of the offer of God's own Self in grace. This would even appear to be the logical consequence of Rahner's insistence that nature exists for the sake of grace: Grace, having "already" been decided upon by God, leads God to produce creatures intrinsically ordained to receive what God has already decided to give. But this is precisely the consequence Rahner denies. Granted that God, in fulfilling his own will, still acts freely in offering a particular individual grace, the issue is that the receiver of this grace, if its reception is no more than the fulfillment of already constituted nature, will receive it as no more gracious than his created existence itself: "God would be creating a creature which would as a whole, together with this natural disposition, be created freely and in this sense unexactedly, but not a creature in respect of which precisely once again grace would be unexacted." Ibid., 308. Rahner's point may be illuminated by reference to the actual experience of Christians: the Christian experience of the life, death, and resurrection of Jesus Christ has never carried with it the sense that God was here merely "finishing the job." He began in Genesis. Christian experience has interpreted Jesus Christ both as God's plan from before the ages, and as the free gift of God's love, and asserted the latter in a way that cannot be reduced to the former through reference to God's eternal, comprehensive will. For instance, do not I, both as creature and sinner, always experience the Eucharist precisely as that which I am utterly and entirely unowed, upon which I, at this moment, can produce no claim, but which comes to me as essentially undeserved, undeserved in a way over and above both my sinfulness and the gratuity of my very existence? Rahner is saying that the failure to make the distinction he defends would result in a real loss of interpretive power for Christian theology, and so conduce to a positive deformation of Christian experience (if, to continue the example, I were to approach the altar of God with the sense that, as a (forgiven) creature, I was merely being given "what was coming to me"). Rahner rejects the very possibility of a created being for which grace could be "the normal, matter-of-course perfection to which it was compellingly disposed." Ibid., 310n.; "Questions of Controversial Theology on Justification," 214–15. Rather, a truly orthodox theology, one faithful to Christian experience, is compelled to acknowledge that God has created us in such a way that "love does not only pour forth free and unexacted, but also so that man as real partner, as one who can accept or reject it, can experience and accept it *as* the unexacted event and wonder not owed to *him,* the real man. As unexacted, not only because he does not deserve it as a *sinner,* but further because he can also embrace it as unexacted when, already blessed in this love, he is allowed to forget that he was a sinner once." Ibid., 310–11. Rahner concludes: In light of God's eternal will for Self-communication to another, he does bestow upon us an intrinsic dynamism for the reception of this Self-communication; and he gives this dynamism not as a part of *natura pura,* but as a perpetual and supernatural offer to the person.

44. "Questions of Controversial Theology on Justification," 212–13.

45. "Existence/III: 'The Existential,'" *Sacramentum Mundi,* 2:304–7; "Existential, übernatürliches," *Lexikon für Theologie und Kirche,* 3:1301.

46. "Concerning the Relationship between Nature and Grace," 302–3.

47. "Questions of Controversial Theology on Justification," 217.

48. *Foundations,* 130.

49. Analyzing the ideas of the "new theology" on this point, as presented by "D.," in "Ein Weg zur Bestimmung der Verhältnisses von Natur und Gnade," *Orientierung 14* (1950): 138–41, Rahner concludes that they make no advance upon the gratuity involved in creation, and that, as a result, "grace is distinguished from other created things only in respect of the greatness of the gift but not in respect of unexactedness itself." "Concerning the Relationship between Nature and Grace," 305.

50. "Questions of Controversial Theology on Justification," 214–15.

51. "Foundations of Christian Faith," in *Theological Investigations,* 19:8–9.

52. "The Concept of Mystery in Catholic Theology," in *Theological Investigations,* 4:67.

53. *Foundations,* 121 (note that Rahner has dropped the "quasi" from his description of the causality involved in grace). See also "Beatific Vision," *Sacramentum Mundi,* 1:153, col. 1; "Grace," *Sacramentum Mundi,* 2:418, col. 2; "Nature and Grace," 175; "Revelation/II: God's Self-Communication," *Sacramentum Mundi,* 5:354, col. 1; *The Trinity,* trans. J. Donceel (Kent: Burns and Oates, 1970), 36; "Some Implications of the Scholastic Concept of Uncreated Grace," 329–37. The concept has met with more than a little criticism, as, for example, George Vass's comment that it is a "bastard category" from a "suspect causal scheme." Vass, *Understanding Karl Rahner,* vol. 2, *The Mystery of Man and the Foundations of a Theological System* (Westminster and London: Christian Classics and Sheed and Ward, 1985), 109.

54. *Foundations,* 79.

55. Ibid., 121, 132.

56. "Grace," *Sacramentum Mundi,* 2:417, col. 2.

57. "Nature and Grace," 176; "Christology within an Evolutionary View of the World," 177–78.

58. "The manifestation in which what is being manifested comes to its own fulfillment and definitiveness can rightly be conceived as the cause of what is being manifested. . . . In other words, you must have a concept according to which the effect, if one can put it this way, can be in a meaningful way at the same time a cause." *Karl Rahner in Dialogue,* 128–29; "Current Problems in Christology," 167.

59. "Jesus Christ/IV: History of Dogma and Theology," in *Sacramentum Mundi,* 3:204, col. 1. Although space does not allow a fuller consideration of the point, this perspective on divinization is rooted in Rahner's theology of the Trinity: "Corresponding to the two Trinitarian processions, immanent in the Trinity and in the economy of salvation, incarnation and grace can be regarded as two self-communications of God, both having their ground in God's one free decision to self-communicate *ad extra.*" "Revelation/II: God's Self-Communication," in *Sacramentum Mundi,* 5:355, col. 1. Thus, when the eschatological culmination of God's Self-communication (i.e., beatific vision) is under consideration, Rahner lays down this principle: "When reference is made to 'sharing in the divine nature,' it must not be overlooked that this participation is necessarily triune and is given for there to be a direct relation between God and the spiritual person of the creature. It is, therefore, implied that there is a direct relation of the creature to God precisely as Father, Son and Spirit." "Beatific Vision," *Sacramentum Mundi,* 1:152, col. 2.

60. For Rahner's understanding of the world as dynamically evolving toward humanity and Christ, see "Christology within an Evolutionary View of the World," 157–92; "Evolution/II: Theological," *Sacramentum Mundi,* 2:289–97; *Hominisation: The Evolutionary Origin of*

Man as a Theological Problem, trans. W. T. O'Hara (New York: Herder and Herder, 1965); "The Unity of Spirit and Matter in the Christian Understanding of Faith," in *Theological Investigations* 4:153–77.

61. "Human being is . . . a reality absolutely open upwards; a reality which reaches its highest (though indeed 'unexacted') perfection, the realization of the highest possibility of man's being, when in it the Logos himself becomes existent in the world. . . . [W]e only radically understand ourselves for what we really are, when we grasp the fact that we are existential beings because God willed to be man." "Current Problems in Christology," 183–84.

62. Rahner writes of his book, *Foundations of Christian Faith,* that "the most fundamental idea of Christianity as presented here is that of the gracious self-communication of God in himself" (10), rather than Christology per se. See also *Foundations,* 116; "Revelation/II: God's Self-Communication," *Sacramentum Mundi,* 5:354, col. 2; *Karl Rahner in Dialogue,* 125–26; "Selbstmitteilung Gottes," *Lexikon für Theologie und Kirche,* 9:627.

63. "[I]f the reality in which God's absolute self-communication is pledged and accepted for the whole of humanity and thus becomes 'present' for us (i.e., Christ's reality) is to be really the final and unsurpassable divine self-communication, then it must be said that it is not only posited by God but is God himself. . . . Hence, if we may put it this way, the hypostatic union does not differ from our grace by what is pledged in it, for this is grace in both cases (even in the case of Jesus). But it differs from our grace by the fact that Jesus is our pledge, and we ourselves are not the pledge but the recipients of God's pledge to us." "Christology within an Evolutionary View of the World," 183.

64. Ibid., 174.

65. "The history of salvation . . . does not consist merely of a series of homogenous single events of equal importance. It tends towards a victorious culmination which gives a direction to this history which is irreversible. It therefore tends towards an 'eschatological' culmination. This culminating point which as goal, as *causa finalis, supports* the whole history of divine self-communication, and in its victorious power brings it to definitive manifestation, is realized when God himself makes this history his own in the God-man." "Salvation/IV: Theology," *Sacramentum Mundi,* 5:431, col. 1; see *Foundations,* 191; "Christology within an Evolutionary View of the World," 175.

66. *Foundations,* 199.

67. "Grace," *Sacramentum Mundi,* 2:418, col. 1; 2:422, col. 2.

68. Among others, see Jn 1:14; Tit 2:11, 3:4; I Jn 1:3.

69. Edward Schillebeeckx, OP, *Christ: The Experience of Jesus as Lord,* trans. John Bowden (New York: Crossroad, 1981), 463.

70. "Transcendental Theology," *Sacramentum Mundi,* 6:288, col. 1; see *Foundations,* 51–55, 208, 273; "Christology within an Evolutionary View of the World," 163.

71. Ibid.

72. *Foundations,* 398.

73. Ibid., 389.

74. Ibid., 132. For Rahner's development of the idea of transcendental grace into his controversial theory of "anonymous Christianity," see "Anonymous and Explicit Faith," *Theological Investigations,* 16:52–59; "Church, Churches and Religions," in *Theological Investigations,* trans. D. Bourke, vol. 10 (New York: Seabury, 1977), 30–49; *Foundations,* 311–21, 429; "Observations on the Problem of the Anonymous Christian," in *Theological Investigations,* trans. D. Bourke, vol. 14 (New York: Seabury Press, 1976), 280–94; see also Peter Hebblethwaite, "The Status of 'Anonymous Christians'," *Heythrop Journal* 18 (January 1977): 47–55.

75. Ibid., 429; *The Church and the Sacraments,* trans. W. J. O'Hara (New York: Herder and Herder, 1963), 13, 18–19, 23; also "The Church's Redemptive Historical Provenance from the Death and Resurrection of Jesus," in *Theological Investigations* 19:321; *Foundations,* 412.

76. Ibid., 18.
77. "On the Theology of Worship," 142.
78. *Foundations,* 419.
79. Ibid., 412, 426.
80. "Virtue/I: Acquired and Infused Virtues," *Sacramentum Mundi,* 6:337, col. 2; "Sanctifying Grace," *Concise Theological Dictionary,* 421–22.
81. "Virtue," *Concise Theological Dictionary,* 483.
82. "On the Theology of Hope," in *Theological Investigations* 10:242; "Justification and World Development from a Catholic Perspective," in *Theological Investigations* 18:261–62.
83. "Merit," *Concise Theological Dictionary,* 285.
84. "*Theos* in the New Testament," 82.
85. Again, this is an eminently Thomistic perspective: "Man was made in order to see God: for this purpose God made him a rational creature, so that he might participate in his likeness, which consists in seeing him." *De Veritate,* trans. R. W. Mulligan, J. V. McGlynn, and R. W. Schmidt, 3 vols. (Indianapolis: Hackett, 1954), 18.1.
86. *The Church and the Sacraments,* 23. Again, the Thomistic provenance is clear: "Persons obtain grace through the Son of God made man. Grace first filled his humanity, and thence was brought to us. . . . Thus it was fitting that grace which overflows from the Word incarnate should be carried to us by perceptible external realities and that perceptible external works should be brought forth from this inner grace by which flesh is subjected to spirit." *Summa Theologiae,* 1–2.108.1.

Theosis in Recent Research: A Renewal of Interest and a Need for Clarity

Gösta Hallonsten

"The Naming of Cats is a difficult matter
It isn't just one of your holiday games;"
—T. S. Eliot, "Old Possum's Book
of Practical Cats"

Theosis: A Renewal of Interest

These words of T. S. Eliot are apt to our present discussion, for it seems to me that the concept of *theosis* is becoming increasingly unclear. The popularity of this concept has risen in Western theology and academic research from the low of Harnack's depreciation of it in the nineteenth century up to today's high interest. *Theosis,* deification, or divinization is no longer a topic limited to Eastern Orthodox thought. It is found almost everywhere: in Luther and Thomas Aquinas, Lancelott Andrewes, and St. John of the Cross.[1] The recent publication of an English translation of Jules Gross's classical *The Divinization of the Christian according to the Greek Fathers* (2002) is just one sign of the renewed interest.[2] The introduction to the English edition, written by Kerry S. Robichaux and Paul A. Onica, testifies to the effort to re-appropriate this doctrine by Protestant theology.[3] I will not comment upon that risky undertaking,[4] but will instead focus upon two substantial contributions to the discussion of possible *theosis* doctrines within the Western tradition. One is the well-known renaissance for Luther Research in Finland by Tuomo Mannermaa and his school.[5] The other is the monograph by A. N. Williams, *The Ground of Union: Deification in Aquinas and Palamas.*[6] A few observations on the terminology used by those two representatives of a renewed interest in deification will be offered, which will lead to a more general deliberation on the doctrine itself. I will then offer a proposal on how to use the terminology in future discussions.

Theosis in Luther?

The Finnish school of Luther research is characterized by ambivalence toward the terminology of *theosis*. Dr. Mannermaa himself, in several passages, states that Luther in fact has a doctrine of deification.[7] Some of his students, such as Simo Peura, on the other hand, consistently speak of a "Theme or Motif" of *theosis* in Luther's writings.[8] The latter way of speaking is certainly to be preferred. No one can doubt that the theme of deification is to be found in the writings of Luther; this was well known even before the rise of the Finnish school. Yet even Peura does not think that Luther's use of this theme is merely rhetorical, for it has a relation to what is in fact the main thesis of the Finnish school: that Luther's doctrine of justification does not exclude but rather implies a "real-ontic" renewal of the justified that in the end leads to union with God. There is a real renewal, a transformation or transfiguration of the justified, which can be described as participation in divine life through Christ. Mannermaa contends that this is the core of patristic and Eastern deification doctrine and that this core is to be found in Luther as well.[9]

This brief description of the Finnish school leads to some immediate conclusions that are of general relevance regarding the revival of interest in the doctrine of deification. First, the presence of the theme of *theosis* is taken as an indication of a doctrine of *theosis*. That this is a premature conclusion, I will argue later. Second, the core or the very point of a doctrine of deification is defined as participation in divine life or union with God.

St. Thomas and St. Gregory Palamas

A. N. Williams's monograph offers more extended references to patristic and Eastern Orthodox doctrines of deification, yet she never expressly defines what she means by a doctrine of *theosis*.[10] She frequently uses this terminology as a characterization not only of Gregory Palamas's theology but also for that of St. Thomas.[11] She concedes, however, that Thomas himself only seldom speaks about *theosis expressis verbis*.[12] Further, while the title of the book seems to equate deification with union with God, sometimes the author, almost in passing, defines *theosis* as sanctification.[13] While these two doctrines are not mutually exclusive, a doctrine of *theosis* traditionally includes sanctification and is in fact much more comprehensive.[14] If we find in Thomas a doctrine of sanctification that is compatible with the concept of sanctification included in the Eastern doctrine of *theosis*, this does not mean that the doctrine of sanctification in St. Thomas necessarily implies a doctrine of *theosis*. This comment applies to the Finnish school as well. If, as the Finnish school maintains, Luther conceives of a "real-ontic" transformation in the justified, this does not necessarily mean that Luther has a doctrine of *theosis,* not even when taking into account the presence of the theme of *theosis* in Luther.[15]

In addition to the lack of clear definition of *theosis* in Williams's book, there is also a methodological flaw. When beginning her analysis of St. Gregory Palamas, she states: "We examine Palamas by the same means we used for Aquinas: by seeking direct references to deification and using the themes we find in these passages as a guide through the work as a whole."[16] This may be an appropriate way to analyze Palamas, who is part of the Eastern tradition. However, with regard to Thomas it is misleading, or rather, it leads to an implied understanding of deification as equal to filiation, adoption, indwelling of God, or union with God.[17] Those themes, as might be expected, are to be found in nearly every Christian author throughout the ages, regardless of provenience. This is quite natural given that the motives referred to are biblical. The problem, however, is that one ends up with a very general understanding of deification, which is not at all helpful if the distinctive mark of the Eastern doctrine of *theosis* is to be singled out. Clearly, therefore, there is a need for a clarification, and I would like to offer the following proposals.

Doctrine and Theme—A Preliminary Distinction

First, a distinction should always be made between the theme and a doctrine of deification. By a doctrine I mean here a rather well-defined complex of thought that centers on one or more technical terms. It is quite natural that the theme of deification can be found throughout the Western tradition. This has been shown in an excellent way by the article "Divinisation" in *Dictionnaire de Spiritualité.*[18] The reason this theme is omnipresent in the Latin tradition is twofold. First, it has a certain connection to places in Scripture like 2 Peter 1:4 and Psalms 82(81):6.[19] Further, these two verses have a clear affinity to other more prominent scriptural themes such as adoption as sons of God, filiation, "indwelling of" and "union with" God, and finally, beatific vision. Second, the presence of the *theosis* theme in Western theology is promoted by the liturgical tradition, especially the Christmas liturgy.[20] Therefore, it's not by coincidence that the clearest references to *theosis* in Luther are found in this context.[21] Yet employing the theme is not the same as making a doctrine out of it. This can be illustrated by reference to St. Augustine, who clearly uses the *theosis* theme, together with adoption and filiation, in his sermons.[22] Yet in his treatises on grace it is almost absent. What is more, the very fact that Augustine developed a doctrine of grace in distinction from the preceding patristic and ongoing Eastern theology, which uses the word in a wider nontechnical sense, illustrates the distinction I'm making here between theme and doctrine.[23]

We must also consider here what exactly is meant by a doctrine of deification in the Eastern sense. The Finnish school, as well as Williams and many other contemporary scholars, seem to think that the core of the doctrine of deification is participation in divine life.[24] This conclusion seems obvious once one takes as the point of departure the theme of *theosis,* which as a matter of fact touches primarily upon the goal in terms of participation in divine life. Further, this is suggested by the two main scriptural references. Yet, if the doctrine of *theosis* according to the Greek Fathers or present-day Orthodox theology is examined, it will be realized that *deification* as doctrine is not solely about the final goal but is conceived of as a comprehensive doctrine encompassing the whole economy of salvation. Before I develop this further, I would like to address a related question.

The Role of Palamas

Current research on deification in the Latin tradition tends to choose St. Gregory Palamas as its preferential point of reference for a comparison between East and West. Whereas the description of the patristic doctrine of deification stands out as unengaged and unsystematic with little or no references in present-day Orthodox theology, Palamas often is subject to a thorough analysis. This is the case not only in Williams but also in the discussion around the Finnish Luther research, as exemplified by the thorough analysis by Reinhard Flogaus.[25] Yet it could very well be asked if Palamas is the most adequate point of reference. Of course, I am not calling into question the fact that Palamas is one of the greatest theologians in the Eastern tradition or that his theology widely influences present-day Orthodox theology. The theology of St. Gregory Palamas is marked by its special polemical context, which focused on the question of knowing and experiencing God through his energies and on the experience of mystical prayer. This, in turn, fits very well with a pre-understanding of deification as meaning primarily participation in divine life. It is far too easy to overlook the elements of this doctrine that are certainly presupposed in the theology of Palamas but not prominent in his polemical writings.[26] Those are the elements, however, that are integral to the doctrine of deification if it is looked at from the perspective of a continuous tradition of Eastern theology.

The Anthropological Fundament of *Theosis*

The doctrine of deification is typically a comprehensive doctrine in the East.[27] It is not as well defined as, for example, the Augustinian doctrine of grace or the Anselmian doctrine of satisfaction. In fact, I would propose that this doctrine is not necessarily dependent upon *theosis* language, nor, alternatively, is the latter necessarily connected to the former. St. Irenaeus is normally taken as the founder of *theosis* doctrine. If this is so, and I think it is, it shows that the doctrine of *theosis* is not necessarily connected to *theosis* language even if it is normally expressed through this language.[28] The comprehensiveness of the *theosis* doctrine, on the other hand, is clearly to be found in Irenaeus. It comprises: a certain view of creation, especially of human beings; a soteriology, including the meaning of the Incarnation; a view of Christian life as sanctification connected to the Church and sacraments; and the final goal of union with God. The whole structure of this comprehensive doctrine is determined by a teleology that implies that creation and human beings from the very beginning are endowed with an affinity and likeness that potentially draws them to God.

As a matter of fact, what is most striking when the Western present-day authors to which I have referred are compared with Orthodox descriptions of the doctrine of deification, or with that of the Greek Fathers, is this: the lack of references to anthropology and especially to the notion of image and likeness.[29] Many present-day Orthodox theologians, on the other hand, put precisely this distinction at the basis of their description of deification.[30] Humanity is created in the image of God—referring to the constitutional aspect of anthropology—and in the likeness of God—referring to the goal of growing into communion with the Creator. The favorite scriptural text of the fathers in this connection is Genesis 2:7; God forms Adam from the earth and breathes his Spirit into him. This text then is combined with the distinction between image and likeness in Genesis 1:26. Although not all of the Greek Fathers link this distinction to the fundamentally dynamic anthropology that characterizes the doctrine of deification, all of them link the fact of being created in the image of God dynamically to the goal. The meaning of Christian life is to assimilate to God, to grow according to the prototype.[31]

This distinction between image and likeness is also to be found in the Latin tradition. There, however, it is not connected to a dynamic anthropology of the Eastern type.[32] It seems that Tertullian, who was highly dependent on Irenaeus, eventually abandoned Irenaeus's "anthropological" model. In the early writings of Tertullian, the thought that the spiritual part of the human being is a partaking of the Holy Spirit breathed into its body can still be found. Hence humanity is dynamically oriented toward full communion with God.[33] Tertullian's later writings, however, are marked by the strong opposition to Gnosticism and hence stress more emphatically that the human as a created being, notwithstanding its spiritual part, is of a clearly distinct genus or species. Through this, Tertullian aims at avoiding the Gnostic thought of a divine spark in human beings and hence a predetermined salvation for the few.[34] Tertullian's emphasis on the relative independence and special character of creature in relation to Creator, however, seems to be a common inheritance in the subsequent Latin tradition.[35] Thus, we see the tendency to distinguish between nature and grace in a way that is foreign to Eastern tradition.[36]

The Concept of Participation

What I have just said means that anthropology is the fundamental feature that marks the Eastern doctrine of deification and is thus the key to an accurate understanding of this doctrine.[37] Further, this anthropology is connected to a view of the relation between God and creation that is significantly different from that of the Latin tradition. In the East, creation from its very beginning is seen as a participation in God; hence grace cannot be separated from creation but inheres in it and potentially leads it to union with God. It is the Platonic concept of participation that is the background here. The world and human beings are seen as caused by God in the sense of formal causality, whereas in the Western view efficient causality takes its place: God and the world are distinct beings, even if the world participates in Being in an analogical sense. As a result the Eastern tradition has worked out the distinction between God's essence and energies, a distinction that makes no sense to the scholastic point of view according to which God is characterized by simplicity. Hence, philosophically speaking, the essence and existence of God coincide.[38]

Referring back, now, to Williams's comparison between Aquinas and Palamas, the striking thing is that she leaves out this whole problem. Her thesis is that both thinkers have a doctrine of participation of human beings in the life of God, which is true. As has been said earlier, the sole fact of having a doctrine of participation of whatever kind, together with the use of words like deification, partaking of divine nature, adoption, and filiation, to Williams equates with having a doctrine of deification.[39] What is lacking in her book is a real discussion of differences between the two types of participation that Aquinas and Palamas teach respectively. This is an inevitable consequence, so far as I can see, of lacking an understanding of the integral doctrine of *theosis* according to the Eastern tradition.[40]

The Finnish contention that Luther teaches a "real-ontic" participation in God exhibits the same shortcoming. It is easy to see that Luther's thought here is clearly original. His notion of participation in God's life does not accord with that of scholastic theology or philosophy, and yet it definitely does not coincide with the Eastern view either.[41] So, what is missing in these two prominent exponents for the renaissance of interest in deification is a clear consciousness not only of similarities but also, and most needed, of differences.

Theosis: A Multiple Phenomenon

To draw our discussion to a conclusion, let me once again quote T. S. Eliot:

> You may think at first I'm as mad as a hatter,
> When I tell you, a cat must have THREE DIFFERENT NAMES.[42]

I think that the discussion of deification could profit from the insight that there are three different names for it, or more accurately, that *theosis* might refer to three different phenomena, which may be interconnected—but not always. They are as follows:

1. First, there is the theme of *theosis,* which most often is connected with similar scriptural themes like adoption and filiation. While the theme of *theosis* is surely to be found in most Christian writers throughout the ages, this should not, however, mislead us into speaking as frequently about a doctrine of *theosis.* For the sake of clarity, I would like to underscore here that the theme of *theosis* includes the theme of "happy exchange," the *admirabile commercium.*[43]
2. Second, *theosis* is connected to a certain anthropology, often based on the distinction between image and likeness and always teleologically oriented in a dynamic way toward the prototype. This prototype, the real Image of God, is Christ. Thus the importance of the Incarnation as the central point in the economy of salvation. This anthropology, further, is based on or implies a view of the relation between creation and its Creator that is characterized by formal causality and implies the continual presence and action of grace or the energies of God from the beginning to the end.
3. Third, *theosis* is a comprehensive doctrine that encompasses the whole of the economy of salvation. The whole plan of God and its accomplishment from the creation through the Incarnation, salvation, sanctification and the eschaton are included in this comprehensive vision.[44]

Points 2 and 3 belong intimately together, whereas point 1 is more independent. No doubt other classifications exist, for the comprehensiveness of this topic is somewhat elusive. Yet, I hope my main point leads to further discussion, namely, that a distinction should be made between the theme and doctrine of *theosis,* and that the label "doctrine of *theosis*" should preferentially be reserved for the integral doctrine of deification as presented by the Eastern tradition. Promoting mutual Christian understanding is a good thing. We do not reach that goal, however, simply through interpreting similarities as identities.

Notes

Eliot's poem in the epigraph is from *The Complete Poems and Plays 1909–50* (New York: Harcourt Brace, 1952), 149. This paper was first given in the Eastern Orthodox Study Group at the Annual Meeting of the AAR in Atlanta, November 2003. Notes have been added.

1. Cf. A. N. Williams, *The Ground of Union: Deification in Aquinas and Palamas* (New York and Oxford: Oxford University Press 1999), 201; and David Bentley Hart, "The Bright Morning of the Soul: John of the Cross on *Theosis,*" in *Pro Ecclesia: A Journal of Catholic and Evangelical Theology* 13, no. 3 (2003): 324–44.

2. Originally published as *La divinisation du chrétien d'après les pères grecs: Contribution historique à la doctrine de la grace* (Edition J. Gabalda, 1938).

3. See viii–xvii.

4. See esp. xii–xiii, where an effort to twist the doctrine to suit Protestant concerns is undertaken.

5. Among many writings produced by this school of research, see esp. Tuomo Mannermaa, *Der im Glauben gegenwärtige Christus: Rechtfertigung; und Vergottung. Zum ökumenischen Dialog,* Arbeiten zur Geschichte und Theologie des Luthertums, N.F. 8 (Hannover: Lutherisches Verlagshaus 1989), and *Union with Christ: The New Finnish Interpretation of Luther,* ed. Carl E. Braaten and Robert W. Jenson (Grand Rapids, MI and Cambridge, UK: Eerdmans 1998).

6. See note 1.

7. Mannermaa's terminology is not altogether consistent, however. In the introductory essay "Why is Luther so Fascinating? Modern Finnish Luther Research," in *Union with Christ,* Mannermaa speaks both of a "doctrine of *theosis*" in Luther (2, 10–11, 17–18, 19) and uses words like "theme" (3) or "concept" of *theosis* (10, 18). Cf. further the following formulations: "doctrine of real participation or divinization" (3), "concept of real participation in God" (9), "idea of participation" (9, 13), "notion of *theosis*" (9) and "theology of participation" (20). It is clear that Mannermaa prefers to speak of a doctrine of *theosis* and/or participation. Concept, notion, and "theme" seem to function as stylistic variations. See further, Mannermaa, "Justification and *Theosis* in Lutheran-Orthodox Perspective," in the same volume, esp. 25–26.

8. See esp. "Die Vergöttlichung des Menschen als Sein in Gott," in *Lutherjahrbuch* 60 (Göttingen: Vandenhoeck & Ruprecht, 1993), 39–71. In this article Simo Peura consistently speaks about "Das Thema der Vergöttlichung" or "Das Motiv der Vergöttlichung" but avoids the term doctrine. He also uses "Vergöttlichung" without further qualification. In his contributions to *Union with Christ,* "Christ as Favor and Gift (*donum*): The Challenge of Luther's Understanding of Justification," 42–69 and "What God Gives Man Receives: Luther on Salvation" 76–95, Peura, however, does not use "theme" or "motif" but rather terms like "notion," "concept," "idea," or "issue" of *theosis.* He also speaks of *theosis* or "participation" without a qualifying term. This slight difference in terminology between the German and English language writings of Peura is illuminating. The primary language of the Finnish Luther Research publications has clearly been German. This is only natural given the subject matter and also the connections between Mannermaa and the German Catholic Luther scholar, Peter Manns. The translation into English language points, however, to a fundamental flaw in the terminology of the Mannermaa school.

9. See "Justification and *Theosis* in Lutheran-Orthodox Perspective," in *Union with Christ,* 27: "Thus, the doctrine of divinization rests more profoundly on the presupposition that a human being can participate in the fullness of life that is in God. It is precisely this participation that is called *theosis* in the tradition of the early church and in the Orthodox Church." Cf. *Der im Glauben gegenwärtige Christus,* 12–21.

10. See Williams, "The Patristic Concept of Deification," in *Ground of Union,* 27–33.

11. Williams very frequently uses wordings like "doctrine of *theosis,*" "the root idea of deification," "doctrine of deification," "doctrine of divinization," "the fact of *theosis,*" alternating with the simple terms such as *theosis,* divinization, and deification. She also speaks expressly about a "Thomistic view of deification" (37), "Thomistic doctrine of *theosis*" (36, 41), and "Thomistic conception of divinization" (38).

12. Williams, *Ground of Union,* 34: "Thus, while Aquinas uses the technical vocabulary of *theosis* sparingly . . ."

13. Ibid., 32: "there is a firm core that distinguishes this doctrine from some other model of sanctification." Cf. also 174.

14. Chapter 1, sec. 3, "The Patristic Concept of Deification," shows that Williams is basically aware of the comprehensiveness of the patristic doctrine of deification. Yet the way she treats it in this part of her book is very confusing and does not contribute to a clarification of her conceptual apparatus throughout the book. The following elements that should have been analyzed and brought into relation with each other can be found in the same chapter: "notion of deification," "*theosis* became the dominant model of the concept of salvation," "The earliest Christian tradition spoke of deification using the same themes and images we will encounter in Aquinas and Palamas" (27); "The most extended early treatment of divinization occurs in the chief works of Irenaeus, *Adversus Haereses*" (28; What is the relation between this statement and the obvious fact that Irenaeus does not yet use the terminology of divinization? Cf. statements on 29 and 30 for the first occurrence of *theopoiein* and *theosis* in Clement of Alexandria and Gregory Nazianzen, respectively. "This simultaneous emphasis on the unbreachable divide between creature and Creator and on the creature's likening to the Utterly Other we will refer to as the two poles of deification. What is most characteristic of a doctrine of deification is the delicate balancing and negotiation of these two themes." Doesn't this statement basically imply that Christian theology generally contains or at least implies a doctrine of deification?); "This, then, is the patristic tradition of deification. While we find few actual definitions of the term, a clear enough pattern has emerged that we may make some generalizations. It asserts the *imago Dei* and the Incarnation as the basis of deification and construes *theosis* overwhelmingly in terms of knowledge, virtue, light and glory, participation and union" (31). On 32, Williams summarizes her survey of the patristic doctrine of deification and lists three characteristics: "First, we can safely say that where we find references to human participation in divine life, there we assuredly have a claim specifically of *theosis.*" This obviously is the fundamental presupposition that guides Williams throughout the book. She clearly singles out some common Christian "themes and images"(cf. 27) as markers for this doctrine of *theosis* = participation in divine life. Here, on 32, however, she warns that this "is carefully to be distinguished, however, from the idea of divine indwelling in the human person. Both schemes of sanctification draw on the notion of union, but whereas the latter locates sanctification within the creature and *in via,* the former locates it at the level of the divine and insists upon the inseparability of life *in via* and *in patria.*" This is an interesting distinction that does not seem to play any role in the analysis of Thomas and Gregory Palamas. If it had played a role, then the use of "themes and images" could not have acted as markers of a doctrine of *theosis* without further qualification. The second characteristic follows from this: "A second infallible marker of the doctrine, then, is the union of God and humanity, when this union is conceived as humanity's incorporation into God, rather than God's into humanity, and when conceived as the destiny of humanity generally rather than the extraordinary experience of the few. Adoption also functions as a signal of a doctrine of deification, albeit a somewhat weaker one than participation and union." According to Williams, union and adoption function as markers for a doctrine of *theosis,* notwithstanding that you might distinguish between union (and adoption?) in the sense of participation in God and as God's indwelling in man. In addition to this obvious contradiction, one might wonder if participation and indwelling necessarily function as alternatives in Christian tradition. Both notions might be possible to use in various combinations with other "themes and images" without necessarily presupposing the same view of the relation between creatures and Creator.

15. Although the discussion on the correctness of the Finnish interpretation of Luther is an important one, my interest in this article is not to take sides in that debate. It could very well be that Luther has a "real-ontic" understanding of the union of the Christian with Christ/God,

but this does not necessarily mean that he teaches a doctrine of *theosis*. On the other hand, if the critics of the Finnish interpretation are right, this does not necessarily diminish the importance of the theme of *theosis* in Luther.

16. Williams, *Ground of Union,* 102; cf. 34, as regards Thomas.

17. This is clear throughout the chapters on Thomas Aquinas. The analysis, however, to some extent is predetermined by chapter 1 ("The Problem and Its History"). Cf. earlier n. 13.

18. *Dictionnaire de spiritualité,* vol. 3 (Paris: Beauchesne 1957), s.v. "Divinisation," cols. 1370–1459.

19. In the recent research I discuss here, the tendency is to put most of the weight upon 2 Pt 1:4 and less on Ps 82(81):6. In patristic literature, however, the latter reference is more important. Cf. Gross, *Divinization of the Christian*; and "Divinisation," in *Dictionnaire de spiritualité.*

20. Cf. preface 3, for Christmas in the present Roman Missal as well as the collect for the Mass of Christmas Day.

21. It is no coincidence that the most important text testifying to the presence of the *theosis* theme in Luther is his Christmas Sermon from 1514. Cf. Flogaus (see below note 25), 301–52. It is also well known that the theme of "happy exchange" is to be found in the Christmas hymns not only of Luther himself but those of later Lutheran authors. Cf. Flogaus, *Theosis bei Palamas und Luther,* 18.

22. For references, see "Divinisation," 1395–97; and Gérard Philips, *L'union personnelle avec le Dieu vivant: Essai sur l'origine et le sens de la grace créé,* rev. ed. (Louvain: Leuven University Press, 1989). After having given several references of this kind, Philips adds: "*On pourrait continuer pendant longtemps pareille anthologie. Elle est abondante à souhait* . . . [One could long continue such a collection of examples. There is an abundance . . .]" (30).

23. For the development of a doctrine of grace in the technical sense by Augustine in contrast to the foregoing patristic theology, see Alfred Schindler, "Gnade," in *Reallexikon für Antike und Christentum,* ed. Theodor Klauser, col. 386–441 (Stuttgart: Hierseman, 1950), esp. 418–30.

24. See notes 7–8.

25. *Theosis bei Palamas und Luther: Ein Beitrag zum ökumenischen Gespräch,* Forschungen zur systematischen und ökumenischen Theologie Bd 78 (*Göttingen:* Vandenhoeck & Ruprecht, 1997). The brief description of the patristic doctrine of *theosis* by Flogaus (19–27) is more consistent than in Williams. Yet Flogaus focuses exclusively on Palamas in his analysis and comparison.

26. Cf. Yannis Spiteris, *Palamas: La grazia e l'esperiecza; Gregorio Palmas nella discussione teologica* (Roma: Lipa 1996). Spiteris writes in relation to the aspect of sacramentality in the theology of Palamas: "Infatti, nel contesto della polemica in cui il dottore esicasta era impegnato, egli si vide constretto a soffermarsi di preferenza sul fatto stesso della divinizzazione, sugli effetti carismatici e sulla collaborazione del fedele affinché la divinizzazione possa svilupparsi. È sintomatico il fatto che la maggior parte dei testi che si referischono alla sacramentalità della divinizzazione si trovino nelle sue Omelie, scritte e pronunziate al di fuori della rovente atmosfera della polemica [As a matter of fact, in the polemical context of the hesychast controversy, Palamas was forced to focus primarily on the very fact of divinization as well as on the charismatic effects and the cooperation of the believer that is necessary for the development of divinization. It is symptomatic that the major part of texts that refer to the sacramentality of divinization are to be found in the *Homilies,* written and held outside the hot atmosphere of polemics]" (79).

27. In addition to Gross's classical book, an important contribution to the understanding of the Eastern doctrine of *theosis* is Myrrha Lot-Borodine, *La Déification de l'homme, selon la doctrine des Pères grecs* (Paris: Editions du Cerf, 1970), originally published as articles in *Revue de l'Histoire des Religions,* 1932–33. My interpretation of the Eastern doctrine of

theosis is further based on writings of contemporary Eastern Orthodox theologians like Vladimir Lossky, John Meyendorff, and Dumitru Stăniloae.

28. As is well known, Irenaeus did not use the terminology itself. Cf. Gross, *Divinization of the Christian,* 120–31.

29. Although Flogaus (*Theosis bei Palamas und Luther,* 20ff.) mentions this aspect of the patristic doctrine, it does not influence his comparison between Luther and Palamas. The same is the case with Williams's comparison between Thomas and Palamas. The distinction is clearly to be found in Palamas. See Spiteris, *Palamas,* 71–74. Further, the Finnish Luther research ignores the distinction altogether and does not even discuss the role of the notion of the image of God in Luther, a point that would most naturally come into mind in a comparison between Orthodox and Lutheran doctrine. For the notion of *imago Dei* in the theology of Luther see Bengt Hägglund, *De Homine: Människouppfattningen i äldre luthersk tradition* (Lund: C.W.K. Gleerup, 1959).

30. Cf. Lossky, *The Mystical Theology of the Eastern Church* (Crestwood, NY: St. Vladimir's Seminary Press, 2004), chap. 6.

31. Both points stand out clearly in Gross's survey. Cf. further John Meyendorff, *Christ in Eastern Christian Thought* (Crestwood, NY: St. Vladimir's Seminary Press, 1975), 114: "There is no *consensus patrum* for a complete exegesis of Gen 1:26–27. . . . There is, however, an absolute consistency in Greek patristic tradition in asserting that the image is not an external imprint, received by man in the beginning and preserved by human nature as its own property independently of its relationships with God. 'Image' implies a *participation in the divine nature.*"

32. An obvious example is St. Hilary of Poitiers in whom the language of *theosis* is prominent. That this is an influence from St. Athansius is clear. However, it seems that St. Hilary is building more upon the foundation of the *salus carnis* theme of Irenaeus and Tertullian than on the specific connection between the theology of image and *theosis* in Athanasius. For this crucial distinction, see further below, note 43. For St. Hilary, see Michael Durst, *Die Eschatologie des Hilarius von Poitiers* (Bonn: Borengasser, 1987).

33. See *De Baptismo* 5:7: *Ita restitutitur homo deo ad similitudienm eius, qui retro ad imaginem dei fuerat. Imago in effigie, similitudine in aeternitate censetur. Recipit enim illum dei spiritum quem tunc de afflatus eius acceperat sed post amiserat per delictum.* CCL 1:282. ["In this way is man being restored to God, to the likeness of him who had aforetime been in God's image—the image had its actuality in the *man God* formed, the likeness *becomes actual* in eternity—for there is given back to him that spirit of God which of old he had received of God's breathing, but afterwards had lost through sin." *Tertullian's Homily on Baptism: Edited with an Introduction,* trans. and commentary by Ernest Evans (London: S.P.C.K., 1964)].

34. See especially Paul Mattei, "Adam, posséda-t-il l'Esprit? Remarques sur l'état primitf de l'homme et le progres de l'histoire selon Tertullian," in *Recherches des Études Augustiniennes* 29 (1983): 27–38. Cf. also Jean Daniélou, *Les origines du christianisme latin* (Paris: Cerf, 1978), 298–306.

35. Tertullian distinguishes between the *spiritus dei* and the *flatus dei.* Man consists of *corpus* and *flatus.* It is because God has blown his *flatus* into man that makes him the image of God. This image/*flatus,* however, is not identical with the Spirit of God. It is of a distinct order and hence image. The spirit is given to human beings only in Christ. See Mattei, "Adam," and Daniélou, *Origines du christianisme latin,* with references to Tertullian.

36. In many ways recent Tertullian research has revised the picture of Tertullian as the "Father of Latin Theology" and especially as the creator of Ecclesiastical Latin. Yet, his influence should not be played down either. In connection with anthropology Tertullian answered to a situation that possibly had long-term consequences for Latin theology. Cf. the verdict of Daniélou, *Origines du christianisme latin,* 306: "Sur ce point, la pensée de Tertullien

est profondemément originale, et elle sera d'une très grand portée pour l'avenir de la théologie latine. C'était donner en effet à la personne humaine, à l'homme intérieur, à la subjectivitè, une place essentielle. [On this point Tertullian's thought was profoundly original and of great importance for the future of Latin theology. As a matter of fact it gave a central role to the human person, to the interior man or to subjectivity]."

37. The first part of Paul Evdokimov, *L'Orthodoxie* (Paris: Desclée de Brouwer, [1959] 1990) is dedicated to anthropology. This is the foundation for the rest of his introduction and contains a chapter entitled "Anthropologie de la deification." Cf. Lot-Borodine, *Déification de l'homme.*

38. The difference is well described by Yves Congar, "*Deification* in the Spiritual Tradition of the East," in *Dialogue Between Christians: Catholic Contribution to Ecumenism,* ed. Yves Congar, 217–31 (Westminster, MD: Newman Press, 1966).

39. Cf. notes 10–14.

40. On the different understandings of participation in the life of God according to Eastern and Western theology, see esp. Congar, "Deification," 223–24. Cf. H.R, Schlette,"*Teilhabe. II. Problemgeschichtlich und systematisch*" in *Handbuch theologischer Grundbegriffe,* II (München, 1963), 634–41, and David L. Balás, *Μετουσια Θεου: Man's Participation in God's Perfections According to Saint Gregory of Nyssa,* Studia Anselmiana 55 (Roma: Herder, 1966). See also André de Halleux, "Palamisme et scolastique," in *Patrologie et oecuménisme: Recueil d'études,* BEThL XCIII, ed. André de Halleux, 782–815 (Leuven, 1990).

41. This has been worked out in an illuminating way by Flogaus, *Theosis bei Palamas und Luther,* in his chapter on Martin Luther (chap. 3). See esp. the summary, 375–80. Cf. 381: "Schon ein flüchtiger Blick auf unsere bisherigen Ergebnisse lässt indes deutlich werden, wie gross die Unterschiede zwischen beiden Theologen sind. Es steht ausser Zweifel, dass Martin Luther, hätte er die Theosislehre des Metropoliten von Thessaloniki gekannt, diese in Baush und Bogen abgelehnt hätte und sein Urteil über ihn sicher nicht wesentlich anders ausgefallen wäre als über den Ps.-Areopagiten. Zu eng ist die Theologie des Palmas mit dessen Theologie [this must be a misprint for "Anthropologie"], als dass man sich hierüber irgendwelchen Illusionen hingeben könnte. Viel zu entschieden ist auch Luthers Ablehnung der scholastischen Metaphysik, als dass man annehmen durfte, er hätte vielleicht doch die Gotteslehre und Anthropologie des Verteidigers der Hesychasten gutheissen können [Already a cursory glance on our findings makes it clear how large the differences are between the two theologians. There is no doubt that if Martin Luther had known the *theosis* doctrine of the metropolitan of Thessaloniki, he would have rejected it outright. His judgement would not have been substantially different from that over against the Pseudo-Areopagite. The anthropology of Palamas is too closely connected to Pseudo-Dionysius that there would have been another possible option. The firm rejection by Luther of scholastic metaphysics, also, makes it difficult to imagine that he would have been willing to endorse the anthropology and doctrine of God that was conceived by the defender of hesychasm]."

42. Eliot, *Complete Poems and Plays,* 149.

43. The theme of "happy exchange" is almost omnipresent in Christian theology since Irenaeus, as is the theme of *theosis.* Those two themes belong basically together but are not necessarily present at the same time in every context. Fundamental to both themes seems to be the energetic rejection of Gnosticism by Irenaeus and Tertullian, which results in the notion of *salus carnis. Salus carnis/admirabile commercium/theosis* make up a common basis for the development of soteriology in East and West. A real *doctrine of theosis,* however, is to be found only in the East. For the development of patristic soteriology and especially the role of the *salus carnis* theme see Basil Studer, *Trinity and Incarnation: The Faith of the Early Church* (Edinburgh: T & T Clark, 1993), and Studer, *Soteriologie in der Schrift und Patristik,* Handbuch der Dogmentgeschichte Bd. III Faszikel 2a. (Freiburg: Herder, 1978).

44. In his article "Redemption and Deification," Vladimir Lossky writes, "Even if

redemption appears as the central aspect of the incarnation, i.e., of the dispensation of the Son toward the fallen world, it is but one aspect of the vaster dispensation of the Holy Trinity toward being created *ex nihilo* and called to reach deification freely—to reach union with God, so that 'God may be all in all.'" *In the Image and Likeness of God,* ed. John Erickson and Thomas Bird (Crestwood, NY: St. Vladimir's Seminary Press, 2001), 102–3.

Resources on *Theosis* with Select Primary Sources in Translation

Compiled by Jeffery A. Wittung

Aden, Ross. "Justification and Divinization." *Dialog* 32 (Spring 1993): 102–7.

Allchin, A. M. *Participation in God: A Forgotten Strand in Anglican Tradition.* Wilton, CT: Morehouse-Barlow, 1988.

Andia, Ysabel de. *Henosis: L'union a Dieu chez Denys l'Areopagite.* Leiden: E. J. Brill, 1996.

———. *Homo Vivens: Incorruptibilité et divinisation de l'homme selon Irénée de Lyon.* Paris: Études Augustiniennes, 1986.

———. "Mystères, unification et divinisation de l'homme selon Denys l'Aréopagite." *Orientalia Christiana periodica* 63 (1997): 273–332.

———. "Philosophie et Union Mystique chez le Pseudo-Denys l'Aréopagite." In *Sofihs Maihtopes: Hommage à Jean Pépin,* edited by Marie-Odile Goulet-Caze, Goulven Madec, and Denis O'Brien, 511–31. Paris: Institut d'Études Augustiniennes, 1992.

Anstall, Kharalambos. *Aspects of Theosis: The Purification and Sanctification of the Human Intellect.* Dewdney, BC: Synasis Press, 1994.

Ardusso, Franco. *Divinizzazione dell'uomo e redenzione dal peccato: Le teologie della salvezza nel cristianesimo di Oriente e di Occidente.* Torino: Fondazione Giovanni Agnelli, 2004.

Aubineau, Michel. "Incorrutibilité et divinisation selon saint Irénée." *Recherches de Science Religieuse* 44 (1956): 25–52.

Bachmann, Claus. "Das Kreuz mit der Alleinwirksamkeit Gottes: Die Theologie des Nürnberger Reformators und protestantischen Erzketzers Andreas Osiander im Horizont der *Theosis*-Diskussion." *Kerygma und Dogma* 49, no. 3 (July–September 2003): 247–75.

Baert, E. "Le Thème de la vision de Dieu chez S. Justin, Clément d'Alexandrie et S. Grégoire de Nysse." *Freiburger Zeitschrift für Philosophie und Theologie* 12 (1965): 439–97.

Bakken, Kenneth. "Holy Spirit and *Theosis:* Toward a Lutheran Theology of Healing." *St. Vladimir's Theological Quarterly* 38, no. 4 (1994): 409–23.

Balás, David L. "Christian Transformation of Greek Philosophy Illustrated by Gregory of Nyssa's Use of the Notion of Participation." *Proceedings of the American Catholic Philosophical Association* 40 (1966): 152–57.

———. *Metousia Theou: Man's Participation in God's Perfections according to Saint Gregory of Nyssa.* Rome: Libreria Herder, 1966.

———. "Two Styles of Theology and Spirituality." *St. Vladimir's Theological Quarterly* 26 (1982): 89–101.

Bartos, Emil. *Deification in Eastern Orthodox Theology: An Evaluation and Critique of the Theology of Dumitru Stăniloaë*. Carlisle, Cumbria: Paternoster Press, 1999.

———. "The Dynamics of Deification in the Theology of Dumitru Stăniloaë." In *Dumitru Stăniloaë: Tradition and Modernity in Theology*, edited by Lucian Turcescu, 207–48. Palm Beach, FL: Center for Romanian Studies, 2002.

Baur, L. "Untersuchungen über die Vergöttlichungslehre in der Theologie der griechischen Väter." *Theologische Quartalschrift* 98 (1916): 467–91; 99 (1918): 225–52; 100 (1919): 426–46; 101 (1920): 28–64, 155–86.

Begegnung mit der Orthodoxie. *"Theosis, die Vergottung des Menschen." Vorträge von dem "Seminar für Orthodoxe Liturgie und Spiritualität," Frankfurt, 1988 und 1978*. München: Kloster des Hl. Hiob von Pocaev, 1989.

Beisser, Friedrich. "Zur Frage der Vergottlichung des Menschen bei Martin Luther." *Kerygma und Dogma* 39 (October–December 1993): 226–81.

Berdyaev, Nikolai. *The Destiny of Man*. London: Geoffrey Bles, 1948.

Berger, Kevin. "Towards a Theological Gnoseology: The Synthesis of Fr. Dumitru Stăniloaë." PhD diss., Catholic University of America, 2003.

Bielfeldt, Dennis. "Deification as a Motif in Luther's *Dictata super psalterium*." *Sixteenth Century Journal* 28, no. 2 (Summer 1997): 401–20.

———. "The Ontology of Deification." In *Caritas Dei: Beiträge zum Verständnis Luthers und der gegenwärtigen Ökumene; Festschrift für Tuomo Mannermaa zum 60 Geburtstag*, edited by Oswald Bayer, et al., 90–113. Helsinki: Luther Agricola Gelleschaft, 1997.

Bilaniuk, Petro. "The Mystery of *Theosis* or Divinization." In *Heritage of the Early Church: Essays in Honor of Georges Vasilievich Florovsky on the Occasion of His Eightieth Birthday*, edited by David Neiman and Margaret Schatkin, 337–59. Rome: Pont Institutum Studiorum Orientalium, 1973.

Blaising, Craig. "Deification: An Athanasian View of Spirituality." In *Evangelical Theological Society Papers*, 1987. Portland, OR: Theological Research Exchange Network, 1988. Textfiche.

Bonner, Gerald. "Augustine's Conception of Deification." *Journal of Theological Studies* 37 (October 1986): 369–86.

Bornkamm, K. *Die Vergottungslehre des Athanasius und Johannes Damascenus*. Beiträge zur Föderung christlicher Theologie 2. Gütersloh: C. Bertelsmann, 1903.

Braaten, Carl E., and Robert W. Jenson, eds. *Union with Christ: The New Finnish Interpretation of Luther*. Grand Rapids, MI: Eerdmans, 1998.

Bratsiotes, Panagiotes. *Die Lehre der Orthodoxen Kirche über die Theosis des Menschen*. Brussel: Paleis der Academiën, 1961.

Brock, Sebastian P. *The Luminous Eye: The Spiritual World Vision of Saint Ephrem the Syrian*. CS 124. Revised ed. Kalamazoo, MI: Cistercian Publications, 1992.

Burghardt, W. J. *The Image of God in Man according to Cyril of Alexandria*. Washington, DC: Catholic University of America Press, 1957.

Burns, J. Patout. "Economy of Salvation: Two Patristic Traditions." *Theological Studies* 37 (1976): 598–619.

Butterworth, G. W. "The Deification of Man in Clement of Alexandria." *Journal of Theological Studies* 17 (1916): 157–69.

Calendine, Caren Ferree. "*Theosis* and the Recognition of Saints in Tenth-Century Byzantium." PhD diss., University of Wisconsin, 1998.

Campbell, John. "Deified to Be the Bride of Christ." *Affirmation and Critique* 7, no. 2 (October 2002): 95–99.

Canlis, Julie. "Calvin, Osiander and Participation in God." *International Journal of Systematic Theology* 6, no. 2 (April 2004): 169–84.

Capànaga, P. V. "La deification en la soteriologia agustiniana." *Augustinus Magister* 2 (1954): 745–54.

Caponi, Francis J., OSA "Rahner and the Metaphysics of Participation." *The Thomist* 67, no. 3 (July 2003): 375–408.

Capsanis, George. *The Deification as the Purpose of Man's Life*. Mount Athos: Holy Monastery of St. Gregorios, 1997.

Carabine, Deirdre. "Five Wise Virgins: *Theosis* and Return in Periphyseon V." In *Iohannes Scottus Eriugena,* edited by Gerd van Riel, Carlos Steel, and J. J. McVoy, 195–207. Leuven: Leuven University Press, 1996.

Casiday, Augustine M. C. "Deification in Origen, Evagrius and Cassian." In *Origeniana Octava: Origen and the Alexandrian Tradition = Origene e la tradizione Alessandrina: Papers of the 8th International Origen Congress, Pisa, 27–31 August 2001*. Leuven: Leuven University Press, 2003.

———. "St. Augustine on Deification: His Homily on Psalm 81." *Sobornost* 23, no. 2 (2001): 23–44.

Chadwick, Henry. "Note sur la divinisation chez saint Augustain." *Revue des sciences religieuses* 76, no. 2 (April 2002): 246–48.

Chae, Isaac. "Justification and Deification in Augustine: A Study of His Doctrine of Justification." PhD diss., Trinity Evangelical Divinity School, 1999.

Choufrine, Arkadi. *Gnosis, Theophany, Theosis: Studies in Clement of Alexandria's Appropriation of His Background*. New York: Peter Lang, 2002.

Christensen, Michael J. "Partakers of the Divine Nature: The Problem, Promise, and Process of *Theosis*." *Journal of Christian Education and Information Technology* 8 (October 30, 2005): 15–30.

———. "*Theosis* and Sanctification: John Wesley's Reformulation of a Patristic Doctrine." *Wesleyan Theological Journal* 31, no. 2 (Fall 1996): 71–94.

Christou, Panayotis. "Maximos the Confessor on the Infinity of Man." In *Maximus Confessor: Actes du Symposium sur Maxime le Confesseur, Fribourg, 2–5 septembre, 1980,* edited by Felix Heinzer and Christoph von Schönborn, 261–71. Fribourg, Suisse: Editions Universitaires, 1982.

———. "Uncreated and Created, Unbegotten and Begotten in the Theology of Athanasius of Alexandria." *Augustinianum* 13 (1973): 399–409.

Clendenin, Daniel. "The Deification of Humanity: *Theosis*." Chapter 7 in *Eastern Orthodox Christianity: A Western Perspective*. Grand Rapids, MI: Baker Academic, 1994.

———. "Partakers of Divinity: The Orthodox Doctrine of *Theosis*." *Journal of the Evangelical Theological Society* 37 (September 1994): 365–79.

Climacus, John. *The Ladder of Divine Ascent*. Translated by Colm Luibheid and Norman Russell. CWS. Mahwah, NJ: Paulist Press, 1982.

Coffey, David. "The Gift of the Holy Spirit." *The Irish Theological Quarterly* 38, no. 3 (July 1971): 202–23.

Cole, Spencer. "The Dynamics of Deification in Horace's Odes 1–3." In *Between Magic and Religions,* edited by Sulochana Ruth Asirvatham, Corinne Ondine Pache, and John Watrous, 67–91. Lanham, MD: Rowman and Littleman, 2001.

Collins, Carr. "*Theosis:* Deification of Man." *Diakonia* 15, no. 3 (1980): 229–35.

Congar, Yves. "Deification in the Spiritual Tradition of the East." In *Dialogue between Christians: Catholic Contribution to Ecumenism,* edited by Yves Congar, 217–31. Westminster, MD: Newman Press, 1966.

Coniaris, Anthony. *Achieving Your Potential in Christ, Theosis: Plain Talks on a Major Doctrine of Orthodoxy.* Minneapolis, MN: Light and Life, 1993.

Contos, L. C. "The Concept of *Theosis* in St. Gregory Palamas, with Critical Text of *Contra Akindynum.*" DPhil diss., University of Oxford, 1962.

Coolidge, Francis P., Jr. "Philosophy, Deification, and the Problem of Human Fulfilment." PhD diss., Pennsylvania State University, 1988.

Cooper, Adam G. *The Body in St. Maximus the Confessor: Holy Flesh, Wholly Deified.* Oxford Early Christian Studies. Oxford: Oxford University Press, 2005.

———. "Holy Flesh, Wholly Deified: The Place of the Body in the Theological Vision of Saint Maximus the Confessor." PhD diss., University of Durham, 2002.

Corneanu, Nicolae, and Luminitsa Niculescu. "The Jesus Prayer and Deification." *St. Vladimir's Theological Quarterly* 39, no. 1 (1995): 3–24.

Cullen, J. A. "The Patristic Concept of the Deification of Man Examined in the Light of Contemporary Notions of the Transcendence of Man." DPhil diss., University of Oxford, 1985.

Dalmais, I. H. "Divinisation." In *Dictionnaire de Spiritualité,* vol. 3, cols. 1376–89. Paris, 1957.

———. "Mystére liturgique et divinisation dans la Mystagogie de saint Maxime le Confesseur." In *Epektasis: Mélanges patristiques offerts au Cardinal Jean Daniélou,* edited by Jacques Fontaine and Charles Kannengiesser, 55–62. Paris: Beauchesne, 1972.

Daniélou, Jean. *Platonisme et theologie mystique: Doctrine spirituelle de S. Grégoire de Nysse.* Paris, 1954.

Danker, Bob. "Deification." *Affirmation and Critique* 7, no. 2 (October 2002): 100–105.

Danker, Frederick W. "2 Peter 1: A Solemn Decree." *Catholic Biblical Quarterly* 40 (January 1978): 64–82.

Dawson Vasquez, David C. "The Mystical Theology of Vladimir Lossky: A Study of His Integration of the Experience of God into Theology." PhD diss., Catholic University of America, 2001.

Devdat, Cletus. *The Acosmic: Human Quest for Liberation and Deification. Revisiting Christian Spirituality at Its Source.* Revised edition. Bangalore, India: Asirvanam Publications, 2005.

Doble, Peter. "'Vile Bodies' or Transformed Persons? Philippians 3:21 in Context." *Journal for the Study of the New Testament* 86 (2002): 3–27.

Dragas, George. "Exchange or Communication of Properties and Deification: *Antidosis* or *Communicatio Idiomatum* and *Theosis.*" *Greek Orthodox Theological Review* 43, no. 1–4 (Spring/Winter 1998): 377–99.

Drewery, B. "Deification." In *Christian Spirituality: Essays in Honour of Gordon Rupp,* edited by Peter Brooks, 33–62. London: SCM Press, 1975.

Dupuis, James. "Theological Foundations for the Interpretation of Man." *Indian Journal of Theology* 27 (1978): 160–70.

Edwards, Dan. "Deification and the Anglican Doctrine of Human Nature." *Anglican and Episcopal History* 58 (June 1989): 196–212.

Edwards, Henry. "Justification, Sanctification and the Eastern Orthodox Concept of *Theosis.*" *Consensus* 14, no. 1 (1988): 65–80.

Emerton, J. A. "The Interpretation of Psalm LXXXII in John X." *Journal of Theological Studies* 11 (1960): 329–32.

Engelhardt, H. Tristram. "Genetic Enhancement and *Theosis:* Two Models of Therapy." *Christian Bioethics* 5, no. 2 (August 1999): 197–99.

Ephrem the Syrian. *Hymns*. Translated and edited by K. E. McVey. CWS. Mahwah, NJ: Paulist Press, 1989.

Ermoni, V. "La déification de l'homme chez les Pères de l'Eglise." *Révue du clergé français* 11, no. 66 (1897): 509–19.

Evangelical Church of Germany. *Rechtfertigung und Verherrlichung (Theosis) des Menschen durch Jesus Christus*. EKD-Studienheft 23. Hermannsburg: Missionsverlag Herrmannsburg, 1988.

Evdokimov, Paul. *L'Orthodoxie*. Paris: Desclée de Brouwer, 1959. Reprinted 1990; see esp. part 1.

Every, George. "*Theosis* in Later Byzantine Theology." *Eastern Churches Review* 2 (Spring 1969): 243–52.

Fairbairn, Dan. "Salvation as *Theosis:* The Teaching of Eastern Orthodoxy." *Themelios,* no. 23 (June 1998): 42–54.

Faller, O. "Griechische Vergottung und christliche Vergöttlichung." *Gregorianum* 6 (1925): 405–35.

Ferguson, Everett. "God's Infinity and Man's Mutability: Perpetual Progress according to Gregory of Nyssa." *Greek Orthodox Theological Review* 18 (1973): 59–78.

Festugière, A. J. "La divinisation du chrétien." *La Vie Spirituelle* 59, suppl. (1939): 90–99.

Finch, Jeffrey David. "Sanctity as Participation in the Divine Nature according to the Ante-Nicene Eastern Fathers, Considered in the Light of Palamism." PhD diss., Drew University, 2002.

Finger, Thomas. "Anabaptism and Eastern Orthodoxy: Some Unexpected Similarities." *Journal of Ecumenical Studies* 31, no. 2 (Spring 1994): 67–91.

Finlan, Stephen, and Vladimir Kharlamov, eds. *Theosis: Deification in Christian Theology.* Eugene, OR: Wipf and Stock, 2006.

Flew, R. *The Idea of Perfection in Christian Theology.* Oxford: Clarendon Press, 1934.

Flogaus, Reinhard. "Einig in Sachen *Theosis* und Synergie." *Kerygma und Dogma* 42 (July–September 1996): 225–43.

———. *Theosis bei Palamas und Luther: Ein Beitrag zum ökumenischen Gespräch*. Göttingen: Vandenhoeck & Ruprecht 1997.

Folliet, Georges. "*Deificari in otio*: Augustin, *Epistula* 10.2." *Recherches Augustiniennes* 2 (1962): 225–36.

Ford, David C. "Saint Makarios of Egypt and John Wesley: Variations on the Theme of Sanctification." *Greek Orthodox Theological Review* 33, no. 3 (1988): 285–312.

Fortino, Eleuterio. "Sanctification and Deification." *Diakonia* 17, no. 3 (1982): 192–200.

Franks, R. S. "The Idea of Salvation in the Theology of the Eastern Church: A Study in the History of Religion." In *Mansfield College Essays, Presented to the Rev. Andrew Martin Fairbairn, D.D., on the Occasion of His Seventieth Birthday, November 4, 1908,* edited by C. Silvester Horne, 249–64. London: Hodder and Stoughton, 1909.

Frary, Joseph. "Deification and Human Freedom." *Sobornost* 7, no. 2 (1975): 117–26.

Galbaito, Enrico. "La deificazione nei padri orientali." In *Simposio cristiano,* edited by Timotheos Moschopulos and Piero Scazzoso, 23–35. Milan: Edizione dell'Istituto di Studi Teologici Ortodossi, 1971.

Garrigues, Juan Miguel. "L'énergie divine et la grâce chez Maxime le Confesseur." *Istina* 19 (1974): 272–96.

Gatta, John. "Little Lower Than God: Super-Angelic Anthropology of Edward Taylor." *Harvard Theological Review* 75 (July 1982): 361–68.

Gebremedhin, Ezra. *Life-Giving Blessing: An Enquiry into the Eucharistic Doctrine of St. Cyril of Alexandria*. Uppsala: Almqvist & Wiksell International, 1977.

George, Martin. "Vergottlichung des Menschen: Von der platonischen Philosophie zur Soteriologie der griechischen Kirchenvater." In *Die Weltlichkeit des Glaubens in der Alten Kirche: Festschrift für Ulrich Wickert zum siebzigsten Geburtstag*, edited by Barbara Aland and Christoph Schäublin, 115–55. Berlin: Walter de Gruyter, 1997.

Gillet, R. "L'Homme divinisateur cosmique dans la pensée de S. Grégoire de Nysse." *Studia Patristica* 6, edited by F. L. Cross. Texte und Untersuchungen 81, 62–83. Berlin: Akademie Verlag, 1962.

Giosanu, Évêque Joachim. *La Déification de l'homme d'après la pensée du Père Stăniloaë*. Iassy: Trinitas, 2003.

Golitzin, Hieromonk Alexander. "A Testimony to Christianity as Transfiguration: The Macarian Homilies and Orthodox Spirituality." In *Orthodox and Wesleyan Spirituality*, edited by S T Kimbrough, 129–56. Crestwood, NY: St. Vladimir's Seminary Press, 2002.

Good, Roger. "Children of God Becoming Deified Sons." *Affirmation and Critique* 7, no. 2 (October 2002): 91–94.

Gowan, Donald E. *When Man Becomes God: Humanism and Hubris in the Old Testament*. Pittsburgh, PA: Pickwick Press, 1975.

Greear, James D. "*Theosis* and Muslim Evangelism: How the Recovery of a Patristic Understanding of Salvation Can Aid Evangelical Missionaries in the Evangelization of Islamic Peoples." PhD diss., Southeastern Baptist Theological Seminary, 2003.

Green, Lowell. "The Question of *Theosis* in the Perspective of Lutheran Christology." In *All Theology Is Christology: Essays in Honor of David P. Scaer*, edited by Dean Wenthe, et al., 163–80. Fort Wayne, IN: Concordia Theological Seminary Press, 2000.

Gregory of Nyssa. *From Glory to Glory*. Translated by Jean Daniélou and Herbert Musurillo. Crestwood, NY: St. Vladimir's Seminary Press, 1979.

———. *The Life of Moses*. Translated by Abraham Malherbe and Everett Ferguson. CWS. Mahwah, NJ: Paulist Press, 1978.

Gross, Jules. *The Divinization of the Christian according to the Greek Fathers*. Translated by P. Onica. Anaheim, CA: A&C Press, 2002. Originally published as *La Divinisation du chrétien d'après les pères grecs: Contribution historique à la doctrine de la grace* (Paris: J. Gabalda, 1938).

Gustafson, Richard. "Soloviev's Doctrine of Salvation." In *Russian Religious Thought*, edited by Judith Kornblatt and Richard Gustafson, 31–48. Madison, WI: University of Wisconsin Press, 1996.

Hampton, Laura Lynn. "The Deification of Man: A Comparison of the Doctrine of Soul in Thomas Aquinas and Rene Descartes." PhD diss., University of Dallas, 1994.

Harakas, Stanley. "Eastern Orthodox Christianity's Ultimate Reality and Meaning: Triune God and *Theosis*—An Ethician's View." *Ultimate Reality and Meaning* 8, no. 3 (1985): 209–23.

Harrison, Nonna Verna. "*Theosis* as Salvation: An Orthodox Perspective." *Pro Ecclesia* 6 (Fall 1997): 429–43.

Hart, David Bentley. "The Bright Morning of the Soul: John of the Cross on *Theosis*." *Pro Ecclesia* 12, no. 3 (Summer 2003): 324–44.

———. "A Gift Exceeding Every Debt: An Eastern Orthodox Appreciation of Anselm's *Cur Deus Homo*." *Pro Ecclesia* 7 (1993): 333–49.

Hart, T. "Two Models of Salvation in Relation to Christological Understanding in the Patristic East." PhD, diss., Aberdeen University, 1989.

Hartnett, J. *Doctrina S. Banaventurae de deiformitate*. Mundelein, 1936.

Hauke, R. *Gott-Haben—um Gottes Willen: Andreas Osanders Theosisgendanke und die Diskussion um die Grundlagen der evangelisch verstandenen Rechtfertigung; Versuch einer Neubewertung eines umstrittenen Gedankens*. Frankfurt: P. Lang, 1999.

Helleman, Wendy E. "Philo of Alexandria on Deification and Assimilation to God." *Studia Philonica Annual* 2 (1990): 51–71.

Hess, Hamilton. "The Place of Divinization in Athanasian Soteriology." In *Studia Patristica* 26, edited by Elizabeth Livingstone, 369–74. Leuven: Peeters, 1993.

Heubach, Joachim. *Luther und Theosis*. Erlangen: Martin Luther Verlag, 1990.

Heibert, Frances. "The Atonement in Anabaptist Theology." *Direction* 30, no. 2 (Fall 2001): 122–38.

Himmerich, Maurice Fred. "Deification in John of Damascus." PhD diss., Marquette University, 1985.

Hinlicky, Paul. "Theological Anthropology: Toward Integrating *Theosis* and Justification by Faith." *Journal of Ecumenical Studies* 34 (Winter 1997): 38–73.

Holladay, C. R. *Theios Aner in Hellenistic-Judaism: A Critique of the Use of This Category in New Testament Christology*. Missoula, MT: Scholars Press, 1977.

Hudson, Nancy J. *Becoming God: The Doctrine of Theosis in Nicholas of Cusa*. Catholic University of America Press, 2007.

———. "*Theosis* in the Thought of Nicholas of Cusa: Origin, Goal, and Realized Destiny of Creation." PhD diss., Yale University, 1999.

Inge, W. R. "The Doctrine of Deification." Appendix C in *Christian Mysticism*. London: Methuen, 1899.

Jenson, Richard. "*Theosis* and Preaching: Implications for Preaching in the Finnish Luther Research." *Currents in Theology and Mission* 31, no. 6 (December 2004): 432–37.

Jenson, Robert. "*Theosis*." *Dialog* 32 (Spring 1993): 108–12.

Jervis, L. Ann. "Becoming Like God through Christ: Discipleship in Romans." In *Patterns of Discipleship in the New Testament,* edited by Richard N. Longenecker, 143–62. Grand Rapids, MI: Eerdmans, 1996.

Jordan, James. "Some Encouragements toward an Evangelical Doctrine of the Deification of Man." In *Evangelical Theological Society Papers, 1985*. Portland, OR: Theological Research Exchange Network, 1987. Text-fiche.

Kangas, Ron. "Becoming God." *Affirmation and Critique* 7, no. 2 (October 2002): 3–30.

———. "Regeneration for Deification, Regeneration as Deification." *Affirmation and Critique* 7, no. 2 (October 2002): 71–83.

Kärkkäinen, Veli-Matti. "The Doctrine of *Theosis* and Its Ecumenical Potential." *Sobornost* 23, no. 2 (2001): 45–77.

———. *One with God: Salvation as Deification and Justification*. Collegeville, MN: Liturgical Press, 2004.

———. "Salvation as Justification and Deification: The Ecumenical Potential of a New Perspective on Luther." In *Theology between East and West: Essays in Honor of Jan Milic Lochman,* edited by Frank Macchia and Paul Chung, 59–76. Eugene, OR: Wipf and Stock, 2002.

Keating, Daniel A. "The Appropriation of Divine Life in Cyril of Alexandria." DPhil diss., Oxford, 2000.

———. *The Appropriation of Divine Life in Cyril of Alexandria*. Oxford Theological Monographs. Oxford: Oxford University Press, 2004.

———. *Deification and Grace*. Fort Collins, CO: Sapientia Press of Ave Maria University, 2007.

———. "Divinization in Cyril: The Appropriation of Divine Life." In *The Theology of St. Cyril of Alexandria: A Critical Appreciation*, edited by Thomas Weinandy and Daniel A. Keating, 149–85. New York: T&T Clark, 2003.

———. "Justification, Sanctification and Divinization in Thomas Aquinas." In *Aquinas on Doctrine: A Critical Introduction*, edited by Thomas Weinandy, Daniel Keating, and John Yocum, 139–58. London: Continuum, 2004.

Kharlamov, Vladimir L. "'The Beauty of the Unity and the Harmony of the Whole': Concept of *Theosis* in the Theology of Pseudo-Dionysius the Areopagite." PhD diss., Drew University, 2006.

Kirov, Dimitar Popmarinov. "The Mysticism of Light in the Scriptures and in the Orthodox Worship Tradition." In *Orthodox and Wesleyan Scriptural Understanding and Practice*, edited by S T Kimbrough, 89–103. Crestwood, NY: St. Vladimir's Seminary Press, 2005.

Knickerbocker, W. E. "The Myth That Saves: C. S. Lewis and the Doctrine of *Theosis*." *Touchstone* 13, no. 6 (July-August): 31–34.

Knight, Duane Winston. "From 'Secret Cell' to Compostella: Medieval Itineraries of *Theosis*." PhD diss., University of Pennsylvania, 1990.

Koester, Helmut. "The Divine Human Being." *Harvard Theological Review* 78, no. 3–4 (July–October 1985): 243–52.

Kolp, A. L. "Partakers of the Divine Nature: The Use of 2 Peter 1:4 by Athanasius." In *Studia Patristica* 17.3, edited by Elizabeth Livingstone, 1018–23. New York: Pergamon, 1982.

———. "Participation: A Unifying Concept in the Theology of Athanasius." PhD diss., Harvard University, 1976.

Kopcke Duttler, Arnold. "Das Licht der *Theosis:* zur Philosophie Nikolaj Berdjaevs." *Ostkircheliche Studien* 35, no. 1 (1986): 34–36.

Krekhovetsky, Yakiw E. Jacob. "Evolution and Divinization: The Orientation of Man to Perfection and His Divinization in the Thought of Pierre Teilhard de Chardin." PhD diss., University of St. Michael's College, 1977.

Kronawetter, Karl Heinz. *Die Vergöttlichung des Irdischen: Die ökologische Lebensphilosophie von Ludwig Klages im Diskurs mit der christlichen Theologie*. Bonn: Bouvier Verlag, 1999.

Laeuchli, Samuel. "Prolegomena to a Structural Analysis of Ancient Christian Views of Salvation." In *Disciplina Nostra: Essays in Memory of Robert F. Evans*, edited by D. F. Winslow, 133–70. Patristic Monograph Series 6. Cambridge, MA: Philadelphia Patristics Foundation, 1979.

Lambrecht, J. "Transformation in 2 Cor 3:18." *Biblica* 64 (1983): 243–54.

Laneau, Louis. *De la deification des justes*. Geneve: Editions Ad Solem, 1993.

Larchet, Jean Claude. *La divinisation de l'homme selon saint Maxime le Confesseur.* Paris: Edition du Cerf, 1996.

Laspides, Chrestos. *He theose tou anthropou: kata tous pateres tes ekklesias*. Thessalonike, 1992.

Lattey, Cuthbert. "The Deification of Man in Clement of Alexandria: Some Further Notes." *Journal of Theological Studies* 17 (1916): 257–62.

Lee, Jeha. "Love or *Theosis?* A Critique of Tuomo Mannermaa's New Paradigm of Luther Research in Light of Luther's Concept of Love in His Commentary on the First Epistle of John." ThD diss., Boston University, 2003.

Leemans, Johan. "'God Became Human in Order That Humans Might Become God': A Reflection on the Soteriological Doctrine of Divinization." In *The Myriad Christ: Plurality and the Quest for Unity in Contemporary Christology,* edited by Terrence Merrigan and Jacques Haers, 207–16. Sterling, VA: Uitgeverij Peeters, 2000.

LeGrys, James. "Blondel's Idea of Assimilation to God through Mortification of Self." *Gregorianum* 77, no. 2 (1996): 309–31.

Le Guillon, M. J. "Lumiere et charité dans la doctrine Palamite de la divinisation." *Istina* 19, no. 3 (1974): 329–38.

Lehninger, Paul. "Luther and *Theosis:* Deification in the Theology of Martin Luther." PhD diss., Marquette University, 1999.

LeMasters, Philip. "The Practice of Medicine as *Theosis*." *Theology Today* 61, no. 2 (July 2004): 173–86.

Levko, John J. "From Discernment to Deification with Athanasius." *Diakonia* 30, no. 1 (1997): 5–19.

Lison, Jacques. "La divinisation selon Gregoire Palamas: Un sommet de la theologie orthodoxe." *Irenikon* 67, no. 1 (1994): 59–70.

Lossky, Vladimir. *In the Image and Likeness of God*. Edited by Thomas E. Bird and John Erickson. Crestwood, NY: St. Vladimir's Seminary Press, 1974. Reprinted 2001.

———. *The Mystical Theology of the Eastern Church*. London: James Clarke, 1957. Reprinted, Crestwood, NY: St. Vladimir's Seminary Press, 1998.

———. *Orthodox Theology: An Introduction*. Crestwood, NY: St. Vladimir's Seminary Press, 1978.

———. *The Vision of God*. Translated by Ashleigh Moorhouse. 2nd ed. Crestwood, NY: St. Vladimir's Seminary Press, 1973.

Lot Borodine, Myrrha. *La Déification de l'homme selon la doctrine des Pères grecs*. Paris: Editions du Cerf, 1970. Originally published as articles in *Revue de l'Histoire des Religions* 105 (1932): 5–43; 106 (1932): 525–74; 107 (1933): 8–55.

———. *Nicholas Cabasilas*. Paris: l'Orante, 1958.

Louth, Andrew. "Manhood into God: The Oxford Movement, the Fathers and the Deification of Man." In *Essays Catholic and Radical,* edited by Kenneth Leech and Rowan Williams, 70–80. London: Bowerdean Press, 1983.

Madden, J. N. "Christology and Anthropology in the Spirituality of Maximus the Confessor." PhD diss., University of Durham, 1983.

Mahoney, Timothy. "A Note on the Importance of the Incarnation in Dionysius the Areopagite." *Diakonia* 35, no. 1 (2002): 49–53.

Malherbe, Abraham J. "Pseudo Heraclitus, Epistle 4: The Divinization of the Wise Man." *Jahrbuch für Antike und Christentum* 21 (1978): 42–64.

Maloney, George. "Ecumenism and Divinization." *Mid-Stream* 40, no. 1 (January–April 2001): 203–10.

———. *The Undreamed Has Happened: God Lives within Us*. Scranton, PA: University of Scranton Press, 2003.

Mannermaa, Tuomo. *Der im Glauben gegenwärtige Christus: Rechtfertigung und Vergottung zum Ökumenischen Dialog*. Arbeiten zur Geschichte und Theologie des Luthertums, Neue Folge, Band 8. Hannover: Lutherisches Verlagshaus, 1989.

———. "Luther ja *Theosis*." In *Pastor et Episcopus Animarum: Studia in Honorem Pauli Verschuren,* edited by Pentti Laukama, 15–29. Vammala: Vammalan Kirjapaino, 1985.

———. "*Theosis* as a Subject of Finnish Luther Research." *Pro Ecclesia* 4, no. 1 (1995): 37–48.

Mantzarides, Georgios. *The Deification of Man: St. Gregory Palamas and the Orthodox Tradition*. Crestwood, NY: St. Vladimir's Seminary Press, 1984.

———. *Methexis theou*. Thessalonike: Ekdoseis "Orthodoxos Kypsele," 1979.

———. "Spiritual Life in Palamism." In *Christian Spirituality: High Middle Ages and Reformation*, edited by Jill Raitt, Bernard McGinn, and John Meyendorff, 208–22. New York: Crossroads, 1987.

Mantzarides, Georgios, M. J. Monsaingeon, and Joseph Paramelle, trans. and eds. *De la deification de l'être humain*. Lausanne: L'Age d'Homme, 1990.

Marks, Ed. "Deification by Participation in God's Divinity." *Affirmation and Critique* 7, no. 2 (October 2002): 47–54.

Marquart, Kurt. "Luther and *Theosis*." *Concordia Theological Quarterly* 64, no. 3 (July 2000): 182–205.

Marrocco, Mary Noreen Rita. "Participation in the Divine Life in St. Augustine's *De Trinitate* and Selected Contemporary Homiletic Discourses." PhD diss., University of St. Michael's College, 2000.

Marshall, Bruce. "Justification as Declaration and Deification." *International Journal of Systematic Theology* 4, no. 1 (March 2002): 3–28.

Martens, P. "Divinization." In *The Westminster Handbook to Origen*, edited by J. A. McGuckin, 91–93. Louisville, KY: Westminster John Knox Press, 2004.

Martikainen, Jouko. "Man's Salvation: Deification or Justification? Observation of Key-Words in the Orthodox and the Lutheran Tradition." *Sobornost* 7, no. 3 (Summer 1976): 180–92.

Martin, Mary Elizabeth. "Orphans, Widows and Sons of God: An Exegetical Investigation of Augustine's Concept of Adoption and Deification." PhD diss., Union Theological Seminary, 2003.

Martin, Walter. "You Shall Be Gods." In *Agony of Deceit*, edited by Michael Scott Horton, 89–105. Chicago: Moody Press, 1990.

Mateo Seco, Lucas. "Salvacion y Divinizacion: La Leccion de los Padres." *Scripta Theologica* 31 (May–August 1999): 453–69.

Mattei, Paul. "Adam, posséda-t-il l'Esprit? Remarques sur l'état primitf de l'homme et le progress de l'histoire selon Tertullian." In *Recherches des Études Augustiniennes* 29, 27–38. Paris: Études Augustiniennes, 1983.

Maximus the Confessor. *On the Cosmic Mystery of Jesus Christ*. Translated by Paul Blowers and Robert Louis Wilken. Crestwood, NY: St. Vladimir's Seminary Press, 2003.

McClymond, Michael. "Salvation as Divinization: Jonathan Edwards, Gregory Palamas and the Theological Uses of Neoplatonism." In *Jonathan Edwards: Philosophical Theologian*, edited by Paul Helm and Oliver Crisp, 139–60. Burlington, VT: Ashgate, 2003.

McCormick, Steve. "*Theosis* in Chrysostom and Wesley: An Eastern Paradigm on Faith and Love." *Wesleyan Theological Journal* 26 (Spring 1991): 38–103.

———. "A Trinitarian Paradigm of *Theosis:* A Context for the Emergence of a Wesleyan Notion of Christ Transfiguring Culture." In *Grace in the Academic Community: Festschrift for Cecil R. Paul*, edited by Maxine Walker, 193–206. San Diego, CA: Point Loma Press, 1996.

McDaniel, Michael. "Salvation as Justification and *Theosis*." In *Salvation in Christ: A Lutheran-Orthodox Dialogue*, edited by John Meyendorff and Robert Tobias, 67–84. Minneapolis, MN: Augsburg, 1992.

McGuckin, J. A. "Deification." In *The Oxford Companion to Christian Thought*, edited by A. Hastings, 156. Oxford: Oxford University Press, 2000.

———. *The Transfiguration of Christ in Scripture and Tradition*. Lewiston, NY: Edwin Mellen Press, 1986.

———. "The Vision of God in St. Gregory Nazianzen." In *Studia Patristica* 32, edited by Elizabeth Livingstone, 145–52. Leuven: Peeters, 1997.

McIntosh, I. M. "The Spirit and Life: An Assessment of Jurgen Moltmann's Pneumatology with Particular Reference to the Theology of Gregory Palamas." PhD diss., London, King's College, 2000.

Mehl, Roger. "La divinisation de l'homme, doctrine problematique." In *Penser la foi: Recherches en théologie aujourd'hui; Mélanges offerts à Joseph Moingt,* edited by Joseph Dore and Christoph Theobald, 971–87. Paris: Assas, 1993.

Merki, Hubert. *Homoiōsis Theōi: Von der Platonischen Angleichung an Gott zur Gottähnlichkeit bei Gregor von Nyssa*. Freiburg, CH: Paulus, 1952.

Meyendorff, John. *Byzantine Theology: Historical Trends and Doctrinal Themes*. New York: Fordham University Press, 1974.

———. *Christ in Eastern Christian Thought*. Crestwood, NY: St. Vladimir's Seminary Press, 1975.

———. *Gregorie Palamas: Defense des saints hesychasts; Introduction, Texte critique, traduction et notes*. 2nd ed. Louvain: Spicilegium sacrum lovaniense, 1973.

———. *A Study of Gregory Palamas*. Translated by George Lawrence. London: Faith Press, 1964. Reprint, Crestwood, NY: St. Vladimir's Seminary Press, 1998. Originally published as *Introduction à l'étude de Grégoire Palamas* (Paris: Editions du Seuil, 1959).

———. "*Theosis* in the Eastern Christian Tradition." In *Christian Spirituality: Post-Reformation and Modern*. Edited by Louis Dupre, Don Saliers, and John Meyendorff, 470–78. New York: Crossroad, 1989.

Meyer, John Rudolph. "Saint Athanasius on Divinization." DTh diss., Universidad de Navarra (Spain), 1991.

Moltmann, Jurgen. "Cosmos and *Theosis*." In *The Far-Future Universe: Eschatology from a Cosmic Perspective,* edited by George Ellis, 249–65. Philadelphia: Templeton Foundation Press, 2002.

Morse, Jonathan. "Fruits of the Eucharist: *Henosis* and *Theosis*." *Diakonia* 17, no. 2 (1982): 127–42.

Mosser, Carl. "The Earliest Patristic Interpretations of Psalm 82, Jewish Antecedents, and the Origin of Christian Deification." *Journal of Theological Studies* 56, no. 1 (April 2005): 30–74.

———. "The Greatest Possible Blessing: Calvin and Deification." *Scottish Journal of Theology* 55, no. 1 (2002): 36–57.

———. "Mormonism and the Christian Doctrine of Deification." PhD diss., Fuller Theological Seminary, 2002.

Moutsoulos, Elias, and Constantine Andrews. *The Incarnation of the Word and the Theosis of Man according to the Teaching of Gregory Nyssa*. Athens: Eptalophos S.A., 2000.

Muckler, J. T. "The Doctrine of St. Gregory of Nyssa on Man as Image of God." *Medieval Studies* 7 (1945): 55–85.

Negrut, Paul. "Orthodox Soteriology: *Theosis*." *Churchman* 109, no. 2 (1995): 154–70.

Nellas, Panayiotis. *Deification in Christ: Orthodox Perspectives on the Nature of the Human Person*. Crestwood, NY: St. Vladimir's Seminary Press, 1987. Reprinted 1997.

Newey, Edmund. "The Form of Reason: Participation in the Work of Richard Hooker, Benjamin Whichcote, Ralph Cudworth and Jeremy Taylor." *Modern Theology* 18, no. 1 (January 2002): 1–26.

Ng, Nathan K. K. "A Reconsideration of the Use of the Term 'Deification' in Athanasius." *Coptic Church Review* 22, no. 2 (Summer 2001): 34–42.

Nicholas of Cusa. *Selected Spiritual Writings*. Translated by H. Lawrence Bond. CWS. Mahwah, NJ: Paulist Press, 1997.

Nichols, Aidan. "Anselm of Canterbury and the Language of Perfection." *Downside Review* 103 (July 1985): 204–17.

Norman, Keith Edward. "Deification: The Content of Athanasian Soteriology." PhD diss., Duke University, 1980.

Norris, Frederick. "Deification: Consensual and Cogent." *Scottish Journal of Theology* 49, no. 4 (1996): 411–28.

O'Keefe, Mark. "*Theosis* and the Christian Life: Toward Integrating Roman Catholic Ethics and Spirituality." *Eglise et Theologie* 25, no. 1 (1994): 47–63.

Oroz Reta, Jose. "De l'illumination a la deification de l'ame selon saint Augustin." In *Studia Patristica* 27, edited by Elizabeth Livingstone, 364–82. Leuven: Peeters Press, 1993.

Palamas, Gregory. *The Triads*. Translated by Nicholas Gendle. CWS. Mahwah, NJ: Paulist Press, 1983.

Papanikolaou, Aristotle. "Divine Energies or Divine Personhood: Vladimir Lossky and John Zizioulas on Conceiving the Transcendent and Immanent God." *Modern Theology* 19, no 3 (July 2003): 357–85.

Patronos, George. *He theose tou anthropou: Hypo to phos ton eschatologikon antilepseon tes Orthodoxes theologias*. Athena: Ekdoseis Domos, 1995.

———. *The Theosis of Man in the Light of Orthodox Eschatology and Theology: A Biblical and Patristic Study*. Athens, 1981.

Perl, Eric D. "St. Gregory Palamas and the Metaphysics of Creation." *Dionysius* 14 (1989): 105–30.

———. "*Methexis:* Creation, Incarnation, Deification in Saint Maximus Confessor." PhD diss., Yale University, 1991.

Pester, John. "The Gospel of the Promised Seed: Deification according to the Organic Pattern in Romans 8 and Philippians 2." *Affirmation and Critique* 7, no. 2 (October 2002): 55–69.

Peura, Simo. *Mehr als ein Mench? Die Vergöttlichung als Thema der Theologie Martin Luthers von 1513 bis 1519*. Stuttgart: Mainz: P. von Zabern, 1994.

———. "More Than a Human Being? Deification as a Subject of the Theology of Martin Luther, 1513–1519." PhD diss., Helsingin Yliopisto, 1990.

———. "Die Vergöttlichung des Menschen als Sein in Gott." In *Lutherjahrbuch* 60, 39–71. Göttingen: Vandenhoeck & Ruprecht, 1993.

———. "Vergöttlichungsgedanke in Luthers Theologie 1518–1519." In *Thesaurus Lutheri: Auf der Suche nach neuen Paradigmen der Luther-Forschung. Referate des Luther-Symposiums in Finnland, 11–12 November 1986,* edited by Tuomo Mannerma, Anja Ghiselli, and Simo Peura, 171–84. Helsinki: Finnische Theologische Literaturgesellschaft, 1987.

Peura, Simo, and Antti Raunio, eds. *Luther und Theosis: Vergöttlichung als Thema der abendländischen Theologie. Referate der Fachtagung der Luther-Akademie Ratzeburg in Helsinki 30.3–2.4.1989*. Helsinki: Luther Agricola Gesellschaft, 1990.

Philips, Gérard. "La grâce chez les Orientaux." *Ephemerides Theologicae Lovanienses* 48 (1972): 37–50.

———. *L'union personnelle avec le Dieu vivant: Essai sur l'origine et le sens de la grace créée*. 2nd ed. Louvain: Leuven University Press, 1989.

Podskalsky, Gerhard. "Gottesschau und Inkarnation, zur Bedeutung der Heilsgeschichte bei Gregorios Palamas." *Orientalia Christiana Periodica* 35 (1969): 5–44.

Popov, I. V. "Ideia obozhenia v drevne-vostochnoi tserkvi" [The Idea of Deification in the Ancient Eastern Church]. *Voprosy filosofii i psikhologii* 97 (1906): 165–213.

Posset, Franz. "'Deification' in the German Spirituality of the Late Middle Ages and in Luther: An Ecumenical Historical Perspective." *Archiv für Reformationsgeschichte* 84 (1993): 103–26.

Preuss, Th. "La Mystique de l'initiation et de d'unité chez Ignace d'Antioche." *Revue d'histoire et de philosophie religieuses* 18 (1938): 197–241.

Pseudo-Dionysius. *The Complete Works*. Translated by Colm Luibheid. CWS. Mahway, NJ: Paulist Press, 1987.

Pseudo-Marcarius. *The Fifty Spiritual Homilies and the Great Letter.* Translated and edited by George Maloney. CWS. Mahwah, NJ: Paulist Press, 1992.

Radin, M. "Apotheosis." *Classical Review* 30 (1916): 44–46.

Rakestraw, Robert Vincent. "Becoming Like God: An Evangelical Doctrine of *Theosis*." *Journal of the Evangelical Theological Society* 40 (June 1994): 257–69.

Riordan, William. "Divinization in Denys the Areopagite." PhD diss., Pontificia Studiorum Universitas a S. Thoma Aq. in Urbe, 1991.

Ritschl, Dietrich. "Hippolytus' Concept of Deification." *Scottish Journal of Theology* 12 (1959): 388–99.

Robichaux, Kerry. "Can Human Beings Become God?" *Affirmation and Critique* 7, no. 2 (October 2002): 31–46.

———. ". . . that we might be made God." *Affirmation and Critique* 1 (July 1996): 21–31.

Rogobete, Silviu Eugen. "Mystical Existentialism or Communitarian Participation? Vladimir Lossky and Dumitru Stăniloaë." In *Dumitru Stăniloaë: Tradition and Modernity in Theology,* edited by Lucian Turcescu, 167–206. Palm Beach, FL: Center for Romanian Studies, 2002.

Romains, Jules. *Manuel de déification*. Paris: Société des amis de Jules Romains, 1990.

Romanides, John. "Notes on the Palamite Controversy and Related Topics." *Greek Orthodox Theological Review* 9 (1963–64): 225–70.

Rondet, H. "La divinisation du chrétien." *Nouvelle Révue Théologique* 17, no. 5–6 (1949): 449–76, 561–88.

Rossum, Joost van. "Deification in Palamas and Aquinas." *St. Vladimir's Theological Quarterly* 47, no. 3–4 (2003): 365–82.

Ruis-Camps, J. *El dinamismo trinitario en la divinizacion de los seres racionales segun Origenes*. Orientalia Christiana analecta 188. Rome: Pontificium Institutum Orientalium Studiorum, 1970.

Rusch, William. "How the Eastern Fathers Understood What the Western Church Meant by Justification." In *Justification by Faith,* edited by H. George Anderson, T. Austin Murphy, and Joseph Burgess, 131–42. Minneapolis, MN: Augsburg, 1985.

Russell, Norman. "The Concept of Deification in the Early Greek Fathers." PhD diss., Oxford University, 1988.

———. *The Doctrine of Deification in the Greek Patristic Tradition*. Oxford Early Christian Studies. Oxford: Oxford University Press, 2004.

———. "'Partakers of the Divine Nature' (2 Peter 1:4) in the Byzantine Tradition." In *Kathegetria: Essays Presented to Joan Hussey on Her 80th Birthday*, edited by Julian Chrysostomides, 51–67. Camberley: Porphyrogenitus, 1988.

———. "Theosis and Gregory Palamas: Continuity or Doctrinal Change?" *St. Vladimir's Theological Quarterly* 50, no. 4 (2006): 357–79.

Rybarczyk, Edmund John. "Beyond Salvation: An Analysis of the Doctrine of Christian Transformation Comparing Eastern Orthodoxy with Classical Pentecostalism." PhD diss., Fuller Theological Seminary, School of Theology, 1999.

Savvidis, Kyriakos. *Die Lehre von der Vergöttlichung des Menschen bei Maximos dem Bekenner und ihre Rezeption durch Gregor Palamas*. St. Ottilien: EOS Verlag, 1997.

Scheeben, Matthias Joseph. "The Splendors of Grace." *Orate Fratres* 17, no. 1 (November 1942): 13–23.

Schonborn, Christoph. "Uber die richtige Fassung des dogmatischen Begriffs der Vergöttlichung des Menschen." *Freiburger Zeitschrift für Philosophie und Theologie* 34, no. 1–2 (1987): 3–47.

Schonherr, Hartmut. "Concepts of Salvation in Christianity." *African Theological Journal* 12, no. 3 (1983): 159–65.

Schumacher, William Wallace. "'Who Do I Say That You Are?' Anthropology and the Theology of *Theosis* in the Finnish School of Tuomo Mannermaa." PhD diss., Concordia Seminary, 2003.

Schnurr, G. M. "On the Logic of the Ante-Nicene Affirmation of the Deification of the Christian." *Anglican Theological Review* 51 (1969): 97–105.

Schwartz, Kirchenrat Klaus. *Rechtfertigung und Verherrlichung des Menschen durch Jesus Christus*. Hermannsburg: Missionshandlung Hermannsburg, 1995.

Scuiry, Daniel. "The Anthropology of St. Gregory of Nyssa." *Diakonia* 18, no. 1 (1983): 31–42.

Scurat, K. E. "The Doctrine of Saint Athanasius the Great on Deification [in Russian]." *Review of the Patriarchate of Moscow* 5 (1973): 61–64; 8 (1973): 63–68.

Sedley, David. "The Ideal of Godlikeness." In *Plato 2: Ethics, Politics, Religion, and the Soul*, edited by Gail Fine, 309–28. Oxford: Oxford University Press, 1999.

Sherrard, Philip. "The Christian Understanding of Man." *Sobornost* 7, no. 5 (Summer 1977): 329–43.

Silcock, Jeffrey. "Luther on Justification and Participation in the Divine Life: New Light on an Old Problem." *Lutheran Theological Journal* 34, no. 3 (November 2000): 127–39.

Sinkewicz, Robert E., trans. and ed. *St. Gregory Palamas: The One Hundred and Fifty Chapters; A Critical Edition, Translation, and Study*. Toronto: Pontifical Institute of Medieval Studies, 1988.

Smith, Morton. "Ascent to the Heavens and Deification in 4QM[a]." In *Archaeology and History in the Dead Sea Scrolls*, edited by Lawrence H. Schiffmann, 181–88. Sheffield: Sheffield Academic Press, 1990.

Solovyov, Vladimir. *Lectures on Divine Humanity*. Edited by Boris Jakim. Hudson, NY: Lindisfarne Books, 1995.

Sophrony (Sakharov), Archimandrite. *We Shall See Him as He Is*. Translated by Rosemary Edmonds. Tolleshunt Knights: Stavropegic Monastery of St. John the Baptist, 1988.

Spearritt, Dom Placid. "Soul's Participation in God according to Pseudo-Dionysius." *Downside Review* 88 (October 1970): 378–92.

Stăniloaë, Dimitru. "Image, Likeness, and Deification in the Human Person." *Communio* 13, no. 1 (Spring 1986): 64–83.

———. "The Procession of the Holy Spirit from the Father and His Relation to the Son, as the Basis of Our Deification and Adoption." In *Spirit of God, Spirit of Christ: Ecumenical Reflections on the* Filioque *Controversy*, edited by L. Visscher, 174–86. Faith and Order Paper 103. London: SPCK, 1981.

———. *The World, Creation, and Deification*. Vol. 2. *The Experience of God: Orthodox Dogmatic Theology*. Translated and edited by Ioan Ionita and Robert Barringer. Brookline, MA: Holy Cross Orthodox Press, 1994.

Starr, James M. *Sharers in Divine Nature: 2 Peter 1:4 in Its Hellenistic Context*. Coniectanea Biblical NT Series 33. Stockholm: Almqvist & Wiksell International, 2003.

Stavropoulos, Christoforos. *Partakers of the Divine Nature*. Minneapolis, MN: Light and Life, 1976. Pages 17–38 reprinted in *Eastern Orthodox Theology: A Contemporary Reader,* edited by Daniel Clendenin, 183–92. Grand Rapids, MI: Baker Academic, 1995.

Stephanopoulos, Robert. "The Orthodox Doctrine of *Theosis*." In *New Man: An Orthodox and Reformed Dialogue,* edited by John Meyendorff and Joseph McLelland, 149–61. New Brunswick, NJ: Agora Books, 1973.

Stogiannidis, Athanassios. *Leben und Denken: Bildungstheorien zwischen Theosis und Rechtfertigung; eine Untersuchung zum Verhältnis von evangelischer und orthodoxer Relgionspädagogik*. Munster: Lit, 2003.

Stoop, J. A. *Die Deificatio hominis in die sermons en epistulae van Augustinus*. Leiden: Luctor et Emergo, 1952.

Strange, C. R. "Athanasius on Divinization." In *Studia Patristica* 16.2, edited by Elizabeth Livingstone, 342–46. Berlin: Akademie Verlag, 1985.

Strange, Roderick. "Newman and Athanasius on Divinization." In *Christliche Heiligkeit als Lehre und Praxis nach John Henry Newman* [Newman's Teaching on Christian Holiness], edited by Gunter Biemer and Heinrich Fries, 43–51. Sigmaringendorf, West Germany: Regio Verlag Glock und Lutz, 1988.

Stuckwisch, Richard. "Justification and Deification in the Dialogue between the Tübingen Theologians and Patriarch Jeremias II." *Logia* 9, no. 4 (2000): 17–28.

Studer, Basil, and Brian Daley. *Soteriologie in der Schrift und Patristik*. Handbuch der Dogmentgeschichte, Bd. III, Faszikel 2a. Freiburg: Herder, 1978.

Swoboda, Philip J. "'Spiritual Life' versus Life in Christ: S. L. Frank and the Patristic Doctrine of Deification." In *Russian Religious Thought,* edited by Judith Kornblatt and Richard Gustafson, 234–48. Madison, WI: University of Wisconsin Press, 1996.

Tamburello, Dennis E. *Union with Christ: John Calvin and the Mysticism of St. Bernard*. Columbia Series in Reformed Theology. Louisville, KY: Westminster John Knox Press, 1994.

Theodorou, A. "Die Lehre von der Vergottung des Menschen bei den griechischen Kirchenvätern." *Kerygma und Dogma* 7 (1961): 283–310.

Thomas, Stephen. "Are St. Gregory Palamas and St. Thomas Aquinas Consistent with One Another after All?" *Sourozh* 85 (August 2001): 1–21.

———. *Deification in the Eastern Orthodox Tradition: A Biblical Perspective*. Gorgias Press, 2007.

Thunberg, Lars. *Man and the Cosmos: The Vision of St. Maximus the Confessor.* Crestwood, NY: St. Vladimir's Seminary Press, 1985.

———. *Microcosm and Mediator: The Theological Anthropology of Maximus the Confessor.* Chicago: Open Court, 1995.

———. *The Vision of St. Maximus the Confessor.* Crestwood, NY: St. Vladimir's Seminary Press, 1985.

Tollefsen, Torstein. "Did St. Maximus the Confessor Have a Concept of Participation?" In *Studia Patristica* 37, edited by Maurice Wiles, Edward Yarnold, and P. M. Davis, 618–25. Leuven: Peeters, 2001.

Tsirpanlis, Constantine N. "Aspects of Athanasian Soteriology." *Kleronomia* 8 (1976): 61–76.

Turner, H. E. W. *The Patristic Doctrine of Redemption: A Study of the Development of Doctrine during the First Five Centuries*. London: A. R. Mowbray, 1952, see esp. chap. 4.

Urbano Lopez de Meneses, Pedro. "The Christian Theology of Human Deification." DTh diss., Universidad De Navarra, 1999.

———. "'*Christus in fide adest*': Cristo presente en el creyente o la teologia de la deificacion en Lutero." *Scripta Theologica* 32, no. 3 (September-December 2000): 757–99.

———. *Theosis: La doctrina de la divinización en las tradiciones cristianas; Fundamentos para una teología ecuménica de la gracia*. Pamplona: Ediciones Universidad de Navarra, 2001.

Vajda, Jordan. *"Partakers of the Divine Nature": A Comparative Analysis of Patristic and Mormon Doctrines of Divinization*. Provo, UT: Foundation for Ancient Research and Mormon Studies, 2002.

Van Dale, Robert LeRoy. "An Understanding of *Theosis* in the Divine Liturgy and Its Implications for the Ecumenical Church." PhD diss., University of Iowa, 1968.

Vandervelde, George. "Justification and Deification—Problematic Synthesis: A Response to Lucian Turcescu." *Journal of Ecumenical Studies* 38, no. 1 (Winter 2001): 73–78.

Van Rossum, Joost. "Palamism and Church Tradition: Palamism, Its Use of Patristic Tradition, and Its Relationship with Thomistic Thought." PhD diss., Fordham University, 1985.

Van Unnik, W. C. "'With Unveiled Face': An Exegesis of 2 Corinthians iii 12–18." *Novum Testamentum* 6 (1963): 153–69.

Veniamin, C. "The Transfiguration of Christ in Greek Patristic Literature: From Irenaeus of Lyons to Gregory Palamas." DPhil diss., University of Oxford, 1991.

Vishnevskaya, Elena. "*Perichoresis* in a Context of Divinization: Maximus the Confessor's Vision of a 'Blessed and Most Holy Embrace.'" PhD diss., Drew University, 2004.

Von Ivánka, E. "Palamismus und Vätertradition." In *L'Église et les églises, 1054–1954: Neuf siècles de douloureuse séparation entre l'Orient et l'Occident; Études et travaux sur l'unité chrétienne offerts à Dom Lambert Beauduin*, vol. 2, 29–46. Belgique: Éditions de Chevetogne, 1955.

Ware, Kallistos. *The Orthodox Way*. Crestwood, NY: St. Vladimir's Seminary Press, 1998.

———. "Salvation and *Theosis* in Orthodox Theology." In *Luther et la réforme allemande dans une perspective oecuménique*, edited by Centre orthodoxe du patriarcat oecuménique, 167–84. Chambésy-Geneve: Éditions du Centre orthodoxe du patriarcat oecuménique, 1983.

Ware, Timothy [Kallistos of Diokleia]. "Deification in St. Symeon the New Theologian." *Sobornost* 25, no. 2 (2003): 7–29.

Watts, Pauline Moffitt. *Nicolaus Cusanus: A Fifteenth-Century Vision of Man*. Leiden: E. J. Brill, 1982.

Wendebourg, Dorothea. *Geist oder Energie: Zur Frage der innergöttlichen Verankerung des christlichen Lebens in der byzantinischen Theologie*. Munchener Universitats-Schriften, Bd. 4, Munchener Monographien zur historischen und systematischen Theologie. Munich: Kaiser Verlag, 1980.

Wesche, Kenneth Warren. "The Defense of Chalcedon in the 6th Century: The Doctrine of 'Hypostasis' and Deification in the Christology of Leontius of Jerusalem." PhD diss., Fordham University, 1986.

———. "Eastern Orthodox Spirituality: Union with God in *Theosis*." *Theology Today* 56, no. 1 (April 1999): 29–43.

———. "*Theosis* in Freedom and Love: The Patristic Vision of Stewardship." In *Consuming Passion: Christianity and the Culture of Consumption*, ed. Rodney Clapp, 118–28. Downer's Grove, IL: InterVarsity Press, 1998.

Weston, Frank. "*Theosis* or Philanthropy?" *Sobornost* 6, no. 10 (Winter 1974): 720–30.

Wild, Philip. *The Divinization of Man according to Saint Hilary of Poitiers*. Mundelein, IL: Saint Mary of the Lake Seminary, 1950.

Williams, A. N. "Deification in Thomas Aquinas and Gregory Palamas." PhD diss., Yale University, 1995.

———. *The Ground of Union. Deification in Aquinas and Palamas*. New York and Oxford: Oxford University Press, 1999.

———. "Light from Byzantium: The Significance of Palamas' Doctrine of *Theosis*." *Pro Ecclesia* 3 (Fall 1994): 483–96.

Willis-Watkins, D. "The *Unio Mystica* and the Assurance of Faith according to Calvin." In *Calvin: Erbe und Auftrage*, edited by W. van't Spijker, 77–84. Kampen: Kok Pharos, 1991.

Wilson, Daniel. "A Comparison of Irenaeus' and Athanasius' Respective Descriptions of Deification in Relation to Adolf Harnack's History of Dogma." PhD diss., Southeastern Baptist Theological Seminary, 2005.

Wilson, Kenneth. *Theosis*. London: Regency Press, 1974.

Winslow, Donald F. *The Dynamics of Salvation: A Study in Gregory of Nazianzus*. Cambridge, MA: Philadelphia Patristics Foundation, 1979.

Wolters, Al. "'Partners of the Deity': A Covenantal Reading of 2 Peter 1:4." *Calvin Theological Journal* 25 (April 1990): 28–44.

Yanguas, Jose Maria. "El Espiritu Santo y la divinizacion del cristiano segun San Basilio." *Scripta Theologica* 30 (May–August 1998): 519–29.

Youngs, F. W. "The Place of Spiritual Union in Jonathon Edwards's Conception of the Church." *Fides et Historia* 28 (1996): 27–47.

Zaitsev, Eugene. "Analysis and Evaluation of Vladimir Lossky's Doctrine of *Theosis*." PhD diss., Andrews University, Seventh-Day Adventist Theological Seminary, 1998.

Zizioulas, John. *Being as Communion: Studies in Personhood and the Church*. Crestwood, NY: St. Vladimir's Seminary Press, 1985.

Contributors

J. Todd Billings, assistant professor of Reformed theology at Western Theological Seminary in Holland, MI; author of *Calvin, Participation and the Gift*.

Thomas Buchan, assistant professor of theology at Asbury Theological Seminary in Orlando, FL; author of *"Blessed Is He Who Has Brought Adam from Sheol": Christ's Descent to the Dead in the Theology of St. Ephrem the Syrian*.

Francis Caponi, OSA, assistant professor of theology at Villanova University; author of various articles appearing in *The Thomist* and *Modern Theology*.

Michael J. Christensen, affiliate associate professor of spirituality at the Caspersen School of Graduate Studies and director of the Doctor of Ministry Program at the Theological School, Drew University; author of "*Theosis* and Sanctification: John Wesley's Reformulation of a Patristic Doctrine," in *Wesleyan Theological Journal*.

Stephen Davis, assistant professor of religious studies at Yale University; author of several books including *The Early Coptic Papacy: The Egyptian Church and Its Leadership in Late Antiquity*.

Jeffery Finch, assistant distance learning coordinator at Holy Apostles College and Seminary; PhD, Drew University, dissertation entitled "Sanctity as Participation in the Divine Nature according to the Ante-Nicene Eastern Fathers Considered in the Light of Palamism."

Stephen Finlan, PhD, Durham; adjunct professor in religious studies at Seton Hall University; author of several books including *Problems with Atonement*, and coeditor of *Theōsis: Deification in Christian Theology*.

Gösta Hallonsten, professor of systematic theology at Lund University, Sweden, and former Carl J. Peter Professor for Systematic Theology and Ecumenism at the Catholic University of America.

Boris Jakim, fellow of Caspersen School of Graduate Studies, Drew University; translator of *The Lamb of God*, *The Comforter*, *The Bride of the Lamb*, and *The Friend of the Bridegroom* by Sergius Bulgakov.

Vladimir Kharlamov, PhD, Drew University; coeditor of *Theōsis: Deification in Christian Theology*; and co-coordinator of the "Partakers of the Divine Nature" Conference at Drew University.

Nathan Kerr, assistant professor of philosophy and theology at Trevecca Nazarene University in Nashville, TN; author of several essays and articles including "Speaking Gracefully: The Dynamic of Language in the Economy of Reconciliation."

John Lenz, associate professor and former chair of the Classics Department at Drew University, and former Fulbright Fellow to Greece.

Jonathan Linman, associate professor of ascetical theology and director of the Center for Christian Spirituality at the General Theological Seminary in New York City, and an ordained minister of the Evangelical Lutheran Church in America.

Andrew Louth, professor of patristic and Byzantine studies at the University of Durham, England; author of several books including *St. John Damascene: Tradition and Originality in Byzantine Theology* and *Maximus the Confessor.*

J. A. McGuckin, professor of early church history at Union Theological Seminary, and professor of Byzantine Christian studies at Columbia University, New York City; author of numerous books including *St. Gregory of Nazianzus: An Intellectual Biography* and *The Westminster Handbook to Patristic Theology.*

James Starr, lecturer in New Testament studies at Johannelund Theological Seminary, Uppsala, Sweden; author of *Sharers in Divine Nature: 2 Peter 1:4 in Its Hellenistic Context*.

Elena Vishnevskaya, assistant professor of religion at Central College in Pella, IA; PhD, Drew University, dissertation entitled "*Perichoresis* and the Context of Divinization: Maximus the Confessor's Vision of a 'Blessed and Most Holy Embrace.'"

Jeffery A. Wittung, PhD candidate, Drew University; editor, Baker Academic; and co-coordinator of the "Partakers of the Divine Nature" Conference at Drew University.

General Index

Scripture Index

Old Testament

Apocrypha

New Testament